Iberian Jewish Literature

IBERIAN JEWISH LITERATURE

Between al-Andalus and Christian Europe

Jonathan P. Decter

Indiana University Press
Bloomington and Indianapolis

Publication of this book is made possible in part by generous support from the Koret Foundation.

This book is a publication of

Indiana University Press
601 North Morton Street
Bloomington, IN 47404-3797 USA

http://iupress.indiana.edu

Telephone orders 800-842-6796
Fax orders 812-855-7931
Orders by e-mail iuporder@indiana.edu

Chapter 1 of this book is reproduced with permission of *Prooftexts,* where it appeared in slightly modified form; part of chapter 7 is a modified excerpt from an article that appeared in *Jewish Studies Quarterly.*

The paper used in this publication meets the minimum requirements of American National Standard for Information Sciences—Permanence of Paper for Printed Library Materials, ANSI Z39.48-1984.

Manufactured in the United States of America

Library of Congress Cataloging-in-Publication Data

Decter, Jonathan P., date
Iberian Jewish literature : between al-Andalus and Christian Europe / Jonathan P. Decter.
p. cm.
Includes bibliographical references and index.
ISBN 978-0-253-34913-2 (cloth)
1. Hebrew poetry, Medieval—Spain—Andalusia—History and criticism. 2. Hebrew poetry, Medieval—Spain—History and criticism. 3. Jewish religious poetry, Hebrew—Spain—Andalusia—History and criticism. 4. Jewish religious poetry, Hebrew—Spain—History and criticism. 5. Jews—Spain—Andalusia—Intellectual life. 6. Jews—Spain—Intellectual life. 7. Andalusia (Spain)—In literature. 8. Spain—In literature. I. Title.
PJ5023.D43 2007
892.4'1209384—dc22
2006038451

1 2 3 4 5 12 11 10 09 08 07

In loving memory of Lawrence K. Horberg

CONTENTS

Preface

I first had the idea for writing this book while I was traveling by train from Boston to New York. I was fortunate enough to have two books as my traveling companions: Bernard Septimus's *Hispano-Jewish Culture in Transition* and Jacob Ben El'azar's *Sefer ha-meshalim* (The Book of Stories). Septimus's book, which detailed the intellectual profile of Rabbi Meir Abulafia between the Jewish intellectual trends of al-Andalus (Islamic Iberia) and northern France, brought to life remarkable transformations in Iberian Jewish culture during the twelfth and thirteenth centuries, as Andalusian Jewry fell into decline and Jews relocated to Christian Iberia. Because Christian Iberia stood at the crossroads, both physically and culturally, between the Islamic and Christian worlds, Jews in cities such as Toledo and Barcelona were touched by competing intellectual trends internal to Judaism and also by Islamic and Christian culture more generally. At some point (I like to imagine somewhere along the scenic shore of Connecticut), I put down Septimus and picked up Ben El'azar, a thirteenth-century Toledan author of Hebrew rhymed prose fiction, and reflected upon the place of the Hebrew author within the culture of transition.

I soon recognized the need for a study of medieval Hebrew literature that used cultural transition as a point of departure and as an interpretive lens. Rather than marking the decline of Andalusian Jewry as the dividing line between two periods, I made it the center of my study in order to highlight literary topoi and thematic concerns that persist from the late eleventh century, when Jews began to migrate out of al-Andalus, through the mid-thirteenth century, the late days of the Reconquista, by which time all of Iberian Jewry was living in Christian domains. I found that Jewish authors who migrated out of al-Andalus and those born on Christian soil who were heir to the Andalusian tradition shared a discourse about the significance of cultural transition and the Andalusian past. Centuries after Jews stopped living under Islamic rule in Iberia, al-Andalus and Andalusian social values remained central topics of concern in Hebrew literature.

The subject of this book is twofold: the literary discourse that surrounds the topic of Jewish cultural transition between Islamic and Christian Iberia in medieval Hebrew literature; and the transformations that took place in Hebrew literary production between the late eleventh and the mid-thirteenth century. Regarding the first topic, Hebrew authors memorialize, romanticize, and repudiate the cultural model of the Andalusian past and exhibit varying degrees of optimism concerning cultural renewal within the Christian environment. Several chapters of this book are dedicated to delineating the medieval Hebrew poetics of estrangement and lamentation. Some authors cast their Hebrew lamentations over Andalusian decline in a distinctly Arabic key by adopting tropes of personal estrangement from Arabic writing. Other Hebrew authors adopt more specifically Jewish discursive strategies to mourn Jewish suffering before a broad community. Another dominant theme of the book is the fate of Andalusian social values (such as aristocracy and social wine drinking) in post-Andalusian Hebrew literature. Authors seldom share opinions about the Andalusian past in a transparent way but speak through a language that is highly symbolic. As such, the enclosed garden (*hortus conclusus*), which became a synecdochic icon of Andalusian culture, emerged as a subject of sustained engagement in literary texts. Discourse about the garden runs through this book as a unifying thread, from its emergence as an Andalusian cultural icon to its existence as a literary object laden alternatively with nostalgia or disdain.

Regarding the second subject, the book studies a broad shift from writing rhymed metered poetry to composing rhymed prose fictional narratives as Jews move from Islamic to Christian Iberia. As is well known, Hebrew poetry by Andalusian Jewish authors (and by those who adopted their style) owes its prosodic features and much of its thematic interest to classical Arabic poetry. The Hebrew rhymed prose narrative that flourished in Christian Iberia likewise owes prosodic and thematic elements to Arabic literature, particularly the rhymed prose form known as the *maqāma*. Indeed, Arabic literature, as well as other intellectual disciplines dominant in the Islamic world, continued to be cultivated by Jews in Christian Iberia.

Yet this book does not read the Hebrew literature of Iberia as a product of the prolonged engagement of Jewish authors with Arabic literature only. In its search for literary parallels and influences, the book turns to the various literatures that converged in medieval Iberia, from the long tradition of Arabic poetry (pre-Islamic to Andalusian), to Arabic learned and popular prose writings and the burgeoning literatures in Christian European vernacular languages (especially the troubadour lyric and Romance fiction). Some Hebrew rhymed prose narratives reveal a remarkable hybridity wherein trends reaching Jews from Arabic and European vernacular literatures intermingle. Contextualizing Hebrew literature within broad literary trends allows us to gauge the cultural orientations of Jewish authors within the competing and overlapping literary worlds of Islamdom and Christendom. Moreover, this book does not understand Hebrew literary production primarily as an imitative process. Rather, this book argues that Hebrew authors of the twelfth and thirteenth centuries drew upon themes, tropes, and forms, many of which resonated against conventions existing in other literatures, in order to create a discourse about the subject of cultural transition.

Iberian Jewish Literature contributes to several areas of scholarship. Scholars of medieval Hebrew literature will find the book innovative for its systematic treatment of topics in literary studies. The field of medieval Hebrew literature has been grounded in philology and aesthetics but is a relative newcomer to the fields of literary theory and comparative literature. The book's organization according to topics in literary studies—such as imagery, structure, voice, landscape, and geography—reflects this methodological approach. Scholars of Jewish history will find a study of this little-understood period useful and will be aided by the thorough treatment of literary texts that often lie beyond the historian's purview or receive cursory treatment only. The book demonstrates that literary theory is an indispensable tool for the historian by exploring how literary texts refract and encode social issues.

Scholars of Arabic literature will find that the book presents Hebrew parallels to several areas of current research, including the poetics of estrangement and nostalgia and studies of specific literary forms such as the *qaṣīda* (a multipartite poem) and the *maqāma* (rhymed prose narrative), upon which many of the Hebrew writings are based. The book should also interest scholars of European vernacular literature in that it contributes to our understanding of the literary climate of thirteenth-century Iberia and to discussions over contested issues such as the role of Andalusian Arabic poetry in the rise of the European courtly lyric.

Finally, the book should appeal to scholars of Iberian studies in that it illuminates the place of Jews between the competing powers of Islam and Christianity. Specialists have long noted that the Iberian Peninsula seems, paradoxically, both unified and disjointed during the Middle Ages; despite fierce political divisions, Muslims and Christians often held shared intellectual and cultural tastes. *Iberian Jewish Literature* explores the contours of this paradox from the perspective of minority authors who recognized al-Andalus and Christian Iberia as different places distinguished by language, culture, and ecology and who were affected by the literary trends of Islamdom and Christendom.

Acknowledgments

This project could not have been completed without essential collegial, institutional, and personal support. I have enjoyed the kindness of all my colleagues in the Department of Near Eastern and Judaic Studies at Brandeis University. In particular, I wish to thank those who have shown a special interest in the development of this project or offered advice on navigating the worlds of publishing and the academy: Tzvi Abusch, Marc Brettler, Sylvia Barack Fishman, ChaeRan Freeze, Benjamin Ravid, Jonathan Sarna, Eugene Sheppard (thrice crowned), and David Wright. Sylvia Fuks Fried, executive director of the Tauber Institute for the Study of European Jewry at Brandeis, has been a veritable fountain of wisdom in all matters pertaining to publishing.

I have been fortunate enough to receive numerous grants and awards that helped provide the training, time, and financial subventions for executing this project. The Koret Foundation's Jewish Studies Publication Program Award offered an important subvention toward publication costs. The Bernstein-Pearlmutter Award for Junior Faculty Leave at Brandeis relieved me of teaching responsibilities for one semester. The Theodore and Jane Norman Fund for Faculty Research at Brandeis provided money toward indexing. Some research and writing was conducted during a glorious year I spent as the Hazel D. Cole Fellow in Jewish Studies at the University of Washington, Seattle. I also benefited from a year at the Hebrew University of Jerusalem as a Fulbright Student Fellow and from a year of Arabic immersion as a Fellow at the Center for Arabic Studies Abroad in Cairo, Egypt. Preliminary stages of this project were undertaken while I was a graduate student at the Jewish Theological Seminary of America. During those years, I enjoyed the support of various grants from the Seminary and other institutions: the Charles H. Revson Fellowship in Advanced Jewish Studies, the Shalom Spiegel Institute for Medieval Hebrew Literature of the Jewish Theological Seminary, and the National Foundation for Jewish Culture Dissertation Grant.

I especially wish to thank the many people who were generous enough to offer comments on sections of the work or on the manuscript as a whole. Their diligence, thoughtfulness, and insight have helped me to improve the work significantly: Raʿanan Boustan, Ross Brann, Benjamin Gampel, Matti Huss, Philip Kennedy, the late Magda al-Nowaihi, Michael Rand, Tova Rosen, Marina Rustow, Raymond Scheindlin, Menahem Schmelzer,

Eugene Sheppard, Suzanne Pinckney Stetkevych, and Joseph Yahalom. Special thanks are owed to Raymond Scheindlin, who taught me this craft, and who offered insightful suggestions during many stages of this project—***kunta** ḥilf al-nadā wa rabb al-samāḥ wa ḥabīb al-nufūs wa al-arwāḥ.*

My family and friends have been an enduring source of love, support, and encouragement. My parents, David and Carole Decter, and grandparents, Aaron and Regina Schultz, were always eager to hear about my progress and to share my accomplishments. My brother and sister-in-law, Adam Decter and Margie Ross Decter, and my three wonderful nephews, Noah, Jacob, and Zack, provided many hours of needed fun, support, and relaxation. My in-laws in Chicago—Lawrence, Debra, Gideon, and Noa Horberg, Samuel and Marilyn Horberg, and Edwin and Paulette Weinfield—saw this project unfold over many years and continents and always offered great encouragement and understanding. My cousins Philip and Jennifer Wickham Decter have given me much warmth and counsel. My dear friend and fellow traveler Raᶜanan Boustan has long been a source of intellectual engagement and emotional support; my relationship with him these many years has been a blessing. Other close friends have been with me to celebrate triumphs and to empathize at moments (sometimes very long moments) of difficulty and doubt. To all of them I owe a deep gratitude: Andy and Nancy Dubin, Edna Friedberg and Stig Tromer, Stuart and Wiebke Light, Aaron Seeskin, Eugene Sheppard, and Gavriel Speyer.

Finally, I thank my wife, Nikki, who, I am happy to say, played no role in the typesetting of this manuscript but was always a thoughtful and challenging conversation partner, reader, and editor. I cannot imagine having done all this without her. My love for her and gratitude to her are immeasurable. Our beautiful daughter, Lila Yaᶜel, was born seven months ago and has brightened our lives ten-thousandfold. To her I offer the pleasure of knowing a father who has published his first book rather than one working to complete it.

Iberian Jewish Literature

Introduction

Estrangement

Al-tagharrub and *al-ightirāb*—emigration and estrangement. Like the English pair "travel" and "travail," these Arabic words share a common root (*ghrb*) that underscores the intimate relation between moving from one place to another and resigning oneself to the burden of alienation. *Al-tagharrub* is the word that the Andalusian Jewish intellectual Judah Halevi (1075–1141) uses in his famous *Kuzari: Book of Refutation and Indication Concerning the Lowly Faith* to describe the patriarch Abraham's faithful emigration from his birthplace of Ur of the Chaldeans to Canaᶜan according to God's command.[1] *Al-ightirāb* is the word that the Jewish spokesman in the book uses to describe the duty to journey to the Land of Israel as an ultimate act of devotion.[2]

Halevi's Jewish spokesman offers a twist on a rabbinic dictum as a prooftext for the obligation to emigrate: *galut mekhaperet avon* (Makkot 2b), "*galut* atones for sin," where the word *galut,* often translated as "exile," is understood as the equivalent of the Arabic *ightirāb,* "estrangement." In the Talmudic context, *galut* refers to the exile from the Land of Israel. In Halevi's usage, the idea is ironically reversed so that the actualization of atonement requires emigration from one's homeland to the Land of Israel with its concomitant hardship of alienation. *Galut* is not the condition of banishment from the Promised Land; it is the acceptance of the yoke of estrangement that results from leaving one's homeland. Even for Halevi, who rhapsodized famously in Hebrew about the ease with which he would renounce "the good things of Sefarad"[3] in order to "behold the dust of the ruined shrine"[4] in Jerusalem, emigration's devotional value lay primarily in estrangement.[5] As important as reaching the land where God's commands can be executed perfectly is the self-sacrifice of becoming a *gharīb*—one who has traveled a distance, a foreigner, a stranger.

Halevi was one of numerous intellectuals who pondered the significance of emigration out of Islamic Iberia, al-Andalus, during a transitional period in Iberian Jewish history. Inasmuch as Halevi's own emigration from al-Andalus to Palestine was undertaken with the devout passion of the rabbinic character in the *Kuzari*, we must bear in mind that the aristocratic Jewish society of al-Andalus, which celebrated Halevi as its doyen, was beginning to deteriorate. Due to the numerous political shifts of the late eleventh and twelfth centuries—including the Reconquista and the invasions of the Almoravids and the Almohads—many Andalusian Jews took flight to relocate in destinations including Christian Iberia, the rest of Europe, and the Islamic East, including Palestine. For many, emigration out of al-Andalus created an experience of estrangement, which might result in personal crisis or, as Halevi suggests, become integral to an act of religious devotion.

The Arabic words for estrangement (*al-ightirāb; al-ghurba*) are layered with connotations that emerge from a long literary and cultural history. Estrangement is the dominant theme of countless Islamic sources, Arabic poems from the pre-Islamic and medieval periods, proverbs, treatises, letters of travelers, and even travelers' graffiti.[6] Travelers often wrote about their sense of *dhull*, humiliation, but also recognized the experience of estrangement as a crucible in which one's manhood and fortitude could be tested. When Judah Halevi's older Jewish contemporary Moses Ibn Ezra (1055–1138) found himself displaced from his Andalusian home of Granada, fated to reside in the Christian kingdom of Navarre at the far north of the Iberian Peninsula, he possessed a broad repertoire of Arabic aphorisms upon which to draw for lamenting his situation of "long estrangement" (*al-ightirāb al-ṭawīl*):

> I am imprisoned in jail, nay, buried in a tomb. It is true what is said, "The intellectual is not more satisfied by that which gives him sustenance than he is by his homeland." It is written in the Qurʾān of the Arabs (4:66), "If we had ordered them to kill themselves or abandon their homes, only few would have done so." "Killing oneself" and "leaving one's home" are considered equivalent. It is also said, "Estrangement [*al-ghurba*] is one of the two prisons." It is also said, "The foreigner [*al-gharīb*] is one who has lost the social companions whose company he enjoys and the confidants upon whom he depends." Another said, "The foreigner is like a plant whose land has been taken by night and has been deprived of drink: it is withered and does not bear fruit; it is faded and does not blossom."[7]

Ibn Ezra, who went into exile following the establishment of Almoravid rule over al-Andalus (1091), longed for the former days of the Andalusian Tāʾifa kings, when Jewish luminaries such as Samuel the Nagid (d. 1056) and his son Joseph (d. 1066) enjoyed royal favor and great prestige: "The community's splendor and luxury existed by virtue of [Samuel and Joseph] for thirty-four or thirty-five years; then these years and their people passed away as if they were but fading dreams."[8] Only a half-century after the death of Joseph, the Tā'ifa period was recalled nostalgically as a fading dream situated in the irretrievable past. For the rest of his life, Ibn Ezra referred to himself as a fugitive longing for the past while disparaging the Jews of Christian Iberia as philistine ignoramuses.

Jewish migration out of al-Andalus instigated a process of establishing Islamic Iberia as a place of memory that could be a recalled as an unrecoverable ideal, as a social and cultural template to be re-created elsewhere, or as an experiment in Jewish-Islamic symbiosis that had failed. What is clear is that the period of political reconfiguration and migration that had begun in the late eleventh century and continued through the mid-thirteenth century had profound effects on the making of Iberian Jewish culture.

A Period of Transition

In its broadest outlines, the transition of Hispano-Jewish society in the twelfth and thirteenth centuries involved the redistribution of the Jewish population from Islamic to Christian territories as Jews emigrated and political borders were redrawn. Prior to 1085, the vast majority of Iberian Jewry lived under Muslim control in al-Andalus, which retained a largely Arabic-Islamic character from the Islamic invasion of 711 through the periods of the Umayyad emirs (756–928), the Umayyad caliphate (929–1031), and the Tā'ifa kingdoms (1031–1091).[9] The year 1085 marks the capture of Islamic Toledo by the forces of the Reconquista, bringing part of Andalusian Jewry within the sphere of Christian domination. One year later, Almoravid troops—originally petitioned by al-Muᶜtamid Ibn ᶜAbbād, the tottering king of Seville, to aid him in his struggle against the Christian invaders—entered al-Andalus and proceeded to dismantle the numerous Tā'ifa kingdoms, instituting a single state under Almoravid rule by 1091. During the Almoravid period, Andalusian Jewry began to decline, leading some intellectuals to emigrate to kingdoms of Christian Iberia and other destinations. Although most Jews continued to live[10] and study[11] largely as they had during the Tā'ifa period, the change in regime forced some Jews (and also Muslims) into exile. The history of the Jews in Almoravid al-Andalus has never attracted the attention of scholars in the same way as the Tā'ifa period; completely omitted from Eliahu Ashtor's influential *The Jews of Moslem Spain*[12] and lightly brushed in the early pages of Yitzḥak Baer's *History of the Jews in Christian Spain,*[13] a comprehensive history of the Jews in Almoravid al-Andalus remains to be written.[14]

The ongoing tensions and skirmishes among the tens of small Ṭāʾifa kingdoms in al-Andalus had provided an ideal situation for Jews with political aspirations before the Almoravid period. Parallel government bureaucracies and competing armies created windows of opportunity for men of talent such as Ismaʿīl Ibn Naghrila (also known as Samuel the Nagid) to serve in Zirid Granada or Abraham Ibn al-Muhājir in Abbadid Seville. It is probably the centralization of power that ensued with Almoravid hegemony that narrowed the opportunities for a Jewish elite, even if such opportunities were not extinguished entirely.[15] Soon after the Almoravid invasion, numerous Jewish notables, Moses Ibn Ezra prominent among them, began to emigrate to the Christian north—perhaps because their lives and property were severely disrupted in the aftermath of the attacks, because their esteemed positions put them at particular risk as associates of the former regime, or simply because they feared worse. Emigration out of al-Andalus continued throughout the Almoravid period, including the notable departures of Abraham Ibn Ezra (1092–1167) and Judah Halevi in 1137 and 1140, respectively.[16]

Almoravid hegemony collapsed when the Almohad revolution, which had already deposed the Almoravids in North Africa, seized control of al-Andalus in 1147. The Almohads persecuted the Jews of al-Andalus, leading to forced conversion and mass flight, mainly to the kingdoms of Christian Iberia but also to destinations in Egypt, the Maghreb, the Islamic East, Provence, and Italy.[17] Although the Almohad era did not witness the absolute end of Jewish life in al-Andalus,[18] Jews of the Iberian Peninsula were largely transferred from Islamic to Christian territories as they emigrated from south to north and as the political border of Christian Iberia moved southward. For some of those who settled in the Christian kingdoms of northern Iberia, their refuge seemed a place that was culturally alien, where language, landscape, and social custom were foreign and inferior. In Christian Iberia, Jews retained some aspects of their Andalusian culture while novel developments occurred in intellectual and spiritual life. These centuries of transition were productive ones for authors of Jewish philosophy, halakhah, and Hebrew belles-lettres, all of which occasionally touch upon the topics of estrangement and renewal.

One great paradox of medieval Iberia is that, as much as al-Andalus and Christian Iberia seem like two places in many ways, in other ways they seem like one. Despite profound divisions between Muslims and Christians, political borders were easily penetrated by trends in philosophy, religion, architecture, and literature; Islamic culture and Christian culture, as well as the Arabic and Romance languages, were never hermetically sealed off from one another.[19] With the exception of the kingdom of Granada following the mid-thirteenth century, al-Andalus always retained a Christian population and was penetrated by Latin-derived vernaculars spoken by members of all religious faiths.[20] In the eleventh century, the Andalusian Hebrew poet Solomon Ibn Gabirol lamented Jews' disregard for learning Hebrew and decried, "Half of them speak Edomese [Romance] and half the language of Qedar [Arabic]."[21] Even Moses Ibn Ezra, a champion of Arabic literary erudition who sometimes denigrated Romance speakers as "stammerers of speech," followed the literary vogue of concluding Hebrew *muwashshaḥs* with Romance *kharjas*. Some have seen al-Andalus not as "Islamic Spain" but as a multi-confessional entity wherein an "Andalusian" cultural identity transcended religious differences.[22]

Likewise, the Christian north possessed a substantial Muslim population that even constituted the majority in regions such as Valencia after the Reconquista. Many cities engulfed by the Christian kingdoms during the Reconquista, notably Toledo, retained their Arabic and Islamic character, preserving Arabic as a spoken or at least a written language for centuries. The impact of Arabic-Islamic culture on the emergence of Spanish and French literature, Spanish architecture, and Christian philosophical and mystical thought has become increasingly accepted.[23] However, the intellectual currents that bypassed confessional and political boundaries to produce a culture that, in retrospect, seems deeply intertwined and perhaps even unified did not prevent émigrés from experiencing crossing boundaries as estrangement and alienation. The complex contours of Iberia's simultaneous unity and division will be revisited numerous times throughout this book.

Andalusian Jews referred to their homeland in Hebrew as Sefarad, a place identified in the Bible as the domicile of Jerusalem exiles (Obad. 1:20) and equated (probably erroneously) in the first-century Aramaic Targum with the Roman province Hispania. Yet mapping the exact borders of Sefarad during the medieval period is tricky. Whereas kingdoms such as Seville, Granada, Castile, and Aragon had actual (albeit shifting) borders, Sefarad never had a political reality; it existed only in the minds of Jews. In the early part of the Middle Ages, Sefarad functioned discursively in Hebrew as the equivalent of al-Andalus in Arabic; this is attested to in a famous tenth-century letter from Ḥasdai Ibn Shaprūṭ to the distant Khazar king: "The name of our land in which we dwell is called in the sacred tongue Sefarad, but in the language of the Arabs, the inhabitants of the land, al-Andalus."[24] With emigration, Moses Ibn Ezra clearly saw himself as leaving Sefarad and coming to a foreign place that was not culturally continuous. When Judah Halevi spoke of the "good things of Sefarad," he probably had al-Andalus only in mind. When Moses Maimonides identified himself as Moses the Sefardi in the introduction to the *Mishne Torah,* he was probably thinking of the Arabic term *Andalusī,* with all the prestige and authority that the term implied.[25] With time, especially as Jews moved from Islamic to Christian territories within the Iberian Peninsula, the borders of Sefarad were reimagined to include the new communities. Only after centuries did the whole of the Iberian Peninsula come to be identified with Sefarad.

It is difficult to approach the subject of Jewish emigration out of al-Andalus without feeling the powerful and romantic position that al-Andalus has occupied in the minds of Muslims, Christians, and Jews in modernity. On many occasions and for various purposes, al-Andalus has been evoked as a model of religious tolerance and multi-confessional cultural glory. Nostalgic expressions may be found in the modern period, from Washington Irving's *Alhambra*[26] to Borges's account of Ibn Rushd[27] and popular reports that North African families of Hispano-Arabic descent preserve the keys to their houses in Spain.[28] In Jewish studies, al-Andalus has been hailed as the paragon of Jewish acculturation within Islam wherein the two faiths nurtured each other in a symbiotic dance.[29] The scholarly consensus has been that Jewish life was better under Islam than under Christianity; given such a narrative, it hardly seems surprising that a displaced intellectual such as Moses Ibn Ezra would pine for the past.

We must remember, however, that the narratives that have become stable in the popular and scholarly imagination held no currency for medieval writers. Nostalgia for al-Andalus was only one of numerous possible responses toward emigration. For some, Christendom provided an attractive refuge from the instability of life in al-Andalus. Even Maimonides, who settled in Egypt after his family's emigration out of al-Andalus, may have believed that the future of Jewish intellectual life lay in the realm of Christendom and in the Hebrew, rather than the Arabic, language.[30] Toward the end of the thirteenth century, the phrase "better under Edom [Christendom] than under Ishmael [Islamdom]" was cited sporadically by Bible commentators, revealing a preference for life in Christendom over (at least a conception of) life under Islam.[31]

Jews who left al-Andalus during the twelfth and thirteenth centuries faced many options. They could settle in Christian Iberia, elsewhere in Europe, or in Arabic-speaking countries in North Africa and the Islamic East. It is difficult to know exactly why individuals chose the paths that they did. Why did Moses Ibn Ezra remain in Castile and Navarre while his friend Judah Halevi set out on a pilgrimage to Palestine and Solomon Ibn al-Muᶜallim immigrated to Morocco? Why did Abraham Ibn Ezra wander the lands of Europe while his son Isaac settled in the Islamic East? Why did Maimonides' family remain in the Islamic world while many of their coreligionists chose Christian Iberian kingdoms or Provence as their refuge? Ultimately, the answers to these questions depend upon an author's particular circumstances, his religious, cultural, or intellectual convictions, and conceptions about the destination to which he was going.

The possibilities for intellectual and cultural expression were as plentiful as the number of physical destinations. The situation in Christian Iberia (and also in Provence) was particularly complex since the territory stood at the crossroads—geographically and culturally—between the domain of Islam and Christian Europe. In short, it may be said that a kind of synthesis between the Judaisms of Islamdom and Christendom took place, though not without significant dissonance between intellectual systems and social values. Scholars such as Bernard Septimus and Yom Tov Assis have studied the strategies of synthesis and accommodation utilized by legal scholars and exegetes in Castile and Aragon who were faced with contradictory traditions such as Andalusian rationalist exegesis versus northern French literalism[32] or the Andalusian practice of polygyny versus northern French monogamy.[33] Jews could continue the intellectual traditions of the Andalusian past, rework them to integrate new interests, or seek paths of expression that were altogether new. Andalusian Hebrew poetic writing, which dealt with sacred as well as secular themes, could be imitated, revised, or abandoned. Topics expounded by Andalusian Jews in Arabic (exegesis, philosophy, science, mathematics, astrology, etc.) could be treated by Jews in Christian Iberia (and in Provence) in the same language, a neologistic register of Hebrew, or in the local Christian vernacular (a choice seldom made).

On a social level, Jews of Andalusian stock had to evaluate whether Arabic mannerisms were integral to their identities in the Christian environment or whether their "Arabness" was an outer skin that was easily shed. Would adopting the customs of Christendom threaten to rupture their communal identity? Regarding communal organization, Jews had to determine whether Jewish leadership should follow the Andalusian model or whether that model had failed or been misleading. To some, Andalusian Jewish leaders embodied the ideal synthesis of Jewish advocacy and secular acculturation by participating in the intellectual and social trends of Andalusian society; to others, these men brought on the downfall of the community through their arrogance, ostentation, and decadent behavior. Indeed, the relationship between Jewish leadership and Andalusian cultural tastes was an issue of great controversy in Christian Iberia.[34]

In this book, I study Jewish belletristic writing emanating from this transitional period of Iberian Jewish history in order to elucidate the discourse surrounding the relocation of Jewish life from Islamic to Christian Iberia.[35] The intent of the book is not to create a comprehensive *Zeitgeschichte* but rather to interpret a corpus of interrelated writings.[36] Iberian Jewish authors—both those who crossed the border between al-Andalus and Christian territories and those who were born in Christendom but saw themselves as the intellectual heirs of Andalusian Jewry—composed Hebrew belles-lettres in the forms of poetry and fictional narratives in rhymed prose that touch on subjects of exile, estrangement, and identity in transition. Several of these authors also composed poetry, travelogues, and other writings in Arabic. The study begins with poetry from the early stages of the Reconquista (after 1085) and the Almoravid invasion (1091) and continues with poetry and fictional narratives composed after the Almohad incursions (1146–1147). No attempt is made to offer a concluding date for the historical narrative; the book does not mark a moment when the transitional period came to an end, when the questions raised by the decline of Jewish life in al-Andalus became resolved or forgotten. Rather, the book contemplates several moments from the early stages of the afterlife of al-Andalus, an afterlife that has undergone many transformations down to the modern period.

The strategies of accommodation formulated by Jewish authors experiencing the transformation of Jewish life in medieval Iberia were manifold. Authors express attitudes toward cultural transition that range from desperate nostalgia for the Islamic past to partial acculturation in the Christian environment. Some experiencing the transition delineate a sharp border between the cultures of al-Andalus and the Christian north and develop a sophisticated poetics of estrangement based in the Arabic tradition. Others see the Christian environment as a viable site for the reestablishment of Jewish culture and adapt to certain norms of Christian society. During the period of transition, Hebrew literature undergoes internal transformations, utilizing forms and themes that maintain a complex and evolving relationship with the Arabic and European literary models that intermingled in medieval Iberia. This book, then, is about both transition in literature and literature in transition. Evolving literary styles between Arabic and Romance help us map changing cultural postures. Just as halakhists and philosophers can be located between the Jewish intellectual traditions of al-Andalus and northern France, so authors of belles-lettres should be understood as individuals negotiating their art between two great literary cultures.

In considering attitudes toward transition reflected in the texts discussed, it should be kept in mind that the authors are representative of only a small segment of Iberian Jewry. This is the case not only because the texts are the products of a cultural elite—men of education, talent, and sometimes wealth—but because the authors' very choice to write Hebrew poetry and rhymed prose already betrays them as bearers of one of Andalusian Jewry's hallmark traditions. One generation after the Almohad invasion, the writing of Arabized Hebrew poetry was revived enthusiastically by the heirs of Andalusian Jewry. Had these intellectuals on Christian soil decided to renounce the Andalusian heritage out of hand, they undoubtedly would have rejected its literary values. Although all of the authors treated in this book continue the tradition of Andalusian Jewish writing in one way or another, a range of attitudes toward cultural transition is apparent among them.

Literature and History

This book explores the discursive practices surrounding the ideas of estrangement and transition in literary texts from a specific historical period. The relationship between belles-lettres and historical moments has been extremely perplexing for scholars of literature and history alike. While historians grapple with the implications of literary criticism on their ability to reconstruct events of the past, literary scholars' interpretative power is checked by their knowledge of social and historical contexts.[37] The dialectical nature of these disciplines is evident in scholarship treating the Jews in the Middle Ages. Some of the fiercest debates that have raged in this field may be reduced to problems of interpretation, both of texts that have been viewed traditionally as "literary" as well as texts that have been considered "historical." Do the Hebrew Crusade chronicles convey facts about the events of 1096,[38] or does their preconceived structure and affected style preclude the possibility of retrieving actual information about the events?[39] Do the records of the Spanish national Inquisition offer an accurate record of crypto-Jewish practices,[40] or does their status as confessions obtained under duress relegate their contents to accusation and fiction?[41] Do references in medieval Hebrew poems to erotic desire for a male beloved indicate homosexual practice,[42] or do they indicate literary fashion?[43] Such problems, often intractable, are always dependent upon how scholars conceive of the relationship between texts and their contexts.

All too often, positivists have mined literary texts for historical facts; medieval Hebrew literature has often been rendered ancillary to the reconstruction of medieval Jewish life, particularly Jewish courtier culture and the biographies of notable personalities.[44] The positivist approach is critiqued by Russian Formalists, New Critics, and other literary theorists who argue that texts may be read for their literary merits alone without having to answer to such questions as social reality or authorial intent.[45] For such theorists, the critic's business is to study how devices such as sound, imagery, rhythm, syntax, and structure function within a textual system, and not to reduce all literature to autobiography. Other critics have argued that it is nearly impossible to interpret texts properly without at least some contextualization. Words and discursive forms have histories; identical utterances can carry one meaning in one period and quite another meaning in another. The present project therefore engages the literature-history conundrum through readings that eschew naïve positivism without banishing history from the interpretation of texts.

Historians must accept that "historical" texts possess a literary dimension while students of literature must accept that texts cannot be wholly severed from their contexts. Of course, the exact interplay between text and context is complex and remains difficult to define. One great trap that readers must avoid is the vicious cycle of interpreting texts in view of a preconceived historical narrative. As mentioned, the subject of transition away from al-Andalus is already circumscribed by several narratives that have become stable among academic and popular communities. If one begins with the simplistic assumption that Jews displaced from al-Andalus must have viewed the past nostalgically, since life was better for Jews under Islam than under Christianity, and then proceeds to read texts under the tyranny of this assumption, misreadings will certainly ensue. Every text will be interpreted as a further piece of evidence, another telling artifact, verifying and ratifying the presumed narrative. Readings must emerge from texts themselves even though, as Seth Schwartz has pointed out, even the most empirical reader cannot approach a text with no preconceptions regarding its meaning.[46] The present work maintains that Iberian cultural transition is a useful vantage point from which literary texts can be interpreted but does not insist upon a singular master narrative (such as "better under Ishmael" or "better under Edom").

Through literary analysis, this book treats Hebrew poetry and rhymed prose fictional narratives, texts that have been designated by scholarship as "literary," as opposed to "historical," "legal," "mystical," or "philosophical." Although these divisions among textual genres may be partly attributed to the organization of academic disciplines, medieval readers considered Hebrew poems and fictional narratives within a single category called *shirah* (poetry, or song), which could be either "composed" (*meḥubar,* a translation of the Arabic *manẓūm*)—what we would call "metered poetry"—or "scattered" (*mefurad,* a translation of the Arabic *manthūr*)—what we would call rhymed prose. These texts form a close-knit corpus wherein texts utilize material existing elsewhere in this corpus, allowing words, phrases, names, places, and themes to reverberate through evocation and reuse. At the same time, these texts cannot be severed from the non-Hebrew literatures with which Jewish authors were in contact. The impact of Arabic literature, for example, is strongly felt in the Hebrew poetics of estrangement wherein the very construction of exile is shaped by the discourse surrounding the "stranger" in Arabic writing.[47] Elements of Hebrew literature derived from European vernacular writing, although still a marginal topic of scholarly interest, are also not without importance.

Organization of the Book

Inasmuch as this book stresses the interdependence of history and literature, the organization reflects concerns that are admittedly more literary than historical. The book is first divided into two main parts, "Poetry" and "Narrative," separated because different strategies of reading are employed for interpreting these different literary forms. The division is also pertinent because there is a rough (though not absolute) correspondence between the literary forms and the division between Andalusian and post-Andalusian periods. Poetry dominated the literary scene during the Andalusian period while the rhymed prose narrative dominated during the Christian period, although this variety of Hebrew fiction originated in al-Andalus while poetry continued to be written in Christian Iberia through the fifteenth century. The significance of the shift to prose in the Christian environment will be contemplated at length in part 2 of this book. For now, let it suffice to say that the switch does not in itself engender a rejection of Arabic models of writing; like metrical Hebrew verse, Hebrew rhymed prose derives its prosodic features from Arabic belles-lettres. However, thematic and structural elements in some Hebrew narratives bear a greater affinity for a European vernacular style, a fact that helps us gauge Jewish engagement with Christian culture.

Within each part of the work, the chapters are arranged according to literary topics—imagery, space, form, structure, and voice—that are pertinent in gleaning attitudes toward cultural transition. Chapter 1, "Space: Landscape and Transition," explores the cultural significance of three landscapes of medieval Hebrew poetry—garden, desert, and forest. The chapter shows how authors exploit these landscapes to create succinctly a sense of place and an ambience of estrangement and nostalgia. Chapter 2, "Form: Varieties of Lamentation and Estrangement," contrasts poems by three authors on the decline of Jewish life during the Almoravid period, the Reconquista, and the Almohad period. Because Jewish authors of the Islamic world were generally reticent about responding directly to incidents of persecution, literary texts remain some of the most telling expressions available.[48] By utilizing different literary forms, Moses Ibn Ezra, Judah Halevi, and Abraham Ibn Ezra situate their mourning within contrasting literary and cultural traditions, lamenting personal or communal loss with the voice of an Arabic poet or with the voice of a Jewish mourner. Chapter 3, "Imagery: The Protean Garden," demonstrates how authors manipulate imagery in garden poetry to create different emotional tenors, sometimes signifying distress and estrangement. In particular, the chapter contrasts two garden poems by Moses Ibn Ezra—one written from the context of al-Andalus and the other from the poet's exile in the Christian north—showing that the poet utilized different fields of imagery for creating the impressions of comfort and distress.

The second part of the book, on narrative, opens with an introduction (chapter 4), "Context: Imagining Hebrew Fiction between Arabic and European Sources," which situates the Hebrew rhymed prose narrative between classical Arabic fiction and the literature of Christian Europe. The remaining three chapters contrast aspects of two Hebrew narrative collections: the famous *Taḥkemoni,* by Judah al-Ḥarīzī (c. 1166–1235); and the lesser-known *Sefer ha-meshalim* (The Book of Stories), by al-Ḥarīzī's younger contemporary Jacob Ben Elʿazar (mid-thirteenth century). This comparison elaborates the contrasting perspectives that these two authors—born in the same city, approximately thirty years apart—held concerning the Christian and Islamic worlds and cultural transition in general. Chapter 5, "Structure: Literature in Transition," introduces the two authors and their works, highlighting differences in literary structure and narrative technique. The chapter shows that, despite numerous innovations, al-Ḥarīzī remains faithful to norms of the classical Arabic *maqāma* while Ben Elʿazar turns to other literary models reaching the Iberian Peninsula from the Islamic world and from Christian Europe. Chapter 6, "Voice: *Maqāma* and Morality," continues the discussion of structure and technique with an eye directed toward the ways in which issues of cultural transition are refracted through the respective compositions. By focusing on authorial voice, it is shown that al-Ḥarīzī allows multiple social voices surrounding aspects of Andalusian culture to collide whereas Ben Elʿazar causes a single voice that is critical of select values to emerge. Chapter 7, "Space: Landscape, Geography, and Transition," shows that the two works, although both written by authors born in Christian Toledo, reflect the perspectives of authors with contrasting worldviews. While al-Ḥarīzī continues to idealize the landscape of the garden so central to the memory of al-Andalus, Ben Elʿazar rejects the aristocratic landscape and turns toward a new vision of nature more consistent with European models. Furthermore, while al-Ḥarīzī retains the geographical perspective of an author of the Islamic world, Ben Elʿazar appears as an author of the Christian world looking outward at the world of Islam.

On Medieval Hebrew Literature

Readers familiar with the field of medieval Hebrew literature have undoubtedly noticed the distinct approach of this book, which departs from previous scholarship with respect to periodization and methods of literary analysis. Whereas most studies choose either al-Andalus or Christian Iberia as a focal point, this book carves out a period spanning the last days of the Jews in al-Andalus through the rebirth of Jewish life in Christendom in order to stress common concerns and a shared discourse. Regarding method, I emulate the ideals of my predecessors who have built this field on a number of pillars: philological rigor, close comparison with contemporary non-Jewish literature, painstaking attention to the conventions of medieval genres, and recognition that the aims and values of medieval authors are vastly different from those of their modern readers. Nevertheless, I do not refrain from employing analytic strategies that have been productive in studying medieval and modern texts alike.

The field of medieval Hebrew literature has been dedicated largely to creating a coherent narrative of literary history. The collection, publication, and analysis of thousands of manuscripts from diverse sources over the past century and a half have brought us closer to having an accurate picture of the evolution of this literature, although the work is still incomplete. Like Iberian Jewish history, which customarily is divided into Islamic and Christian eras, the Hebrew literature of medieval Iberia has generally been segregated into two main periods: the Andalusian period, often referred to as the "Golden Age" or the "classical period"; and the post-Andalusian period of activity in Christian Iberia and Provence, sometimes called the "Silver Age" or "postclassical period."[49] Through the efforts of numerous scholars, we have learned that a literary revolution took place in al-Andalus toward the end of the tenth century owing to the importation of Arabic poetry's prosodic and thematic features into Hebrew poetry. Great Hebrew poets such as Samuel the Nagid (993–1056), Solomon Ibn Gabirol (1021–1053?), Judah Halevi, Moses Ibn Ezra, and Abraham Ibn Ezra displayed their educations in Arabic learning—ranging from poetry to mathematics, astronomy, social etiquette, and Qurʾān—in their Hebrew compositions. In addition to liturgical poems for use in the synagogue, Hebrew authors in al-Andalus through the mid-twelfth century composed poems of entertainment on themes such as wine drinking, sexual desire, and palace gardens.[50]

Following the Almohad invasion, Hebrew poetry lay dormant for the duration of a generation and was reborn on the soil of Christian Iberia, largely adhering to the aesthetic tastes and prosodic requirements of Andalusian Hebrew poetry. Some have seen the poetry of this period as epigonic and a pale reflection of the Andalusian model.[51] The greatest innovation in Hebrew literature on Christian soil was the development of the Hebrew rhymed prose narrative[52] (sometimes called the Hebrew *maqāma* or *maḥberet*), which mimics the prosodic features of the Arabic *maqāma* but exhibits a wide variety of structures, plots, and character types. The Hebrew narratives have generally been studied in the context of the Arabic tradition and, to a lesser extent, the literatures surfacing in the Iberian Peninsula in European languages.

This bipartite schema of literary history is given its finest expression in the masterful (posthumous) publication of Jefim Schirmann's two-volume literary history *The History of Hebrew Poetry in Muslim Spain* and *The History of Hebrew Poetry in Christian Spain and Southern France*. However, the tension inherent in this model becomes apparent when we consider that a liminal figure such as Abraham Ibn Ezra lived between the Islamic and Christian worlds. Ibn Ezra was born in Tudela (in Christian Iberia) in 1092 and was educated and active in al-Andalus, leaving circa 1140 for Italy, France, and finally England, where he died in 1167. Straddling the temporal border between classical and postclassical periods and crossing the physical border between the Islamic and Christian worlds, Abraham Ibn Ezra is a transitional figure whose place is difficult to pin down. He has been portrayed as a proponent of Judeo-Arabic symbiosis, a conduit of Andalusian Jewish culture to the burgeoning Jewish communities of the Christian world,[53] a literary innovator and harbinger of a new literary age, the poetic mourner over the devastated cities of al-Andalus,[54] and a tragic wanderer able to endure his suffering with a measure of humor.[55] The ambiguity of his place is reflected in his leap from being the last poet in volume 1 of Schirmann's anthology *Hebrew Poetry in Spain and Provence* (locating him in Muslim Iberia) to being the first poet in volume 2 of Schirmann's history of that poetry (locating him in Christian Iberia and Provence).[56] Abraham Ibn Ezra not only traveled great distances during his lifetime but has "traveled" in the imagination of scholars.

In order to study the Hebrew poetics of estrangement and Jewish identity in transition in medieval Iberia, we must imagine periodization somewhat differently. This is not to say that the Almohad invasion does not mark a significant dividing line; the testimonies of medieval authors suggest that it did (though some place the division earlier, with the Reconquista or the Almoravid invasion). Rather, I maintain that we should not pigeonhole authors into singularly Islamic or Christian contexts when, in one way or another, they exist both in al-Andalus and outside of it. For authors such as Moses Ibn Ezra, Judah Halevi, and Abraham Ibn Ezra, who leave al-Andalus themselves, Islamic Iberia is a subject in need of pondering; they reflect upon the meaning of the Jewish experience in al-Andalus and the significance of life outside of it. For authors born in the kingdoms of the Christian north, such as Judah al-Ḥarīzī and Jacob Ben Elʿazar, al-Andalus stands out in their writings as a place of origin, a font of intellectual life approached with a mixture of nostalgia and ambivalence. Although these authors may never have even set foot on the soil of Muslim Iberia, al-Andalus remains a topic of their consciousness that is evoked through a number of discursive strategies.

Concerning literary analysis, I introduce methods that have not gained much attention in scholarship on medieval Hebrew literature, which has been grounded in philology, comparison with Arabic literature, and literary categories presented by medieval critics. As in Arabic poetry, the basic syntactic unit of Andalusian Hebrew poetry is the individual line, which medieval critics and modern critics after them have studied for the intricacies of poetic meter, different types of wordplay, and various constructions of metaphor.[57] Scholarship has been appropriately wary about applying topics popular in modern literary theory, many of which address postmedieval forms such as the novel, to the study of medieval writings. Still, a scholar such as Dan Pagis, who generally insists upon a conservative approach by situating compositions vis-à-vis medieval genre conventions, turns to contemporary theory to argue that medieval poems are not devoid of individual expression or emotional transparency.[58]

Discussions of method within the discipline of classical Arabic literature are illuminating for the student of medieval Hebrew literature. Some have asked whether analysis that extends beyond the methods of medieval criticism is justifiable, since classical critics were certainly closer to the literature in its original context than modern scholars. The Arabist G. J. H. van Gelder, for example, questions why medieval Arab critics should not be allowed to represent Arab culture themselves and argues that studying medieval criticism is tantamount to the study of poetry itself.[59] Others, such as Wolfhart Heinrichs, have noted the deficiencies of medieval Arabic criticism for treating subjects that interest modern students of literature, such as thematic development.[60] Recent studies of Arabic literature have turned to myth analysis, structuralism, post-structuralism, and anthropology as analytical approaches.[61]

Although there is a need for a careful and consistent application of the many literary methods employed today, van Gelder's comments seem overly restrictive. To study criticism is not to study poetry. The relationship between poets and critics was undoubtedly complex in the medieval period, as it is today.[62] Innovative poets flout the conventions praised by critics precisely to keep poetry from becoming stale. Also, it is simply possible that those aspects of writing that are most interesting to modern readers were either uninteresting to medieval critics or so deeply entrenched in medieval culture that no critic would think to comment on them. For a corpus such as pre-Islamic poetry, there is little reason to assume that a medieval Muslim scholar—who may have been a Persian speaker who read poetry as a means toward interpreting the language of the Qurʾān—is necessarily a better interpreter of the poetry than a modern scholar. Classical critics developed reading strategies that suited their religious, political, and philosophical needs, and modern readers need not limit their methods to those of their predecessors.

In addition to reconstructing literary history, modern studies of medieval Hebrew literature have treated specific poets, genres,[63] forms,[64] and themes.[65] Less common have been works that offer close readings of individual poems.[66] Even more limited have been studies dedicated to topics current in literary disciplines outside of medieval Hebrew literature such as imagery, poetic or narrative structure, gender, space, time, comparative, or post-structuralist approaches.[67] By treating some of these topics systematically, this book draws out the complex relationship between literary texts and their historical moments in order to illuminate a transitional period in Jewish literature and Jewish history. My hope in this book is to stress the importance of systematic engagement with literary theory for the field of medieval Hebrew literature, to give prominence to literary texts alongside halakhic and philosophical texts for reconstructing Hispano-Jewish culture in transition, and to make medieval Hebrew writing more accessible and relevant for students of comparative literature, especially those with an interest in the themes of estrangement, exile, and cultural transition.

PART I
POETRY

One

Space

Landscape and Transition

"O Sir," said [Don Quixote's] niece, "pray order these [books of poetry] to be burnt with the rest; for should my uncle be cured of this distemper of chivalry, he may possibly, by reading these books, take it into his head to turn shepherd, and wander through the woods and fields singing and playing on a pipe."

—Miguel Cervantes, *Don Quixote*

Had *Don Quixote* been set in eleventh-century al-Andalus rather than the unified Spain of the sixteenth century, the delusional knight-errant's niece would have feared that her uncle, upon reading books of poetry, would think himself a courtier sipping wine in palace gardens rather than a shepherd wandering woods and fields. *Don Quixote* is heir to the classical tradition wherein the bucolic poets created an intimate bond between the creation of poetry and the pastoral landscape.[1] Not only was poetry about forests, but forests were about poetry. The Arabic and Hebrew poetry of al-Andalus, in contrast, was an urban poetry that idealized the aristocratic palace garden as poetry's font and natural setting.

Scholarship treating Andalusian Hebrew literature has generally approached poems depicting natural settings—especially the garden and the desert—as "nature poetry" without considering "landscape" as a distinct literary topic. It is generally assumed that the poet's aim in writing is to describe an observed setting, usually the palace garden, or to imitate the fashion of Arab poets by depicting the desert, a landscape inherited from the Arabic literary tradition.[2] This chapter reconsiders Andalusian Hebrew poetry from the perspective of landscape, focusing on the associations between natural settings (garden, desert, and forest) and cultural meaning. In particular, the contrast between the garden and its counterpoints in the desert and forest is linked with the poetics of estrangement and nostalgia that surfaced briefly following the destruction of Cordoba (1013) and became prominent following the establishment of Almoravid hegemony over al-Andalus (1090). As Islamic Iberia began to fade into Jewish memory, the palace garden emerged as an icon of Andalusian culture, while the desert and forest represented landscapes of exile, each bearing specific cultural connotations. This chapter begins with a theoretical discussion about landscape as a construct in geographical descriptions of al-Andalus and then treats the three dominant landscapes of the Andalusian Hebrew canon: garden, desert, and forest.

Describing Al-Andalus: Landscape and Culture

Landscape has long been a pivotal construct in the definition both of Self and Other. Latin authors, identifying themselves as refined urban dwellers, derided the barbarians by portraying them as primitive forest dwellers dependent upon the hunt for sustenance. Germanic authors reclaimed the forest as a locus of spiritual and artistic virtue, immune to the decadent seductions of urban life.[3] Pre-Islamic poets depicted the desert as a wasteland in which individuals and tribes displayed bravery, generosity, and chivalry while animal protagonists faced the dangers of thirst, starvation, heat, and human hunters. In the urban ᶜAbbasid empire, Arabic poets of Persian descent mocked Arab origins by stripping the desert of its noble associations and portraying Bedouin customs as primitive and backward.[4] In Romance literature, the wooded forest appeared paradoxically as an anti-courtly refuge and as an unknown place of peril and exploitation.[5]

Medieval Arab geographers unanimously extol the landscape of al-Andalus as a lush garden signifying wealth, power, comfort, and intellectual culture. Throughout the *Nafḥ al-ṭīb min ghuṣn al-andalus al-raṭīb*, the exhaustive compendium of Andalusian history and literature compiled by al-Maqqarī in the seventeenth century, the impression is given that al-Andalus was covered by a continuous garden. Quoting the ninth-century sheikh Aḥmad Ibn Muḥammad Ibn Mūsā al-Rāzī, al-Maqqarī notes:

> The land of al-Andalus is the western extreme of the fourth clime. In the opinion of the wise it is a land plentiful in lowlands with good, arable soil, fertile settlements [*janāb*], flowing copiously with plentiful rivers and fresh springs. There are few poisonous beasts. [It possesses] a temperate climate and pleasant breezes. Its spring, fall, winter, and summer are relatively temperate and well-balanced such that no season generates excess. . . . Its fruits are ripe at most times, not wanting.[6]

What al-Rāzī omits from the landscape are the desolate and arid regions abutting the areas of growth, resembling desert more than verdant garden. As Thomas Glick has pointed out, wide stretches of the southern peninsula resembled "the face of the moon" because of the effective deforestation projects of the Romans.[7]

Yet, according to medieval Arab historians and geographers, Islamic Iberia was considered a naturally cohesive region. It was temperate and constant because of its location at the edge of the fourth clime, whose limit was somehow just beyond the border of Muslim settlement. A similar description of al-Andalus was composed in Hebrew by Menaḥem Ben Sarūq (c. 910–c. 970), scribe of Ḥasdai Ibn Shaprūṭ, in a famous letter to the Khazar king:

> The name of our land in which we dwell is called in the sacred tongue Sefarad, but in the language of the Arabs, the inhabitants of the land, al-Andalus. . . . The land is rich, abounding in rivers, springs, and aqueducts; a land of corn, oil, and wine, of fruits and all manner of delicacies; it has pleasure-gardens and orchards, fruitful trees of every kind, including the leaves of the tree upon which the silkworm feeds, of which we have great abundance. In the mountains and woods of our country the cochineal [insect] is gathered in great quantity.[8]

Centuries after al-Rāzī and Ibn Shaprūṭ, the traveler Ibn Baṭṭūṭa (1304–1377) encountered a similar landscape in Granada, then capital of the last remaining stronghold of Muslim Iberia:

> [Granada] is the capital of al-Andalus and the bridegroom of its cities. Its environs are unparalleled on earth. It covers forty miles and is crossed by the well-known Genil River and many rivers like it. Many types of gardens [*riyāḍāt, jannāt, basātīn*], palaces, and vineyards surround it on every side.[9]

In this account, Granada is a remnant of al-Andalus, fully continuous with it in landscape and cultural values. Still absent is mention of landscapes other than the garden.

The gardenlike appearance of al-Andalus was as much the result of technological coercion as of nature. One of the earliest Arabic poems from al-Andalus calls attention to the lack of such species as the palm tree in the eighth century. In the famous poem of estrangement, ʿAbd al-Raḥmān I, the Umayyad prince who had fled Damascus for Cordoba (ruled 756–788), confronted his sense of displacement in al-Andalus by addressing a palm tree planted in his garden at the palace of al-Ruṣāfa:

A palm tree set for us upon the pavement in the Western Land
[al-Andalus]
remote from the Land of the Palm [Syria],
I said, "[You are] like me in estrangement, remoteness
and long separation from children and family;
You have grown in a land in which you are a stranger,
you and I in our alienation and separation."[10]

Syria is remembered foremost through the vegetation of its landscape; the palm is a symbol both of the author's place of origin and of his present estrangement. The lone sapling marked the initiation of a process of re-creating the lost culture of Syria and making a new cosmopolitan home for the Umayyad refugees. The garden at al-Ruṣāfa epitomized a cultural transformation whose most physical manifestation was the remaking of landscape. The introduction of Syrian methods of agriculture, which included an irrigation system suited to the needs of a predominantly urban economy, made the landscape of al-Andalus a mirror of the original seat of the displaced Umayyads.[11] For this reason, early geographers often compare al-Andalus with Syria,[12] and Andalusian cities, particularly Granada, with Damascus.[13]

The Syrianization of al-Andalus was executed so thoroughly that the direction of association between the two regions was ironically reversed; although al-Andalus was modeled after Syria and not vice versa, the twelfth-century Andalusian author Ibn Saʿīd al-Andalusī remarked that no place in the East reminded him of his native home of Granada, with the exception of Damascus.[14] Muslim and Jewish heirs of Andalusian culture praised the beauty of cities such as Alexandria and Damascus between the thirteenth and seventeenth century by describing them as gardens.[15] Although there were certainly physical commonalities among the Islamic cities, the similar depictions point not to an absolute continuity of landscape but to a certain typology of place. The garden landscape carried specific cultural connotations; it represented a tame, cultivated environment that was suited for human settlement and ultimately for the advancement of intellectual, especially literary, culture.

In the nineteenth century, Washington Irving portrayed al-Andalus in opposite terms for a European readership. Following his journey from Seville to Granada in 1829, the English author described a desolate desert "partaking of the savage and solitary character of Africa."[16] Although Irving's description of Granada does incorporate remnants of the landscape described by Ibn Baṭṭūṭa, these elements are contextualized within the narrative of al-Andalus as a barren desert:

> Vast sierras or chains of mountains, destitute of shrub or tree and mottled with variegated marbles and granites, elevate their sunburnt summits against a deep-blue sky, yet in their rugged bosoms lie engulfed the most verdant and fertile valleys, *where the desert and the garden strain for mastery,* and the very rock is, as it were, compelled to yield the fig, the orange and the citron, and to blossom with myrtle and the rose.[17]

Verdancy seems to come forth miraculously from the desert, the underlying landscape, which is forced to violate its very nature and give forth life. The gardens and groves are perceived as oases rather than as the perpetual ecology of the fourth clime, normative in the medieval accounts. For Irving, al-Andalus was created by a people who were paradoxically sophisticated urban innovators and primitive desert Bedouin. While surveying the "boundless wastes" of the Andalusian landscape, he observed a lone herdsman leading a long train of mules, likened in the text to a "train of camels in the desert," and concluded that "the country, the habits, the very looks of the people, have something of the Arabian character."[18]

Of course, a certain amount of ecological transformation did occur between the centuries of Ibn Baṭṭūṭa's visit and Irving's. The southern Iberian ecology changed as the agrarian methods of Muslim Iberia, which were ideal for an economy in which countryside and urban centers were interdependent, were (partially) abandoned following the Reconquista. Northern habits of land-devouring pastoralizing were rapidly adopted, thereby creating the ravaged landscape that Irving perceived as desert.[19] Irving's depictions are fueled by his expectations of finding in al-Andalus the remnants of the medieval Moors and the ancient Arabians. However, his lone herdsman was more likely descended from a family of northern Christian herders than the Bedouin of Najd.

Authors find landscapes that they expect to find and project cultural significations onto natural settings. Descriptions of places are molded by authors' associations with the given landscape. The gardens of the Arab geographers signify prosperity, security, power, and thriving intellectual culture. Irving's desert serves as the backdrop necessary to create a sense of adventure for a readership that identifies the desert landscape with "primitive" Arab culture. To borrow from Simon Schama's insightful comment, "landscapes are culture before they are nature."[20] This point is as important for reading medieval Hebrew authors as it is for reading Ibn Baṭṭūṭa and Washington Irving. In the Hebrew poetry of nostalgia, the author's sense of place and displacement is conveyed through memories of the past garden landscape and reactions to the actual landscape of Christian Iberia.

Three Landscapes of Andalusian Hebrew Poetry

Garden

It is well known that the palace garden is one of the favorite subjects of Hebrew and Arabic poetry from al-Andalus.[21] Muslim and Jewish aristocrats elevated the palace garden into the ultimate manifestation of urban glory. The garden was a *hortus conclusus,* an enclosed garden bounded by an organized conception of space and a scripted set of cultural practices including wine drinking, conversation, relaxation, and entertainment. This garden was an artificial landscape that hovered among the realms of the natural, the human, and the paradisial. Forged by artful and technologically skilled landscapers, the palace garden simultaneously mimicked nature and recreated it in an idealized form. The palace garden proclaimed to its beholder the values of the Islamic state encompassing order, agriculture, cosmopolitanism, and faith.[22] Poetic descriptions of the garden further emphasized these values through the infusion of images of power, social order, and paradise.[23]

The garden took on the status of a cultural icon in Andalusian Hebrew literature.[24] It stood out not only as the meeting place of literati and aristocrats but also as a microcosm of the celebrated culture. In Moses Ibn Ezra's poem "Kotnot passim lavash ha-gan" (The garden wears an ornamented coat), a rose is metaphorically described as a king borne high on his throne while the other flora, all dressed in courtly garments, greet him with supplication.[25] When the Andalusian context began to break down, the garden remained a persistent symbol of the cosmopolitan culture that poets recognized as their own.

In Andalusian writing, both Arabic and Hebrew, nostalgic poetry associated with political and social upheaval began to be composed following the fall of Cordoba (1013) and continued with the destruction of cities during the Reconquista (after 1085), the Almoravid invasions (1090), and the Almohad invasions (1147). In this poetry, the fixed identity between the garden and cosmopolitan values is commonly exploited in such a way that personal and communal loss is expressed by remembering the past as a lost garden. The garden is the landscape with which wandering, estranged authors most intimately identify.

The Arabic tradition preserves a large corpus of poems specifically dedicated to mourning the destroyed cities of al-Andalus.[26] In the lament of Ibn Shuhayd (992–1035) over Cordoba, the glory of the lost city is conveyed through garden imagery:

The scent of [Cordoba's] flowers appeared to them with winds,
exposing the sleeping quarters. . . .
How good they were in its palaces and women's quarters.
In its palaces full moons came to rest. . . .
Tigris and Euphrates, Nile and Kawthar,
all overflowed between your banks,
While you were suckled by a cloud with the water of life,
reviving your gardens and causing them to blossom.
My grief is for a dwelling whose spring encampments I knew well
and whose gazelles would strut through its open courtyards.[27]

The scent of flowers, flowing waters, suckling clouds, palaces, and strutting "gazelles" (i.e., love objects) are all elements that derive from the Andalusian poetic corpus that idealizes the garden as the locus of sophisticated culture.

Hebrew expressions of lost Andalusian culture first appear in the poetry of Ibn Shuhayd's contemporary Samuel the Nagid, who was displaced from his native Cordoba in 1013, and exist in greater numbers following the establishment of Almoravid hegemony in 1090. Garden imagery figures prominently throughout this poetry, both as a means of evoking the past and as a device utilized in praising social confidants and their poems. In one poem by the Nagid, which the scribe introduces as "a poem from his youth, when he departed Cordoba,"[28] the wandering poet pledges to "sew together the edge of one desert with another / and traverse the sea in every sailed[29] ship" to regain his status and fame. He boasts that friends will find salvation in him and swears allegiance to his loyal companions. Turning to the addressee of the poem, he writes: "In [my soul] there is a garden for you / planted along the river of love." With the poet severed from the familiar landscape of the Andalusian garden and (figuratively) caught between deserts and seas, the garden is refashioned into a portable miniature of itself.

The two outstanding Hebrew poets to write nostalgic poems following the Almoravid invasions are Moses Ibn Ezra, who resettled in the Christian north, and Judah Halevi, who died just before or after completing a pilgrimage to Palestine.[30] For each of these poets, the garden remained a symbol of cultural refinement. In a poem addressed to Moses Ibn Ezra, Halevi laments Ibn Ezra's departure and stresses the two poets' kindred spirits: "We were [both] raised on spice gardens, nursed on the breasts of vines."[31] The garden, metonymically representing sophisticated Andalusian culture, is the shared place of origin for the poet and his addressee and their very source of sustenance. In another poem, Halevi expresses longing for a friend by internalizing elements of the garden: "In my heart there are flourishing plantings for you. When I remember your name I gather the finest of spices."[32] Because of the separation, the poet seeks comfort in a dream: "[You are] a friend because of whom I call out to my dream: 'Be gentle until I behold a garden of delight.'" Yearning for the garden is dialectically bound up with longing for the friend; remembering the friend produces a garden within the poet, yet the poet hopes for a vision of the garden in order to remember his friend.

After leaving al-Andalus, Halevi found other gardens in place of the lost garden. Most concretely, he discovered a new garden in Egypt, a stopping ground on his journey to Palestine. Halevi describes what he calls a "Garden of Eden along the Pishon [Nile]," using standard images of the Andalusian garden repertory.[33] The earth is dressed in fine weaving and embroidery, the planted area is chequered, and dwellings are girded with the colors of the high priest's breastplate. He beholds precious maidens[34] and handsome male youths along the river and declares, "The heart is enticed and forgets its old age." More than merely extolling Egypt's beauty, these images allow for continuity between al-Andalus and Egypt, thereby blurring the spatial and temporal gaps and allowing the poet to forget his "old age." The poem is part of the broad discourse that invokes the garden as a typological place embodying cultural refinement.

Unlike Halevi, Moses Ibn Ezra never embarked upon a pilgrimage to Palestine but spent his final years in the northern Iberian kingdoms of Castile and Navarre. Until the end of his life, Ibn Ezra referred to himself as a refugee and fugitive, wasting away in a prison of isolation. In many poems written from the Christian north, Ibn Ezra includes evocative garden descriptions that refer to past memories. In one example, an endless night of wandering is juxtaposed with the felicitous memories of garden soirées. The poetic speaker is forlorn, for the long night refuses to pass; he waits for the stars to diminish, but they multiply oppressively. Desperate in his state of separation, the poet remembers the garden, drinking, and friendship, all of which seem to hasten toward self-annihilation.[35]

The development in this poem from the slow night of wandering to the harried night of companionship exploits a time sequence common in a form of Arabic poetry known as the *qaṣīda*—a distressing present that leads to a flashback of a felicitous past (that here passes far too quickly).[36] The use of this time sequence allows the poet to distinguish between one period of time and another, to call one moment present and another past. The poem is not so much about describing a garden as it is about evoking the garden as a nostalgia-laden icon of former delight.[37]

In the introduction to his well-known Judeo-Arabic work on Hebrew poetics, *Kitāb al-muḥāḍara wa al-mudhākara,* Ibn Ezra apologizes to the addressee of his book (who had asked numerous questions concerning poetry) for his delayed response.[38] Writing from Navarre toward the end of his life, Ibn Ezra dwells upon the subject of estrangement and the loss of intellectual companions. Part of this passage was quoted in the introduction to this book but merits repetition here:

> Your request of me met weakness, idleness, languor, and difficulty due to two reasons: one was out of fear that the masses would designate me one of the empty-minded people because of the enmity most people of our era hold toward refined culture.[39] . . . The second reason is due to that which Time has hurled at me at the end of my life: long separation from my native country and the disappointment[40] attained in a distant land and a remote frontier. I am imprisoned in jail, nay, buried in a tomb. It is true what is said, "The intellectual is not more satisfied by that which gives him sustenance than he is by his homeland." It is written in the Qurʾān of the Arabs (4:66), "If we had ordered them to kill themselves or abandon their homes, only few would have done so." "Killing oneself" and "leaving one's home" are considered equivalent. It is also said, "Estrangement is one of the two prisons." It is also said, "The foreigner is one who has lost the social companions [*julasāʾ*] whose company he enjoys and the confidants upon whom he depends." Another said, "The foreigner is like a plant whose land has been taken by night and has been deprived of drink: it is withered and does not bear fruit; it is faded and does not blossom."[41]

Ibn Ezra's notions of displacement and estrangement are informed by the traditions of Arabic proverbial literature and Qurʾānic exegesis.[42] The final image of the withered plant deprived of its soil is most significant, since Ibn Ezra frequently refers to himself as a "withering plant" in his poetry.[43]

Unlike Halevi, Moses Ibn Ezra never found another garden in a new land, not even temporarily. This is not to say that he stopped imagining the garden or writing about it. In fact, the garden continued to occupy his literary imagination, perhaps persisting with even greater vigor because it went unreplaced. However, Ibn Ezra did find certain substitutes for the garden in small groups of refined intellectuals and in writing. In another Judeo-Arabic work on poetics and exegesis, Ibn Ezra introduces himself as a "refugee from his homeland, a fugitive from his resting place, alone without his people or dwelling." He invites his readers in the "frontiers" (*thughūr*),[44] the "remaining notables among the loved ones and vanquished, brothers who possess fine lineage and pure fugitives among the people of refined culture" to join him in "gardens of kinship and refined culture" rather than gardens of flowers.[45]

In his poetry from Christian Iberia, Moses Ibn Ezra creates "new gardens" by projecting the garden onto other objects. Through this displacement of the iconic image, the culture represented by that icon is allowed to persist. In some panegyrics, Ibn Ezra refers to the *mamdūḥ,* the "one praised," as a garden. While this in itself is not uncommon, Ibn Ezra specifically identifies friends as replacements for something larger that has been lost. In one instance, he writes that the "waters of desire" satiate the "plantings of love" whose fruits will be gathered now that the "garden of love has been laid waste."[46] Longing for friends, of course, is not unique to the Hebrew poetry following the Almoravid invasions. It is a highly conventional way of addressing patrons and friends in panegyrics whether reunification is expected soon or not. However, in the poetry following the Almoravid invasion, the longing intensifies as it becomes inextricably linked with the sense that a way of life has been lost.

Poetry itself also serves as the site of the replacement garden. In a poem written from Castile in response to a letter that arrived "like the descent of cold water upon a soul burnt by the flame of desire,"[47] Ibn Ezra describes poetry as "a garden bed of spices but plucked only with the hand of my wisdom's thought."[48] This imaginary garden provides a stark contrast with the bleak description of the Castilian landscape wherein the soil of the earth is figured as "brimstone" and the waters of the rivers as "pitch."[49] Over against this landscape, polluted and populated with wild beasts, the letter and poetry stand out as fresh waters and gardens. Ibn Ezra perceives and describes the landscape of the Christian north through his prism of displacement, just as Washington Irving and Ibn Baṭṭūṭa depict landscapes according to cultural expectations and desired effects.

The associations of al-Andalus with specific species of plants and trees belonging to a cultivated landscape may also lie at the root of Abraham Ibn Ezra's (1092–1167) cryptic comment on Lev. 23:40, the verse from which the laws of sukkah are derived for the festival of Sukkot (during which Jews commemorate their wandering through the desert between Egypt and the Land of Israel). The verse reads: "On the first day, you shall take the product of the citron[50] trees, branches of the palm trees, boughs of the leafy trees, and willows of the brook, and you shall rejoice before the Lord your God seven days." Associating the Israelites' wandering in the wilderness with his own wandering and remembering the Andalusian garden with its citrus and palm, the willow by the brook, Ibn Ezra writes, "The wanderer from the land of Qedar [Islamdom] to the land of Edom [Christendom] knows the secret of this commandment if he has eyes."

More than the garden landscape stands for a specific place in the Andalusian Hebrew tradition, it functions as a cultural icon.[51] Poets identify one another as social equals in a refined culture through their mutual sense of belonging to the garden landscape. They remember places of the past as idyllic gardens and express comfort in new environments by portraying them as similar and continuous. When new gardens are not found, poets project the garden onto other objects that are accessible, such as friends and poetry. With this in mind, we turn to the landscapes of desert and forest, both of which provide contrast with the garden, in the Hebrew poetry of wandering.

Desert

The desert stands out in the Western imagination as the seat of Arab culture, as noted above in reference to Washington Irving's *Tales of the Alhambra*. In Arabic literature, this landscape is the repository of many cultural meanings. In pre-Islamic and early Islamic poetry, the desert is the ubiquitous backdrop of life's experiences and conveys sentiments ranging from loss, nostalgia, and death to love, courage, and rebirth. The most famous of poetic desert themes is *al-bukāʾ ʿala al-aṭlāl*, "weeping over the ruins": the poet, traveling through the desert, arrives at the remnants of an abandoned campsite. Remembering the tribe that once resided there, especially the women departing (*ẓuʿun* or *zaʿāʾin;* singular, *ẓaʿīna,* from the root *ẓʿn*, "to wander, depart") with the breaking down of the camp, he weeps and bids his companions to join in the nostalgic musing.[52] The sight of the ruins triggers a series of memories that whisk the listener back in time to the idyllic days of the tribe's presence. The poet's memories often include his erotic exploits.

The desert holds numerous functions in the ʿUdhrī love lyric of the early Islamic period, a tradition marked by a love that is frustrated and unconsummated.[53] The star-crossed lovers Jamīl and Buthayna first develop affection for each other as children, herding camels in the pastoral landscape of a desert wadi. After Jamīl's marriage proposal is thwarted by Buthayna's family, the desert remains the site of the lovers' trysts, physically and symbolically beyond the confines of the tribe. Ultimately expelled from the Hijāz, Jamīl wanders the desert and settles in Egypt, where he dies. Similarly, the tragic lover Majnūn banishes himself to the desert after his love for Layla is frustrated.[54]

During the ʿAbbasid era, a period of urbanization, the desert becomes a landscape remembered, both for good and for ill. It emerges as a place of origin, the pristine idyll where life and language were pure, untainted by urban decadence or the linguistic distortions of non-native Arabic speakers. At the same time, the desert—along with its associated themes—is lampooned by poets, particularly those of Persian descent. These so-called *shuʿubiyya* poets brandish their pedigrees as urban sophisticates by mocking the primitive and unsavory customs of the desert Arabs.[55] In the Andalusian

Arabic tradition, the desert, particularly specific places of the Hijāz, retains the status of a noble place remembered, less mocked than used to create a sense of nostalgia.[56] The desert is an archetypal landscape in which one expects a certain range of activities (such as wandering, weeping, and decay) and emotions (such as loss, desperation, and nostalgia).

In the medieval Hebrew tradition, the use of the desert landscape is rare and generally conventional. The most common motifs include the departure of tribes and weeping over the ruins.[57] The earliest uses are found in the poetry of Samuel the Nagid, whose "Ohalei bat nasi ha-ḥarevim" (The ruined tents of the princess) expresses resignation toward the natural cycle of life, death, and life's rebirth.[58] The poet recalls former days when companions (the tribe, as it were) drank together, the subsequent effacement of the ruins by storms, and the growth of new grasses. The first instance in the Hebrew corpus of the departure of tribes motif is also found in the poetry of the Nagid, where the poet laments the departure of drinking companions whom "Evening and Morning sentenced . . . to wander [*lehiṣaʿen*] like a Bedouin tent."[59] The use of the word *lehiṣaʿen* for "to wander" is particularly significant since it resonates against the Arabic cognate root *ẓʿn*, which is strongly associated with the departure of tribes motif.[60]

A different desert function inherited from pre-Islamic poetry is found in Joseph Ibn Ḥasdai's famous panegyric to the Nagid, "Ha-li-ṣvi ḥen" (Does the gazelle have grace). Here the poet evokes the *raḥīl* (journey) motif of the classical Arabic *qaṣīda*, referring to the lover who, in search of the beloved, valiantly "wraps himself in a veil of darkness like a garment to pasture the stars of twilight and to wander the waste of the desert, a dwelling of terror and fear."[61] Also, Solomon Ibn Gabirol refers to the departure of his companions figuratively set on camelback to designate the finality of the departure.[62] Thus, beyond the impulse of convention, there is a strong and logical association between the desert and the themes of departure, wandering, distance, and longing. In the generation of Moses Ibn Ezra and Judah Halevi, there is a sharp increase in references to the desert and its associated motifs. Ibn Ezra, in particular, brings the desert to life through the expansion of conventional motifs and by furnishing the landscape with species of carnivorous beasts and herbivores.

The conventional use of desert themes in Hebrew poetry and parallels in the Arabic corpus have been noted by scholars for many years.[63] However, the poetic *function* of the desert landscape has received relatively little treatment in scholarship. Israel Levin has argued that the desert landscape was employed by Moses Ibn Ezra because the author "esteemed the later *badīʿ* style"; that is, in his emulation of the conventions of manneristic Arabic composition, the Hebrew poet displayed his dexterity in the classical genre of desert composition.[64] While Levin admits that the theme of ruins might have had some basis in reality, since Ibn Ezra did see palaces abandoned, he finds the surfacing of desert themes surprising. Because the desert landscape appears only in limited cases before the generation of Ibn Ezra, Levin concludes that Ibn Ezra imitated Arabic norms more freely than his predecessors because of his greater "confidence." For Levin, the instinct to imitate signifies an assimilation-positive cultural posture that far outweighs the author's desire to create a nostalgic discourse.

More recently, scholars have suggested that Ibn Ezra's predilection for desert motifs stems from his specific experience as one whose friends departed for Christian Iberia, leaving him isolated, and who later wandered to Christian Iberia himself. Arie Schippers writes: "In many of Moses ibn Ezra's poems we find the departure motif from the *nasīb* [prelude] used to indicate his own feelings of being abandoned by his friends and family."[65] Raymond Scheindlin notes: "It would seem that the nostalgia of the *aṭlāl* motif provided a suitable way of introducing the tone of self-pity that would become an important part of the poem."[66] It is certainly the case that the use of desert motifs is conventional. This does not mean, however, that convention serves as the poet's foremost purpose or that the motifs do not carry associations essential for reading the poems. By referring to a camel, tribal tents, ruins, weeping, and wandering, the poet utilizes the repertoire of images and meanings bequeathed to him as a member of a literary and cultural group. While a certain amount of acculturation is prerequisite for accessing this literary system, the significance of the poetic discourse cannot be relegated to acculturation alone.

The nostalgic significance of Moses Ibn Ezra's poetry hinges on meanings that are mediated through the history and interpretation of Arabic verse. Central to his poetry is the contrast between garden and desert, landscapes whose opposition is rooted in the Arabic tradition. In one example, the poet juxtaposes the landscapes along with appropriate species of non-carnivorous and carnivorous animals: doe, gazelle, swift, and crane for the garden; leopard, lion, buzzard, and falcon for the desert. Caught in the landscape of desert ruins, the poetic speaker wanders upon "tilting walls," longing for the stones and dust to be revived.[67] In another poem, wherein Ibn Ezra exploits the weeping over the ruins motif to create an ambience of nostalgia, "lovers" call out in vain to dwellings that "listen like the deaf" for friends who wandered (*ṣaʿanu*) at the "Head of Exiles with their tents" by Time's command.[68] As heir to the Arabic literary and cultural traditions, Ibn Ezra is able to draw on motifs such as weeping and deaf ruins and the semantic depth of roots such as *ṣʿn* in order to alert his readers of the intended emotional tone of the poem.

In addition to the references mediated by the Arabic language, the Hebrew poet also had at his disposal the history of biblical phrases. In the poem discussed above, the aristocratic identity of the wandering friends is implied through the reference to the "Head of Exiles" (*rosh golim*), mentioned in Amos 6:7 as those who recline on comfortable beds, satiate themselves with food and drink, and take delight in music.[69] Unlike the usage in Amos, in which the group is marked by decadence and indulgence, Ibn Ezra's usage is laudatory and recalls a lost way of life.[70] The Andalusian exiles are aristocrats and, like the poet, have been forced to give up their way of life and wander in culturally barren places.

Interestingly, Ibn Ezra occasionally defends the use of conventional themes such as "weeping over the ruins." In a Hebrew *qaṣīda,* he writes:

The days of my life were satiated with the honeycomb of love,
    intoxicated only with the wine of youth,
In a land more pleasant than all other lands,
    its inhabitants created according to their will.
Slivers of my liver are in its tracts of land,
    scraps of my heart in its plots.
I left it for its people passed away;[71]
    [the lands] are like prisons without them.
The people are dwellings' souls;
    when [the people] are lacking, [the dwellings] search for ghosts
        in vain.
I yearn for inhabitants, not dwellings,
    for the people of good grace, not chambers,
And for people of understanding, not bricks,
    for those who come, not entryways.[72]

This is not an attempt to undermine the conventional motif but is rather a defense of conventionality. The language suggests that Ibn Ezra may have been critiqued for holding confused priorities in utilizing the motif so liberally. Because he mentions dwellings so frequently, one might think that he had no feelings for people. The verses are meta-poetic; they explain that the motif of weeping over ruins *means* longing for friends and that evoking it is an efficient manner of expressing the precise emotion of yearning for lost relationships. In the same poem, Ibn Ezra goes on to exploit further the desert landscape as a vehicle for expressing nostalgia and displacement:

My Time has purged me from among them
and appointed me to live in a *desert of wild beasts;*
[They are] beasts though they starve for a morsel of intellect,
thirsting for waters of faith,
[They act like] knowledgeable men but they devise to destroy;
[they act as though] they are guiltless but they sin against the pious.
They pretend to be wise but wise they are not;
they prophesy but not with the visions of prophets.
The wind of their love is not a wind to winnow
but is like *a dry wind that lays bare.*[73]

In migrating to the Christian north, the displaced poet encounters a landscape that is both familiar and foreign. He expresses the foreignness by projecting the desert landscape, a place familiar as a literary motif, onto the actual landscape of the Christian north. In wandering this "desert," the poet is always in search of "new gardens," remnants of and replacements for the lost culture of al-Andalus. Continuing to the *madīḥ,* or panegyric section, the poet praises his friend as a "shoot of spice":

But there [in the desert], Time allowed me to meet
a shoot of spice amid a garden of weeds,
A rose amid thorns and high weeds,
a myrtle amid forest trees and high grasses.[74]

The friend is identified with fixtures of the Andalusian garden (spice, rose, myrtle), found in a foreign environment (weeds, forest). The poet has almost seamlessly transformed the landscape depiction from a barren, desolate desert to an overgrown and weed-ridden forest. This brings us to the landscape of the forest, which is associated with its own layers of cultural and literary meaning.

Forest

One landscape that has gone virtually unnoticed in the corpus of medieval Hebrew poetry is the forest, quite different from the desert but equally distant from the garden. The desolation and waste of the desert and the unruly wilderness of the forest both provide similar contrasts with the tame verdancy of the *hortus conclusus* that the Andalusian poets recognize as their own. In one poem written in Christian Iberia, Moses Ibn Ezra rebukes his former social peers for abandoning the cultural manners of al-Andalus. According to the poet, the Andalusians have "adopted their neighbors' ways";[75]

this is not a fulmination against religious conversion but rather against assimilating into the social customs of the "barbaric" north. The Andalusians' perfidy is expressed through the language of landscape with the garden and forest pitted against each other: "In the days of youth they pastured in the *garden of righteousness* but in old age they gather wood in the *forest of treachery*."[76] The forest is clearly meant to be the Christian north while the garden, not surprisingly, represents al-Andalus.

Unlike the desert, a landscape known mainly from literature, the forest constitutes a real dimension of the northern landscape. Thus, the employment of the motif has some basis in the actual perception of a shifting landscape. This is not to say that there were no forests in the Muslim south. Rather, the forest in the south was less pervasive. It was perceived as a place distant from urban culture that carried a different range of connotations. As Thomas Glick has shown, above and beyond the differences in temperature and rainfall, there was a perception of different ecologies between Islamic and Christian Iberia, determined more by culture than by climate.[77]

Arabic texts about al-Andalus express ambivalent attitudes toward the forest. As urbanization expanded in Muslim Iberia, trees were utilized for goods, agriculture, and naval supplies. As was the case already in Roman Iberia, deforestation was a natural stage of urbanization that was met with little resistance or lamentation. The low status of the forest as compared with other aspects of the landscape is reflected in the *Nafḥ al-ṭīb*. Sultan Yūsuf Ibn ʿAbd al-Muʾmin (mid-twelfth century) explains that the Umayyad kings made Cordoba their capital because of "the many spacious dwellings, the broad streets, the magnificent, imposing structures, the flowing river, the temperate climate, the verdant environs, the wondrous soil, the *adequate* forest [*al-shaʿrā al-kāfiya*]."[78] Following this list of superlatives, the "adequacy" of the forest indicates that it was valued as a source of raw materials but not as a source of beauty or pleasure.

The forest served a utilitarian purpose but was not intrinsically associated with sophistication, delight, or high culture. It appeared as a place unowned, where people went at appointed times of the year to gather raw materials for industrial use in urban culture. Forest trees such as the oak were valued for building, but they existed beyond the area of settlement and were not emphasized as beautiful species. In one anecdote, city dwellers go out to the forest (*al-shaʿrā*) to collect the kermes (*qirmīz*) insect from oak trees; a red dye would be extracted from the insects' bodies.[79] Also, a story is related about Abū Ḥusayn ʿAlī Ibn al-Ḥamāra, a musician of Granada who became famous for tearing down a branch from a forest tree with his bare hands and carving from it an *ʿūd* (lute).[80] Here we find the ideal of taming nature for cultural—in this case, musical—consumption. More than the trees of the forest, Andalusian culture identified with "tame" trees such as the olive and pomegranate.[81] In some instances, Muslim territory could be distinguished from Christian settlement by the defining border of dense olive growth.[82] While the olive tree was also known in the agriculture of the north, it was not emphasized as a primary and profitable crop. Following the Christian conquest of regions of the Muslim south, the conquerors often tried to learn Muslim farming techniques and sustain the system of agriculture. However, in many places fields were abandoned for pasture, turning cities into herding centers.[83]

In the Christian north, the forest held a very different value. In ordinances and charters, the forest appears as a pervasive and precious landscape. For example, in a Latin charter issued in 1153 by Ramon Berenguer, count of Barcelona, the inhabitants of Siurana are granted the "houses and lands" given by the count's representative, the knight Bertrand of Castellet. The people of Siurana are also given "all pastures and springs and hunting rights and all improvements in the forest and mountains and wood and all things which are used by people, and free exits and access for all of them and all their cattle and animals."[84] Unlike the settlements of al-Andalus, the towns of the Christian north commingle with the forest. This charter, expressly designed with urbanization in mind, reflects the pastoral lifestyle of the north, where the forest appears as valued grazing land. There is little interest in reshaping the natural ecology of the forest. As forest space began to grow scarce, lords and kings protected their resources. These early acts of conservation restricted the communal use of forests and timbering in the town forest. An ideology that is more than merely utilitarian is alluded to in one of the anti-deforestation statutes of Alfonso X, in which the "great pleasure that [forests] afford men when they behold them" is cited among the policy's justifications.[85]

Whereas the forest emerges only occasionally in the Arabic literature of Muslim Iberia,[86] it is the most prominent landscape in the emerging literatures of the European vernacular languages. It occupies a prominent role despite the emphasis placed on the courtly world. The landscape has no singular meaning, representing (often simultaneously) idyll and exile, refuge and terror, love and violence. It is a place of refuge from social convention, the standard backdrop of the quest, the primary context for displaying chivalry and valor, and sometimes a place of terror.[87] These meanings confront one another in the *El Poema de Mío Cid*. Having been banished from the court of Alfonso VI, the Cid (Ruy Díaz) exits the city gate and crosses the river Arlanzón. He dismounts along a river beside the town of Burgos "as if he were out in the woods,"[88] which places him in the tradition of the chivalrous knights of French Romance. Later in the poem, the Cid marries his daughters to the nefarious Infantes of Carrión, who dishonor the Cid by abusing their wives. Following the marriage, the Infantes and the Cid's daughters enter the

> oak forest of Corpes, where the branches of the lofty trees seemed to stretch up to the clouds, and the wild beasts roamed at large. They found a grassy clearing with a fresh spring, and there the Infantes ordered a tent to be set up. On this spot they spent the night with all their company, and with their wives, to whom they showed signs of tender love.

In the morning, pleasure turns to terror when the Infantes "strip their wives to their shifts and beat them, hacking their flesh with straps and spurs, leaving them for dead in the oak forest of Corpes."[89]

Identifying with the cultural perspective of the urban Arabs, Andalusian Jewish authors consistently depict the forest as a foreign territory. It is a place associated with exile, estrangement, and destruction, possessing none of the noble associations of refuge, beauty, love, or chivalry found in the European tradition. In his eleventh-century Hebrew-Arabic dictionary *Kitāb al-uṣūl,* Abū al-Walīd Marwān (Jonah) Ibn Janāḥ translates the Hebrew word *yaʿar* as *shaʿrā,* meaning "forest, densely wooded area, etc.,"[90] the same term used above in the numerous references to the forest in the *Nafḥ al-ṭīb.* In a *geʾulah* (poem of redemption) by Halevi, the poet laments "pleasant girls banished from cities" now dwelling amid "unlearned folk" and "stammerers of speech" and questions God for forsaking Israel to "wander in forests."[91] The forest is exile's abode and is perceived as an entangled, threatening environment. Already in Moses Ibn Ezra's earliest poetry of estrangement, written while the poet lingered without his companions in al-Andalus, the earth becomes overgrown with "foreign shoots" that transform the familiar landscape into something strange and dreadful. In the poem, even wandering itself is figured as a tree nourished by the poet's tears.[92]

In his poetry written from Christian Iberia, Ibn Ezra conveys his encounter with the foreign forest landscape and, in turn, uses this landscape as a device to create a discourse about loneliness and estrangement. In one poem, the poetic speaker complains that Time has isolated him from his intimates, tossed him about violently, and "made me like *a bud withering in the forest,* like a rose picked among thorns."[93] The image of the "bud withering in the forest" is consistent with Ibn Ezra's simile for estrangement in the introduction of his *Kitāb al-muḥādara wa al-mudhākara:* "The foreigner is like a plant whose land has been taken by night and has been deprived of drink:

it is withered and does not bear fruit; it is faded and does not blossom." The poet is planted in a foreign soil and is struggling for survival. Elsewhere, Ibn Ezra extends the simile even further: "In anger [the sons of Time] purged us from the palaces of pleasure and hastened to lead us to Christendom [*bat Edom*]. . . . Among them we are like *myrtles among the trees of the forest,* our leaves withering."[94] The myrtle (*hadas*) is a plant of the Andalusian garden often praised in Hebrew (and Arabic) verse. For Ibn Ezra, it symbolizes all that is urban, cultured, and refined. This myrtle is uprooted from "palaces of pleasure," now withering in the foreign landscape of Christendom's forest.[95] In contrast with the balanced landscape of al-Andalus, the untamed wilderness of the Christian forest signifies the lack of a sophisticated literary culture that was so central to the poet's sense of home.

It is not difficult to observe new attitudes toward the forest landscape emerging in the Christian environment. Todros Halevi Abulafia (1247–d. after 1298), a Jewish court poet in urban Toledo, wrote a response to a poem by Rabbi Meir Ben Shoshan, who had left the city for a sort of forest retreat. In praising the superiority of Rabbi Meir's poem to his own, Todros extols the clarity of thought that the retreat, free of urbane distractions, afforded his friend:

In the land of honey and the Village of Forests,[96]
  you cut trees of knowledge in forests,
While we in the cities cut
  dry wood, food for asses.
You browse through henna in the villages
  while we consume straw like steer.
You have fastened to yourself links of the necklace
  while we have bound pebbles in bundles.
Before you poets stop their words
  and nobles hide themselves in holes.
Can stones be compared to corals?
  Can thistles be likened to pearls?
You can magnify wisdom as long as men
  are fruitful and multiply like fruits.
You became honored by virtue of separating yourself,
  you became exalted by not beholding haughty brutes in cities.[97]

While Todros was never a "forest poet" and generally favored the urban garden landscape, this poem reflects an attitude toward the forest that would have been unthinkable in al-Andalus. The forest does not appear as the foreign landscape of estrangement but rather as the landscape that affords "great pleasure when men behold it," as Alfonso X had stated.

This study of landscape in Andalusian Hebrew verse testifies to authors' perceptions of al-Andalus and Christian Iberia as different places, distinguished from each other by language, culture, and ecology. The authors project meanings onto natural phenomena and express their sense of home and estrangement by evoking particular landscapes. References to gardens, be they to the real *hortus conclusus* or the figurative gardens that exist in poets' hearts, convey a persistent memory of Andalusian culture. The garden has two counterpoints in the desert and forest: one the archetypal realm of estrangement adopted from Arabic letters; and the other the perceived region of anxiety, based in the actual experience of Christian Iberia's ecology.

Two

Form

Varieties of Lamentation and Estrangement

The three major Jewish poets who left al-Andalus permanently between 1090 and 1142—Moses Ibn Ezra, Judah Halevi, and Abraham Ibn Ezra—all wrote poems about the decline following changes in political regimes. Moses Ibn Ezra composed several personal complaints concerning the abandonment of Granada by Jewish intellectuals after the Almoravid conquest and his own wandering to Castile and Navarre. Halevi composed several poems associated with events befalling the Jewish community during the early stages of the Reconquista and expressed nostalgia for al-Andalus in some poems from his pilgrimage to Palestine. Having already left al-Andalus, Abraham Ibn Ezra composed a famous lament over the collapse of Andalusian and Maghrebi communities during the Almohad era.

Whereas the previous chapter treated authors' reactions to cultural transition collectively, this chapter contrasts three authors' poetic responses to decline and to their own displacement. Focusing on the significance of poetic form offers insight into how each author chose to represent communal calamity and personal displacement and how he wished his audience to perceive his expression and sentiment. The term "form" in this chapter signifies the shape of the poem itself, comparable to its use in "sonnet form" or "quatrain form" for English verse. The term overlaps with "genre" to some extent but is nonetheless distinct, since a single form might serve multiple genres while a single genre might be cast in multiple forms. What is *not* meant here by the analysis of "form" is a treatment of the peculiar qualities of literary language (e.g., the relationship between sound and meaning or between signifier and signified) as studied by the Russian formalists and their structuralist successors. The purpose here is to investigate how a medieval reader/listener might have reacted to a given poem given the literary traditions against which the poem sounded.

In choosing a literary form, an author quickly indicates his poetic voice and identifies himself as a speaker within a given community. Moses Ibn Ezra, although writing in Hebrew, adopts a classical Arabic form—the *qaṣīda*—and hence speaks with the voice of a nostalgic Arabic poet to an audience with a taste for Arabized Hebrew poetry. Judah Halevi chooses an indigenous Hispano-Jewish form—the *petiḥa*—which is associated with Jewish public mourning; the poet locates political events within the theological framework of exile and redemption specific to Jewish literature and culture and addresses a broad community. Abraham Ibn Ezra also utilizes traditional Jewish tropes of exile in a strophic poem that conflates personal, local, and national modes of lamentation.

The three authors responded to unique events that had different effects on their communities. The Almoravid attacks were not directed against the Jewish community specifically and resulted in the displacement of only a small minority of Jews, including Moses Ibn Ezra. The Reconquista, even if not specifically anti-Jewish in character, had a broader effect on Jews and led to the physical destruction of some institutions of Jewish life. Halevi wrote not about the moment that Christian conquerors wrested control of Muslim cities but about the instability in Jewish life that soon followed. The Almohad attacks did involve a pronounced dimension of anti-Jewish persecution that gravely affected the Jewish communities of al-Andalus (and the Maghreb). Still, it is useful to compare the compositions of these three authors within the rubrics of cultural transition and the representation of calamity in Hebrew literature. The divergence in poetic expressions is shaped as much by the authors' literary styles and personal identities as the particulars of each event. By treating these poems together, this chapter makes a methodological point by transcending a barrier that has been imposed by scholarship between "sacred" and "secular" verse. The discussion is sensitive to the diverse functions of poetic forms while highlighting the difficulties that arise when a strict division between "sacred" and "secular" verse is insisted upon.[1]

Moses Ibn Ezra: The *Qaṣīda*

1. Will you seek my blood from the mouths of lions,
   will you seek my sleep from the hands of gazelles?
2. Can the blood of a lover be avenged?
   Can sleep be sent to him when his pains interfere?
3. As if his eyes were painted with burning flame[2]
   and painful thorns filled his pupil,
4. And his eyelids could not be closed[3] as if
   they were suspended from their backs,

5. As if the night were thrust into a sea
of darkness, silent, no rising waves.
6. In my eyes, its expanse[4] is broader than the sea,
no shore and no passage for those arriving.
7. The moon on its course in glory is like a shepherd
slowly leading his flock in a wide pasture,
8. Or the sun sent him to muster his battalions
and made him general over the troops.
9. And I know not whether [the night] will be long or short;
how can a diseased man understand?
10. I would be ransom for a heart that concealed its love
and rendered all people of this world enemies,
11. Yet my wrong is in my eyes, not in my heart,
for the tear is truthful speech for those who see,[5]
12. As if my eyes were fashioned as clouds
or pitchers to tilt[6] upon my cheeks.
13. Companions left me to wander;
they are no more though they exist in my thoughts.
14. Their forms dealt treacherously with me to a point
that they feared approaching me in my sleep.
15. Alas, for Time that plotted to separate my confidants
and heaped together the griefs of my heart.
16. [Once] the days of my life were satiated with the honeycomb of love,
intoxicated with the wine of youth only,
17. In a land more pleasant than all other lands,
its inhabitants created according to their will.
18. Slivers of my liver are in its tracts of land,
scraps of my heart in its plots.
19. I left it for its people passed away;[7]
[the lands] are like prisons without them.
20. The people are dwellings' souls,
when [the people] are absent [the dwellings] seek after ghosts in vain.
21. I yearn for inhabitants, not dwellings,
for the people of good grace, not living chambers,
22. And for people of understanding, not bricks,
for those who come, not entryways.
23. My Time has purged me from among them
and appointed me to live in a desert of wild beasts;
24. Beasts, though they starve for a morsel of intellect,
thirsting for waters of faith.

25. [They act like] knowledgeable men but they devise to destroy,
[they act] guiltless though they sin against the pious.
26. They pretend to be wise but wise they are not,
they prophesy but not with the visions of prophets.
27. The wind of their love is not a wind to winnow or cleanse,
but is like a dry wind that lays bare.
28. But there Time allowed me to meet a shoot of spice
among a garden of grasses,
29. A rose rising amidst thorns and high weeds,
myrtles among forest-trees and grasses.[8]

For the reader not familiar with the conventions of classical Arabic poetry, Ibn Ezra's opening might seem strange for a poem about cultural decline. The speaker's self-referential statements treat his insomnia, his affliction, and his perception of the night sky. Only in line 13 does the speaker explain the reason for his distress: the departure of friends. In line 19, the poet's circumstance becomes clearer. Completely abandoned, he, too, has departed his homeland, which he calls "a land more pleasant than all other lands" (17). Following line 23, the speaker's predicament comes into even sharper focus. He is residing in Christian Iberia, a "desert" of boorish "beasts" and false prophets. Through a gradual transition in the final lines of the excerpt, the poet changes subject to praise a *mamdūḥ* ("one praised"), Ibn Ezra's distant friend and cultural confidant.

The excerpt is the opening of a Hebrew *qaṣīda,* a multithematic form popularized in Andalusian Hebrew poetry through contact with Arabic models. More than merely emulating a literary model, Ibn Ezra contextualizes his response to cultural decay within the collective experience offered by the Arabic literary tradition. The following discussion introduces the Arabic and Hebrew *qaṣīda*s and ultimately returns to the poetry of Moses Ibn Ezra and this poem in particular. By properly contextualizing the form and motifs of Ibn Ezra's complaint, we can see that the poet represented loss through the eyes of an Arabic poet and directed reception among a readership with Arabic tastes.

The Arabic *Qaṣīda*

The *qaṣīda* is a formal poetic structure originating in the pre-Islamic Arabic tradition that takes on various manifestations in subsequent periods of Arabic and non-Arabic letters.[9] On the level of prosody, Arabic and Hebrew *qaṣīda*s conform to the standard requirements of classical Arabic verse—monorhyme and quantitative meter. In most scholarly literature, the *qaṣīda* involves a further requirement of being multithematic, usually binary or ternary in structure, joining together disparate subjects by linking them in succession. Unlike the Hebrew *qaṣīda,* the Arabic *qaṣīda* has been the subject of much research in Western scholarship. Scholars have sought to unravel the mysteries of the form's origins,[10] to study its evolution throughout various historical periods and literary trends,[11] and to consider its formal organization and meaning from performative,[12] structuralist[13] and anthropological perspectives.[14] What emerges from this scholarship is a loose affiliation of poems dedicated to tribal values in one period, the power of Islamic kingship in the next, and the triumph of urban glory in the next.

Thematic choice and organization vary considerably from period to period, from poet to poet, and from poem to poem. A poet might begin with the theme of wandering and end with a personal boast; he might begin with garden description or weeping over desert ruins and conclude with panegyric or invective. The idealized topos of the pre-Islamic *qaṣīda*'s *nasīb* (prelude), one that would be emulated and then satirized in subsequent periods of Arabic literature, begins with the nomad poet wandering the desert with friends and happening upon an abandoned campsite, now ruins in decay. The poet charges his companions to halt and weep over the ruined encampment where his tribe, or perhaps his beloved, once resided. Weeping triggers a flashback to the past, now lost, through which the poet recalls tribal life and erotic encounters.

Because of its role as a vehicle for past memories, the *qaṣīda* became Arabic literature's nostalgic form par excellence. The relationship between the *qaṣīda* and nostalgia has been treated in a number of works, including Fāṭima Ṭaḥṭaḥ's study on estrangement and longing in Andalusian poetry, Muḥammad al-Zayyāt's study of Andalusian city laments (*rithā' al-mudun*), and Jaroslav Stetkevych's study of nostalgic elements in the *nasīb* of the classical *qaṣīda.*[15] All these studies have shown that Arabic literature possesses a distinct nostalgic mode—a set of forms, motifs, and semantic uses that resonates within a deep matrix of longing and loss specific to Arab culture. By merely evoking *qaṣīda* form and hinting at its pre-Islamic themes—weeping over ruins, the departure of tribes, wandering deserts, pasturing stars, insomnia—the poet is able to create an emotional backdrop that charges the poem and molds the listener's response.

Jaroslav Stetkevych unearths layers of symbolic reference in the *qaṣīda* that hark back to an originary nostalgic core. According to Stetkevych, the *nasīb,* throughout its development, evokes emotions of mournful longing harmonized with the literary and performative expectations of an Arab audience. The motifs of pre-Islamic poetry that make up the *nasīb* remained

Arabic writing's language of nostalgia and elegy. Following an earthquake that struck Syria in 1157 CE, Usāmah Ibn Munqidh (d. 1188) compiled his *Kitāb al-manāzil wa al-diyār* (Book of Campsites and Abodes), an anthology of Bedouin laments over effaced dwellings, to mourn the "courtyards, formerly so full of life, [that] were now turned desolate."[16] Anthologizing pre-Islamic odes was a form of memorialization and consolation that allowed the compiler (and the reader) to experience loss within the context of a broad community limited neither by space nor time.

Stetkevych also addresses the "pastoral" motif of Arabic literature, specifically the theme of "pasturing stars" as a form of nostalgic expression. Typically, the poet describes the slow movement of the night sky as his pasture, wherein the constellations are herds of sheep. The motif has been identified by Western scholarship at least since 1902, when Ignaz Goldziher understood it as reflective of "the circumstances of Arabic Bedouinity," for "the watching of stars" is perceived as watching herds and "is connected with the fact that the ancient Arabs had viewed the stars from the perspective of herdsmen."[17] Stetkevych moves beyond such a panoramic view and considers the motif an expression of the poet's loneliness and concludes that the Arabic pastoral motif is "permanently elegaic."[18]

Ṭaḥṭaḥ's study of estrangement (*ghurba*) and longing (*ḥanīn*)[19] in Andalusian poetry traces the evolution of these motifs throughout successive waves of political upheaval—the siege of Cordoba in 1013 with the disruption of the Umayyad caliphate, the Almoravid invasion of 1090, and the Almohad invasion of 1147. The author recognizes the same nostalgia-laden motifs inherited from pre-Islamic poetry studied by J. Stetkevych and also delineates personal modes of expression of individual authors, including Ibn Shuhayd, Ibn Zaydūn, Ibn Darrāj, al-Aᶜmā al-Tuṭaylī, Ibn Ḥamdīs,[20] al-Muᶜtamid Ibn ᶜAbbād, Ibn Khafāja, and others.[21] Al-Zayyāt's work on Andalusian city laments anthologizes and analyzes elegies composed following the destruction of cities during the same political periods treated in Ṭaḥṭaḥ's book. The most common form for the city lament is shown to be the *qaṣīda*, exploiting the fixed solemnity of the formal ode, although other forms (*muwashshaḥ, zajal*) are also used.

The first Andalusian Arabic poem to address a fallen city is the lament over Cordoba (destroyed 1013) by Ibn Shuhayd, a contemporary of Ibn Zaydūn's, Ibn Darrāj's, and the Hebrew poet Samuel the Nagid's. Remembering Cordoba, Ibn Shuhayd laments the fallen ruins, petitions Time to restore the city's courtyards, and remembers the city as a verdant, fragrant garden:

There is none among the ruins to inform us about loved ones;
whom shall we ask about their circumstance?
Ask none but separation for it keeps you far from them
when they travel in the highland or the lowland.
Time persecuted them and they dispersed
in every direction, most of them perishing.
Misfortune fell upon their dwellings and upon them
so that they all changed for the worse.
So invoke Time to create in their courtyards a light
[so bright] that hearts are nearly illuminated by it,
For the weeping of one who weeps with gushing tears
is insufficient for a city such as Cordoba. . . .
I was well acquainted with it, its state of affairs
brought together its people; life in it was verdant.
The scent of its flowers appeared to them with winds,
exposing the sleeping quarters.
Perfection set up its quarters in its dwelling
while want could not make itself known.
The people were secure that its beauty would not come undone,
they wrapped and veiled themselves in its beauty.
How good they were in its palaces and women's quarters,
in its palaces full moons came to rest. . . .
O dwelling place upon which and upon whose people
the bird of separation has alighted so that they changed and
became unknown,
Tigris and Euphrates, Nile and Kawthar,
all overflowed between your banks,
While you were suckled by a cloud with the water of life,
reviving your gardens and causing them to blossom.
My grief is for a dwelling whose spring encampments I knew well
and whose gazelles would strut through its open courtyards.[22]

Ibn Shuhayd preserves the themes and organization of the pre-Islamic *qaṣīda,* beginning with the lament over silent ruins, leading to a recollection of Cordoba. The poet wishes for the city's restoration and then returns nostalgically to the idyllic memory of a past state and time. He remembers gatherings, dwellings and palaces, waters, and clouds suckling gardens. The poem braids together classical desert motifs and courtly motifs in a pattern of contrast, creating a sharp separation between present and past that is central to nostalgic expression. Of all the elements of the classical *qaṣīda,* it is perhaps this temporal pattern that is the most persistent, beginning in a lamentable present and returning to a distant idyllic past. In this way, the *qaṣīda* form is able to enframe one period within another, to call one moment present and another past, and to convey a solemn memorialization. The *rithāʾ al-mudun* (city lament) continued to be evoked in later generations following the destruction of other Andalusian cities—including Toledo, Madinat al-Zahrāʾ, Valencia, Elvira, and Seville—during the Berber and Christian conquests.

The Hebrew *Qaṣīda*

The use of the Hebrew *qaṣīda* to commemorate cultural loss begins in the poetry of Samuel the Nagid, a contemporary of Ibn Shuhayd's.[23] The Nagid fled Cordoba following the city's destruction in 1013 by wandering for a time before ultimately settling in Granada. The scribes of the Nagid's *dīwān* occasionally identify "estrangement" (*ghurba* or *ightirāb*) as the dominant subject of poems composed following the Nagid's flight from Cordoba.[24] The *qaṣīda* excerpt below is introduced following the poet's petition to his soul to weep on the occasion of departure:[25]

By him on the occasion of his departure from Cordoba in his youth wherein he mentions estrangement

7. One who asks about the location of wandering's flame,
 I answer, "It is lit in my heart!"
8. When the heart-blood boils up to my head,
 it descends from my eyes.
9. How can anyone deny what I say
 when my tears testify,
10. Just as the Pleiades can testify for my tears[26]
 since she was teaching her children until morn![27]
11. Through my wandering my eyes have wasted away
 and my bones have shriveled as grains have shriveled.[28]
12. I measure the face of the earth with my legs
 as if they were two measuring cords.
13. The blood of my eyes was [the only] bread in my house
 and [the only] provision on the journey.
14. Were it not for the letter my friend sent
 with a kind word for my trembling soul,
15. And with news of his well-being, Awaiting Death
 would have come to my soul prematurely.
16. The words were like shade to the laborer,
 a redeemer to people in a city under siege,

17. Like rain for a thirsting land,
    like peace for a frightened soul.
18. I read it, calling aloud,
    "Liberty is proclaimed for my downtrodden soul!
19. My distress and punishment are over!
    Peace has come and horror departed!"
20. My friend remembered me with a letter,
    my soul is appointed among the redeemed.
21. Comfort has come to my troubled hand,
    freedom to my shackled leg.
22. I am caught in the hand of foreigners
    as if I were an accomplice to the husband of Ṣillah.[29]
23. I wander in a net of wandering.
    My friends, are you too weak to break open the net?
24. He who can free his friend but ignores him is like one
    who makes sacrifices to a demon!
25. Friends, I am enslaved to a member [of an alien family]![30]
    You are my kin, free me from slavery!
26. Like Benjamin I am stolen from among my brothers;
    may you be like Judah![31]

The poet represents estrangement through common motifs of wandering: tortured weeping (8–10, 13) witnessed by the stars throughout a long night (10), and the speaker's measuring the earth with his legs (12). The poem suggests affinities between the circumstance of the speaker and the predicament of the *ṣuʿlūk,* or brigand poet, of pre-Islamic poetry:[32] the speaker is wandering, his feet his only riding steed, starving along the journey with his tears as his only provisions (13). Like the brigand poet, he is a social outcast accused of violating the taboos of society's moral code, for he identifies with Lamekh (22), a murderer in Gen. 4:23. Although the poem contains praise for the reception of a letter from a friend (14–21), the poet is also severed from society, caught in a net of wandering from which his friends refuse to free him (25). Unlike Ibn Shuhayd's poem, however, this poem contains no direct expression of nostalgia for a lost time or place; it is concerned with estrangement and present distress more than nostalgia per se.

Many of the same themes of estrangement surface in the following poem by the Nagid, now with the added dimension of distinguishing present from past:[33]

By him, mentioning brothers and estrangement

1. Must I journey and encamp every day
    like a vulture dwelling in darkness by night,

2. When every morning Wandering mocks my household
and at evening my eyes weep because of departure?
3. My Time hurls me from one place to another
like a spear, dart and lance!
4. One day I am a friend to the fawn,
but the next I neighbor the kite.
5. I do not stay two days in a house,
nor rest two nights in a structure.
6. As if my legs were obligated to wander
through every city and village!
7. I am the man who rushed through wastelands
with a strong hand and an outstretched arm,
8. But in my city I had two companions,
Yehoshuᶜa and Yaḥya ben Aḥiyya.
9. In friendship they seemed to us like the sons of the Pleiades
and drinkers gathered in a palace.
10. But Time put one in prison
and the other in captivity.
11. This separation set scorching in my heart—
it is a raw wound!
12. I mentioned him when I was naked and bare,
the desert my [only] dress and [only] the Pleiades over
my head.[34]
13. Orion taught its sons the path of the heavens,
but me it taught the paths of ruin.
14. He who forgets a brother in good times or bad
is like one who is deceitful in performing the work
of God,
15. Who gave me as a portion wasteland and wilderness,
a parched place, desolate and barren,
16. And gave my friends a furnace, hot pokers,
the house of the grave, bitterness and sorrow.
17. Will they return from separation,
or will they rise from their descent?
18. Will we sit to expound Torah,
and [drink] new wine as we did before?

A number of themes work in concert to create the mood of estrangement: the relentless cycle of journeying and encamping (1), the lengthy desert journey accomplished without a riding animal (6–7), the poet's vulnerability and exposure beneath the constellations of night (12–13), weeping (2), and the hammering effect of densely packed terms for desert that nearly exhaust the biblical lexicon (15).[35] Estrangement borders on nostalgia in line 4 with the poet's transformation from being companion to the fawn, an animal associated with courtly culture (and similar to Ibn Shuhayd's memory of strutting gazelles), to being neighbor of the kite, a scavenger bird especially associated with frequenting ruins (cf. Isa. 34:15). With respect to the poem's temporal organization, it is largely grounded in the distress of the present though it also reaches into the past (4, 8–9, and 18) to recount former days of companionship and Jewish courtly culture (Torah and new wine). Concluding the poem with questions that are simultaneously hopeful and desperate befits the poem's mood of nostalgic yearning. Unlike Ibn Shuhayd's city lament, there is no mention in the Nagid's poetry of the city Cordoba, though his nostalgia for life there seems evident. Nostalgia and longing seem more associated with culture, people, and a generalized sense of place than in the Arabic corpus. Still, with the exception of omitting actual city names, many Hebrew *qaṣīda*s closely adhere to the form and style of the Andalusian Arabic city lament.

The nostalgic themes introduced by the Nagid—insomnia, wandering, pasturing stars—all become extremely prevalent in the poetry of Moses Ibn Ezra.[36] Ibn Ezra dedicates a vast amount of verse to the misery of his prolonged wandering, including a dimension of nostalgia for people, gatherings, and Islamic Iberia in general. The poet begins to utilize the *qaṣīda* form for nostalgic expression even before his departure from al-Andalus. The first stage of Ibn Ezra's estrangement occurred not with his own wandering but with his abandonment when members of his social circle left Granada to resettle in Christian Iberia. In his poem, familiar surroundings are transformed into a wasteland, at least in a literary sense:

To one of his friends praising him and complaining about separation[37]

1. The dwellings of my loved ones have become ruins,
 their palaces have become like deserts.
2. A place designated for doe to tread
 and a trampling place for gazelles,
3. But today leopards crouch in their place
 and lion cubs growl within them.
4. And in gardens where the swift and crane had nested,
 buzzards and falcon gather to lament.[38]
5. I wander over collapsing walls
 and roam the thrust-down fences,
6. Gently, I feel compassion[39] for their dust and hope
 that the stones will be revived from their ruined heap.
7. From the blood of my eyes I pour forth rivers
 that a sailor could not traverse by ship.

8. I address [the ruins] but there is none to pay attention
or respond, only jackals wailing.
9. Time, with its mighty hand and outstretched arms,
cast out their inhabitants.
10. Our joys went after[40] them,
our souls captive in their hands.
11. How can we live without them,
when they were like spirits in our bodies?
12. Do I weep for my companions or for the departure
of brothers and the appointed place of sisters?
13. Or do I grieve for separation from Shelomo
whose love was like honeycomb to mouths?

In order to express extreme loss, the poet transforms the theater of his experience into the desert, a place strange yet oddly familiar, known intimately through centuries of literary reference.[41] Finding himself among ruins, the poetic speaker weeps, selecting the proper response for a member of Arabic culture. Without trying to answer the vexing question of whether Ibn Ezra considered himself an "Arab," we may conclude that his poetry shares the atavistic yearnings of contemporary Arabic poets. The poet evokes nostalgia by recognizing a sharp contrast between the present (desert, ruins, home to leopards, jackals, and buzzards) and the past (palaces, treading ground of fawns and gazelles). Still, the theme of ruins and weeping in this example is not identical with its pre-Islamic archetype. Traveling through the desert, the pre-Islamic poet happens upon an abandoned campsite, which evokes memories of the past and leads him to weep. Here, the poetic speaker is a stationary witness to the dwellings' transformation and decay. As much as the expression contained in this poem is dependent upon convention, the adaptation befits the poet's circumstance of abandonment following the departure of friends. The progression is not identical with the temporal blueprint found in Arabic poetry ranging from pre-Islamic odes to Ibn Shuhayd's city lament: weeping leading to a flashback, reviving a former epoch and way of life.

The temporal pattern of the lamentable present leading to a memory of an idyllic past is observed in the following example by Ibn Ezra:

1. How long shall lovers call out for naught
to the ears of ruined dwellings?
2. Like the deaf they listen or, like the dumb,
they fail to answer their cries.

3. [The lovers] halted,[42] weeping because their inhabitants departed
   at the Head of the Exiles[43] by Time's command.
4. With their tents they wandered,[44] the sons of fraternity hid
   in the shade within our bodies.[45]
5. The stars of light rose on the circuit of the land,
   even at noon they came.[46]
6. I know not whether [the friends] loathed the lands
   or whether the lands vomited up their inhabitants.
7. They departed and soon their dwellings inherited [new inhabitants]
   for they were expelled from within and did not leave
   [willingly].
8. Jackals spread throughout their landings
   and crumbling abodes,[47] and wailed,
9. Their mouths' laments are heard from the corner of their ruined dwellings
   though they are not seen.
10. I lament thus and thus[48] more than they
    until they take notice of me and are amazed.
11. I set my grievance[49] upon tears that drip
    so such that they destroy them [the dwellings].[50]
12. Woe for the gazelles who cried shrilly [with joy]
    in [the dwellings] and in their places ostriches gathered as
    a host to lament.[51]
13. Alas for the days when my locks were drenched with the dew of youth,
    the days of black hairs on head and beard,
14. And the plaits of hair on my head where the ravens of youth
    gathered together, but now they dart away!
15. During the days of youth, the hems of joy
    trailed on high and the wine of love was imbibed;
16. [I wonder] if they were fashioned from flowing myrrh
    or if they were created solely from the spices of deeds of
    Joseph's son.[52]

Like the pre-Islamic poet presenting the departure of tribes, the poetic speaker remembers the shocking departure of contemporaries without even understanding the reason for their separation (6). The speaker halts and weeps over ruined dwellings, for the dwellings' inhabitants have departed with their tents (1–4). Clearly, we are in the world of pre-Islamic poetry. The speaker's tears grow so intense that they drive the ruins into further stages of disrepair (11). His sense of estrangement is so powerful that the stars of night, those symbols of loneliness and yearning, shine and haunt him even in the day (5). The singing of gazelles has turned to the lament of ostriches (12), and wailing jackals have spread throughout the abodes (8). Most significantly, the time sequence is similar to that of many Arabic *qaṣīdas*, opening with the lamentable present and leading to a nostalgic reminiscence over former days. In this manner, the poem draws a sharp contrast between a lost past and a lachrymose present. From this point in the irretrievable past, the poet returns to the present and makes a transition to the *mamdūḥ,* here made the very source of the past's mirth.[53]

Returning to the *qaṣīda* by Moses Ibn Ezra quoted at the beginning of this section, we can see that many of the standard *qaṣīda* themes are present. The poetic speaker is a wretched insomniac, forced to gaze at the limitless, expansive darkness (2–6). He appoints the moon the pasturer of stars, which are both a flock and a battalion (7–8). In his desperation, he weeps (12), recalling his departed companions and "a land more pleasant than all other lands," a land that became like a prison once companions left (13–27). As discussed in chapter 1, Hebrew poets rarely make reference to specific cities in their poetry.[54] However, the identification of this land with al-Andalus or Granada is unmistakable. Al-Andalus and its culture evoke a powerful and bittersweet memory for Ibn Ezra. The poem follows the common time sequence of the *qaṣīda,* beginning in a lamentable present and returning to a lost, idyllic past. From the past, the poem returns to the present, to the speaker's own wandering and the treachery of his contemporaries, finally reaching the *mamdūḥ,* a rose among thorns. With the exception of omitting an actual city name, there is little to distinguish this poem from contemporary Arabic city laments. Exploiting the time sequence of the classical *qaṣīda* and enframing the past as a lost, idyllic time over against a tormenting present, the poem is a type of cultural memorialization.

Moses Ibn Ezra laments Andalusian decline with the voice of an Arabic poet. Although writing in Hebrew, he reaches into the storehouse of forms and motifs available to the Arabic author to represent estrangement and nostalgia. The poet does not write for a general Jewish audience but rather for an Arabized elite that shares his tastes and values. By adopting the *qaṣīda* form, the poet pronounces his cultural affiliation as an Andalusian strongly affiliated with Arabic culture. Throughout his poetry, Ibn Ezra denigrates the non-Arabized Jews of Christian Iberia as philistine ignoramuses, calling them everything from fools to wild asses, stammerers, and even murderers. In Christian Iberia, Ibn Ezra does his best to retain a social circle of intellectuals while pining for former days in al-Andalus. His writings show a particular concern for preserving contacts with men of fine "lineage," a category that transcends both religion and nationality.[55]

It was perhaps because of the personal nature of his experience that Ibn Ezra did not write liturgical poems on displacement and exile from al-Andalus. Since the Almoravid attacks did not affect Israel as a whole, a poem in Israel's collective voice might seem unfitting. One wonders why the poet was so reticent about the Reconquista in general, since he was a contemporary of the events. Ultimately, Ibn Ezra chose to privilege his own experience of displacement over the broader experience of his fellow Jews. The *qaṣīda* form thus served a dual purpose for Ibn Ezra. First, it proved an efficient vehicle of nostalgic expression for an author who interpreted the world through the lens of Arabic culture. Second, it served as a bonding mechanism between the poet and his distant companions seeking to maintain Arabic cultural values in the post-Andalusian environment. Absent from Ibn Ezra's *qaṣīdas* is a sense of Israel's collective consciousness or reflection upon the Jewish people's predicament of exile and hope for redemption. These sentiments characterize the poetry of Judah Halevi.

Judah Halevi: The *Petiḥa*

1. You who wait for deliverance,
 do not be downhearted at the rumor
  heard in the land!
2. Ask those who flee and escape,
 the remnant and refugees about crimes
  against men and wrongs against lands!
3. The refugee[56] was tranquil and quiet
 in the cities of Sefarad since
  the exile from the Land,[57]
4. Until iniquities became mighty
 and my glory and scent disappeared,
  making me odious among the inhabitants of the land.
5. The Lord brought it about
 to awaken the heart of a multitude,
  the earth rocked and quaked.
6. As dawn broke,
 the angels of destruction rose
  and the land grew dark,
7. The day the fierce and impetuous nation
 that crosses the earth's broad spaces[58]
  rushed at me like an arrow.
8. O Lord, my foes were so many,

[I was] a nation surrounded by copious waters,
a unique nation on earth.
9. They ruined my house and my land,
destroyed my holy synagogues,
all God's tabernacles in the land.
10. All that was desirable in me was lost at morning,
and with my departure[59] [went Israel],
the praise of every land.
11. The comely girl[60] became
despised, a terror, contemptible
to all kingdoms of the world.
12. She could not find peace
when the curse went out
over all the earth.
13. The songs of His[61] mansion fell silent,
my palaces became desolate,
deserted sites became many in the land.
14. They divided up my clothing
and there was none to gather my wandering
from the four corners of the earth.
15. We were hiding in inner rooms,
fearing terror lest
the earth swallow us.
16. He turned the hearts of their enemies
to hate them for their sin,[62]
and the land could not support them.
17. How my treasures were ransacked;
those seeking my stores came
to search out the land.
18. From morning my dawn was gloom;
the enemy rejoiced because
a bird[63] fell into a trap on the land.
19. I was cut off from my house of delight.
After glory [was gone] I remained
a wandering vagabond in the land.
20. The earth did not rise up
until it made my house desolate;
all the earth was still and quiet.
21. Men of no name plundered my glory
while men of reputation were glad at my distress
with none in the land to molest them.
22. Is God's hand still stretched out,

His sword unsheathed and brandished,
His spear stuck in the ground?
23. If He will not mind the covenant,
the remnant will be lost[64]
and effaced from the earth.
24. Though He slay me, I have trust in Him,
for He is a wall and rampart for us
when He rises up to instill the earth with awe.
25. God of vengeance, arouse your wrath
like a man of war
to seize the ends of the earth!
26. Shake out the wicked from it!
Lest the seed[65] of the wicked say,
"God has abandoned the earth!"
27. Serve a cup
of the four punishments[66]
to make the whole earth drunk!
28. Your servant is bound up;
when one shakes [sand] in a sieve,
not a pebble falls to the ground.[67]
29. North and South will know that
in the heavens we have a God
who judges the earth.
30. [You are] a refuge for the lowly and poor,
a signet-ring of might.
Therefore we fear not though the earth reels.[68]

Despite the lack of detail identifying the foreign nation or even the location of the lost community, this poem is somewhat historical in character. It was probably written as a response to an attack on the Jewish community of Toledo during the early decades of the Reconquista. Ezra Fleischer suggests that the poem was written during a period of unrest after the death of Alfonso VI in 1109.[69] The details about the event are sparse; it was probably more anti-royal than specifically anti-Jewish in nature, though Jews may have been affected disproportionately. There is no sign that Halevi viewed the Christian conquest of Toledo pessimistically when it occurred in 1085; instead, the poem is about the precarious nature of Jewish existence that evolved over two decades later. The religiously charged atmosphere that characterized the period of the Reconquista, although directed against Muslims primarily, undoubtedly contributed to the feeling of Jewish instability within Christendom.

The themes of Halevi's poem may be divided as follows: address to listeners (1–2); account of events (3–21); and plea to God (22–30). Unlike Ibn Ezra's responses to the Almoravid conquest, Halevi's poem dwells on the theological implications of the attack and its destructive effect on the Jewish community. The theological problem that underscores the poem also occupies Hebrew writing from the book of Lamentations, the *piyyuṭ* (liturgical poetry) of Roman Palestine, the laments written following the First Crusade (1096), and beyond: How can an omnipotent God allow destruction to befall His chosen people?[70] Halevi's response is conventional; God punishes Israel for her iniquities but will redeem her from oppression in the future. The people of Israel should not lose faith, for God will remember the covenant and unleash His wrath against Israel's enemies.

God's active role in the tragedy is made explicit in the poem. Line 5 begins "the Lord brought it about," and line 16 begins "He turned the hearts of their [i.e., Israel's] enemies." Lines 5–7 highlight the coordinated nature of the attack against Israel by celestial and earthly beings, including God, the "angels of destruction," and the "fierce and impetuous nation." Following traditional theological formulations, the cause of the destruction is identified as Israel's sin. In line 4, the loss of tranquility is attributed to iniquities, and in line 16, God turns the hearts of Israel's enemies to despise Israel for its sin. The concluding plea to God is also conventional, reminding the reader of the earlier *piyyuṭ* tradition. The poet implores God to rise up against Israel's enemies as a mighty warrior (25), to remember His covenant with Israel and spare the holy remnant (28). Despite recent tragedies, the poet retains his faith in God as Israel's protector (24).

A few details overlap with themes of Moses Ibn Ezra's poems of wandering: the poet remembers a time of former tranquility (3), nostalgically recalls a "house of delight" (19), and laments the rise of men of low reputation (21) while palaces are transformed into deserted ruins (13). There is some influence from the Arabic poetics of nostalgia. Still, the theological preoccupation and the form of this poem make it quite distinct from Ibn Ezra's *qaṣīda*s and Arabic poetry generally. Although Halevi was a master of the *qaṣīda* form and composed *qaṣīda*s over separation from friends in a nostalgic mode, the poet did not utilize the form to commemorate the decline of communities.[71]

From the perspective of prosody and form, this poem does not adhere to the Arabic-inspired innovations of the Andalusian school. Each line consists of three stichs, with stichs 1 and 2 ending with the same rhyme syllable and stich 3 ending with the word *haʾareṣ* (translated as "land," "earth," and "ground"). The rhyme scheme may be represented as follows:

1. a/a/*haʾareṣ*
2. b/b/*haʾareṣ*
3. c/c/*haʾareṣ*

. . . .

The final stich is always a quotation from a biblical verse. The meter is syllabic (not the quantitative system adapted from Arabic), with each stich consisting of seven long syllables (excluding the biblical verses).[72] An almost identical form is utilized in the following poem, which opens with the same two words (*loʾ ʾaleikhem*) and is associated by scribal tradition with the "fall of Toledo":[73]

Arabic superscription: *By him, a* petiḥa *concerning the fall of Toledo*

1. May it never befall you,[74]
    hearers of my words who mourn my affliction,
        who are all alive today!
2. Ask if you have not heard!
    I will tell you if you do not know.
        Take [it] to heart from this day!
3. Let us pursue how
    the misfortune occurred
        and how this guilt was incurred today.
4. Announce to the Exile of Ariel
    that a tribe of Israel
        was cut off today!
5. I was a mistress,
    content among the daughters of exile,
        before the coming of day.
6. Since the day I discovered
    that I dwelled with Seʿir[75]
        I did not lack God's kindness all the day.
7. My sons were [Seʿir's] generals' advisers,
    my people dwelled between his[76] shoulders,
        he protected them each day.
8. I was honored with the glory of elders;
    with my teaching I appointed
        watchmen all the day.
9. A company of wise men and students

would recite learned teaching as
I would fulfill my vows each day.
10. An adviser of the king favored me;[77]
he feared God and
kept brightening until noon.[78]
11. Esau's power was with me
but in his heart he was scheming for my blood,
only evil all the day.
12. He seized my community with his cords
and [pronounced] a decree stating,
"You know not what will happen today."
13. They fashioned plots against me and,
on the Sabbath, [the city] was forsaken,
and they were ready for the day.
14. It was the day on which we were judged[79]
and they said, "Alas for us,
for the day is declining![80]
15. Leave the slaughtering for tomorrow!
Do not tarry in the morning!
Let no one be put to death today!"
16. They raided my settlements,
my sight grew dim,
and the day grew dark upon them.
17. They came to utterly annihilate,
their generals rushed to say,
"Finish your deeds today!
18. Kill them through the evening!
Do not turn back the blade
until the day declines!"
19. They set me before the arrows of their quiver.
They killed me, [laying me] like dung[81] [on the ground],
[making me] a butt and derision all the day.
20. My children were dashed to pieces before my eyes,[82]
elders were shown no respect,[83]
leading to the present state.[84]
21. When the synagogues were polluted
with the blood of young men and maidens,
they wailed, "Alas, for the day!"
22. My wise, experienced, and discerning men
were killed for the name of the Lord.
Blessed is the Lord, day by day.[85]
23. Mourn and lament!

Perform there what we
perform here today!
24. They reproached me, shouting,
"Where is the salvation that
[the Lord] will work for you today?"[86]
25. They filled my synagogue with blood,
for there my children were concealed
by base men all the day.
26. The Torah was rolled in blood,
[. . .] in the blood of the fallen,
On the holiday of Hoshanah Rabbah.[87]
27. My eyes look on my sons and students,
who were murdered between my breasts,
and strain for them all the day.[88]
28. My enemies prepared the slaughter
saying, "This
is the day for which we hoped."[89]
29. They defiled and divided [spoils] for shame,[90]
day and night for three
nights and days.
30. Woe! Woe for the nation against which You made a decree!
The promise You made them with Your mouth
is now fulfilled by Your hand.
31. Rouse the vengeance of those who wait for You,
who shout, "God, it is for Your sake
that we are killed all the day."
32. Declare that their fallen ones should live!
Instead of mourning,
they will rejoice in Your name all the day.

As in the previous poem, meter is syllabic, with each stich (excluding the biblical verses) consisting of seven syllables. Again, each line consists of three stichs, with stichs 1 and 2 rhyming and stich 3 ending with a repeating word—in this case, *yom* (translated here as "day," "today," "present," "holiday," and "noon"). Again, the third stich of every line contains a quotation from a biblical verse. The rhyme scheme may be represented as follows:

1. a/a/*yom*
2. b/b/*yom*
3. c/c/*yom*

. . . .

Evoking words of the biblical prophets, the poet stands as the announcer of calamity before a broad community: "Ask if you have not heard! I will tell you if you do not know. . . . Announce to the Exile of Ariel that a tribe of Israel was cut off today!" (2, 4).[91] The poet speaks with a voice that is at once personal and communal. It is likely important that this poem and the previous one open with the same two words; Ezra Fleischer suggests that the two poems were written following the same attack. The first poem, which offers less detail about the violence, is directed toward those who actually witnessed the events. The second is directed toward another community (or several communities) that did not experience the destruction firsthand (1, 23). Halevi enjoins it to bolster its faith in God's promises of salvation (24) and to join in the lamentation. The poem was probably circulated in order to raise awareness, arouse sympathy, and build solidarity. It is striking but logical that the less gory poem was intended for the victims, who had no need to be reminded of their suffering; the more vivid poem attempts to re-create through language the violence that the audience was spared.

The nation that attacked Israel is clearly identified as Seʿir and Esau (6, 11), both epithets for Christians. Halevi remembers dwelling in Christendom fondly, focusing on the high station of Jews in government and the success of learning academies (6–10). The sweet memories of the past set up a contrast with the poet's surprise at Christian perfidy and duplicity. Unlike Ibn Ezra, Halevi was active in both al-Andalus and in Castile; he did not portray Castile as a foreign and backward region that was culturally vacuous. Were it not for the violence perpetrated against Jews during the Reconquista, Halevi may not have been mournful that Andalusian Jewish communities were engulfed by Christian expansion.

The poem places the events within the framework of traditional Jewish modes of mourning over exile from the Land of Israel. The opening quotation from Lamentations immediately evokes Israel's mourning tradition, recalling agony at the destruction of Jerusalem. In line 3, the theological cause of the destruction is pursued, using the traditional formulation of destruction as punishment for sin. The poem concludes with the poet calling upon God to initiate vengeance on behalf of the faithful.

The scribe identifies the events described with the fall of Toledo and designates the poem a *petiḥa,* meaning "introduction." The term is generally reserved for a public elegy written in the same form that would introduce a eulogy over a deceased individual.[92] Here the term is extended to elegize the fall of an entire community. In this poem and in the previous one, the poet exploits the sound of mourning inherent in the form; the audience would have associated the meter and rhyme scheme with the tradition of the elegy and public lamentation. There is at least one other poem by Halevi treating the fall of a community in this form, also identified by a scribe as a *petiḥa*.[93] Modern scholars have designated the *petiḥas* dedicated to communities "sacred" verse but those dedicated to individuals "secular" verse.[94] The sharp division between sacred and secular verse (*shirat qodesh* and *shirat ḥol*) made during the modern period is useful but requires qualification. While a *qedushta* (a poetic variation on the Eighteen Benedictions prayer) might be called "sacred" and a wine poem might be "secular," the border between sacred and profane becomes hazy around quasi-historical poems cast in theological frameworks such as Halevi's *petiḥas*.

In reality, there is little that separates the elegies over communities from those over individuals. They all share the same prosodic and formal qualities and are strongly associated with one another in the scribal tradition.[95] In the community *petiḥas*, the poet laments in the tradition of Israel's collective mourning and ponders the theological implications of communal loss. The elegies over individuals are also concerned with theology; the poet questions the justice of the individual's death but ultimately proclaims faith in God's decree.[96] Elegies over individuals and communities sometimes employ identical imagery; for example, of both Israel and a deceased individual, Halevi writes, "She/he fell like a bird into a trap on the land."[97] Moreover, both types of poems espouse theological positions that preserve God's ultimate justice.

Thus, when Halevi wished to commemorate the loss of a Jewish community, he adopted the voice of a public mourner, using the elegy over the individual as a model. The elegizing voice in both these *petiḥas* speaks to the community in the second person, urging it to reflect upon historical events within the framework of traditional theology and offering a message of consolation. Whereas Moses Ibn Ezra's *qaṣīdas* would have been read by an elite of Arabized Jews only, Halevi's *petiḥas* were intended for public performance, much like the funerary *petiḥas*. They would have been heard by those who witnessed the destruction and were in need of consolation and also by neighboring communities. In lamenting the destruction of Jewish communities in the *petiḥa* form, Halevi does not adopt the personal voice of an Arabic poet but rather the public voice of a Jewish mourner. Halevi causes the reader to situate the poems within a tradition of loss and mourning specific to Jewish culture. The poems show that Halevi interpreted events through the lens of Israel's prolonged exile and urged his audience, a broad community of Jews, to do the same.

In addition to the *petiḥas*, Halevi wrote poems in strophic form on Jewish suffering during the period of the Reconquista.[98] Three of these poems are preserved in documents from the Cairo Genizah.[99] These poems likely had a different performative function from the *petiḥas*, though it is difficult to know exactly what that function was. None of the poems discloses where events unfolded, while all three recount details of bloodshed and plundering and clearly identify the perpetrators as Christians (e.g., "One extended his hand and the other shrieked, 'Woe!'. . . . The voice is the voice of Jacob and the hands are the hands of Esau!," which is a brilliant play on Gen. 27:22).[100] Only one of the three addresses an audience in the second person ("Exile, that has been exiled to Sefarad and Ṣarfat [France] / have you heard about the plunder that has come upon the wondrous community? / Ask him who is fleeing and her who is escaping, say, 'What happened?'" [Jer. 48:19]).[101] The others speak of the community in the third person. In only one of these poems does the poet lament in the first-person singular at all: "How the children of my people were banished from the house of their delight! . . . My heart [mourns] for their plundered, my innards for their murdered!," and even here the personal voice is not sustained.[102] Halevi also wrote some laments over individuals in strophic form, though they are few in comparison with his *petiḥas*;[103] there is thus some association between the strophic form and the sound of lamentation, though it is not as firmly established as in the case of the *petiḥa*.

A more personal experience of estrangement surfaces in some of Halevi's poems written during the course of his pilgrimage to the Land of Israel. In one example, the poet links a nostalgic introduction with a pronouncement of desire to reach the ruined Temple in Jerusalem:

1. My desire for the Living God pressed me to seek
   the place of the anointed's throne at morn,
2. To such an extent that it did not even let me kiss
   my children, friends and brethren [goodbye].
3. I did not weep for the orchard I planted
   and watered so that my plants blossomed,[104]
4. And I did not mention Judah and Azraʾel,
   two precious youths, the choice ones of my flowers,
5. And Isaac, whom I considered like a son,
   the yield of my sun, the fine crop of my moon.
6. I nearly forgot the synagogue
   in whose study house was my rest,
7. And forgot the pleasures of my Sabbaths,
   the glory of my festivals, the honor of my Passover.
8. I bequeathed my stature to others
   and left my renown to idols.[105]

9. I exchanged my chambers for the shade of timber,[106]
the security of my [home's] bars for a thicket covering.
10. My soul was satiated with the finest of spices,
but I have made my perfume the scent of bark.[107]
11. I have ceased groveling [before men][108]
and set my paths in the heart of the sea
12. So that I may find my God's footstool[109]
and there pour out my soul and my speech.
13. I will stand at the threshold of His holy mountain
and make my doors face the doors of heaven's gates.
14. I will cause my nard to flower in the waters of the Jordan,
plant my shoots in the Shiloaḥ [river].
15. The Lord is on my side. How can I fear[110]
or dread when the angel of His mercy bears my weapon?
16. I will praise His name
the rest of my life and thank Him forever.[111]

At first glance, the formulation of the poem suggests an *absence* of nostalgia; the speaker maintains that the depth of his religious passion obviated his need for kissing his children good-bye, weeping for his "orchard," and so on. However, recounting so many aspects of his life in al-Andalus (filial, social, intellectual, religious) amounts to a nostalgic reminiscence. The scribe of the *dīwān* certainly identified nostalgia and estrangement as the dominant themes of the poem and introduced it: "He said concerning longing for his family and homeland." Despite its personal tone, the nostalgic mode here differs from Ibn Ezra's, wherein *qaṣīda* form and topoi are central. Although the poem preserves the basic prosodic elements of Arabized Hebrew verse (quantitative meter and monorhyme), it does not follow the typical thematic development of the *qaṣīda*.

Following the opening verse that states the impetus for Halevi's journey, the poem may be divided easily into three main parts that correspond to the temporal progression past/present/future: 1) Recollection of a former life in al-Andalus (2–7); 2) estrangement during the present journey (8–11); and 3) fulfillment of the pilgrimage in the future (12–16). Moses Ibn Ezra's reluctant, if not forced, migration to Castile and Navarre amounted to the poet's life ending in a state of estrangement. For Halevi, estrangement at sea—symbolized by the boat (shade of timber, thicket covering, perfume of bark)—was only a stage, albeit one of great significance, of a journey that began in al-Andalus and would terminate in Jerusalem. Halevi writes from the liminal point of estrangement between the stability of al-Andalus and the spiritual destination of Jerusalem. Like other stages of liminality that have been described by anthropologists and scholars of religion, this one is marked by the "initiate's" separation from familiar surroundings and a heightened sense of danger.[112] The stage is a test that the pilgrim must endure before completing the ritual.

Halevi's nostalgia and estrangement should be considered signs of devotional sincerity more than indications of ambivalence over leaving al-Andalus (though they might be this as well). By embarking upon a pilgrimage, Halevi subjected himself to a volitional experience of estrangement from his homeland, much like the patriarch Abraham as depicted in the *Kuzari*.[113] The poet *chose* estrangement over security and assigned the experience a religious valence inextricably linked with the pilgrim's quest. Pining for the past and experiencing the vicissitudes of estrangement in no way undermine the pilgrim's purpose; on the contrary, the spiritual imperative of pilgrimage can only be fulfilled if longing and estrangement wrack his soul and purify him. As the Jewish spokesman of the *Kuzari* expounds just before embarking upon his journey to the Land of Israel, estrangement is preparatory for divine service: *galut mekhaperet ʿavon,* estrangement atones for sin.[114]

Abraham Ibn Ezra: Strophic Form

1. Woe, for calamity has descended upon Sefarad from the heavens!
2. My eyes, my eyes flow with water.[115]

3. The weeping of my eye is like an ostrich's[116] for the city of Lucena!
4. Without guilt, the exile dwelled there untroubled,
5. Unchanged for one thousand and seventy years.
6. When her day arrived and her people wandered, she became like a widow.
7. [She was] without Pentateuch or Bible; the Mishnah was hidden.
8. The Talmud was like desolation[117] for all of its glory had passed away.
9. There were murderers and others seeking[118] everywhere for a place [to hide].
10. A place of prayer and praise was renamed a house of moral indecency.[119]
11. For this I weep and strike my hand;[120] lamentation is constantly in my mouth.
12. I cannot be silent and say, "Would that my head were water!"[121]

13. I shave[122] my head and shout bitterness over the exile of Seville,
14. Over noble ones, now fallen ones, their sons in captivity,

15. Over refined girls passed over to the strange faith.
16. How the city of Cordoba was abandoned! Can it be ruin like the sea?
17. There were sages and mighty ones who died in famine and drought.
18. There is neither Jew nor friend in Jaén or Almería.
19. In Majorca and the city of Málaga there remains no sustenance.
20. The remnant of Jews was given a fresh wound.
21. For this I wail and teach bitterness, still I utter a bitter lament.
22. I groan in my distress, "They have vanished like water!"

23. Woe! I call like a woman in travail[123] over the communities of Sijilmasa,
24. A city of intellectuals and sages whose light covered darkness.
25. The pillar of Talmud was brought low, wisdom ruined.
26. The Mishnah was taunted, trampled underfoot.
27. The enemy's eye did not show mercy toward fine men pierced through, wounded.[124]
28. The whole community of Fez became naught when they were given to plunder.
29. Where is the treasure of the community of Tlemsan? Its greatness has melted away.
30. I raise my voice with bitterness over Ceuta and Meknes,
31. I tear my robe over Dar^{c}i, which had been captured.
32. On the Sabbath sons' and daughters' blood was shed like water.

33. What can I say when this was because of my sin?
34. From my Lord, the Rock of my strength, harm was carried out against me.[125]
35. For whom can I hope? What can I say? My hand did it all!
36. My heart is hot within me, because of my soul that has sinned
37. And been exiled from her land, the haven of her desire, to a defiled land.
38. Humiliated and dumbfounded, too weary to speak of her weariness.
39. Yet, with pain in her heart, she hopes for the kindness of her Rock,
40. That He will order freedom from slavery so that she may take shelter in His wings' shade.
41. Imprisoned at every moment, if she remembers His name she is allowed to live.
42. Her weeping is upon her cheek; she is in the hand of a maidservant[126] who
43. Will shoot her bow harshly until God will look down from the heavens.[127]

Although we do not know exactly where Ibn Ezra was when he composed "Aha yarad ᶜal sefarad" for the communities of al-Andalus and the Maghreb (he was probably somewhere in France), it is clear that he was not an eyewitness to the events, having left al-Andalus for Christian Europe several years prior to the establishment of Almohad hegemony. We do not know why Ibn Ezra left al-Andalus when he did, although it is likely that he was aware that an ominous change in political climates was ensuing. As stated in the introduction to this book, it is also unclear why he chose Christian Europe over the Islamic East as his destination. In any case, he maintained a strong identity as an Andalusian Jew displaced from his homeland. He identified himself as a native of Sefarad in almost all of his writings composed outside of al-Andalus; for example, in the introduction to his commentary on the book of Lamentations, he writes, "I am Abraham the son of Meir from a distant land. The wrath of the oppressors drove me out of the land of Sefarad."[128] In his poetry, he characterized himself as "Abraham the old man [*ha-zaqen*] who wandered like a bird from his nest [*ke-ᶜof mi-qen*]."[129] Like Moses Ibn Ezra, he lamented the dim intellectual culture of Christendom in comparison with Islamdom: "In Edom, the wise man has no glory, but in the land of Qedar he is a pearl."[130] As Israel Levin has written:

> When Abraham Ibn Ezra left Sefarad, he went into poverty, suffering and wandering. He did not find a home again that took the place of Sefarad. He would linger in a given city for several years, abandon it ultimately and move to a new place. He was in many places, and in every place he was not in his own place. A lack of inner peace drove him to depart. More than once he felt that he was like a stranger among his people, whose spiritual world was different from his.[131]

On the other hand, Abraham Ibn Ezra was more open to and successful at integrating into his new environment than Moses Ibn Ezra and established friendships with prominent Jews in Christendom.

The form of "Aha yarad" is strophic; as mentioned, some of Halevi's poems written during the Reconquista follow strophic form and may have served as models for Ibn Ezra. In Arabic poetry, strophic forms originated in the Islamic East with the *musammaṭ* and flourished in al-Andalus with the invention of the *muwashshaḥ* and the *zajal,* forms whose popularity was not limited to a courtly audience.[132] In Hebrew poetry, strophic forms were used prior to the Andalusian period in the East and became very common in al-Andalus under the influence of the *muwashshaḥ*.[133] In comparison with the stringent meter and rhyme of classical Arabic prosody, the strophic forms allow for greater flexibility with respect to the number of stanzas, the number of lines per stanza, rhyme, and even meter. (Arabic strophic poems adhere to more varied quantitative meters; meter in Hebrew strophic poems can be quantitative, syllabic, or neither.) Strophic forms are used in Andalusian Arabic and Hebrew poetry for a wide variety of genres and are not associated exclusively with lamentation. Hence casting a communal lament in a strophic form does not evoke the sound of mourning to the same degree that styling it as a *petiḥa* does.

"Aha yarad" consists of four strophes of ten lines each (except for the final strophe, which contains eleven); these strophes are abnormally long (most poems employ strophes of five or six lines). The first nine lines of each strophe (ten lines of the final strophe) share a common rhyme, which changes from strophe to strophe, while the ultimate line of each strophe ends with a common rhyme. The rhyme of the final line of each strophe is established in the first two lines of the poem preceding the strophes (called the *maṭlaᶜ* in Arabic terminology) with the words *shamayim* (heavens) and *mayim* (water). *Mayim* then becomes the final word of strophes 1, 2, and 3, while strophe 4 ends with the word *shamayim,* recalling the opening line. Each line of the poem (excluding line 2) consists of three stichs that follow syllabic meter (3/3/6) according to the rules of Hispano-Jewish devotional verse. The poet's first name, Avraham, appears in the acrostic.[134]

Many of these features are to be found in other examples of Abraham Ibn Ezra's verse; the poet uses strophic form for several genres (such as love poetry, panegyric, devotional petition, and a poem on sea travel), although he left no other poem that fits this form precisely.[135] Significantly, the poet wrote two laments upon the death of his son Isaac in strophic form, one of which ("Avi ha-ben") also consists of four strophes and includes the poet's name in the acrostic (though there are fewer lines per strophe and a freer use of meter).[136] Among all of Ibn Ezra's laments over individuals, it is only in the laments over Isaac that he uses the strophic form; the others follow the *petiḥa* form and are very impersonal, even generic, in character.[137] For Ibn Ezra, the use of the strophic form in lamentation seems to signify that his subject is very close to his heart.

"Aha yarad" has usually been counted among Ibn Ezra's "secular" poems in modern scholarship.[138] However, like Halevi's *petiḥas*, this poem does not fit neatly into a "sacred" or "secular" category. Although the poem certainly contains historical information, which is what suggested the "secular" label to scholars, it also offers a theological dimension; the opening verse identifies "the heavens" as the origin of the destruction, and a theory of divine retribution for human sin is expanded upon in the final strophe. Heavenly decree is also the opening theme of the lament over Isaac, "Avi ha-ben"—"Father of the child, come and mourn, for God has separated you from your son, your favored one, whom you loved, Isaac" (cf. Gen. 22:2)—and is resumed in the final strophe, though this lament does not pursue the topic of divine justice per se.

In "Aha yarad," the poet stands apart from the scene of destruction, lamenting from afar and taking a bird's-eye view. This is the first Hebrew poem to name cities of al-Andalus (and the Maghreb) explicitly by simply transliterating their names as faithfully as possible. In Halevi's poems on Toledo, the city is not mentioned at all; in the rare instances in which Moses Ibn Ezra mentions Granada, the city name is always rendered in a Hebrew formulation such as *beit rimon,* "house of pomegranate." It is worth considering what inspired Abraham Ibn Ezra to depart from the practice of the Hebrew Andalusian school. Schirmann suggests that Ibn Ezra followed the model of Ashkenazi post-Crusade laments, which often offer historical details, including town names.[139] Indeed, the author was in Christian Europe at the time of the poem's composition and may have seen himself as writing for an audience with a taste for Ashkenazi laments. It is also possible that Ibn Ezra was following the Arabic city laments (*rithāʾ al-mudun*), which also include historical details and place names and sometimes utilize strophic forms. In either case, commemorating Andalusian and Maghrebi cities with their actual names became significant for the poet as he grew distant from them in space and time. Unlike the Reconquista, the Almohad invasion resulted in the virtual end of Jewish settlement in these cities, which may have heightened the need for preserving their names lest they be forgotten, especially outside of the region.

The first strophe is dedicated to a single city, Lucena, well-known for its rabbinic academy and activity in the study of the Hebrew language. In the second strophe, other cities of al-Andalus are remembered in rapid succession: Seville, Cordoba, Almería, Jaén, and Málaga. In the third strophe, the poet expands the circle of vision even wider to recall destroyed communities of the Maghreb.[140] The extraordinary length of the strophes mirrors the weighty subject matter. Throughout these strophes, the reader is aware of a first-person speaker who expresses mourning through biblical phrases of distress and lamentation.[141] The speaker here is most easily identified with the poet, although we will see that his speech may have simultaneously represented the community.

The fourth strophe is the most complex. It begins with a continuation of the first-person voice ("What can I say when this was because of my sin," 33). Since it is unlikely that the poet was literally placing blame for the calamity on his own actions, it would seem that the "poetic I" here now represents a communal voice. Yet, as Ross Brann has discussed, there is still an ambiguity of voice, since the poet conflates the local experience of Andalusian and Maghrebi Jewry with traditional tropes of Israel's exile and hope for redemption.[142] In lines 36–37, the poem makes a transition to speak about the community in the third-person feminine. It is not uncommon in the Hebrew tradition to speak of the community in the first-person singular and also in the third-person feminine within a single poem; this phenomenon is observed in the *petiḥas* by Halevi above.[143] However, here the poet makes the transition from first person to third by locating the community within himself ("My heart is hot within me, because of my soul that has sinned and been exiled from her land," 36–37). Communal or national exile seems to exist within the poetic speaker.

Like Halevi, Ibn Ezra focuses on the long-standing security of Israel in Iberia and the subsequent loss of synagogues and academies of religious learning. Yet the tone of this poem is far more personal than in the poems by Halevi. The two *petiḥas* by Halevi open by addressing an audience in the second person—"*You* who wait for deliverance," "May it never befall *you* hearers of my words."[144] The *petiḥas* focus on offering words of consolation for survivors who are still in Iberia; Halevi's strophic poems from the Reconquista are also not particularly personal. In contrast, Ibn Ezra's lament is turned inward; although one imagines that the poem was recited or circulated publicly (indeed, it was incorporated and expanded upon within the liturgical rites of some North African communities), the poet assumes the individualized posture that characterizes the laments over his son. The first three strophes open and close with the speaker's mournful first-person utterances and rituals of lamentation. The personal voice continues even in the fourth strophe, in which the poet speaks on behalf of the broader community (whether it is the Jews of al-Andalus and the Maghreb, the Jewish people as a whole, or, as Ross Brann has argued, both). The poem undoubtedly works on several levels simultaneously; rhetorically, it is the personal, suffering voice of the author that predominates.

The notion of divine punishment presented in the fourth strophe is largely conventional. Lines 33 and 35 posit the traditional rubric of exile as punishment for sin, as in Halevi's poems written during the Reconquista; punishment is meted out by God, and Israel waits for God's redemption. However, the theological formulation is less consistent than it is in Halevi's *petiḥas*. The theory of divine retribution for communal sin is tempered by the premise that Lucena was "without guilt" (4). Also, "Aha yarad" offers none of the consolation of Halevi's *petiḥas*. Halevi's speaker stands confidently before his audience and calls upon God to initiate salvation through His wrath and fury: "God of vengeance, arouse your wrath! . . . Shake out the wicked [from the earth]!" and so on ("You who wait," 25). In "Aha yarad," the tone is simply mournful and despondent. Line 35 begins, "For whom can I hope?" Because we might assume that the speaker can usually hope for God, the rhetorical nature of the question suggests that there truly might be none for whom he can hope when even God has turned against him. There is no confidence in an imminent redemption but only meek hope: "with pain in her heart, she hopes for the kindness of her Rock" (39). In the final strophe of the poem, one senses the poet grasping for answers, trying to find a satisfying interpretation for the bewildering events.

What is the significance of the strophic form in this poem? Is it completely incidental to the content, or does it convey meaning? Unlike the *qaṣīda* and the *petiḥa* forms, strophic form does not immediately evoke a long-standing tradition of mourning and estrangement. Still, it seems to have two functions for Ibn Ezra. First, lamenting in strophic form may signify that the subject was of personal importance for the poet (although it was also used by Halevi, it does not seem to bear the same valence). As stated above, among his laments Ibn Ezra uses the strophic form only in for lamenting the cities of al-Andalus and the Maghreb and his son, subjects dear to his heart. Distant from the scene of the destruction and the people of his former homeland, the poet presents the destruction as his personal loss as much as he integrates his voice with traditional tropes of mourning. With respect to thematic structuring, the division of the poem into four strophes allows each strophe a certain degree of autonomy. The poet is able to zoom out progressively from Lucena, to al-Andalus, to the Maghreb to create a swelling sense of scale and a deepening sense of lamentation. By postponing theological content until the poem's conclusion, the poet allows the personal mourning of the first three strophes to dominate. One is struck far more by the poet's keening through the haunting phrasing of the Bible than by the conventional theological ruminations. The weight of "Aha yarad" falls on the poet's lamentation over the destroyed communities of his memory and the city names that had never before been uttered in Hebrew verse.

Even if "Aha yarad" does not situate itself within a long-standing tradition of lamentation, it seems that the poem became a template for later laments over Jewish communities of the Islamic West; "Aha yarad" was expanded upon by scribes and other poets several times, and the poem "Eikh neḥerav maʾarav" (How the West was destroyed), which addresses communities of the Maghreb only, imitates the form, meter, and rhyme of "Aha yarad."[145]

In choosing literary forms, Andalusian Jewish poets drew upon the methods of memorialization conveyed in two literary traditions, Arabic and Hebrew. Moses Ibn Ezra gave precedence to his cultural identity as an Arabized Jew by locating his experience of estrangement within the resonant tradition of Arabic mourning and nostalgia. The *qaṣīda* form provided a succinct vehicle of nostalgic expression that continued to represent the poet's cultural ideals in the post-Andalusian environment. Judah Halevi interpreted the fall of communities during the Reconquista through the voice of a public mourner before the community of Israel, a community of survivors needing consolation, and stressed the theological significance of events and the expected redemption. Halevi's more personal poems written during his journey to the Land of Israel incorporate nostalgia and estrangement as themes but avoid *qaṣīda* form and topoi such as "weeping over the ruins"; the poems written at sea accentuate the author's persona as a pilgrim during a liminal stage who willingly accepts the yoke of estrangement as a devotional practice. As Halevi did by selecting the *petiḥa,* Abraham Ibn Ezra chose a form that cannot easily be labeled "secular" or "sacred." The strophic form is common in several genres of Ibn Ezra's verse, though the closest analog of "Aha yarad" is the lament over his son Isaac, "Avi ha-ben," a point that emphasizes the highly personal character of each poem. Although "Aha yarad" presents a theological interest, its emphasis is concentrated in the opening strophes that memorialize the lost communities through a personal voice, an effect that is accomplished by the thematic segregation possible in the strophic form.

Moses Ibn Ezra, Judah Halevi, and Abraham Ibn Ezra all ascribed different weights to personal, historical, and theological aspects of their experiences. Still, it would be an error to separate their poems according to the categories of "secular" and "sacred" verse. More is to be gained by piercing the synthetic barrier between the two types of verse than by segregating poems according to a preconceived division of genres that is more modern than medieval. It is better to allow for a flexible conception of genre and to let classifications emerge from the poems themselves. By reading the poems treated in this chapter together, the variety of responses to cultural transition comes into sharper focus.

Three

Imagery

The Protean Garden

> "Image, all image," he cried to the fallen tower as the night came on. "Whose harp is the sea? Whose burning candle is the sun?" An image of a man, he rose to his feet and drew the curtains open. Peace, like a simile, lay over the roofs of the town. "Image, all image," cried Marlais, stepping through the window on to the level roofs.
>
> —Dylan Thomas, "The Orchards"

It is generally recognized that the gardens described in Hebrew Andalusian garden poems are idealized. The poems always describe similar garden beds, flowers, trees, watercourses, fountains, couches for reclining, entertainers, wine goblets, and wine. Throughout the corpus, the poems seem to describe the "same" garden, pointing to the social setting of a courtier class.[1] However, a garden poem is seldom about a garden only. Through poetic imagery, the poet links the garden to some external reality of a social, devotional, or personal nature. In fact, the external theme is often more central to the poem's meaning than the ostensible subject of the garden. While the idealized garden is stable with respect to its physical accoutrements, its poetic existence is protean, always changing identity through imagery.

This chapter reconsiders Hebrew Andalusian garden poetry from the perspective of poetic imagery, a topic that has not gained sufficient attention in scholarship. The chapter begins with a general discussion of poetic imagery and an analysis of select garden poems by Dunash Ben Labrat, Samuel the Nagid, Solomon Ibn Gabirol, and Moses Ibn Ezra. In the final section, two poems by Moses Ibn Ezra are contrasted from the perspective of imagery. One of the poems was composed while the poet resided in al-Andalus whereas the other was composed from his exile in Castile following the Almoravid conquest. The discussion demonstrates the centrality of imagery analysis for reading the medieval Hebrew poetics of estrangement and exile.

Imagery

Modern Western Criticism

Like many terms in literary criticism, "imagery" has been used in modern criticism to signify various aspects of literature, and as such, its meaning has been unstable and imprecise. Even a quick glance at major works on literary terms and theory reveals that imagery has been construed in any number of ways. Most basically, and closest to the term's original sense, is the understanding of an image as a "mental picture," though such a definition is of limited value for literary studies. In criticism, most authors agree that images are "sensuous"—that they are artistic expressions of the sensual (visual, audible, tactile, olfactory) world and allow the reader to re-create that world through the mental faculties. They also generally differentiate between "concrete," or literal, images and "abstract," or figurative, ones. An example of a concrete image is "red roses covered the white wall"—the words signify something sensuous and allow the reader to re-create a picture through the mental faculties. "Figurative" images—for example, "she is a rose"—make use of tropes, or figures of speech (metaphor, simile, metonymy, synecdoche, and so on), and also relate to mental pictures, even if the picture suggested by a phrase is not strictly obvious.

In its broadest applications, the term "image" has referred to a sensuous effect provoked by literary language, a striking use of language, symbol, metaphor, or other figure of speech.[2] Some critics have pronounced this shifting application, particularly the contradictory senses of "mental picture" and "figure of speech," as treacherous and advantageous only to "lazy criticism."[3] Still, "imagery" remains more valuable than "metaphor" or "simile" as independent terms for it emphasizes the common ground of tropes over the subtle distinctions of their construction.

Until the New Criticism, imagery was considered an ornamental aspect of literature that contributed little to the meaning of a work. As a manifestation of style, imagery was relegated to mere decoration. For nineteenth-century theorists, imagery could inspire pleasure in the reader who would appreciate reality in a new way upon recognizing the similarities between seemingly disparate objects. An image might have been considered beautiful but did not participate in the meaning-making of a poem. Among theorists identified with the New Criticism,[4] the concept of imagery claimed a new prominence in both the study of prose—in which it figured more centrally than author, narrator, plot, and argument—and poetry, which was considered nothing if not a complex amalgam of images.[5] No longer seen as mere ornament, imagery became a fundamental tool for interpreting the very meaning of literature. A new interest developed not only in the ostensible object (tenor) being described in a poem or verse but also in the comparate (vehicle)[6] used to describe that object. Thus, when a poet states *A* (the object) is like *B* (the comparate), the reader is intended to think of *B;* ultimately, *B* might be more significant to the meaning of the poem than *A*. The New Critics were especially insistent upon revealing patterns or clusters of images wherein comparates belong to related semantic fields.

As an extension and corollary of this area of interpretation, some critics became interested in the psychological analysis of texts and their authors through poetic imagery. Some scholars followed dubious methods, such as literally counting the occurrence of types of images (for example, household goods, heavenly bodies, and sex) throughout an author's entire corpus and concluding that the predominant categories revealed something fundamental about the author's personality.[7] Image categories were considered more essential in the analysis of meaning than the text's "deliberate" effects. Inspired by Freudian analytic methods, the imagery on the page was said to present a trajectory of the author's subconscious yearnings and inclinations. Poetic images are like images in a dream, the theory goes, operating according to a system of codes that can be interpreted. Problems of interpretation in this area of analysis are as plentiful as they are in dream interpretation (for example, is the code by which an image may be interpreted universal or specific to a given author?). Appropriately, critics have attacked such readings as mere "message hunting" and the foundationless pursuit of "psychological biography."[8] Still, some modern authors themselves have described imagery production as a semiconscious process; Dylan Thomas remarks in a letter to his friend Henry Treece: "I make one image—though 'make' is not the word; I let, perhaps, an image be 'made' emotionally in me and then apply to it what intellectual and critical forces I possess."[9]

After the New Criticism, imagery analysis continued in several directions. It remained important for critics who linked imagery in particular works with aspects of the poet's personality (more in the service of understanding the work than analyzing the author),[10] with broader societal myths and rituals,[11] and with specific historical situations.[12] Structuralists were interested less in how imagery affected the meaning of a work than in how images (as tropes) were constructed, how they were able to carry meaning, and what they revealed about the relationship between signifier and signified.[13]

Medieval Arabic Criticism and the Study of Medieval Hebrew Poetry

Medieval Arabic poetics is deeply mindful of rhetoric and the figures of speech that are included within the rubric of modern concepts of imagery.[14] Medieval critics usually focus on the construction of isolated images without relating them to the meaning of whole poems. The unit of analysis is usually the individual line; hence the analysis of imagery clusters in whole poems is by definition beyond the scope of the medieval critic's interest. In *maʿānī* (motifs) literature, critics compile related images taken from different poems by different poets in an order of hierarchical abstraction and show no concern for the pattern or function of imagery within a single poem.[15]

The only premodern theorist to develop a psychological theory of imagery is the eleventh-century Arabic critic al-Jurjānī (d. 1078 or 1081). In the view of Kamal Abu-Deeb, al-Jurjānī's opinions prefigure the conclusions of modern Western linguists and literary theorists.[16] Al-Jurjānī maintains that there is a psychological dimension of imagery that reveals something about the psychological profile of the poet.[17] Similar to Dylan Thomas's reference to images being "made" within, al-Jurjānī writes that in choosing an image, the poet looks *fī nafsihi,* into himself, his psyche, his soul.[18] In order to illustrate al-Jurjānī's method of psychological interpretation, let us consider his reading of the following verses by Ibn al-Muʿtazz (d. 908) describing the crescent moon at the end of Ramaḍān:

> The reign of fasting is now over, and the illness
> of the crescent moon heralds the coming of the *ʿīd.*
> The moon chases the Pleiades like a greedy eater
> opening his mouth to eat a bunch of grapes.

Clearly, the metaphors and similes in the verses suggest a mental picture, one that the reader can readily associate with the sky being described. The moon is "ill," meaning that it is lean and slight like a crescent. Its concave shape resembles a mouth in profile facing, hence "chasing," the Pleiades, a cluster of stars likened to a "bunch of grapes." Thus, the lines state that the month of Ramaḍān is over, and the appearance of the crescent moon announces the arrival of the *ʿīd.* The imagery is effective in that the metaphors employed fit together logically and accurately describe the moon and the Pleiades. The reader may even experience pleasure, reflecting upon the affinity between the objects and their comparates.

Al-Jurjānī ventures beyond such an interpretation and incorporates biographical information about the author into his reading. He maintains that Ibn al-Muʿtazz was irreverent and that his life and poetry were consumed with drinking and eating. For the poet, Ramaḍān was tantamount to supervised deprivation and compulsory abstinence, causing him to experience the month as "the *reign* of fasting" (*dawlatu al-ṣiyāmi*). The "illness" of the moon refers to the poet's own emaciation. For Ibn al-Muʿtazz, the *ʿīd* did not arouse thoughts of religious contemplation but only of ravenous consumption; hence the moon is a "greedy eater" about to consume "a bunch of grapes"—a fine simile for the Pleiades but representing food and, more importantly, drink (i.e., wine) on a deeper level.[19]

This type of analysis might also be performed in the analysis of Hebrew poetry. Let us consider the following couplet by Solomon Ibn Gabirol, which also describes a crescent moon:[20]

> The moon between white and black is like
> a maiden peering[21] through a hole,
> It stuck out its lip from the darkness[22]
> but retracted as if on account of your lip.[23]

The images are descriptive and provide a fine simile (like a maiden, line 1) and metaphor (attribution[24] of a lip, line 2). The crescent moon, part light and part dark, is like a woman's face behind a lattice, partly viewable yet partly obscured. In line 2, the moon protruding through the darkness also resembles a single lip because of its concave shape. However, this analysis leaves aspects of the verse unexplained; what is the significance of the *action* of the lip? Whether the lip is about to be kissed, is refusing to be kissed, or has already been kissed, its likeness to the moon is not altered. If the moon's action of having "retracted as if on account of your lip" is not essential for conjuring up the intended mental picture, then does it have a function?

One might read a psychological dimension into these images along the lines of al-Jurjānī's method. Ibn Gabirol is a poet believed to have been frustrated in love. Scholars generally find his love poems unconvincing and unrealistic and believe that he led a lonely life, deprived of intimacy and social companionship. He was haughty, acerbic, afflicted with a disfiguring disease, and lacking in social grace, generally incapable of personal or romantic intimacy.[25] Thus, the reader should not be surprised to find that the moon conjures up a cloistered maiden kept at a distance, love impossible, and desire unfulfilled. The moon is a lip that is offered but then retracted when an attempt at intimacy is made; "your" lip in the verse is surely that of the poet. For this reason, the moon is not a luscious lip waiting to be devoured by a capable lover nor one that has been satiated with lovemaking, even though such metaphors would serve the visual quality of the image equally well. Indeed, alternative images would have changed the emotional quality of the verse. The two visual suggestions are linked through their shared concern with desire and frustration and, according to a psychological reading, may be said to betray the emotional state of the author. The couplet's true subject is frustrated love and is not determined through its object, the crescent moon, but through its comparates. While such an analysis provides useful insights, it also presents methodological difficulties that will be discussed below.

Al-Jurjānī's evocative method of criticism made little impact on subsequent critics of Arabic literature, medieval or modern, let alone critics of medieval Hebrew literature. The heyday of modern imagery criticism also came and went, barely affecting the study of medieval Hebrew poetry. This is not altogether surprising, since the progenitors of this field are philology, Jewish history, and aesthetics to some extent, but not literary criticism.[26] Insofar as scholars of medieval Hebrew literature laid traditional Arabic literary criticism as the foundation of their analyses, the critical sources explored also presented little interest in imagery as an explanatory concept of meaning in poems. Scholarship on medieval Hebrew literature has treated imagery as an ornamental aspect of poetry, itself defined as "ornate speech" (following the medieval definition by Moses Ibn Ezra).[27] David Yellin's treatment of imagery in his classic explication of Andalusian Hebrew poetics is limited to categorizing the various figures of speech as understood within medieval Arabic criticism.[28] The concept of imagery dominating the field of medieval Hebrew literature thus derives from the limited contextualization characteristic of medieval Arabic criticism and is ratified by nineteenth-century notions of reading.

In two articles treating imagery in medieval Hebrew poetry (one in Hebrew and one in English), Dan Pagis also focuses on imagery's formal and ornamental aspects.[29] Pagis accurately portrays the conception of imagery within the Iberian school and primarily looks at areas of poetry that are particularly dense in imagery and ornamentation. Pagis discusses the various types of imagery wherein figures of speech (metaphor, simile, metonymy, and so on) are combined with rhetorical figures (antithesis, wordplay, alliteration, and so on) to produce novel effects. Thus, Pagis is specifically interested in the areas of writing wherein the *raison d'être* is the manneristic interplay of images, sometimes revolving around a central conceit.

Toward the end of the English article, Pagis redirects his thinking and departs from medieval conventions of reading. He offers an interpretation of the sophisticated imagery suffused throughout Ibn Gabirol's famous storm description in "Ani ha-ᵓish" (I am the man). The passage analyzed reads as follows:

> Then the wind assailed the moon with sailing clouds, and they covered his face with a mask. . . . The skies robed themselves in darkness. It seemed as if the moon had died, and the cloud had buried him. . . . Then the night put on an armor-plate of darkness; thunder, with a spear of lightning, pierced it; and the lightning flew about the skies . . . spreading its wings like a bat; the ravens of the dark fled when they saw it.[30]

Pagis calls attention to the recurring imagery of war and death, which is not limited to this section of the poem but also surfaces in a personal key near the poem's conclusion, "And God closed in my thoughts. . . . He bound my heart with ropes of darkness. Yet it arose like a warrior breaking out of a siege." Pagis, who lauds Ibn Gabirol for introducing "searching introspection" into Hebrew poetry, finds significance behind the imagery that can only be called psychological. He writes, "The entire passage [the storm description], with all its local metaphors of battle and death, in fact depicts an actual storm; but the point is also an *extended metaphor of the poet's mind*" (emphasis mine). If Pagis is correct, there is greater significance to imagery than ornament or the sheer pleasure experienced upon recognizing the relationships between seemingly incongruous objects. In stepping beyond the categories of imagery as delineated by medieval criticism, Pagis enters an area of modern criticism that touches upon difficult areas of interpretation.

One wishes that Pagis had developed his passing yet pregnant suggestion into a fuller theory of interpretation. Although he is hardly explicit here about a methodology, one may glean a few points from his terse comments: 1) interpretation relies upon finding a pattern of imagery; Ibn Gabirol supplies the storm not with one but with several images of war and death; 2) in a multipartite poem, the imagery crosses over between parts of the poem—in this case, between the description of the storm and the personal conclusion; and 3) there is some relationship between the poet's personal experience, his biography, and disposition and his writing. These points have more in common with the New Criticism and al-Jurjānī's psychological strain of analysis than with mainstream medieval poetics.

Pagis's analysis raises more questions than it answers. How do we know that the link between author and imagery is truly psychological? Is it not possible that Ibn Gabirol utilized similar imagery in different parts of the poem to create a sense of cohesion and unity and that nothing can be learned about the poet's inner life? If Ibn Gabirol did infuse imagery with a personal aspect, did he do so consciously or unconsciously? What is the relationship between emotive, expressive imagery, and conventional, ornate writing? Are they mutually exclusive, or might imagery convey emotion even in a writer such as Moses Ibn Ezra, who explicitly defines poetry as "ornate speech"?

As mentioned, critics since the New Criticism have been appropriately skeptical concerning poetry's ability to provide a window into the author's subconscious emotions. Poems contain intentionally created representations of emotions, which the author might ascribe to himself or to some other speaker. Imagery criticism does not require a theory of poetry as unconscious or subconscious creation; a method such as cluster analysis is equally valid when one assumes an author who carefully constructs his work. Even within highly conventional writing, the poet is faced with choices. Is the crescent moon a greedy eater, or a delicate lip? Is the Pleiades a bunch of grapes, or an intimate gathering of friends? Is the full moon a beautiful face, or a love-struck insomniac wandering through the night? Are the stars wine goblets soaring across a table, or military troops poised to wage war? Are roses red from the bloody tears of a lover, the blood of grapes, an infection? Such differences are essential for creating meaning within poems.

The method used in reading Hebrew garden poems below is not like that of New Critics who viewed the preponderance of image types across an author's corpus to be a reflection of his predilections, preoccupations, and subconscious yearnings. Rather, imagery analysis is confined to patterns of images occurring within individual poems, and the production of images is not viewed as a necessarily subconscious process. Imagery is seen as a device used by poets to create meaning beyond the single line. Authors control their selection of images in order to indicate subject matters beyond the poem's ostensible object of description (in this case, the garden) and to create a desired emotional tenor. In the following analyses, images are situated vis-à-vis convention; unconventional images are considered the most suggestive substrates for interpretation, although a dense concentration of related conventional images can also be significant.

Of God, Disease, and Aristocracy: Imagery in Andalusian Hebrew Garden Poems

Scholarship on medieval Hebrew literature has been interested in the garden on cultural and literary levels and has focused on three primary areas of research: 1) tracing the repertoire of motifs found in Hebrew poems to precedents in the Arabic poetic tradition;[31] 2) making inferences from the poems about the material, social, and cultural environment in which the poems were composed;[32] and 3) tracing the development of the genre within

Hebrew letters in order to isolate earmarks of individual authorship and style.[33]

These three areas—influence, realia, and development—while useful, are all extrinsic and fall short of interpreting poetic meaning. In contrast, the present discussion explores a new direction for research based upon imagery analysis. Before returning to the topic of cultural transition through the analysis of two long poems by Moses Ibn Ezra, a number of short poems by various authors will be discussed. These analyses are intended as études in imagery criticism that demonstrate various uses of imagery in the Hebrew corpus. The discussion shows that the descriptions of gardens utilizing comparates as distinct as a woman, a scroll, a weapon, and so on, are not created haphazardly, motivated only by a poet's desire to describe and to reveal links between ostensibly disparate objects. Rather, the images participate in the production of meaning within the poem.

Medieval Hebrew poetry is hardly monolithic in its use of imagery. Some poems include almost no figurative imagery while others group together several figurative images, sometimes in the service of describing a single object. The earliest Andalusian Hebrew poem to include a garden description, Dunash Ben Labrat's "Ve-omer al tishan" (Someone said, "Don't sleep!"), makes almost no use of tropes:

1. Someone said, "Don't sleep! Drink aged wine!"
2. With camphor and rose, frankincense and aloe.
3. In an orchard of pomegranate and date, and grapevines too,
4. And flourishing[34] plantings and varieties of tamarisk trees,
5. The tumult of pipes and the sound of lutes
6. On the lips of singers with harps and lyres.
7. Where every tree is raised high, its branches' fruit lovely,
8. And every bird of every feather sings among the leaves.
9. The doves coo as if they were singing melodies,
10. And the turtledoves answer and flutter like flutes.
11. We drink on garden beds enveloped in roses,
12. We banish worries with all types of carousing,
13. We eat delicacies and drink from basins.
14. We act like giants and drink from bowls.
15. In the morning I rise to slaughter bulls,
16. Fattened choice ones, rams and sheep too.
17. We anoint with fine oil and burn a tender branch.
18. Before the Day of Destruction comes, we will attain peace. . . .[35]

The furnishings of the garden are presented in an almost list-like fashion. The imagery is almost exclusively of the "literal, concrete" type and offers little room for the interpretation of comparates. The similes in lines 9 and 10 are not very suggestive, except that they echo the musical theme introduced in lines 5 and 6. The most suggestive comparison is the likening of drinkers to "giants," *ʿanaqim,* in line 14, connoting indulgence, pleasure, and perhaps even gluttony.[36] The reader is alerted to the various accoutrements of the garden—wine, trees, vines, flowers, birds, musicians, and so on—but is offered no sense of the arrangement of space or emotional associations, apart from general joy and revelry.

The garden figures as a central topic of description in the poetry of Samuel the Nagid, who employs figurative imagery much more liberally than his predecessors. Central to his depictions is the organization of space, as in the following poem. The Hebrew poem is introduced in the *dīwān* with an Arabic superscription by the poet's son, Joseph, giving the occasion for the poem's composition:

I planted a circular garden and enclosed it with a circular stream. I entreated [my father] to go there and relax; he did so and took pleasure in it and because of it. He said:

1. With a word, Joseph inclined his father's heart
   to grant any request, great or small,
2. And said, "Let us go to a garden
   for its buds and flowers are full of bloom.
3. There I planted a round space for my relaxation,
   I made it a treasured place for my rest.
4. A canal rings around it
   as the heavens encircle the earth."
5. We went out to the flower beds of the garden,
   which were arranged in it like lines in a scroll.
6. In the heart of every generous person are highways,
   and to their doors every petitioner has access.
7. In the palace, we sat in the shade of pomegranate and plane trees,
   not in the shade of terebinth and oak.[37]
8. Beneath us we had grasses for couches
   while the leaves above our heads were a swaddling-band.[38]
9. With rubies the wine pourer filled a cup
   and placed it on a boat of variegated papyrus.
10. He sent the cup like a bride in her palanquin
    over water to the drinker, her groom,
11. Who drank and returned his cup
    and addressed the pourer as at the start.
12. [The pourer] never tired from extending his hand to the drinker
    and saying to him, "Drink, there is no roaring sound!"[39]

13. It is a wonder and its sight is magnificent,
    whoever has not beheld its like has not beheld greatness!
14. There is no activity like the activity
    of brethren drinking in a round garden along a canal.[40]

The entire scene is suggestive of comfort, ease, and repose. The garden described is a garden of plenty full of buds, flowers, water, and wine. The drinkers recline in the garden, surrounded by trees on all sides, leaves and grasses above and below.

The physical space of this garden is highly organized. In particular, the poet and also the scribe emphasize the idea of roundness and the circularity of space. In the superscription, Joseph relates that he planted a ***marjan mustadīran,*** a round garden or grassy area, which is rendered in Hebrew as ***kikar*** (lines 3, 14), itself suggesting the idea of roundness.[41] On a semantic level, the root of the word is ***krr,*** evoking the Arabic cognate meaning "to repeat, return." Surrounding the circular space is yet another circle, a river, ringing it as the heavens encompass the earth (4); the repetition of the root *ʿgl,* "to be rounded," in the verse reinforces the feeling of roundness. The garden is likened to a scroll (*megillah,* line 5), derived from the root *gll,* "to roll," in which the garden beds are arranged like lines of writing. The garden is a magnification of the scroll and a reduction of the sky. Thus, the object (***kikar***) and the comparates in figurative images constitute a clear pattern of roundness.[42] Figuring the leaves as a swaddling-band (8) is also appropriate.[43]

The physical dimension of this description is complemented by the action of the poem, which emphasizes the idea of repetition. In lines 9–11, the wine pourer fills the glass with wine and offers it to the drinker, who empties it and returns it to the pourer, restoring matters to their original state. Line 12 emphasizes the perpetual nature of this arrangement, for the process will continue ad infinitum—in other words, as long as the pourer keeps pouring wine, an action from which he never tires. Thus, the cyclical and repeating action taking place within the ***kikar*** mirrors the roundness of the space. The idea of circularity is even echoed phonetically in the poem's final verse, which (roughly) begins and ends with the same word (*ve-khi-peʿulat . . . ʾein peʿulah*). The parallel patterns of circularity and repetition permeate the different parts of the poem, imbuing the text with a feeling of comfort and repose.

The wine pourer is a stock character of the medieval wine poem. He (sometimes she) often plays an erotic function. Common depictions of the wine pourer entail comparing his beauty to that of celestial bodies, lamenting the treacherous hairs that sprout on his pubescent face, praising his murderous glances and the ironic "power" of his languid, lisping speech.[44] He is generally associated with illicit behavior and the rampant (if repressed) desire of his admirers. In this poem, the wine pourer is hardly a murderous or powerful figure, nor is he described as erotic. He merely appears as a dutiful and indefatigable servant. In fact, the licit quality of the scene is complemented by infusing the wine pourer's action with the imagery of bridegroom and bride, of proper rather than illicit union. This is accomplished in line 10, the densest string of comparisons in the poem; the wine drinker is likened to a groom receiving his bride, the wine cup, which the pourer has sent over water in "her palanquin," the variegated boat of papyrus. The wine pourer thus mediates proper matches between drinkers and their drink. These images also suggest a certain mutuality of relation, which matches well with the themes of circularity and repetition. The poet creates the emotional tenor of the poem through such carefully chosen metaphors.

From the perspective of Romantic definitions of unity, this poem is well crafted, characterized by a consistency of imagery and emotional balance. It would be erroneous to draw any far-fetched conclusions such as "the Nagid had marriage on his mind" or "he only emphasized licit imagery because he was in the presence of his young son." Still, the poem does suggest ease, luxury, and generosity. Moreover, this poem emphasizes perpetuity, the cyclical quality of time in the garden. The poem is at ease with the culture that it is describing and conveys the expectation that this culture should continue indefinitely.

Distant from the gardens of Samuel the Nagid are those that appear in the poetry of Solomon Ibn Gabirol. The following garden description, which refers to wine, flowers, and other traditional aspects of the garden, is set in a quasi-devotional key:

1. When [a cloud's] waters pile up like a heap,[45]
   God sends forth His word and melts it;
2. It drips eternally upon the branch
   even as its wine drips upon me.
3. The garden bed blossoms,
   every crocus opening its hooks for us.[46]
4. It sends myrrh to our nostrils
   as [our nostrils] set out to greet its myrtles.
5. Should you go, it will offer you every blossom.
   Give yourself wings[47] lest you tread upon it.
6. The semblance of the sun's face is the face of a bride,
   her finery illuminated by her face.

7. It flees along the pavement of the sphere
without a pursuer to chase it,
8. So that we thought it the chariot of a king,
bounding with his horses.
9. Should you pass by a garden,
you will see its earthen vessels silver-plated.
10. At the time when day turns to evening,
[the sun] spreads [the garden's] ends with yellow gold.
11. You will think that when [the sun] departs, bending low,
that it prostrates itself upon the ground before its Maker.
12. As it hurries to set, you will imagine
that God has covered it with violet.[48]

The poem begins and ends with God. In the opening phrase, the image of "waters piled up like a heap" leads the reader to reflect upon God's miracles, specifically the miracle of dividing the waters of the Sea of Reeds (Exod. 15:8). God then creates another miracle through a command and causes the waters to rain down. As mentioned, the poem does not fail to incorporate standard aspects of conventional garden poetry: rain (1), garden beds (3), flowers (2, 3, 4), vessels (9), and wine (2), although notably there is no wine pourer. In contrast with the garden poems of Samuel the Nagid, the poem has an ethereal quality; the poetic speaker is not concerned with comfort and pleasure in the garden but rather gazes upward toward the heavens (6–12). Although wine drips figuratively on the poetic speaker (2), he does not seem to stand within the garden nor are there wine drinkers present. The speaker tells the reader that if he goes to the garden, he will "fly" above the scene (5). The reader is more cognizant of the "ends" (10) of the garden than its center. The perspective is that of one hovering above the garden rather than one relaxing within it.

In contrast with the perpetuity in the Nagid's garden—the cause of which is human action—Ibn Gabirol portrays the process behind nature in the garden as eternal with God as the cycle's cause (2). The sun is likened to three comparates in the poem: a bride's luminous face (6); a king's chariot bounding with horses (8); and a supplicant bending prostrate before the Creator (11). Despite its superlative beauty and speed, the sun is still God's petitioner, guaranteeing God's superiority over worldly beauty and power. Although this garden is the "same" garden as the one in the poem of the Nagid, it has a very different identity, bearing testimony to the power of God more than the leisure of aristocrats.

In reconstructing Ibn Gabirol's biography, scholars have been fascinated by references to skin disease in the poet's verse.[49] The poet often refers to his disfigurement explicitly, while in other cases, the language of disease penetrates the descriptions of other objects. In one poem, Ibn Gabirol describes a garden through the language of sacrifice and disease:[50]

. . . .

5. My heart beheld the wonders of God
 when it beheld the cloud weeping while [the garden]
 laughed.
6. [The cloud] sprinkled its drops with a skillful hand
 like the hand of Aaron sprinkling [blood] at the altar.[51]
7. It tattooed[52] a design in the buds,
 inscribing a setting[53] of crimson and byssus.
8. The spice field offered[54] the smoke of frankincense
 before a cloud that broke open and rushed to suckle.
9. Upon seeing its plants, they said, "They have been covered"[55]
 but they were not covered, not with green plague nor with
 inflammation.[56]

Again, Ibn Gabirol opens a garden description with a reference to God. The scene re-creates cultic Temple practice wherein the cloud is the high priest sprinkling blood and the garden is an offering of pleasing odor to God. The foremost image is one of blood on skin; Aaron's hand (and the altar, of course) is covered. The art of tattooing draws blood with its incisions. The plants appear diseased, with scabby lesions. Even though the poet denies that the garden is truly afflicted, the reader cannot help but imagine plague and infection. The red and green colors of disease, of course, do have a logical relationship with the colors of the garden. Still, the density of related images creates a world of flowing blood and diseased skin that does more than demonstrate the apparent likeness of seemingly unrelated objects.

Numerous scholars hold that it is because of Ibn Gabirol's own affliction that the poet sees disease in flowers, filtering images through his personal experience of suffering even when it seems inappropriate to a social situation.[57] In one poem, Ibn Gabirol thanks a friend for sending a gift of roses whose appearance he describes as "plaguish green like a sick girl"[58] (i.e., thank you for the roses; they are lovely, like the plague!). Interpreting imagery as a reflection of self implicitly accepts a psychological model of imagery analysis; still, one need not conclude that Ibn Gabirol creates imagery haphazardly or subconsciously. In the longer poem treated above, Ibn Gabirol might even be suggesting that the ruptures of his skin are a kind of offering to God.

In the following poem ("Kotnot passim lavash ha-gan") by Moses Ibn Ezra, the garden stands out not only as the meeting place of aristocrats but also as a veritable microcosm of aristocratic culture:

1. The garden wears an ornamented coat,
   the grasses' raiment is an embroidered robe.
2. Every tree wears chequered shifts,
   displaying wonder to every eye.
3. Every bud in springtime comes out laughing
   to greet the coming of his lord.
4. Before them a rose passes,
   a king, his throne borne on high,
5. Going out from the guard of his leaves,
   and casting off his prison clothes.
6. Whoever does not drink to his honor,
   must accept the blame for his sin.[59]

The poem's subject is hierarchy; it is about flower courtiers and a flower king, all dressed in finery and putting on courtly airs. The predilection for metaphor over simile is highly effective in bringing the reader to visualize an actual court scene. The rose *is* a king; the garden and the trees *are* wearing fine clothes. The idealized social order is re-created through the imagery of the description and the ritual choreography imposed on the objects, enabling the garden to function as a self-contained court scene. In comparison with the circular arrangement of space in the garden of Samuel the Nagid's poem, space here is arranged hierarchically. Buds hasten to greet their lord; the rose/king is before them and above them. The poem closely mimics the aristocratic world outside. In fact, it is unclear whether the "whoever" in the final verse—those who are charged to drink—are human observers outside the wondrous scene, or the grasses, buds, and trees of the garden—the rose's courtiers, as it were. In this manner, the poet breaks down the barrier between the two elements of the metaphor and blurs the distinction between the microcosm and the macrocosm. The garden has become court, and the court has become garden.

This extended introduction has shown that the garden's protean character is discernible through its imagery, now conveying perpetuity, now eternity, now divinity, now disease, and now aristocracy. The garden carries different meanings for different poets and within the corpuses of individual poets. Although the garden described is ultimately the "same" garden, poetic writing should not be viewed as an exercise in description only. Through poetic imagery, the poet privileges less tangible subject matters over the ostensible subject of the garden. Returning to the topic of Hispano-Jewish culture in transition, we must recognize that the gardens of medieval Hebrew verse—despite their conventionality—exhibit mutable identities and significations.

Imagery and Transition: Gardens of Life and Death in Moses Ibn Ezra's Verse

The following discussion contrasts imagery in two lengthy garden poems by Moses Ibn Ezra, one written during the poet's years in al-Andalus and one from his exile in Castile. When asking whether a substantive change in imagery can be detected between poems written within and beyond the Andalusian context, one problem immediately presents itself: With respect to poets who spent part of their lives in al-Andalus and part elsewhere, how do we know which poems emanate from which context? It is sometimes difficult to know whether poems treating Andalusian themes—such as wine, love, and the garden—were necessarily written within the borders of al-Andalus.[60] Ezra Fleischer asserts that Isaac Ben Abraham Ibn Ezra, who spent his youth in al-Andalus and later emigrated to Egypt and Iraq, composed love poems and wine poems in al-Andalus but only monothematic panegyrics elsewhere, reflecting a shift in cultural context.[61] While this may be true on the whole, it is not clear that every poem addressing Andalusian subjects was necessarily composed on Andalusian soil.[62]

In the case of Moses Ibn Ezra, there is more evidence available for determining the provenance of poems, and it is certain that he treated Andalusian themes while residing in Castile and Navarre. First, there are many premodern scribal superscriptions in manuscripts identifying the location of the poet at the time of the poem's composition. While these superscriptions do not supply incontrovertible facts—for it is possible that the scribe is making a subjective analysis based on the poem's content—they do point to a tradition of reading that is close to the original context. Second, the poems themselves often offer details that suggest the poet's location; there are references to "wandering amidst a foreign folk," residing among "stammerers of speech" or "men of no reputation who are like wild beasts," and so on, all of which refer to the Christian environment in Ibn Ezra's corpus.

The two poems discussed below, "Qeraʾani gevir" (The lord who bid his guests) and "Gedudei leil nedod" (The troops of a night of wandering), are *qaṣīdas* that contain lengthy garden descriptions before the transition to panegyric.[63] "Qeraʾani gevir" is the poet's response to an invitation to a wine feast. As such, the poem not only reflects a thriving aristocratic culture but is also an artifact of that culture. "Gedudei leil nedod" derives from Ibn Ezra's wandering in Castile before reaching his final place of settlement in Navarre. The gardens in the two poems contrast each other like a photograph and its negative; the poems describe one and the same place, yet their portrayals and meanings could not be more divergent. These opposing depictions, created through patterns of imagery, may be logically associated with the poems' respective contexts.

"Qeraʾani gevir"[64]

Superscription (Arabic): *And by him describing the invitation*[65] *of Abū Isḥāq Ibn Maṭar,*

1. The lord who bid his guests invited me and brought me
 together with the company of his friends,
2. To loved ones sweet to my mouth as his love,
 and companions precious like his thoughts.[66]
3. In a palace garden surrounded with grace,
 beauty in its four sides,
4. Dressed in silken robes, wrapped in a coat
 of scarlet and linen, its colors variegated,[67]
5. Without an embroiderer or designer its garden beds
 are inlaid, its couches are roses,
6. As if Time whittled their surfaces with statues
 of palm trees and carvings of colocynths.
7. The sun's light is like hammered gold
 above them and the trees are its firmament.
8. Its waters pour earthward like my tears for the absence
 of my heart's brethren and companions.
9. A turtledove seeks out myrtles for his singing
 and a swift rejoices on the height[68] of its plantings,
10. Singing amongst the choice vine, chirping and ringing out
 like a drunkard because of his wine.[69]
11. Birds break open all of its breaches;
 there they gather together as a brood and hatch their
 eggs.[70]
12. When those who slept through joy awoke,
 Time blocked up its eyes and its misfortunes[71] were
 dispersed.
13. [Time's] moments hustled to satiate its weary ones
 with joy at the proper time,[72] its seconds to give comfort.
14. The table had the semblance of a sphere
 and the basin was like the moon, its cups like stars.
15. Its platters were full of delicacies,
 its shovels and fire pans with the finest of spices.
16. A cup of beryl that rose like a star in the hand of a wine pourer,
 red water in [the cup's] innards,

17. [Was] like a lover whose tears froze on his cheek
while a flame [burned] within his ribs.
18. From the gold of Ophir [the cup] cut threads
upon its hand to illuminate its arms,
19. To remove sorrow from a pained heart
and to comfort an agitated heart with its rest.
20. Gently it murmurs so that the head grieves,
infatuated with its love, and its wounds are enduring.
21. Its preciousness is without end or limit,
like Abraham in his praiseworthy qualities and knowledge,
22. Flowing like the dew of his speech; and as for kindness,
its very coming and going[73] are in his hand. . . .

"GEDUDEI LEIL NEDOD"[74]

Superscription (Arabic): *And by him belonging to the art of description;*[75] *he appended to it the praise of Abū al-Ḥasan Ibn al-Battāt. He wrote it while residing in Castile.*

1. The troops of a night of wandering are too tired to run,[76]
too weary to move across the sky,
2. I thought them silver nails planted
in the firmament, or narrow[77] portals.
3. The moon is sleepless like a lover
while [the stars] watch him like scouts.
4. I imagine that their numbers are diminishing
but no, they multiply at every moment;
5. But on a night of companionship, they are immediately
swept away, driven out by the stars of morn,
6. As if taskmasters were urging them on,
hastening and pressing to make them vanish.
7. A night whose end[78] is mixed with its beginning,
its extremes gathered together.
8. A night whose color is like the color of coal,
the wind like a bellows, and the lightning like sparks.
9. There is no light except the light
of plated goblets full of golden waters.
10. Warriors set out to wage war against distress
until they were smitten by its swords.
11. The wine pourer, languid of speech
though mighty men fall prey to his words.
12. His eyes are wide with magic,
they are beautiful, they are sorcerers.

13. He gives life with them though sometimes he murders
for they are [both] powerful and weak.[79]
14. To the humble they teach the ways of innocence
but paths encompassed [with evil][80] to those who go astray.[81]
15. Likewise, the righteousness of cherubs is upon his cheeks
though the deception of idols is upon his hair.
16. Might rests upon his neck,
flowing myrrh has dispersed droplets upon his face.[82]
17. A rose garden upon his cheek for which
he appointed seraph serpents[83] to keep guard.
18. In thought we kiss his lips
and pluck his buds with the pupil's hand,
19. Our eyes are satiated with every good thing
though our lips are faint with hunger.
20. We drank until we hurried to exchange the dross
of gloom for the silver of twilight.
21. The buds of the heavens disappeared for they were
swept away by the waters of the dawn's rivers.
22. They were quickly snatched up by the hand of twilight
while light grasped the end of the earth.
23. There, the stars of the garden beds rose
and were scorched by the sun's eye.
24. The waters of the channels are like flowing liquid silver
though they are the unsheathed blade of a sword.
25. Dew rests upon buds as if there were
grains of crystal gathered upon them.
26. Upon the red surface of the garden bed, they resemble
drops of sweat upon the faces of the exhausted.
27. The scent of every spiced tree
restores souls to bodies after death.
28. The bird sings out among the branches like
songstresses behind veils[84] of branches.
29. With a stammering tongue they sing,
changing their tune from one moment to the next.
30. And a breeze blows the myrtles,
their heads swaying to the voice of the bird.
31. Without wine they reel like a drunkard,
by the wind they stagger, bent over.[85]
32. As if they heard the mention of Joseph
and hurried to bow down to the earth. . . .

These two masterful poems, both *qaṣīda*s, exhibit complex and composite structures. "Qeraʾani gevir" opens with mention of the *mamdūḥ* (the one praised, the patron) and the occasion of the gathering (1–2), turning quickly to a description of the garden and everything in it (3–21). Line 21 is the "escape verse" (*takhalluṣ*), marking a transition from the wine cup to Abraham, pivoting on the shared quality of unlimited preciousness. Praises (21–30) and blessings (31–32) for the *mamdūḥ* continue until the poem's conclusion (not translated here). In "Gedudei leil nedod," less obviously unified motifs intermingle. The poet begins by describing the long night of wandering (1–4), a theme harking back to pre-Islamic poetry and evoking emotions of loss and nostalgia.[86] Through contrast, line 5 opens the transition to the night of companionship and hence the themes of the garden and wine feast (5–32). Line 32 is the transitional verse (*takhalluṣ*), in which the movements of the birds of the garden evoke thoughts of the *mamdūḥ*. The praise continues until the poem's conclusion (33–54, not translated here).

It is worth noting that "Qeraʾani gevir" is written to a friend in gratitude for being invited to a wine party, whereas "Gedudei leil nedod" is written from the context of Christian Iberia and opens with the theme of complaint. Because the first poem was produced for the occasion of a garden wine party, garden description is a logical theme for its content; the poem participates in the very culture it describes and idealizes. "Gedudei leil nedod," on the other hand, places the garden, a memory of the past, in stark contrast with the poet's current reality of displacement and wandering. The poet is contrasting what is with what was. Yet, even as the garden section of "Gedudei leil nedod" is an idyll and the night of companionship stands in opposition to the night of wandering, the pessimistic complaint of the introduction persists in coloring the tenor of the garden description.

As expected, both garden descriptions are highly conventional and depict the "same" idealized garden. The physical spaces and furnishings are almost identical; both contain garden beds, species of trees and birds, water channels, a table, wine goblets, a wine pourer, and drinking companions. Still, the imagery of the poems, although overlapping in some respects, reveals that the poems are describing gardens with very different identities. While one tends toward life and leisure, the other tends toward destruction and death.

"Qeraʾani Gevir"

The poet creates an overall positive emotion in this poem through a carefully chosen cadre of images tending toward slowness, comfort, leisure, and life. Given that the poem is composed as a gift for a gracious host, it suggests a mood for the actual gathering. The only hints of separation and complaint are found in lines 8 and 25–27; here, the theme is hardly pronounced and functions as a convention, even a requisite courtesy, lamenting the temporary separation of friends. In fact, the theme is merely a setup for praising the patron, who is able to relieve the suffering of "wanderers" by inviting them to gatherings. The poem is noteworthy for its remarkable use of Time and images of plenty and life. These points are detailed here:

Slowness—Time, the dreaded force of inevitability that pursues human beings through so much medieval verse,[87] here appears as pliant and comforting. Ironically, it works slowly, always for good and not for ill. In line 5, it is figured as the carver who fashions the surfaces of the garden with palm trees and colocynths. The act of carving is slow and deliberate, artfully executed with concentration and intent. In line 12, Time violates its expected fierce nature and blocks up its eyes so that those who had missed out on joy might take part in the festivity. The only rushing in the poem is found in line 13, where the subunits of Time hasten to satiate and bring comfort to the weary, acting zealously because the proper moment has arrived.[88]

Life—Although birds are constant fixtures of garden poems, in this poem they are assigned a specific action apart from the conventional weeping; they gather as a brood and hatch their eggs (11). The bringing forth of life and the succession of generations are themes that befit the poem's celebratory emotional quality. The process of hatching eggs is also suggestive of the slow-moving model of Time. As in Samuel the Nagid's garden poem discussed above, an ambience of perpetuity is created so that there is no hint of an ensuing end to the delight.

Comfort and Plenty—As mentioned, Time plays the opposite of its usual role and brings comfort to the weary. In lines 19–20, the wine cup murmurs gently, lifts sorrow, and comforts those in pain. Similarly, in line 26, the patron restores the souls of the embittered and grants the weary rest. The resources of the garden are extremely plentiful; it is full of delicacies and fine spices (15).

The images in this poem work in concert to produce a general feeling of continuity and comfort. Metaphors describing different aspects of the garden setting belong to the same semantic field and occur in a clear pattern. The flourishing culture being described seems timeless, as enduring as the generations of birds and as deliberate as Time's carvings. In "Gedudei leil nedod," the imagery works to quite the opposite effect.

"Gedudei Leil Nedod"

Unlike "Qeraʾani gevir," this poem begins with a description of the long night that harks back to the nostalgic longing of pre-Islamic poetry. The poet creates the impression of loneliness by contemplating the limitless night sky and projecting the poetic speaker's insomnia onto the wandering moon.[89] This topos is common in Ibn Ezra's poetry from the Christian north. Although describing a very similar garden with respect to its accoutrements to that of "Qeraʾani gevir," "Gedudei leil nedod" draws upon an almost antithetical repertoire of images. A few images are common to both poems, such as the resemblance between the wine cups and stars. However, even this stock image may bear a different valence in "Gedudei leil nedod" because the stars remind the reader of the other stars in the poem, the marshaled troops of the long night that oppress the lonely poetic speaker. The garden of "Gedudei leil nedod" is not imagined to be dressed in courtly robes and thus is not majestic like the garden of "Qeraʾani gevir." Time is a dominant theme of "Gedudei leil nedod," although it functions in its more conventional role as the aggressive pursuer of humans and their delight. The overall imagery is hardly one of slowness, comfort, and life but rather conjures up pictures of rushing, war, and death.

Rushing—A dominant theme of this poem is the notion that pleasure is fleeting whereas the misery of separation is endless. This stands in direct opposition to "Qeraʾani gevir," in which Time works as an advocate for pleasure and beauty in the garden. In the opening complaint, the poet laments the slow passage of the night of wandering. He watches the motionless stars as if he were watching the second hand of a clock that did not seem to move at all. This long night of wandering stands in direct opposition to the night of companionship, every aspect of which seems to rush toward its end. Lines 5 and 6 contain a striking concentration of adjectives of force and speed (*nisḥafim,* swept away; *hadufim,* driven out; *meʾiṣim,* urge; *mevohalim,* hastened; *deḥufim,* pressed), which are complemented by the subject *nogsim,* taskmasters, specifically the taskmasters of Egypt who violently press the Israelites to accelerate their work (cf. Exod. 5:13). In line 20, the drinking companions hurry (*ḥashnu*) to exchange night for morning. In line 22, the buds of the sky are quickly (*ḥish*) snatched up. In line 29, the birds among the branches change their tunes from one moment to the next (*le-regaʿim*). In lines 32 and 33, the myrtles hurry (*ḥashu, miharu*) to prostrate themselves at the mention of the patron's name.

Even the weather on this night of companionship suggests quick degeneration; in line 8, the night is described as "a night whose color is like the color of coal, the wind like a bellows and the lightning like sparks." On one level, the verse provides logical similes of appearance. However, the similes possess more profound implications; the bellows is *fanning* the flames, causing the coals to burn quickly and spark wildly. The pattern of rushing thus permeates many parts of the poem; beyond functioning to create unity, the images act together to forge an emotional backdrop of urgency.

Exhaustion—Not surprisingly, the themes of rushing and exertion are complemented with that of exhaustion. The theme is introduced in the first line of the poem with reference to the troops of night (the stars) that are too tired to move. Even though we might expect the garden to stand in contrast with the stars, exhaustion resurfaces in the imagery of line 26, wherein the dewdrops on flowers are likened to drops of sweat on the face of the fatigued. The repetition of the image is reinforced by the syntactic repetition of the synonymous and paranomastic roots *yʿf* and *ʿyf* in the final words of the lines (1 and 26).

Death and War—Other repeating images relate to death and war, a register of imagery that does not appear at all in "Qeraʾani gevir." In line 1, the stars of night are depicted as troops. Further, the waters of the channels in line 24 are like the unsheathed blade of a sword. In line 10, the drinking companions are described as warriors bearing swords; they fall prey to the words of the wine pourer (11), who is a murderer (13). The wine pourer (11–19) is, as a beautiful ephebe, a complex of innocence and treachery (both of which are meant to be seductive) while in "Qeraʾani gevir," he appears as a willing and docile servant. Both poems set up parallel relationships between Time and the wine pourer, each to quite a different end. The tameness of Time and the wine pourer in "Qeraʾani gevir" provides a stark contrast with their violent, treacherous dispositions in "Gedudei leil nedod."

In "Gedudei leil nedod," the drinkers are nearly impotent before nature and Time. Every aspect of the poem conveys the message that the seeds of destruction are inherent in beautiful moments. The idea is stated most succinctly in verse 7: the night's end is mixed with (i.e., inherent in) its beginning. Lines 23–27 share the rhetorical quality of presenting something positive but then shifting to a metaphor of exhaustion and danger. The garden flowers rise but are soon scorched by the sun; the waters seem like flowing silver but are really an unsheathed sword; dewdrops resemble sapphire but are really the sweat of the fatigued. The listener imagines flowers, water, and dew but also the burning sun, a brandished sword, and droplets of sweat. The garden bears witness that beauty is deceptive and that pleasure is fleeting.

Moses Ibn Ezra paints the gardens of "Qeraʾani gevir" and "Gedudei leil nedod" with very different strokes and hues. Through careful patterns of imagery, the poems create gardens with different identities, conveying divergent meanings and evoking opposite emotional responses. Although both poems draw on many images that are "conventional," the images work together in patterns to create vastly different results. It is difficult to imagine that the poet's only drive for consistency among motifs is the achievement of cohesion or unity. The divergent depictions are understood best in the contexts of their cultural settings. In "Qeraʾani gevir," the garden is part of the same enduring aristocratic culture as that celebrated by Samuel the Nagid. It is the emblem of a life of leisure and the shared cultural space of the poet and his addressee. The garden is a fixed space of the poet's cultural world; he has experienced it in recent memory and anticipates his return to it. The poem emanates from the context of al-Andalus before the poet fled to the Christian north and functions in the economy of gifts of Andalusian Jewish aristocratic culture. "Gedudei leil nedod" was clearly written from the context of the poet's exile in Christian Iberia. The distress that characterizes the introductory passage of the poem also penetrates the poem's garden description. Flowers are scorched and exhausted and stand before weapons of war. These images, with their natural affinities for the themes of estrangement and exile, provide logical associations for the tenor of distress that characterizes the poem as a whole. The garden described is not within the poet's grasp but is a specter produced through memory, now recognized as ephemeral and even deceptive.

Beyond aiming to create a sense of "organic unity," the poet looks *fī nafsihi,* into himself, his psyche and soul, to produce images expressive of mood and circumstance. It seems unlikely that such consistent patterns of imagery would be created by an author subconsciously, although this is impossible to verify. Without reducing poetry to biography, we can say that poetic imagery is an indispensable measure of shifting cultural mentalities across a corpus of highly conventional writing.

PART II
NARRATIVE

Four

Context

Imagining Hebrew Fiction between Arabic and European Sources

The opening scene of the French film *Ridicule* is set six years before the French Revolution, "when Louis XVI still ruled . . . but *wit* was king."[1] Wit—the practice of acerbic raillery grounded in learning and wordplay—was the key to opening all doors in government. With wit, one could display intellectual prowess before court and king and publicly ridicule one's enemies. Every courtier lived in fear of ridicule, that he would stumble in a battle of wits and be exposed as a dullard. One courtier, recently returned from England, reports that the English do not cultivate wit but practice instead another craft called "hew-mah" (humor)—funny and perhaps even clever, but impassive and victimless. In the film, the Marquis de Bellegard is a kindhearted aristocrat who collects lists of witty remarks, filing them by category: double entendres, repartees, quips, wordplays, retorts, and paradoxes. In the film's final scene, now months after the Revolution, the Marquis stands with a friend on a cliff by the jagged shore of England, where he and other aristocrats had found refuge. Looking back toward France over the channel, he laments, "Wit was the very air we breathed!" A gust of wind blows his hat from his head down to the water below. "Oh, my hat!" he exclaims. "Better your hat than your head!" his companion replies. The Marquis laughs and sighs with satisfaction, "Ah, humor, it's wonderful."

The Marquis, who passed through a transitional moment of history (i.e., the French Revolution), identifies wit with France, the court, aristocracy, and the past while humor represents England, refuge, the present, and future. This point highlights the intimate bond between cultural locus and literary form (although the dichotomy between France and England is oversimplified in the film, since one need only look at "Mac Flecknoe," Dryden's assail on Shadwell, to see that wit was alive and well in Restoration England).[2]

A great shift occurred in Hebrew belles-lettres from poetry to rhymed prose narrative as the centers of Jewish writing moved from al-Andalus to

Christian Iberia. However, there is not an exact correspondence between literary forms and the division between Andalusian and post-Andalusian periods. The associations poetry-al-Andalus/prose-Christian Iberia are not as neat as wit-France/humor-England (at least as presented in *Ridicule*).[3] Poetry continued to be written in Christian Iberia through the late fifteenth century, and the rhymed prose narrative took root in al-Andalus during the twelfth century. Still, a general trend from a literary world dominated by rhymed, metered poetry to one dominated by rhymed prose fictional narrative is apparent. The shift to prose allowed authors much more freedom, not only prosodically but also with respect to ways of presenting discourse and world-making. Authors could juxtapose opposing voices in a lively debate, build representations of the wide-ranging world, and enframe traditional themes in new contexts in order to uphold or degrade them. This transition in belletristic writing is one aspect of the complex flux into which Hispano-Jewish culture was thrust during the twelfth and thirteenth centuries.

The first part of this book addressed poetic responses to transition by Andalusian Jewish poets who witnessed the political upheavals of the eleventh and twelfth centuries. This part continues this discussion by analyzing the narrative fiction of Jewish authors from thirteenth-century Christian Iberia, authors who did not witness the demise of Andalusian Jewry but whose culture circulated memories of the Andalusian past and conceived of itself in relation to it. Al-Andalus, with its luminary figures and intellectual achievements, remained a powerful and persistent memory for Jews in Christian Iberia. At the same time, Jews in Christian Iberia were touched by social and intellectual trends emanating from the north, both from the rabbinic centers of northern France and from Christian Europe more generally. Jewish intellectuals found various solutions to the problems of continuity and cultural redefinition. Some held fast to the identity provided by the Andalusian past while others were more open to cultural and intellectual influences from the new environment. Attitudes toward cultural transition are seldom stated explicitly in the narratives; however, the subject of transition is never far beneath the surface in these texts and can be explored through literary analytical techniques.

This introductory chapter has two main purposes: 1) to present briefly the social and intellectual climate of Jewish culture in thirteenth-century Christian Iberia; and 2) to introduce the Hebrew rhymed prose narrative as a form that emerged through a complex interaction of Hebrew, Arabic, and European literatures (mostly in Romance languages but not excluding Latin).[4] The chapter shows that modern scholarship has privileged the Arabic environment in which Hebrew writing developed to the detriment of underestimating the possibility of European impact. The remaining chapters of the book continue this discussion by looking closely at two nearly contemporary Hebrew rhymed prose narratives of the thirteenth century: the *Taḥkemoni,* by Judah al-Ḥarīzī; and *Sefer ha-meshalim* (The Book of Stories), by Jacob Ben Elᶜazar. The discussion strives to go beyond the concept of thematic influence and considers narrative structure, authorial voice, geographical orientation, and the use of landscape as tools for gauging the cultural affiliations of these medieval Hispano-Jewish authors. It is shown that al-Ḥarīzī and Ben Elᶜazar, despite their similar origins, imagined literature and the world in very different ways.

The Jews of Christian Iberia: Conduits, Continuities, Challenges

The transfer of the Andalusian Jewish population, with its communal structures and distinct way of life, to Christian Iberia is at the heart of Abraham Ibn Daud's *Sefer ha-qabbalah.* Writing in Toledo in 1161 after being displaced from Cordoba by the Almohad invasion, the artful chronicler constructs his history in such a way that the transition of Jewish glory from al-Andalus to Christian Iberia seems divinely ordained, just like the initial rise of Jewish power in al-Andalus.[5] The seeds of transition are planted already following the decline and destruction of Cordoba (1013), formerly the glory of al-Andalus:

> With the termination of the ᶜĀmirid dynasty and the seizure of power by the Berber chiefs, the city of Cordoba dwindled and its inhabitants were compelled to flee. Some went off to Saragossa, where their descendants have remained down to the present, while others went to Toledo, where their descendants are still known until today.[6]

The Jews of Christian Saragossa and Toledo are thus the very descendants of the Jews who graced the streets and academies of Islamic Cordoba. Similarly, just before the Almohad attacks, the sons of Rabbi Joseph Halevi, head of the yeshiva in Lucena, fled to Toledo, where they trained disciples.[7] According to the text, God caused King Alfonso the Emperador to appoint Rabbi Judah the Nasi Ibn Ezra ruler over Calatrava, a city of refuge for the exiles, in anticipation of the Almohad attacks. According to the text, Ibn Ezra was a descendant of "the leaders of Granada, holders of high office and men of power."[8]

Ibn Daud's response to transition is not exactly mournful. Although he is clearly concerned with the possible demise of the Andalusian cultural model, Christian Iberia provides a viable site for the courtly and intellectual culture of al-Andalus to survive and flourish through the leadership of those possessing untainted lineage. Despite the frequently quoted dictum that the Jews fared better under Muslim aegis than under Christian control, there is little to indicate that, through most of its history, the Jewish community suffered more in Christian Iberia than it had in al-Andalus. Christian rulers utilized Jews as positive colonizing and urbanizing agents, just as Muslim conquerors had done during the siege of al-Andalus.[9] In new and revived cities (some in formerly Islamic territories), Jews were assigned land for cultivation, workshops, and construction. In Castile and in Aragon, Jews enjoyed an unprecedented degree of legal autonomy and professional freedom. As during the Muslim period, aristocratic Jews worked as political functionaries who mediated between rulers and the Jewish community, went on diplomatic missions outside the kingdom (particularly to the Muslim south), and patronized Jewish cultural activities. Such individuals were often given special privileges that sometimes afforded them the legal status of nobility.

The unique position and extensive authority of select Jewish leaders, especially those modeling themselves after the Andalusian courtier typology, gave rise in the thirteenth century to what has been characterized as class revolts. Bernard Septimus details two such revolts in Catalonia, noting the rise of an anti-aristocratic class that characterized the ruling elite as lax in religious observance, corrupt in leadership, and immoral in sexual behavior.[10] Practices such as indulgent wine drinking, polygamy, and the keeping of concubines—all associated with Andalusian culture—were at the center of this critique.[11] From the aristocratic camp, we hear voices of rebuke directed toward "slaves who have revolted against their kings and rebelled against their masters."[12] While noting that an integrated cultural history of thirteenth-century Catalonian Jewry is still far off, Septimus suggests a general continuity between the aristocrats and the political and social style of Muslim Iberia while the anti-aristocrats seem at odds with such values. He writes, "The *nesi'im* [princes] are aristocrats, courtiers, literate and rationalistic and perhaps not untouched by decadence. Their opponents are 'new men,' merchants, talmudists, and mystics, striving for spirituality and full of fresh energy."[13] While Yitzḥak Baer may not have been correct in assuming that the aristocrats were of pure Andalusian descent while their opponents were indigenous Catalonians, a certain continuity of values is easy to discern.[14]

In the twelfth and thirteenth centuries, significant intellectual circles were sprouting up in Toledo, Saragossa, and Barcelona. In Christian Iberia and in Provence, the Hebrew language was enjoying a renaissance as Arabic and

Judeo-Arabic texts were translated into Hebrew and new Hebrew writings appeared on topics usually treated in Arabic (such as astronomy, astrology, biblical exegesis, mathematics, medicine, and philosophy).[15] The most incendiary intellectual dispute during the thirteenth century was the controversy over Maimonides concerning his codification of Jewish law and the allegorical interpretations of biblical passages that emerged from his rationalist thought.[16] Jewish intellectual life was negotiated between two intersecting currents, one from al-Andalus and another from northern France. The former was rationalist, allegorical, and engrossed in Arabic and Islamic thought. The latter was antirationalist, literalist, and averse to contact with Greco-Arabic philosophy. Both in halakhic and philosophical disciplines, the intellectuals of Christian Iberia struck balances between these currents.[17] In addition to these issues that were essentially internal to Jewish culture, Jews were affected by broader intellectual trends. They were situated between the cultural and religious styles of Islamdom and Christendom, and Hebrew authors were touched by the literary trends of Arabic and European literatures.

The Hebrew Rhymed Prose Narrative

Between Islamic and Christian Iberia, there is a clear shift in Hebrew belletristic writing from the composition of freestanding poems to rhymed prose fictional narratives with rhymed, metered poems interspersed. By the twelfth century, rhymed prose had become a stylistic feature of virtually all genres of Arabic writing—epistolary, literary, scholarly—that made pretensions of being sophisticated; most significantly, rhymed prose with rhymed metered poems interspersed became dominant in the fictional form called the *maqāma* (further below). Rhymed prose had also enjoyed a more limited usage in Hebrew liturgical, historical, and epistolary writing, which undoubtedly paved the way for the incorporation of rhyme into narrative fiction.[18]

The earliest example of rhymed prose in Hebrew fictional writing is *Ne'um asher ben yehudah* (Asher, Son of Judah, Spoke), by Solomon Ibn Ṣaqbel, produced in al-Andalus, probably during the Almoravid period.[19] The story begins when an enticing maiden behind a lattice beckons the protagonist Asher and tosses him an apple inscribed with a love poem in golden ink. Not sophisticated enough to play the game of courtly love, Asher is subjected to a series of humiliations in his pursuit of his beloved. These humiliations culminate when Asher is led to a veiled woman whom he believes to be his beloved. He lifts the veil and finds "a long beard, a face like death and a mouth open wide as a steaming cauldron." The bearded man turns out to be a "friend" of Asher's, a trickster called the "Adulamite" who has ensnared Asher in a ruse. Asher is ultimately wedded to the Adulamite's daughter.

Ibn Ṣaqbel's work was followed by Joseph Ibn Zabarra's (born c. 1140) *Sefer shaʿashuʿim* (The Book of Delights) in Barcelona.[20] This book presents a cornucopia of tales, proverbs, and scientific teachings set within the frame narrative of an imaginative journey. The story begins when a mysterious stranger calling himself "Enan Hanatash son of Ornan Hadesh" wakes Ibn Zabarra from slumber and urges him to forsake his homeland and travel to a place worthy of his wisdom. Throughout their journey together, Joseph and Enan exchange knowledge, lodge in various cities, and encounter characters who share hospitality, parables, and stories. The travelers ultimately alight in Enan's city, rife with sin and mischief, where Enan reveals that he is not, in fact, a human but a demon. His name, Enan Ha*natash* son of Ornan Ha*desh,* is actually a cloak for his true identity, which one deciphers by reversing letters of the name: Enan Ha*satan* son of Ornan Ha*shed,* meaning Enan the Satan son of Ornan the Demon.

In the Toledan Judah Ibn Shabbetai's (1186–1225) *Minḥat yehudah soneʾ ha-nashim* (The Gift of Judah, the Misogynist), the youth Zeraḥ, along with three companions, swears off women to devote himself to the pursuit of Wisdom (the story invites immediate comparison with Shakespeare's *Love's Labors Lost*).[21] Central to the group's identity is the belief in the wanton and nefarious nature of women. Zeraḥ preaches the misogynist cult of celibacy abroad, eliciting a venomous response from women everywhere. The women devise to trick Zeraḥ by exposing him to a beautiful and eloquent maiden and pressing him into marriage before he knows what hit him. Using the ruse of the veil, the beauty Zeraḥ had beheld is switched with a hideous and quarrelsome hag. A debate ensues among the populace as to whether Zeraḥ may divorce his wife, and the case is brought for judgment before (the historical figure) Abraham al-Fakhkhar, Ibn Shabbetai's patron. Before a verdict is passed, the character Judah (i.e., the author's persona) enters the scene and declares the whole story fiction, undermining the misogamic claims of the text.[22] Soon after its composition, the story inspired several responses in defense of women, which are also written in rhymed prose.

In the second decade of the thirteenth century, Judah al-Ḥarīzī translated the famous Arabic *maqāma* collection of al-Ḥarīrī of Basra into a rhymed prose Hebrew version called *Maḥberot ittiʾel* (Ittiʾel's Compositions)[23] and composed an original collection of fifty narratives, the *Taḥkemoni,* soon afterward.[24] This collection of Hebrew *maqāmāt* will be discussed in detail in the coming chapters. Following al-Ḥarīzī, the rhymed prose narrative form remained popular in Christian Iberia. Jacob Ben Elᶜazar's (thirteenth century) *Sefer ha-meshalim,* which will also be treated in depth in the chapters to come, is a collection of ten stories told by a single narrator, some of which focus on rhetorical and moral themes while others have been called allegories and "love stories."[25]

Following these authors, the rhymed prose narrative tradition continued in the Iberian Peninsula, being utilized by Jacob ha-Kohen (thirteenth century) in his *Megilat ha-ᶜofer* (The Scroll of the Fawn),[26] Isaac Ibn Sahula (b. 1244) in his *Meshal ha-qadmoni* (Tale of the Ancient One),[27] Don Vidal Benveniste in the allegorical love story *Meliṣat ᶜefer ve-dinah* (The Eloquent Tale of Efer and Dinah),[28] and others. Hebrew authors in Italy, Egypt, Yemen, Turkey, and Greece continued to utilize the rhymed prose form for centuries to come.[29]

The Hebrew rhymed prose narrative could not have taken form but for the interaction of Jewish and non-Jewish literatures. To some extent, the new literature was an outgrowth of the Hebrew poetry of al-Andalus. Rhymed prose authors remained largely committed to preserving a diction of biblical Hebrew and paid homage to the Andalusian poets by praising their skill and sometimes incorporating snippets of Andalusian Hebrew verse into their narratives. At the same time, the narratives exhibit features whose origins are traceable to Arabic sources, even though most of the authors stemmed from a Christian environment, and possibly to European sources as well. The Hebrew rhymed prose narratives of Christian Iberia are essential for studying Hispano-Jewish culture in transition on two levels. First, with respect to "transition in literature," the narratives frequently touch upon the subjects of estrangement and renewal by recalling the Andalusian past and refracting debates on social issues. Second, with respect to "literature in transition," the narratives testify to the complex literary environment in which they developed. Just as halakhists and philosophers can be located between the Jewish intellectual traditions of al-Andalus and northern France, so authors of belles-lettres should be understood as individuals negotiating their art among competing and overlapping literary cultures.

Imagining Contexts

In modern scholarship, influences on the Hebrew rhymed prose narrative have been imagined to derive either from Arabic sources only or from a mixture of Arabic and European sources, depending upon how scholars view the flow of literary information in the Iberian Peninsula. The following discussion explores why scholarship has privileged the Arabic context over the

European and advocates a more nuanced perspective on the literary environment in which Hebrew fiction flourished in Christian Iberia.

Several factors help explain Hebrew authors' shift to rhymed prose in Christian Iberia. Dan Pagis describes one aspect of the shift in sociological terms, postulating that the Hebrew reading audience expanded in the twelfth century to include non-aristocrats, thereby requiring a medium more flexible than poetry.[30] The most widely accepted thesis understands the shift as an imitative trend inspired by the dissemination and growth in popularity of Arabic rhymed prose narratives, or *maqāmāt* (singular, *maqāma*), in the Iberian Peninsula. According to this theory, when the Arabic *maqāma*, which originated in Persia during the late tenth century, became popular in Iberia, Hebrew authors sought to emulate it just as they had imitated Arabic poetry previously. Another suggestion that has attracted less attention points out that some Hebrew narratives bear similarities with Romance literature and other European sources. As such, the Hebrew rhymed prose narrative, often called the Hebrew *maqāma* or *maḥberet*,[31] has been situated between two great world literatures.

Rather than seeing Hebrew literary texts as mere products of "influence" derived singularly from one culture or the other, they should be viewed as the fruits of authors aware of multiple literary models who created their texts through a process of negotiation. Several Hebrew texts from Christian Iberia bear markings both of Arabic and European literary influences, sometimes mixed in novel and surprising ways. Furthermore, Arabic and European literatures should not be regarded as two dead, inert literary poles. Both literatures were developing rapidly—and not completely independently of each other—in the thirteenth century; some scholars maintain that the rise of some European literatures is intimately indebted to Arabic sources and literary conventions.[32] In order to properly elucidate the complex literary environment of Christian Iberia, brief introductions are given below to select Arabic and European sources focusing on the Arabic *maqāma* and the French Romance. Most texts introduced here synoptically are discussed in later parts of the book; the reader familiar with these materials may wish to proceed to the section below entitled "Between Arabic and European Literatures." The chapter concludes with scholarly visions of the dynamics of influence upon Hebrew authors within the vibrant literary crucible of Christian Iberia.

Literatures of Medieval Iberia

The literary climate of late-twelfth- and thirteenth-century Christian Iberia is one of the most complex and heterogeneous imaginable. A writer could be aware of Arabic sources from al-Andalus (past and contemporary) and the Islamic East, poems, epics, and Romances from France, Latin texts, and the first glimmerings of a Spanish national literature. As discussed in the introduction to this book, the borders of the intellectual worlds of al-Andalus and Christian Iberia were extremely permeable, even during the Reconquista. In Christian Iberia, Arabic literature (and also philosophy) maintained its prestige—being studied by Christians, Jews, and Muslims through the fifteenth century—and nascent literary forms being cultivated in Christian Europe also gained prominence.[33] Arabic belletristic and philosophical texts were studied and often translated into Hebrew, Latin, and the vernacular dialects of Spanish. It is clear that the troubadour lyric circulated in Iberia, especially after the expulsion of the troubadours from Provence during the Albigensian Crusade (1209), when exiled troubadour poets relocated within the courts of James I and Pedro III of Aragon and Alfonso X of Castile.

María Rosa Menocal, in delineating the "heartland of the lyric," depicts eleventh-century Iberia as a hybrid, multicultural, multilingual society, part of a map whose borders reached "from al-Andalus in the southwest through Provence at the center to Sicily and Tuscany in the east."[34] The heartland of narrative during the twelfth and thirteenth centuries entails a map that is even more extensive, including not only the land of *oc* (southern France, Provence) but also the land of *oil* (northern France), the font of Romance fiction. This is not to say that this broad region was culturally unified; rather, this only means that narrative traditions were popular throughout these areas and that some literary motifs and styles crossed linguistic and political boundaries. It is impossible to give a sufficient introduction to all of the relevant literatures within the constraints of a few pages. However, in order to illuminate the context for the emergence of Hebrew rhymed prose fiction, basic background is given about Arabic and European literatures focusing on the Arabic *maqāma* and French Romance.

Arabic

MAQĀMA

The most significant Arabic form treated in the discussion of the Hebrew rhymed prose narrative is the *maqāma*. The *maqāma* genre was invented by Badīᶜ al-Zamān ("the Wonder of the Age") al-Hamadhānī in tenth-century Nishapur, perhaps intended as a fictional diversion at the learning sessions of experts in *adab* literature.[35] His *maqāma* collection draws upon the content of *adab* texts—including many genres, themes, motifs, situations, verses of poetry, and figures of speech—and refashions it into lively fictional narratives focusing on the travels and encounters of two main characters, a narrator and a protagonist rogue (named ʿĪsa Ibn Hishām and Abū al-Fatḥ al-Iskandārī, respectively).[36] The *maqāmāt* are composed in a sophisticated rhetorical register, making liberal use of intertextual references, double entendres, and rare words. Rhymed, metered poems are placed in the mouths of the narrator, the protagonist, and other characters and are interspersed throughout the rhymed prose.

Each of al-Hamadhānī's *maqāmāt* was composed independently, being gathered into a collection of approximately fifty texts by a later redactor.[37] Narrative development is limited in the *maqāmāt* to a number of standard formulas, though appearing with numerous variations.[38] Most (although not all) episodes involve a scene of recognition (anagnorisis) in which the narrator discerns the protagonist's identity. Some episodes are largely lexicographic or aesthetic in nature and are dedicated to discussions of poetry, riddles, or descriptions of objects such as food. Other episodes have been called "comic" or "picaresque" and usually involve some sort of ruse. One scenario that originates with al-Hamadhānī and is imitated by later *maqāma* authors involves the appearance of the protagonist in the guise of a mendicant preacher. Standing before a congregation of supplicants in a mosque, the protagonist preaches an eloquent sermon in poetry and prose, admonishing the people to live righteously and give to charity. After filling his pockets with the money of the devout, the mercurial protagonist absconds. The narrator then recognizes the protagonist, offers a few words of mild rebuke, but is generally impressed with the ruse and the protagonist's eloquence. The motifs of disguise, mendicancy, eloquence, ruse, and recognition repeat throughout many *maqāma* plots.

Al-Hamadhānī's *maqāmāt* merited the esteem of some littérateurs in the Islamic West soon after their creation, with samples being included in the *adab* anthology *Zahr al-ādāb,* by the Qayrawani scholar al-Ḥuṣrī (d. 1022). Andalusian authors of the eleventh century likewise explain the inception of al-Hamadhānī's *maqāmāt* and occasionally quote the inventor of the *maqāma* genre. Yet, as Rina Drory explains, "[i]t seems that al-Hamadhānī's early fame in al-Andalus neither made his maqamat an identifiable productive model for narration nor gave them exemplary status."[39]

The *maqāma* remained peripheral for a century after al-Hamadhānī until it was revitalized by al-Ḥarīrī of Basra, whose collection of fifty *maqāmāt* would greatly outshine al-Hamadhānī's in popularity and canonical status.[40] Al-Ḥarīrī's *maqāmāt*—collected, organized, and publicly recited in Baghdad by the author himself—may be characterized by an even higher degree of lexicographic virtuosity but a more formulaic vision of plot. Al-Ḥarīrī's plots are reducible to a few models, still revolving around the travels and encounters of a narrator and a protagonist (named al-Ḥārith Ibn Humām and Abū Zayd al-Sarūjī, respectively). Still prevalent are the themes of mendicancy, disguise, ruse, and recognition. In addition, al-Ḥarīrī gives special prominence to debate by assigning characters to competing sides of an argument, arming each speaker with munitions of eloquent speech.[41]

Al-Ḥarīrī's *maqāmāt* were received in al-Andalus with far greater reverence than al-Hamadhānī's collection already during the author's lifetime. Among the attendees of al-Ḥarīrī's recitation of his own *maqāmāt* in Baghdad in 1110 was the Andalusian traveler al-Quḍaʿī, who returned to al-Andalus and repeated the words of the renowned Eastern author.[42] In the twelfth century, the *maqāmāt* took root firmly in al-Andalus, meriting extensive commentary by the Andalusian al-Sharīshī and other scholars and inspiring new *maqāma* creations. The appearance of the Hebrew *maqāma* at about the same time parallels this proliferation.

The only collection of Andalusian Arabic *maqāmāt* to follow the classical model closely was written by al-Saraquṣṭī, also known as Ibn al-Ashtarkūwī (d. 1143), who explicitly composed his *al-Maqāmāt al-luzūmiyya,* a collection of fifty narratives, as a challenge to al-Ḥarīrī's collection.[43] As in the classical *maqāmāt,* al-Saraquṣṭī's narratives revolve around the encounters of a narrator, Abū al-Ghamr al-Saʾib Ibn Tammām,[44] and a protagonist, Abū Ḥabīb al-Sadūsī. Al-Saraquṣṭī's narratives not only retain the sophisticated rhetorical register of al-Ḥarīrī's *maqāmāt* but do so with the additional requirement of a stricter rhyme scheme,[45] upping the literary ante, as it were.

Yet al-Saraquṣṭī's *maqāmāt* are not mere imitations of earlier models with the added prosodic requirement. Although the narratives are deeply dependent upon earlier models, al-Saraquṣṭī is often innovative with story lines and subtle aspects of structure. The narrator, for example, plays a somewhat different role, occasionally appearing as a dissimulating rogue himself and collaborating with the protagonist in his ruses (though the protagonist also dupes him in the end). James Monroe argues that the sensitive reader will realize that the narrator's tales are sometimes planted with inner contradictions, indicating that his speech, like the protagonist's, cannot be trusted. Another significant divergence from the classical *maqāma* is the final *maqāma* of the collection, which records the death of the protagonist, giving the collection a sort of "ending."[46] Although al-Saraquṣṭī's *maqāmāt* predate those of the Hebrew author Judah al-Ḥarīzī by approximately seventy-five years, *al-Maqāmāt al-luzūmiyya* has never been introduced into the scholarly discussion of the Hebrew *maqāma.*

Significantly, al-Saraquṣṭī's were not the first Arabic *maqāmāt* to be composed in the Iberian Peninsula. Other Andalusian *maqāmāt* have merited some discussion, though significant texts still remain in manuscript.[47] Rina Drory points out that the "Andalusi court maqama," while still a fictional narrative, abandons common Eastern features such as the mendicancy theme, the inclusion of two protagonists, scheme-based plots, and final exposure.[48] Noting these same points, Iḥsān ᶜAbbās also comments that "many of the Andalusian *maqāmāt* have become descriptions of a journey in the lands of al-Andalus."[49] H. Nemah incorporates several types of texts under the rubric *maqāma,* which he defines prosodically as rhymed prose with poems interspersed whether or not the text exhibits narrative development.[50] Significant among the *maqāmāt* described by Nemah is that of Abū ᶜAbd Allāh Ibn Abī al-Khisāl (1073–1146),[51] which weaves together several typical *maqāma* scenarios into a single, continuous narrative.[52] Nemah concludes: "[E]vidently it was the intention of Ibn Abi ᵓl-Khisāl to show off his virtuosity in word-painting by combining several *maqāmāt* in one."[53] In addition to the goal of "word-painting," the shift to a more complex narrative form may reflect a different aesthetic in al-Andalus.

The *maqāma* collections by al-Hamadhānī, al-Ḥarīrī, and al-Saraqusṭī all give the sense of being composed after some "golden age" has come to an end. The current age is oppressive; people are ignorant and miserly, and refined culture is difficult to find. The protagonist is a "half-outsider" who complains over his fate and ekes out a living through petty scams wherever his reputation has not preceded him.[54] Al-Hamadhānī's Abū al-Fatḥ is from Alexandria, a city that fell into decline with the ascent of the Fāṭimid dynasty.[55] Al-Ḥarīrī's Abū Zayd, even if he is misrepresenting himself, complains that he took up wandering when his home was destroyed by Byzantine Christians.[56] Al-Saraqusṭī wrote during the Almoravid period, after the Tāᵓifa period had passed, and looked to an idyllic place and time outside of the Iberian Peninsula. Although he was born in Saragossa and settled in Cordoba, his *maqāmāt* are set almost exclusively outside of the Iberian Peninsula, with a strong preference for the East (the Arabian Peninsula, Iran, Iraq). It is perhaps for these reasons that one biographer wrote of al-Saraqusṭī that he is "Saragossan with regard to his physical place of origin, Iraqi with regard to his intellectual homeland."[57]

The aesthetic value of *maqāmāt* has often been denigrated in modern Western scholarship.[58] Because of the texts' penchant for rhetorical play, they have often been deemed mere rhetorical pyrotechnics. Plots have been considered flat, predictable, contrived, and simplistic. Narrative frames have been discounted as insignificant or as mere pretexts for the presentation of rhetorical material. More recent scholarship has valued the playful subtleties of these fascinating texts and appreciated the narratives from structuralist and post-structuralist perspectives.[59]

ARABIC POPULAR LITERATURE AND THE ROMANCE GENRE

In addition to the *maqāma*, other Arabic sources that have received less attention should not be ignored as potential sources for parallel comparison and direct inspiration. These include various fictional sources, learned literatures whose focus is not primarily fiction, and also more "popular" sources.[60] One suggestive genre for illuminating Hebrew narratives is the medieval Arabic romance as represented in learned sources, popular epics (*sīra shaʿbiyya*), which have only begun to be studied by Arabists, and in the popular *Thousand and One Nights.*[61] ʿUdhrī romances contained in the erudite Eastern compilation *Kitāb al-aghānī* sometimes seem so fanciful that the redactor, Abū al-Faraj al-Iṣfahānī (897–967), judges them (negatively) to be fabricated.[62] The popular epics and *The Thousand and One Nights* (which sometimes contain overlapping stories) were related in colloquial Arabic rather than in high literary Arabic (*fuṣḥā*); as such, they stood outside of the prestigious classical tradition of the East that Andalusian authors sought to emulate. Still, thematic elements and plotlines of these stories may have been influential upon Hebrew authors on some level. Although these texts did not attempt to match the *maqāma*'s rhetorical or lexicographic sophistication, they often resemble the *maqāma* prosodically by utilizing a (somewhat clumsy) rhymed prose with rhymed, metered poems interspersed.

Arabic popular epics, which flourished in Egypt during the Mamluk period (1250–1517), generally revolve around the prowess and chivalry of famous individuals, refer to hundreds of characters, and span thousands of pages.[63] *Sīrat ʿAntar* (based on the life of the pre-Islamic poet ʿAntara), for example, is presented by Peter Heath as a four-part heroic cycle in which the black slave protagonist achieves freedom and respect, engages in a love affair with his cousin ʿAbla, displays chivalry in adulthood, and ultimately dies.[64] Although some epics are set in a distant past, others evoke the more recent events of the Crusades and unfold across the border of the Christian and Islamic worlds. A common motif includes the crusader woman who falls in love with a Muslim man, converts to Islam, and possibly even turns to battle against her former coreligionists.[65] Traces of this topos can also be found in the romances of *The Thousand and One Nights.*

Little is known about the circulation of the *sīra* literature in medieval Iberia or among Jews. One piece of suggestive evidence is that Samawʾal Ibn Yaḥya al-Maghribī (d. circa 1174), a famous Jewish convert to Islam of Andalusian background, testifies that as a boy he read "long works" (*al-dawāwīn al-kibār*) such as the stories of ʿAntara, Dhāt al-Himma, and Alexander the Great.[66] Whether the texts that have come down to us are similar to those Samawʾal read in childhood is difficult to say, since Arabic popular epics survive in several recensions and are the products of hundreds of years of development by a host of relaters and redactors. In fact, transmission was often more oral than textual. For these reasons, it is difficult to know whether a parallel theme in an Arabic epic and a Hebrew narrative is a product of direct influence.

The Thousand and One Nights preserves several episodes that have been identified as romances, albeit in somewhat different respects. Scholars have compared the lengthy "Tale of King ʿUmar Ibn al-Nuʿmān" with the epic romances in that it relates military confrontations between Christians and Muslims while incorporating a love story that crosses religious boundaries. The "History of Gharīb and ʿAjīb" follows a similar pattern, though the enemies are not identified as Christians but as infidels and idol worshipers more generally.[67]

Peter Heath views a broader number of *Nights* episodes, many that do not involve martial themes, as romances in that they investigate "the concerns of honor balanced between the demands of love and social propriety, within the context of Fate" (as we will see, Heath's definition is informed by, but not identical to, genre definitions associated with French Romance). As an illustrative example, Heath refers to the story of Niʿma and the slave girl Nuʿm, who fall in love as children and later become man and concubine (a socially sanctioned relationship). Because of her beauty and talent, Nuʿm is kidnapped by a local governor and offered to the caliph as a gift. Niʿma and Nuʿm pine for each other to the point of lovesickness (her illness keeps the caliph from making sexual advances). Through many plot twists involving a female go-between and a Persian physician, Niʿma (disguised as a slave girl) sneaks into the palace, where he loses his way and ends up in the chambers of the caliph's sister, with whom he shares his story. The sister brings the couple together and persuades the caliph to permit the union; the caliph bestows gifts upon them and appoints the physician as an adviser. Heath argues that the competing demands of love and social propriety are met, since the couple's love was true (having fallen in love as children) and licit (especially in that she did not have intercourse with the caliph); for this reason, Fate—the pervasive force of cosmic justice, which Heath calls the true protagonist of the *Nights*—watches over the couple and concludes their story with a kind of poetic justice.[68]

As Heath shows, the standard pattern of development in such romances is a three-part movement from an initial state of security, to one or a series of trials, and a return to a state of security. For the protagonists, these stages represent:

> developmental progressions within moral and psychological matrices, movements from innocence to experience, ignorance to knowledge, naïveté to maturity. It is for this reason that protagonists of *Nights* romances are so often adolescents, for the transition stage between childhood and adulthood is ideal for treating the themes the genre wishes to explore.[69]

As will be discussed below, basic elements of romance as a genre are also observed in French and other European literatures and in some Hebrew narratives.

Is the influence of tales known from *The Thousand and One Nights* on Iberian Jewish literature of the thirteenth century plausible? The earliest references to a written text containing the "Tales of a Thousand Nights" dates from the ninth century. The earliest evidence for the full title "A Thousand and One Nights" appears in a notebook, found in the Cairo Genizah, belonging to a Jewish physician and bookseller and attests to the interest in popular tales among Jews.[70] Yet the earliest surviving manuscript of *The Thousand and One Nights* dates no earlier than the fourteenth century and is likely even later.[71] Romances such as the tales of Niᶜma and Nuᶜm, ᶜUmar Ibn al-Nuᶜmān, and Gharīb and ᶜAjīb all date from manuscripts that are later still. Thus *The Thousand and One Nights* cannot be understood as a stable corpus (at least not one that we can reconstruct) that Hebrew authors could have drawn upon in thirteenth-century Christian Iberia. Still, thematic and structural motifs are worth documenting, since they may reveal something about their oral circulation.

European Literature

In exploring the range of sources that might have played a role in the emergence of Hebrew rhymed prose fiction, we should consider the various literatures of twelfth- and thirteenth-century Iberia that existed alongside Arabic. While it is somewhat problematic to group the numerous literatures produced in the languages of Christian Europe under the single rubric "European literature," this simplification allows here for general comparison with Arabic. Spanish literature (or, more properly, literature in dialects such as Castilian or Catalan) was a "late bloomer" among the vernacular literatures of Europe. Apart from the Hebrew and Arabic *muwashshaḥs*' concluding *kharjas* in Ibero-Romance, which may be remnants of a broader lyric tradition, the earliest texts in Spanish dialects date to the middle of the twelfth century. The first national poem of Castile, *El Poema de Mío Cid*, which narrates events of the late eleventh century, can be dated to 1140 at the earliest.[72] The epic recounts the exile of Rodrigo Díaz de Vivar (the Cid) from the court of Alfonso VI of Castile and León and his subsequent rise to fame as the conqueror of Muslim Valencia in the name of the kingdom that had renounced him. The poem shows a clear concern for French courtly ideals and the model of the knight. It bears signs of influence from French literary models and likely signs of Arabic influence.[73] The earliest purely fictional narratives in Spanish dialects date to the early thirteenth century.[74] While such examples need not be viewed as direct sources for Hebrew narratives, they do constitute a part of the literary environment in which the Hebrew narratives emerged.

In addition to texts in the dialects of Spanish, texts in Latin and French helped shape the literary culture of the Iberian Peninsula. There is a tendency to consider Latin literature irrelevant in studies of Hispano-Jewish literature because Hebrew authors generally did not know the language of Church learning. However, given the powerful influence that Latin had on the rise of European vernacular literature,[75] the contents of this literature should not be ignored. It is unlikely, for example, that Jacob Ben Elʿazar read Latin, even though portions of his *Sefer ha-meshalim* remind the reader of moments in Latin allegorical writing.[76] Even if Latin sources were not read by Hebrew authors, their contents may have been transmitted in oral form, perhaps in intellectual circles. Latin even had its own rhymed prose narrative tradition, which has never been studied alongside the Arabic *maqāma*.[77]

The European sources that hold the most promise as sources for Hebrew narrative are the various literatures in medieval French. Although the focus of the following discussion will be on Romance fiction, mention will be made of other genres that might have touched Hebrew authors, however indirectly. These include the *Chansons de Geste*, the troubadour lyric, and allegorical writing.[78]

CHANSONS DE GESTE

Toward the end of the eleventh century, French epic poems narrating events that took place three centuries earlier, during the reigns of Charlemagne and his son Louis the Pious, began to appear. The *Chansons de Geste* (*chanson* = song; *geste* [*gesta*] = things done, high deeds, exploits) are about warfare, specifically the battles between the Carolingians and the Iberian Saracens (Muslims), who are portrayed as a mysterious Other in the literature.[79] The earliest surviving poem, the *Chanson de Roland,* dates from 1098 and recounts the journey of Roland, Charlemagne's nephew, back to France following a victorious seven-year expedition against the Saracens in Iberia.

The protagonists of the other *Chansons* are Charlemagne's barons. The *Chansons* were retold and rewritten many times throughout the Middle Ages and often reflect events from the time of composition, particularly the conflict with Islam during the Crusades. The stories of conquest often interweave love stories that cross religious boundaries. Hence these texts bear striking generic similarities with the Arabic popular romances; the two sets of texts may be seen as counter-narratives in that they depict similar events from opposite sides of the military and political divide, only inverting the religious identities of conqueror and conquered and lover and beloved.

THE TROUBADOUR LYRIC

The rise of the troubadour lyric is approximately contemporaneous with the *Chanson de Roland*. The first lyric poet was a Provençal prince, William IX, count of Poitiers and duke of Aquitaine (1071–1127), whose style was soon emulated by the troubadours in Provence and later by the trouvères in northern France in the early thirteenth century.[80] The origins of the lyric have been the subject of much debate. Many have argued that it arose sui generis, growing out of the new social environment of the French courts; others have ascribed different weights to the influence of Latin and Arabic precedents.[81]

At the risk of oversimplification, we might say that the troubadour lyric was preoccupied with two subjects: courtliness; and one of its subcategories, *fin'amor* (refined love). To be courtly meant the possession of a good education, skills in hunting, fighting, and conversation, and the cultivation of values such as impartiality, liberality, and nobility of heart. Above all, to uphold the courtly ideal meant to love, to seek the favors of a lady—the *dame* before whom the lover submitted himself—despite obstacles.[82] Troubadour love, although sensual, was seldom about consummation but focused on the demonstration of the lover's worth.[83] The social position of the lady above her suitor is the greatest distinguishing factor between the courtly poetry of al-Andalus and the Provençal lyric; although some scholars posit that the lady's origin is to be found in the beloved of Arabic courtly poetry, the motif was quite distinct by the time that the Hebrew rhymed prose narrative burst onto the scene.[84]

ROMANCE

In the middle of the twelfth century, in northern France, there arose a new literary genre that was intended to be read rather than sung. These texts are known as Romances (for purposes of clarity, this book uses "romance" to designate a text in any language possessing certain generic features, and "Romance" to designate the French tradition specifically; "Romance" is also used to designate the language). The first Romances—such as the *Roman d'Alexander,* the *Roman de Thebes,* and the *Roman d'Eneas*—were adaptations of Latin works.[85] Soon afterward, the settings in which Romances unfolded shifted from Rome to Britain, with Romance authors—usually church clerks trained in Latin—basing stories on works of recent history.[86]

The nature of Romance, and of Western literature, would change in the work of Chrétien de Troyes, a poet of the late twelfth century first associated with the court of Champagne and later with Flanders. All of Chrétien's Romances revolve around the court of King Arthur (although Arthur himself is never featured as a protagonist). The author assumes prior knowledge on the part of the reader about Arthur, the roundtable, and the cast of knights and ladies. Although readers probably considered characters to be real historical figures, they probably did not consider all of the events described in the narratives to be reliable.[87] Rather than choosing history for his subject, Chrétien made the principal topics of his Romances love (following the ideals of the troubadours) and the evolution of protagonists through their adventures. Concerning the centrality of adventure, Michel Zink writes:

> The adventures experienced by the hero are simultaneously the cause and the sign of his evolution. The external adventure is simultaneously the source and the image of an internal one. . . . The solitary figure of the knight-errant, almost entirely Chrétien's invention, emblematizes the concerns of his romances: the discovery of one's self, of love, and of the other.[88]

Adventure is also at the heart of some anonymous Romances, such as the mid-twelfth-century *Le Conte de Floire et Blanchefleur* and the thirteenth-century *Aucassin et Nicolette.* These texts involve love stories that evolve over the border of the Christian and Islamic worlds. *Floire et Blanchefleur* tells the story of Floire, the son of an Iberian Muslim king, who falls in love with Blanchefleur, the daughter of a Christian slave who had been taken captive by Floire's father. The two are born on the same day, are raised together, and later develop affection for each other in Muslim Iberia. Disapproving of their love, the king sells Blanchefleur into slavery in Babylon and tells Floire that she is dead, even building a fake tomb where she was said to lie. Inconsolable, Floire threatens suicide, until he learns that Blanchefleur is alive and sets out in search of her in Babylon, where the lovers are ultimately reunited and married. When Floire learns of his father's death, he returns to Iberia with Blanchefleur, converts to Christianity, and spreads his new faith within his kingdom.[89] The work circulated in Iberia no later than the late fourteenth or early fifteenth century, when the first (surviving) Spanish version appeared.[90] Parallels with Arabic sources, including *The Thousand and One Nights,* have been documented, though the precise nature of the relationship remains speculative.[91]

Aucassin et Nicolette refers to itself as a *chantefable,* composed half in prose and half in verse. It is the story of Aucassin, son of the count of Beaucaire, who is forbidden by his father to marry his love Nicolette, a girl of unknown lineage who was bought from Saracens in North Africa and later baptized. Unable to realize their forbidden love, they both steal off to the forest, where they reunite and then journey together by ship away from Beaucaire. Through a complex series of shipwrecks, Aucassin is returned to his native Beaucaire while Nicolette turns up in Carthage, the Muslim kingdom whence she was stolen as a child. Ultimately, Nicolette flees Carthage dressed as a minstrel and reunites with Aucassin in Beaucaire. The book is believed to have Byzantine and possibly Arabic influences.[92]

A comparison of the French Romances with the romance genre in medieval Arabic literature yields several similarities. Texts from both traditions feature movement from a state of security, to a state of crisis, to a new state of security and structure plot around character maturation. As mentioned, significant parallels can be documented among some French and Arabic texts, such as affinities between *Le Conte de Floire et Blanchefleur* and episodes from *The Thousand and One Nights.* One difference, however, is the pervasive force of Fate as the controller of events in the Arabic tradition whereas protagonists in French Romance are more self-reliant and active figures.

ALLEGORY

Allegorical writing came into French through the classical tradition, wherein the Latin *Psychomachia* (The Battle of the Soul) by Prudentius (fourth century) has been called the first "full-fledged allegorical poem."[93] This narrative presents a battle of the Vices and Virtues as a great military confrontation wherein each Vice is personified as a warrior who is ultimately slain by his opposing Virtue. C. S. Lewis interprets this story as a basic expression of the "inner life," the inner struggle of a moral being.[94] With time, simplistic plots such as battles and dialogues gave way to more complex forms such as drama, journey, biography, and romance.[95] The turn to these forms made the interpretation of allegorical texts more elusive. It need not be the case that each object in an allegory correspond to a single, specific object outside of the text. In fact, allegories seldom make their meanings completely transparent; the reader is always working to uncover new meanings, to reconcile them with previous assumptions, and to negotiate through contradictions. David Hult has remarked, concerning *Le Roman de la rose,* the most famous of medieval French allegorical romances: "This massive and centrifugal text, characterized by large-scale digressions and repetitious wordplay, defies attempts to control its meaning, to identify a unified message."[96] Like non-allegorical Romances, *Le Roman de la rose* is set in a courtly setting and treats courtly behavior, including, above all, love (the speaker in the poem is infatuated by his love for the rose, whose virginity he ultimately takes). The garden is at once an allegorical realm and the earthly garden of the court; characters are simultaneously human players and conceptual abstractions.

Between Arabic and European Literatures

As mentioned, the Hebrew rhymed prose narrative has often been called the Hebrew *maqāma* or the *maḥberet,* thus emphasizing continuity with the Arabic form. There has been significant disagreement among scholars concerning which Hebrew texts may be designated *maqāmāt* properly, largely because it has not been fixed whether the term "*maqāma*" refers to a literary form or a genre. The narrowest definition is suggested by S. M. Stern, who only considers Hebrew rhymed prose narratives modeled after the *maqāmāt* of al-Hamadhānī and al-Ḥarīrī to be *maqāmāt.*[97] On the opposite extreme, Jefim Schirmann uses the term "*maqāma*" in referring to all Hebrew texts written in rhymed prose.[98] Israel Levin sees Abraham Ibn Ezra's *Ḥayy ben meqiṣ*—a Hebrew adaptation of Ibn Sīnā's *Ḥayy ibn yaqẓān*—as a *maqāma* because it is written in rhymed prose (*without* metered poems being interspersed).[99] Dan Pagis is the first to stress the variety of rhymed prose narratives:

> We are here [in Hebrew rhymed prose narratives] dealing not only with a chronological evolution of one specific genre, but also with a multitude of genres, some completely unconnected with the maqama. . . . The blurring of distinctions seems to have led to regrettable results. One of these was a somewhat normative approach which judged various works by their proximity to the maqama proper, occasionally evaluating them as lesser ramifications of the pure genre and evolving a theory of flowering and decline in keeping with this principle.[100]

Like the Arabic *maqāmāt,* the Hebrew narratives have been viewed primarily as vehicles for rhetorical display. For this reason, little attention has been paid to literary aspects of the texts, such as the diversity of introductions and conclusions among episodes, plot development, narrative style, the interplay between truth and falsehood, and the dynamic relationship between narrator and protagonist. Only a few studies of the Hebrew narratives have taken notice of such topics and given readings of texts that strive to do more than ferret out Arabic parallels.[101] Studying the literary techniques of Hebrew narratives not only leads to their greater appreciation but also to a more nuanced view of their position on the map of world literature.

Scholarship has exhibited disagreement regarding the extent to which Hebrew rhymed prose narratives may be viewed as products of Arabic or Christian European environments. The vast majority of studies assume a context that is either entirely or mostly Arabic. There is little doubt that the prosodic features of the Hebrew narratives—rhymed prose with poems interspersed—are borrowed from the Arabic *maqāma*. Judah al-Ḥarīzī's *Taḥkemoni* has gained the most attention by modern scholars, perhaps because the narratives follow the classical model most faithfully. Many of al-Ḥarīzī's narratives are borrowed from Arabic *maqāmāt* by al-Hamadhānī and al-Ḥarīrī, as well as other Arabic texts.[102] However, the Hebrew narratives written before the *Taḥkemoni* are less classical in their content even though they share the prosodic features of the *maqāma*.[103] In essence, there is a curious development in Hebrew writing from a less classical model to one that is more classical, from the innovative to the imitative. Only some of the Hebrew narratives truly seem fully at home in the Arabic *maqāma* tradition.

Links made by scholars between themes appearing in the Hebrew narratives and parallels in European literature are extremely rare. Raymond Scheindlin considers Ibn Ṣaqbel's *Neʾum asher ben yehudah,* composed in Muslim Iberia in the early twelfth century, to be more closely related to Romance literature than to the Arabic literary heritage of Andalusian Jewry: although "the story's cultural environment is clearly Arabic, its main point, the lampooning of the protagonist because of his immature understanding of the rules of love, gives it more the character of a romance than a *maqama*. . . . [*Neʾum asher ben yehudah*] might reflect the emergence of the vernacular love story in Romance languages."[104] In *Minḥat yehudah,* Matti Huss considers the theme of *molestiae nupitarum,* distinct from the "wiles of women" motif of Arabic literature, to be inspired by misogamic European literature and debates over celibacy within the Church.[105] Ayelet Oettinger attempts to link the satire of social types in Judah al-Ḥarīzī's *Taḥkemoni* with the *satira communis* (estates satire) of the Latin tradition.[106] Romance roots have been posited for Jacob Ben Elʿazar's *Sefer ha-meshalim* by Schirmann, Scheindlin, and Rosen, although a comprehensive study of the book has not been undertaken.[107] Pagis considers some rhymed prose narratives to be influenced by European literature.[108] In general, however, scholars view the Hebrew narratives primarily as products of the Arabic environment, discounting the possibility of other influences, even when the attribution to Arabic seems somewhat forced.[109]

Scholarship on Hebrew narratives has tried to link themes to the Arabic context whenever possible. An enlightening example of this tendency may be demonstrated by Schirmann's treatment of race and racism in chapter 8 of Jacob Ben El^cazar's *Sefer ha-meshalim*. In the story, the narrator witnesses an aristocrat carousing with a woman who is described as "a worn-out black woman, her lips like a firebrand[110] plucked from burning, her eyes like flames."[111] Witnessing the licentious encounter, the narrator becomes enraged, leading him to fulminate against this "deviant" behavior and physically assault the couple. In an article of 1939, Schirmann posited that the origin of the attitude toward blackness might be found in early European literature, since the racist attitude seemed inexplicable against the background of Arabic literature.[112] Forty years later, after Bernard Lewis published an article delineating negative attitudes toward blackness in Arabic sources,[113] Schirmann revised his opinion:

> This [example from Jacob Ben Elᶜazar], of course, is an example of racism in our literature. . . . For a long time, I held that, concerning this point, the author adapted himself to the system of his Christian environment. I did not even venture to consider Arabic influence, since, according to the common wisdom, the Arabs did not know discrimination in this world between white and black Muslims; members of all races were equal before their Creator. . . . Today I must admit that I erred in this matter as many have erred before me. A few years ago, the well-known British Orientalist Bernard Lewis published detailed research on the relationship of Arab Muslims toward blacks. . . . [Lewis concludes that] the great majority of Arabs did not view blacks as their brethren; rather, they related to them with disdain, mockery, and even hatred. Although the Christians did not love them either, there is no need to attribute only them with the racist influence on Jacob Ben Elᶜazar; the motif of the black fits more naturally with the rest of the motifs whose origins are Arabic.[114]

For Schirmann, the default vector of influence is Arabic-Hebrew, with Romance-Hebrew only existing as an outside possibility when the default seems insufficient. After positing the possibility of Romance influence, Schirmann retreated to the more accepted vector of influence as soon as it seemed plausible. Schirmann did this even though he remained open to Romance influence for other aspects of the same book.[115] It is true that "racist" (or, at least, color-sensitive) attitudes are discernible in both Arabic and Romance literature. What Schirmann fails to do is to consider the possibility of multiple influences or compare systematically the nature of "racist" attitudes in Arabic and Romance literatures and *then* contemplate the Hebrew expression against these models.

Why has scholarship been so insistent about the predominance of Hebrew narrative's Arabic environment? The answer to this question is intimately related to a scholarly vision about medieval Jewish culture that governs the reading of Hebrew literature in medieval Iberia. Medieval Hispano-Jewish verse has been viewed as one of the products of the great Arabic-Jewish symbiosis that characterized medieval Jewish communities from Iraq to al-Andalus. S. D. Goitein called the emergence of medieval Hebrew poetry in al-Andalus the "apex" of this symbiosis whereby Jewish intellectuals invigorated the Jewish tradition by infusing it with Arabic learning and style.[116] As shown in the introduction to this book, the Hebrew literature of Iberia has been viewed according to a model of efflorescence and decline, wherein quality has been equated with adherence to Arabic forms. From this perspective, the Hebrew rhymed prose narrative has been viewed as a later manifestation of the symbiosis phenomenon, exhibiting itself even after Arab hegemony had dwindled. The field of Jewish studies has also been governed by a thesis that medieval Jews were seldom influenced by the intellectual trends of Christendom, where Jews were generally more insular and isolated.[117] Thus, the possibility of Christian European literature's positive influence on Hebrew writing would seem unlikely from the outset.[118]

The problem of determining the sources of Hebrew rhymed prose narratives is extremely complex. A theme that seems to be of Arabic origin at first glance may prove to have a more proximate European relative (e.g., Romance). Conversely, a theme that resembles a European text might be found to have a precedent in an Arabic text. To argue definitively that a given theme does not derive from Arabic sources, one must submit that it appears nowhere in the vast corpus of medieval Arabic literature, a position that would be foolhardy given that so much of this corpus has yet to be explored properly. Similarly, the case for pure Arabic influence would entail demonstrating the impossibility (or at least unlikelihood) of European influence.

Arguments affirming influence from Arabic and European sources in general must rely upon conjectures about the circulation of materials in thirteenth-century Christian Iberia. To argue that a given theme definitively originates from, let us say, Romance, it must be maintained that the theme was known in the Iberian Peninsula before the presence of an actual Romance text can be documented.[119] Similarly, very little is known about the circulation of Arabic literature, especially popular literature, in Christian Iberia. As will be discussed in the following chapters, some Hebrew narratives seem related to popular Arabic romances, including those contained in *The Thousand and One Nights.* Yet popular writing was being committed to writing only in the thirteenth century and largely in Egypt, which would require instantaneous absorption in Christian Iberia (or the earlier transmission of an oral form). Many of the Arabic romances postdate the earliest manuscript of *The Thousand and One Nights,* and even this manuscript postdates the period of the Hebrew narratives under discussion. Moreover, Arabic authors, and Hebrew authors after them, generally recognized a sharp division between learned and popular literatures even if the boundary between the two was not as hermetic as was once thought.[120] The claim that authors of high Hebrew literature borrowed materials from popular Arabic sources (either in written or oral form) requires a violation of this division between learned and popular literatures.

The problem of influence is further compounded by debates regarding the relationship between Arabic and European literature in general. As stated, some scholars view the troubadour lyric as sui generis or as indebted to the classical tradition only, while others argue that Arabic literature contributed to its rise. Looking beyond the thirteenth century, scholars have posited direct influence of certain episodes and themes from *The Thousand and One Nights* upon European classics, including the anonymous *Le Conte de Floire et Blanchefleur,* Boccaccio's (1313–1375) *Decameron,* Chaucer's (1340–1400) *Canterbury Tales,* and other works.[121] Thus, motifs of Arabic popular tales enjoyed significant circulation over centuries and across language barriers.

If one imagines that European works served as immediate sources for Hebrew literature but that Arabic texts, in turn, served as sources for European literature, then are not the Hebrew texts somehow still the result of Arabic influence? Could Hebrew and European literatures have inherited from Arabic literature simultaneously and independently of each other? Is it not possible that Hebrew authors were aware of similar literary trends reaching them from more than one language? One wonders whether the question of making a binary choice—Arabic influence or European—is a good one when the two parts of the binary are somewhat intertwined. Ultimately, we are dealing with a period in literary history whose exact contours have only been sketched in part.

Systematic comparison of Hebrew with Romance and other European literatures is in great need,[122] as is the exploration of many Arabic texts, particularly those from the Islamic East and popular sources, which have been introduced into the discussion only rarely.[123] When a given Hebrew theme has parallels in Arabic and European literatures, we do not necessarily need to discard one in favor of the other. It is possible that the emergence of a literary ideal in European literature allowed the Hebrew author an opportunity to revive a theme of the Arabic tradition that had not been favored by Hebrew authors previously. It is not enough to show that Arabic precedents can be found for sections of Hebrew narratives; we must consider why a particular Arabic topos was favored by an author at a particular time. Also, we must unlearn or rethink some of the dominant academic narratives that discount a priori the possibility of European influence over Hebrew writing. By reimagining the context of Hebrew rhymed prose fiction, much more will be understood about Hispano-Jewish culture in transition and the interplay of literary texts in the multi-confessional atmosphere of thirteenth-century Christian Iberia.

The following chapters do not attempt to resolve issues of literary influence definitively. Rather, they compare and contrast two thirteenth-century Hebrew rhymed prose fictional narratives from various literary perspectives while pointing out parallels with Arabic and European literatures. Importantly, the analysis strives to go beyond conventional concepts of "literary influence" wherein an author's work is merely shaped by his literary environment. All too often, Hebrew authors have been portrayed as passive vessels through which literary influences pass indiscriminately. Instead, Hebrew authors are viewed as individuals aware of multiple literary traditions who select and rework existing materials in innovative, ironic, and even subversive ways. Thus, the presence of Arabic themes does not necessarily prove that an author was "influenced" by a particular text or genre. Rather, it shows that the author chose to make use of that material, possibly inverting its original signification and using it toward a different end. Also, an author's adoption of a European theme is not tantamount to his abandonment of the Arabic literary tradition. Hebrew narratives of the thirteenth century reflect authors' belonging to a dynamic and hybrid cultural environment wherein colliding and overlapping literary traditions were synthesized and reworked.

The two texts compared in the following chapters are the *Taḥkemoni,* by Judah al-Ḥarīzī, and *Sefer ha-meshalim* (The Book of Stories), by Jacob Ben Elʿazar. Both authors were born in Christian Toledo in the latter half of the twelfth century and composed their works during the first half of the thirteenth century. While it seems that Ben Elʿazar spent his whole life in the Iberian Peninsula, traveling, perhaps, only to Provence, al-Ḥarīzī traveled widely, ultimately reaching the Islamic East as far as Iraq and then settling in Aleppo, where he died. Both authors exhibit a strong familiarity with Arabic literature and the *maqāma* tradition in particular, though they relate to it in different ways. Al-Ḥarīzī largely remains a faithful transmitter of the *maqāma* genre, rarely creating textual moments that are not recognizable against the backdrop of the *maqāma* and learned Arabic literature more generally. Although, as will be shown in chapter 5, al-Ḥarīzī was probably not untouched by other currents of the Iberian literary environment, his notion of literature as a whole adhered to the conventions of the *maqāma.* Ben Elᶜazar's relationship with the *maqāma* genre is more complex. Although he mimics some aspects, he also parodies central *maqāma* conventions and turns instead to a new literary sensibility. Unlike the classical *maqāma,* in which characters are static and show no signs of development, Ben Elᶜazar's very idea of fiction hinges on character transformation. In this respect, his narratives fit well within the literary trends of the romance genre as it was developing both in Christian Europe and in the Islamic world. Whether his inspiration can be attributed to Arabic romance, French Romance, or both will also be treated in chapter 5.

Chapter 6 investigates the two authors' use of authorial voice in portraying social issues central to the changing world of thirteenth-century Jewry. Both al-Ḥarīzī and Ben Elᶜazar appear as authors who share the Andalusian Jewish preoccupation with Hebrew as a language of literary possibility. Still, they seem to possess differing views concerning other Andalusian values, such as aristocratic leadership and the related social practice of wine drinking. In fact, it will be shown that the courtly ideal embraced by Ben Elᶜazar is more readily associated with that of Provence than al-Andalus.

Chapter 7 asks whether al-Ḥarīzī and Ben Elᶜazar imagined themselves as members of the Christian or Islamic worlds, by examining the representation of landscape and geography in their respective works. Both authors reveal a certain degree of cultural hybridity, though al-Ḥarīzī seems more rooted in the Islamic world and Ben Elᶜazar in the Christian world. The *Taḥkemoni* reflects the perspective of an author nostalgic for the Andalusian Jewish past, contemplating the transfer of culture from the Islamic West to the East. *Sefer ha-meshalim* reflects the perspective of an author more firmly planted in the Christian world, looking outward at the world of Islam; although Ben Elᶜazar remained closely attuned to trends in Arabic literature, the Islamic world appears unfamiliar in his narratives.

Five

Structure

Literature in Transition

The twentieth century produced a welter of ideas concerning narrative. Once excluded from the serious study of literature, which occupied itself with poetry only, narrative became a central topic of inquiry. The novel, which had been viewed as a light literary diversion, became recognized as a sophisticated form wherein genres mixed and competing social voices collided.[1] Naturally, scholars also turned an eye backward toward the history of narrative by studying Greek epics, chivalric Romances, early novels (*Don Quixote* usually being cited as the first), and non-Western forms.[2] Scholars considered devices such as authorial voice, point of view, the sense of an ending, and the structures of space and time that underlay narratives. Some contemplated whether narrative types adhered to uniform structures, and others asked whether narratives followed a logical "grammar" like the grammar of a sentence writ large.[3] Post-structuralists called attention to the role of the reader in imposing a plot on a narrative and the cognitive processes that make narrativity possible.[4]

Although studies of Hebrew rhymed prose narratives have grown increasingly mindful of structural issues, locating the place of Hebrew narratives on the map of medieval literatures has generally been approached from the perspective of thematic comparison only.[5] The technique used by scholars has been to trace a given theme of a Hebrew text to its "origin" and conclude that the earlier text "influenced" the Hebrew text; some scholars also discuss how Hebrew authors "Judaize" or "Hebraize" the foreign text.[6] While the presence of themes from Arabic and European literatures in Hebrew texts may point to authors' awareness of these literatures, the "influence" model has done little to describe how Hebrew authors work with existing material. Themes cannot be viewed in isolation; they must be read within the framework of the narrative as a whole. Authors can alter themes, manipulate them, and co-opt them for novel purposes.

Of course, medieval Hebrew narratives are not modern novels and cannot be read as such. However, narrative texts all possess certain qualities and are subject to related types of analysis by virtue of being narratives. The present chapter draws attention to narrative techniques such as plot, character development, authorial voice, devices of conclusion, and chronotope (Mikhail Bakhtin's term for the "time-space" blueprint of a narrative) in the works of Judah al-Ḥarīzī and Jacob Ben Elʿazar. The divergent structures of these works attest to the various literary currents of Christian Iberia and to the modes of cultural hybridity of Jews within this environment.

Judah al-Ḥarīzī (1166?–1225) and the *Taḥkemoni*

Until Joseph Sadan's discovery of an entry on "Yaḥya Ibn Suleiman Ibn Shaʾul Abū Zakariyya al-Ḥarīzī the Jew from the people of Toledo" in a medieval Arabic biographical dictionary by Ibn al-Shaʿār al-Mawṣali (b. Mosul, 1197–d. Aleppo, 1256), determining al-Ḥarīzī's place of birth was mainly guesswork. Early scholars designated his birthplace as Toledo, Barcelona, or Granada, each representing different assumptions about the nature of Jewish culture in the twelfth and thirteenth centuries.[7] Several scholars doubted the possibility of Toledo, then in the Christian kingdom of Castile, precisely because al-Ḥarīzī was so well versed in the Arabic tradition and adept at writing Arabic belles-lettres. For this reason, al-Ḥarīzī was inscribed into the tradition of Granada, the former home of Samuel the Nagid, Moses Ibn Ezra, and Judah Halevi and an illustrious seat of Jewish-Arab symbiosis. Subsequent scholarship, however, has proved beyond doubt that Arabic culture was alive and well in Castile and that such a context could well explain the education of a literary phenomenon such as al-Ḥarīzī.[8]

The aforementioned biographical dictionary of Ibn al-Shaʿār al-Mawṣali reveals vital information about the author such as the place and year of his death and miscellaneous facts such as the author's uncommon height, his inability to grow a beard, and his Maghrebi accent. Naturally, the dictionary is mostly interested in al-Ḥarīzī's Arabic works; it preserves six Arabic poems (subjects include passion, nature, and panegyric) and offers the name of al-Ḥarīzī's Arabic *maqāma, al-Rawḍa al-anīqa* (The Elegant Garden), a text that had been known to scholars without a title for many years. The dictionary also recognizes al-Ḥarīzī as an author of "numerous works in the Hebrew language such as the Book of *Maqāmāt*" (probably the *Taḥkemoni*).[9]

Al-Ḥarīzī's first Hebrew writings were translations of Judeo-Arabic and Arabic halakhic, philosophical, and belletristic works, often commissioned by Jewish intellectuals in Christian Iberia and Provence. Among his translations are:[10] Moses Ibn Ezra's *Maqālat al-ḥadīqa fī maʿnā al-majāz wa al-haqīqa* (Treatise of the Garden of Figurative and Literal Speech), entitled *ʿArugat ha-bosem* (The Garden Bed of Spice) in Hebrew;[11] Maimonides' *Dalālat al-ḥāʾirīn* (Guide of the Perplexed), entitled *Moreh nevukhim* in Hebrew;[12] Maimonides' *Introduction to the Mishnah*[13] and the commentary on the first five tractates of *Zeraʿim;*[14] Maimonides' "Essay on Resurrection";[15] ʿAli Ibn Riḍwān's *Epistle on Morals,* entitled *Iggeret ʿali ha-ishmaʿeli* (The Epistle of ʿAli the Ishmaelite) in Hebrew;[16] Ḥunayn Ibn Isḥaq's *Ādāb al-falāsifa* (Dicta of the Philosophers), entitled *Musrei ha-filosofim* in Hebrew;[17] Galen's *Dialogue on the Soul;*[18] and al-Ḥarīrī's Arabic *maqāmāt.* The translation of al-Ḥarīrī's *maqāmāt,* entitled *Maḥberot ittiʾel* (Ittiʾel's Compositions) in Hebrew,[19] is the transitional work between al-Ḥarīzī's early translations and his original fictional masterpiece, the *Taḥkemoni.*

Unlike *Maḥberot ittiʾel,* which was translated while al-Ḥarīzī was still in Toledo, the *Taḥkemoni* is the work of an author who had left his homeland.[20] The many dedications of the *Taḥkemoni* to patrons of the East, both in Hebrew and in Judeo-Arabic, indicate that the author had left Iberia to seek patronage in thriving cultural centers where his Arabic, Judeo-Arabic, and Hebrew works could all be appreciated.[21] The *Taḥkemoni* survives in many versions, and a critical edition has never been attempted. In fact, the book stubbornly resists the idea of an "Urtext." The differences in the versions show that the author was constantly reworking his text, not in order to revise drafts with the goal of creating a superior, final text, but rather to fit the exigencies of the moment. Most conspicuously, as Joshua Blau and Joseph Yahalom have shown, individuals who are praised as generous patrons in one version are lampooned as miserly miscreants in another, and vice versa.[22] For these reasons, a critical edition that aims to provide a single "correct reading" should never be made; the most faithful representation of al-Ḥarīzī's masterpiece is the parallel publication of numerous versions, as Blau and Yahalom have done with select chapters.

As with the poetry of the Andalusian period, the *Taḥkemoni* has been viewed primarily as a testimony to Jewish-Arab symbiosis and the influence of Arabic literature on Hebrew literature. Even with al-Ḥarīzī's birthplace firmly set in Toledo, the impact of the Christian context on the *Taḥkemoni* continues to be debated. Rina Drory argues that al-Ḥarīzī's zealous attempt to ennoble the Hebrew language through the *Taḥkemoni* stems from the author's cultural background as a Jew of Christian Iberia.[23] In Drory's view, the *Taḥkemoni* is an artifact of the Jewish intellectual enterprise (represented also by the translations of the Ibn Tibbon family in Provence) to transplant

Arabic knowledge into an invigorated Hebrew language in the Christian context:

> If not for the prevailing cultural climate in northern Spain and Provence at the time, al-Harizi would most probably never have written his Hebrew maqamat. . . . In other words, it took a non-Muslim and non-Arabic cultural atmosphere, that of Christian Spain, to produce a literary work so notably Arabic-Hebrew in nature.[24]

Joseph Sadan tacitly critiques Drory's view (her articles are conspicuously absent from his bibliography) and emphasizes the direct influence Arabic had on al-Ḥarīzī, both in Christian Iberia and in the East, where the *Taḥkemoni* was composed. For Sadan, the *Taḥkemoni* need not be seen as a part of the transfer of Jewish-Arabic learning to Christendom. In fact, the study views al-Ḥarīzī foremost as an Arabic author who left Castile in search of a professional venue in the Ayyubid East.[25]

Scholarship on the *Taḥkemoni* has been occupied with revealing the sources of al-Ḥarīzī's narratives by uncovering influences from the *maqāmāt* of al-Hamadhānī, al-Ḥarīrī, and other Arabic sources.[26] While important, such an approach does little to go beyond the imitative aspects of al-Ḥarīzī's work. Other studies of the *Taḥkemoni* have attempted to use the text as a testimony to the author's biography and realia of thirteenth-century culture.[27] Matti Huss considers the complex interplay between fiction and reality in the *Taḥkemoni* and other rhymed prose narratives, and Tova Rosen situates chapters of the *Taḥkemoni* within the rubric of gender in medieval Hebrew literature.[28] Little effort has been made to read the book as a text emanating from a culture in transition following the decline of Andalusian Jewry.[29] Even if Drory's study does make the context of Christian Iberia visible by considering the impetus for the *Taḥkemoni*'s creation, it does not read a dimension of cultural transition within the narratives themselves. Beneath the *Taḥkemoni*'s layers of rhetoric and irony, there is a sophisticated discourse about al-Andalus, the past, and cultural transition.

Like the *maqāmāt* of al-Ḥarīzī's Arabic predecessors, the *Taḥkemoni* makes elaborate use of rhetorical play and intertextual allusion. Each of the *Taḥkemoni*'s fifty narratives (assembled by the author) involves an interaction between a narrator and a protagonist. The main characters (and other characters) possess symbolic names that can be deciphered through semantic and intertextual analysis.[30] The title of the book derives from the name of one of King David's warriors in 2 Sam. 23:8. The root of the name, *ḥkm,* means "to be wise"; hence the title evokes both might and wisdom. The narrator is Heman ha-Ezraḥi, a name that reverberates against several usages in the

Bible. The name appears in this exact form as the author of Psalms 88. Another Heman is a wise man with whom Solomon is compared (1 Kings 5:11),[31] and there is yet another Heman who is a Levite called "Heman the poet" (*ha-meshorer,* 1 Chron. 6:18). The name "Ezraḥi" should be considered for its semantic sense, derived from the root *zrḥ,* "to rise from the soil" (and the root of the modern Hebrew word for "citizen"). Thus, it is not surprising that the narrator reveals his native land (i.e., the soil from which he rises) to be Sefarad.[32] The author has thus bestowed upon the narrator a name that evokes wisdom, poetry, and Sefarad.

The narrator's status as "one who rises from the soil" places him in stark contrast with the protagonist, Ḥever ha-Qeni, the namesake of a character from Judg. 4:11 who had "pitched his tent at *elon be-ṣaᶜananim.*" He is Ḥever, not only because he is a "friend" (*ḥaver*) to the narrator but also because he "brings together" (from the root *ḥbr*) scattered bits of rhetoric and teaching.[33] While his home *elon be-ṣaᶜananim* is a simple place name in the Bible, it is significant here because of the force of the root *ṣᶜn,* "to wander."[34] Thus, he comes from a place of abstract and eternal wandering.

The constant movement from place to place in the *Taḥkemoni* imbues the text with the ideal of wanderlust common in *maqāma* literature. While there is no certain evidence that al-Ḥarīzī knew al-Saraqusṭī's *maqāmāt,* there is a strong point of overlap between the two texts with respect to character names. Like Ḥever ha-Qeni, al-Saraqusṭī's narrator is a wanderer; he is Abū al-Ghamr[35] al-Sāʾib, "the Possessor of Naïveté, the Wanderer." As mentioned, al-Ḥarīrī's protagonist also claims to have taken up wandering after his home was destroyed by Byzantine Christians. It is perhaps al-Ḥarīzī's own experience of wandering that led him to select the *maqāma,* with its tales of itinerant rhetoricians, to convey aspects of his social world, one that is concerned with estrangement and continuity during a transitional chapter of Jewish history.[36]

There is an overtly polemical dimension to the *Taḥkemoni.* The author states that he composed the book in order to ennoble the Hebrew language, which had "declined appallingly" in his day, especially as Jews remained enamored with Arabic writing and with al-Ḥarīrī's *maqāmāt* in particular.[37] In Christian Iberia and in the Islamic East, Hebrew remained caught in a lingering polemic with Arabic wherein the Bible competed with the Qurʾān for status as God's revealed speech. Although Hebrew had enjoyed a kind of renaissance in the twelfth and thirteenth centuries, being employed for a wide range of topics that had previously been treated in Arabic only, al-Ḥarīzī lamented the decline of belletristic writing in the tradition of the Andalusian poets.

Most prominently, the *Taḥkemoni* is about representing different types of speech and social types. Al-Ḥarīzī writes in the introduction:

> I gathered together in this book many parables and sweet themes. Among them all types of rhetoric and striking riddles, words of teaching, songs of friendship, proverbs of rectitude, words of admonition, events of history, and tidings of the years. The remembrance of death and the place of the shadow of death; words of repentance and pardoning of guilt. The delights of love and love songs. The betrothing of women, bridal canopy and marriage, and matters of divorce; the drunkenness of drunkards; the asceticism of ascetics; wars of heroes and events of kings; the adventures of travel; songs of praise, and supplications of prayers; instruction of the sages, and associations of the upright. The desire of fawns; gardens and villages; words of princes; the speech of children; the hunt of hunters; the cunning of tricksters and the folly of fools; the slandering of scorners, the blaspheming of revilers. And wondrous songs and epistles in amazing words.[38]

Like the Arabic *maqāma,* the *Taḥkemoni* is meant to entertain and astound the reader with eloquent speech and bring delight through humorous scenarios. However, the diversionary nature of the text should not prevent us from considering its narrative dimensions seriously. Perhaps more than any other form before *Don Quixote,* the *maqāma* resembles the modern novel in its penchant for genre mixture.

European Themes?

One question that has seldom been asked is whether, in addition to Arabic sources, al-Ḥarīzī utilizes themes or plots from European literatures.[39] Although the *Taḥkemoni* indisputably endeavors to emulate Arabic literary norms for the tastes of an Eastern audience, this does not require that themes from the other literatures of the Iberian Peninsula never surface in the book. Despite his dedication to Arabic poetry and style, al-Ḥarīzī was not necessarily impervious to the literary trends of Christian Iberia and France. Some elements of the *Taḥkemoni* may bear earmarks of the European tradition. This is not to say that al-Ḥarīzī necessarily read European sources in their original languages. It is not even clear what languages the author spoke, apart from Arabic; it is difficult to imagine that he did not know at least some Castilian or that he was oblivious to the types of stories that were circulating in Christian Iberia and in Provence (where he also spent time). While we cannot attribute particular sources, a few thematic parallels are suggestive.

First, in the *Taḥkemoni*'s introduction, when the author is in a state he describes as "I was asleep but my heart was awake" (Song of Songs 5:2), the Hebrew Tongue comes to him in the form of a woman and charges him to gird his loins and battle zealously on her behalf, to bring dignity to the Holy Language, which has fallen into decline. While personification, particularly the personification of Israel as a woman, is known in earlier Jewish sources, this episode is strikingly similar to encounters with the goddess Natura (Nature) in Christian sources.[40] For example, Alan of Lille's Latin *The Plaint of Nature* (*De planctu naturae*)[41] begins with the author forlorn because of the loose sexual morals of his age (homosexuality had become rampant, threatening the normal course of reproduction). When the author enters a state described as "half-way between wakefulness and sleep," Natura (who oversees reproduction on earth) descends from heaven adorned in beautiful garments and addresses the author.[42]

Second, in *maqāma* 19, one of the *Taḥkemoni*'s rhetorical episodes, the narrator comes to the river Euphrates, where seven youths are debating which is the best of seven virtues: humility, zeal, courage, faithfulness, wisdom, refinement,[43] or a good heart. While these virtues might be somewhat universal, such lists of virtues (either moral or chivalrous), frequently seven in number, are often enumerated in classical and European sources. The list of seven virtues in the Latin *Psychomachia* of Prudentius includes faith, chastity, patience, humility, moderation, generosity, and concord. In the thirteenth-century Castilian *La leyenda de los Infantes de Lara,* a father pronounces a eulogy over seven murdered sons, enumerating their virtues that, taken together, epitomize the seven qualities of the ideal knight: loyalty, justice, truth, valor, fidelity, generosity, and fondness for good company.[44] While Arabic does possess a genre of biographical-hagiographical literature called *manāqib* literature, which records the *manāqib* (qualities and characteristics) and *faḍāʾil* (virtues) of notable individuals, we do not find comparable enumerations of seven virtues.[45]

Third, in *maqāma* 31, the protagonist relates an adventure in which he and a band of travelers encounter a "man" riding a horse who reveals "himself" to be a lovely maiden. The maiden tells a story that she was cloistered in a royal chamber until a robber kidnapped and assaulted her. She escaped and wandered the wilderness until she met Ḥever ha-Qeni and his companions. She leads the travelers to a spring behind a mountain, where she reveals her beauty and impresses the men with her marksmanship by shooting an arrow into the air and splitting it in twain. Suddenly, she redirects her bow and shoots one of the travelers in the chest and forces the remaining companions to bind one another with ropes. The tale ends with the protagonist's narrow escape, when he unsheathes a knife from his boot and stabs the maiden.

The story, as it is known, is based on al-Hamadhānī's sixth *maqāma,* the "*maqāma* of the Lion," which includes many of the same details (the spring behind the mountain, splitting the arrow in twain, shooting a companion in the chest, the protagonist's narrow escape). However, in al-Hamadhānī's version, the rider is not a woman in disguise but a man. Al-Ḥarīzī's variation alters the sense of the story. While both versions are meant to entertain (and al-Hamadhānī's is not devoid of erotic overtones), al-Ḥarīzī's is based on an inversion of the expected gender hierarchy. This technique is common in French narrative, as is the theme of the cross-dressed knight.[46] However, the theme is also not absent from Arabic sources, and ultimate judgment on the matter of "influence" should be reserved.[47] In any case, with respect to the structure of the narrated tale, the story remains al-Hamadhānī's.[48] Even if al-Ḥarīzī did utilize certain themes that were reaching him from or being reinforced by the European environment, his conception of literature as a whole remained that of the *maqāma.*

Structure

The distinctions in structure between the *Taḥkemoni* and its Arabic forerunners are usually quite subtle.[49] The following discussion reviews structural elements and narrative devices of the *Taḥkemoni;* the book has obvious affinities for the Arabic *maqāma* tradition that place it in contrast with Jacob Ben Elʿazar's *Sefer ha-meshalim.*

PLOT

The plot structures of the *Taḥkemoni* are fairly consistent, revolving around the encounters of the narrator and the protagonist according to the pattern of the classical *maqāma.* In each episode, the two characters meet up in a city or another setting, have some exchange, and then depart, only to meet again in the subsequent episode. Thus, every episode ends as it began, with the narrator and protagonist traveling separately and ready to encounter each another.[50] Heman ha-Ezraḥi is traveling in search of learning, culture, and rhetorical excellence. Ḥever ha-Qeni is a sort of antihero, a mercurial master of eloquence whose disregard for social convention makes him an entertaining, if not exemplary, character. Also a master of disguise and chicanery, he earns a living through petty scams, duping unsuspecting citizens with an eloquent tongue while flouting social mores beneath the surface.

Ross Brann categorizes al-Ḥarīzī's *maqāmāt* according to four basic patterns, although, as Brann recognizes, not every *maqāma* fits neatly into a category while some exhibit elements of more than one category:[51] 1) rhetorical anecdotes in which the narrative element exists as a setup for rhetorical exercises;[52] 2) episodes in which the narrative element is a vehicle for descriptive or didactic discourse;[53] 3) tales involving a ruse or some other deception;[54] and 4) accounts of adventure and rescue.[55] In rhetorical episodes (category 1), the narrative frame seems but a thin veneer for rhetorical display, as when the narrator arrives at a poetry tournament and is dumbfounded at the skill of an unknown master who is revealed to be the protagonist. Recognition is usually followed by a departure scene, although sometimes this is altered or omitted. Descriptive and didactic episodes (category 2) can have equally few plot twists. For example, in *maqāma* 18, the narrator joins a group of intellectuals discussing Hebrew poetry, among them an old man sitting silently yet appearing to mock their words. The old man ultimately speaks and instructs the others in the ways of composing poetry. At the conclusion, the narrator recognizes the old man as Ḥever ha-Qeni, who quickly quits the scene.

In the remaining categories, the narrative can be more dynamic. An example of a tale of deception (category 3) is the plotline of the mendicant preacher that al-Ḥarīzī borrows from al-Hamadhānī (discussed in chapter 4); similar stories can also be found in the corpus of al-Ḥarīrī.[56] In al-Ḥarīzī's version, Heman ha-Ezraḥi arrives at a synagogue where a certain mendicant, along with his young son, is preaching to the public about his plight and misfortune. As a man of means now fallen upon hard times, he appeals to the congregation and gathers contributions.[57] The narrator approaches the mendicant, recognizes him as the protagonist, and the two depart without Ḥever's identity being exposed. *Maqāma* 28 (discussed above), which recounts Ḥever's narrow escape from the attack of a mysterious horseman, is an example of a tale of adventure or escape (category 4).

The most constant and salient structural element of the *Taḥkemoni,* following the classical *maqāma,* is the moment of recognition (anagnorisis), wherein Heman ha-Ezraḥi realizes that the man he has encountered is Ḥever ha-Qeni. This can happen in any number of ways. It is often not until the end of an episode that the narrator recognizes the protagonist, usually after a ruse has been executed. In other instances, Ḥever is discernible from the first moment of the encounter. This method is used in episodes wherein the protagonist relates a self-contained story to the narrator. Following the protagonist's tale, the narrator takes delight in the protagonist's intelligence and the fictitious quality of his speech.

CHARACTER DEVELOPMENT

As is typical of the classical Arabic *maqāma*, the characters in the *Taḥkemoni* exhibit no signs of development. Ḥever ha-Qeni is always deceitful, mercurial, eloquent, and unremorseful. Heman ha-Ezraḥi is always in search of rhetoric and remains ever gullible, (somehow) never learning that the disguised rhetoricians whom he encounters all over the world all turn out to be the same person.[58] The characters are fixed types whose qualities are completely static.[59] Even the protagonist's protean nature is unchanging. The lack of character development is not a sign of low art, as some earlier commentators who compared the *maqāmāt* with Western aesthetics maintained. Rather, the pattern of interaction that makes the *maqāma* possible is entirely dependent upon the main characters' predictability.

TIME

The reader of the *Taḥkemoni* senses that events in the book are roughly contemporary with the life of the author, especially as al-Ḥarīzī sets several stories in prominent cities of his day and makes mention of a number of nonfictional personages. On the other hand, the reader should not understand the book as a testimony to thirteenth-century life, especially since several episodes are rewritings of narratives written centuries earlier (such as the numerous *maqāmāt* that are based on al-Hamadhānī's work).

As a literary whole, the *maqāmāt* do not add up to any logical biography of either main character nor do they recount episodes of life that are somehow formative in the lives of the characters (in contrast with the standard Western bildungsroman).[60] Ḥever ha-Qeni, who was born at an unspecified time in an imaginary place, has a wife and child who mysteriously appear and disappear according to the fictional exigencies of specific episodes. In no episode does a character face a personal challenge that he overcomes to emerge matured and ennobled. The book recounts neither characters' whole lives from birth down to the present (what Bakhtin calls "biographical-time") nor formative episodes in characters' development (what Bakhtin calls "adventure-time"). Rather, the reader is shown numerous short clips whose basic elements (encounter, exchange, anagnorisis, departure) repeat.

Within narratives, time is generally linear and limited within a short span. The narrator usually relates events in the form: "I came to place *x*, I saw *y*, I heard *z*." In some instances, the narrator meets the (undisguised) protagonist, who relates a story of his own, following the form: "I was in place *x* and had experience *y*, which explains how I came to meet you here." We assume that the protagonist is relating an event that has occurred recently (or that he has invented a story that is supposed to have occurred recently). We do not find devices such as the simultaneous unfolding of multiple plots, flashback, or leaps to the future. The *Taḥkemoni* thus exhibits a time structure typical of the classical *maqāmāt,* which, we will see, distinguishes it from literary techniques in *Sefer ha-meshalim,* medieval Arabic romance, and French Romance.

AUTHORIAL VOICE

In the introduction to the *Taḥkemoni,* al-Ḥarīzī informs the reader that he does not speak with his own voice but has placed speech in the mouths of two fictional characters: Heman ha-Ezraḥi and Ḥever ha-Qeni.[61] The narrator is always an actor in the *maqāmāt* (an intradiegetic narrator), although his actions are sometimes limited to meeting and recognizing the protagonist (in addition to his obvious role of narrating).[62] At times, the reader feels the author surfacing in each of the two main characters. Like al-Ḥarīzī, the narrator is a native of Sefarad who travels the world to enjoy the company of the literary intelligentsia. Occasionally, the author allows himself to shine through the protagonist's speech, suggesting that the protagonist's perspective might be the author's, at least for a moment. The most famous example occurs when Ḥever exploits a biblical quotation bearing the author's first name to describe his (i.e., Ḥever's) departure from Iberia to journey to the Islamic East: "At that time *Judah* went down from his brothers" (Gen. 38:1).[63] There is undoubtedly a bit of the author in both characters. As symbols of Sefarad and wandering, Heman ha-Ezraḥi and Ḥever ha-Qeni embody the two poles between which the author moved during his life. Still, one must not confuse either of the main characters with the author himself. The author appears, disappears, and reappears elsewhere; sometimes we are allowed glimpses of him, but we cannot pin him down.

As mentioned, the *Taḥkemoni* is occupied primarily with bringing together various species of speech. Al-Ḥarīzī represents many types of characters, including children, women, simpletons, aristocrats, ascetics, and charlatans, each possessing a unique style of speech. The chameleon Ḥever ha-Qeni can simulate the speech of virtually any recognizable social type. When he appears as a seller of remedies (*maqāma* 30), for example, his speech is ontologically twice removed from the author; it is invented by Ḥever, who is invented by al-Ḥarīzī. Heman ha-Ezraḥi exhibits a distinct and largely consistent pattern of speech. He is not ineloquent (he is able to improvise poems and even wins the praise of the protagonist), though his speech compares dimly with that of Ḥever ha-Qeni.[64] Authorial voice is not to be found in any one speaker in the *Taḥkemoni* but is centered in the tension created among several characters. This point will be expanded upon in the following chapter.

In sum, the *Taḥkemoni* largely preserves the structural elements common in the classical *maqāmāt,* especially the standard patterns followed so persistently by al-Ḥarīrī. Time within episodes is limited to short unfragmented clips while time across episodes is not chronologically or logically ordered. Literariness is achieved through the fulfillment of the reader's expectations for sophisticated rhetoric, debate, dissimulation, trickery, and anagnorisis. Like his Arabic predecessors, al-Ḥarīzī does not allow authorial voice to be centralized in the speech of any one character but creates it through the interactive speech of a cast of characters. Unlike his Arabic predecessors, however, at times al-Ḥarīzī identifies strongly with his two main characters, even inserting himself into the text in a manner that the reader cannot overlook.

Al-Ḥarīzī chose the classical *maqāma* model among several of which he would have been aware. He was undoubtedly familiar with other forms of learned Arabic writing and possibly even the popular epics and stories of *The Thousand and One Nights* variety. He was likely familiar with some trends in European literature (at least, he seems familiar with certain themes). Although "Neʾum asher ben yehudah" is only one of two Hebrew rhymed prose narratives that al-Ḥarīzī mentions by name, it is likely that he knew less classical examples, such as *Minḥat yehudah* or *Sefer shaʿashuʿim.*[65] Still, al-Ḥarīrī's model of eloquent poetry and prose spoken through the mouths of wanderers remained the gold standard of literary style in al-Ḥarīzī's eyes. Al-Ḥarīzī's Eastern literary tastes parallel his fixation on the East as the new center for high Jewish culture and his physical movement from West to East in search of patronage and prestige.

Jacob Ben Elʿazar and *Sefer ha-Meshalim*

The rhymed prose narratives of Jacob Ben Elʿazar have received far less attention than the *Taḥkemoni,* both in the medieval and modern periods. *Sefer ha-meshalim* is preserved in a single manuscript only, despite (or perhaps because of) the fact that it is a unique example of medieval Hebrew fiction.[66] Still, Ben Elʿazar, a younger contemporary of al-Ḥarīzī's who was also born in Toledo, was not altogether unknown.[67] He is glossed by David Qimḥi (c. 1160–1235) some seven times regarding grammatical points.[68] According to an anonymous Judeo-Arabic biographical dictionary, the author composed twelve works in various disciplines; the biographer identifies Ben Elʿazar as the author of the Judeo-Arabic grammatical work on the Hebrew language, *Kitāb al-kāmil* (The Complete Book), for which he seems to have been best known.[69] Of his works, five have survived:

1. *Sefer ha-meshalim* (further below).
2. A Hebrew translation (from Arabic) of *Kalīla wa dimnā,* a famous book of didactic fables about animals and people.[70]
3. *Kitāb al-kāmil,* a book on Hebrew grammar written in Judeo-Arabic.[71]
4. *Sefer pardes rimonei ha-ḥokhmah ve-ʿarugat bosem ha-mezimah* (Book of the Orchard of Pomegranates of Wisdom and the Spice Garden of Thought), a philosophically oriented work in a rhetorically sophisticated Hebrew rhymed prose.[72]
5. *Sefer gan ha-teʿudot ve-ʿarugot ḥuqot ḥamudot* (Book of the Garden of Teachings and Garden Beds of Precious Statutes), an ethical and philosophical treatise written during the author's later years. It is structured as a debate among the Soul, Wisdom, and the Intellect and is also in rhymed prose.[73]

Apart from scant details of birthplace, works, and patrons (who were in Beaucaire), nothing is known about the author's life. Ben Elʿazar never left a record of travels, as al-Ḥarīzī did.[74] Although the author's works are dedicated to dignitaries in Iberia and Provence, there is no evidence that the poet was an itinerant artist.

Sefer ha-meshalim was known to early scholars such as Moritz Steinschneider and Abraham Geiger, who did not hold the book in very high regard.[75] Jefim Schirmann, who did value the literary qualities of the work, published five chapters (the so-called love stories) and the author's introduction.[76] The remaining chapters were published subsequently by Jonah David.[77] Neḥemiah Allony estimated that *Sefer ha-meshalim* was composed sometime between 1180 and 1240,[78] although we can safely date the book after the composition of al-Ḥarīzī's *Maḥberot ittiʾel* and probably after the *Taḥkemoni,* since Ben Elʿazar seems to be familiar with both of al-Ḥarīzī's works. Geiger dated the book to 1233.[79] Apart from the publication of the narratives, the work has seldom been discussed in modern scholarship.[80]

The book consists of an author's introduction plus ten chapters loosely tied together by the personality of the narrator, whose full name is Lemuʾel Ben Ittiʾel Rav Peʿalim me-Qavṣʾel.[81] Following the *maqāma* tradition, there are episodes dedicated to poetic competition (chapter 3) and rhetorical debates over such topics as poetry versus prose (chapter 2) and the pen versus the sword (chapter 4). The other episodes offer dynamic plots of several varieties (further below).

As in the *Taḥkemoni,* the narrator's name is layered with connotations of wisdom, since Lemuʾel and Ittiʾel are both wise men in Proverbs. The particular significance of the name Lemuʾel will be elucidated in chapter 6.

Itti᾿el evokes the name of the narrator in al-Ḥarīzī's translation of al-Ḥarīrī's *maqāmāt.* Ben Elᶜazar's narrator is thus the son of a narrator who is both al-Ḥarīzī's and al-Ḥarīrī's. The last part of the name, Rav Peᶜalim me-Qavṣ᾿el (meaning "a man of great deeds, from Qavṣ᾿el"), refers to one of King David's soldiers in league with Yoshev ba-Sheveṭ of the tribe of Taḥkemoni (2 Sam. 23:8, 20).[82] Again, Ben Elᶜazar seems to be placing his book within the *maqāma* tradition. In the introduction to *Sefer ha-meshalim,* Ben Elᶜazar states that he adopted his fictional device from Arabic storytelling: "I did not mention my name in my stories, but I altered it and changed it to Lemu᾿el Ben Itti᾿el, for it is the practice of Ishmaelites to change their names in stories."[83]

In addition to such clear identifications with the *maqāma* tradition, scholars have pointed to other aspects of the book that ground it within the tradition of Arabic writing. Stories are set in cities of the Islamic world (e.g., Cairo and Aleppo) and describe Islamic architectural styles and cultural scenarios. One story (chapter 5) portrays a pederast, a common character in the *maqāma* literature and other Arabic forms.[84] However, one argument of the following chapters is that this evidence has been partly misinterpreted. This is not to say that such themes do not derive from Arabic sources as suggested. Rather, the discussion considers Ben Elᶜazar's selective and sometimes manipulative use of Arabic source materials. Several conventions of the *maqāma* and poetic genres, such as wine poetry and the poetry of sexual desire, for example, are evoked only to be carefully subverted. The book exhibits remarkable hybridity in that standard Arabic literary and cultural values are sometimes complemented or replaced by conventions reaching Iberia from the Christian north. In only a few cases is it possible to demonstrate that a literary theme or technique is necessarily of European rather than Arabic origin; in most cases, one can find precedent for Ben Elᶜazar's practices in both traditions, either of which could plausibly have been known by the Hebrew author.

Sefer ha-Meshalim *and Romance Literature*

In 1939, the year in which he first published chapters from *Sefer ha-meshalim,* Schirmann suggested that the future sources of the "love stories" might be found in French Romance. In his later writings, Schirmann largely retained this line of argumentation while accepting that specific sources might indeed be unknowable:

> It is reasonable, therefore, to assume that Ben Elᶜazar was influenced in his stories by his Christian environment. However, it is difficult to resolve the

> question of whether he used specific Christian stories that he knew or merely borrowed isolated motifs and employed them freely. There is room in this area for further research, and it is not impossible that the problem of Ben Elᶜazar's Christian sources will never be fully resolved.[85]

As is the case with al-Ḥarīzī, we do not know the extent of Ben Elᶜazar's exposure to European literature or even what languages the author knew (apart from Arabic and Hebrew); given that the author probably remained in Toledo for his entire life, it is difficult to imagine that he did not speak Castilian at the very least. The literary trends that were developing in Christendom likely reached the author's ears, if not his eyes. Although we do not have direct testimony concerning the author's contact with Christians, we can readily imagine such encounters, given that they were common for his contemporaries.

Most prominently, Schirmann attributed the love ideal of *Sefer ha-meshalim* to a Romance rather than an Arabic background even though he recognized that the Arabic corpus preserved a wide variety of texts on love such as the ᶜUdhrī lyric, court poetry, and Ibn Ḥazm's love treatise *The Ring of the Dove.*[86] Schirmann saw the love ideal in *Sefer ha-meshalim* as the reverse of that found in Arabic (and Andalusian Hebrew) poetry, largely because Ben Elᶜazar idealized "spiritual love" over "carnal love" and because women in *Sefer ha-meshalim* play active roles in their courtships.[87]

As stated, Ben Elᶜazar clearly had knowledge of Arabic literature. He knew Arabic well enough to write a grammatical treatise in that language and to translate *Kalīla wa dimnā* from Arabic into Hebrew. If we were to seek Arabic precedents for Ben Elᶜazar's treatment of love, the ᶜUdhrī tradition, with its emphasis on non-consummation and the pining of the lover for the beloved, and also Ibn Ḥazm's concluding chapter on spiritual love in *The Ring of the Dove* are suggestive. Schirmann realized that Ben Elᶜazar may have drawn on some Arabic materials but doubted that spiritual love would have surfaced in Hebrew literature under the influence of Ibn Ḥazm two hundred years after the composition of *The Ring of the Dove.*

In reality, "spiritual love" is not the best way to describe the love topos of *Sefer ha-meshalim,* nor is it the best way to capture the ideal in troubadour poetry or its descendant Romance. In all these models, love is "courtly" in that the lover must adhere to a set of rules and prove himself worthy of his beloved.[88] A. J. Denomy's definition is instructive:

> Courtly Love is a type of sensual love and what distinguishes it from other forms of sexual love, from mere passion, from so-called Platonic love, from

> married love is its purpose or motive, its formal object, namely, the lover's progress and growth in natural goodness, merit and worth.[89]

It is some of the behavioral ideals and the notion of the "lover's progress" (more than an idea of "spirituality") that *Sefer ha-meshalim* shares with troubadour poetry and Romance. The love topos of Arabic poetry might also be called "courtly" in that it functions according to a set of prescribed and proscribed behaviors, though it does not ascribe the same weight to the lover's "progress." Although Schirmann may not have understood the overlap between the courtly love topos of Europe and *Sefer ha-meshalim* properly or appreciated the possible influence of the ᶜUdhrī tradition sufficiently, his conclusion is still largely correct:

> It is fair to assume that the poets were influenced in this respect [i.e., their interest in "spiritual love"] by Christian authors who lived during this period. The poetry of the Provençal troubadours was known and accepted at this time in many countries, not only in southern France, but also in Spain, Portugal and Italy.[90]

This is not to say that Ben Elᶜazar simply wrote Hebrew versions of troubadour poetry; the lover never boasts over such skills as hunting the hare and ox. Yet *Sefer ha-meshalim* presents lovers who acquire their beloveds through the demonstration of behavioral virtues and progress. Raymond Scheindlin recognizes this point in a study that ties the function of love in the overall plots of *Sefer ha-meshalim* to Romance literature, noting a number of significant points of consistency: 1) The lover must endure some test before being united with the beloved; 2) Quarreling is part of the practice of lovers;[91] 3) The lover must learn to balance his desire for his beloved and his obligations to society.[92]

Ultimately, the question is not whether we can isolate a single source of influence for the love topos of *Sefer ha-meshalim*. One can imagine themes such as chastity, quarreling, or showing signs of lovesickness deriving from Arabic or Romance sources. The question is why, if Ben Elᶜazar was turning toward ᶜUdhrī or Arabic romance sources, he did so in thirteenth-century Christian Iberia whereas Hebrew authors prior to him neglected these areas of the Arabic tradition. Ben Elᶜazar likely found this love topos, which stood at odds with the one embraced by the Hebrew authors of al-Andalus and most authors of Arabic literature, appealing because it fit well within the literary and cultural environment of Christendom.

Another theme that has generally been attributed to the Romance tradition is that of the cross-dressed knights in the story of Yoshfeh and his two loves (chapter 7). Sleeping in bed with his lover Yefefiyah, Yoshfeh is kidnapped by Yemimah, who had acquired military arms and a horse. Throughout the ordeal, Yoshfeh does not realize that his kidnapper is a woman. The next morning, another rider (Yefefiyah, also dressed as a male knight) approaches on horseback and challenges Yemimah. Throughout their battle, Yoshfeh believes the two knights to be men.[93]

Tova Rosen has investigated the possible roots of this theme in European and Arabic sources.[94] Thirteenth-century Romance preserves tales of female militancy and women who cross-dress as men to fight in battle.[95] The theme of women who dress as men may have a historical basis in the Crusades, when some women joined the military expeditions of men as an act of faith.[96] However, medieval Arabic popular epics also preserve similar themes. Several examples involve "warrior women," some dressed in men's garb as they are in the European parallels.[97] There are even examples of two women who challenge each other in battle. To these examples from popular literature we can add a story from the *Kitāb al-aghānī* that involves a lover's passion for a woman whom he first encounters as a cross-dressed hunter.[98] In short, it may be impossible to conclude definitively whether the source of this theme is Arabic or Romance, especially since the French and Arabic traditions were developing simultaneously. As stated earlier in this chapter, al-Ḥarīzī grafts the theme of cross-dressing onto a *maqāma* by al-Hamadhānī; there is no reason to assume that al-Ḥarīzī's source for the motif was Arabic while Ben Elʿazar's was French; indeed, the motif seems to have belonged to multiple literary traditions that converged in Christian Iberia.

Allegory

One general question faced when encountering *Sefer ha-meshalim* is whether the stories relate to some philosophical or moral reality beyond the surface meanings of the texts. How should we translate the title of the book, *Sefer ha-meshalim:*[99] The Book of Allegories? The Book of Parables? The Book of Fables? The Book of Proverbs? The Book of Exempla? The Book of Stories?[100] The Book of Poems? The Book of Prophetic Discourses?[101] The word *meshalim* can certainly convey each of these meanings. Aspects of the book suggest a philosophical allegorical reading. Chapter 1 explicitly identifies itself as a philosophical allegory of the Intellect and the Soul expressed through the language of love. Rosen has recently discussed this extremely complex amatory allegory wherein the dramatis personae consist of the narrator; his heart (a synecdoche for the body); his rational soul (portrayed as a woman); the soul's beloved, who is the Intellect (embodied as a handsome army general); and the general's paramour (a feminine personification of

Wisdom).[102] Through a dramatic sequence of erotic dreams, love quests, and jealous interlopings, the soul seeks her beloved, the Intellect, who is the gardener of Wisdom. At the conclusion, the immortal soul teaches the mortal narrator basics of Neoplatonic philosophy (emanation, hypostases, the four elements, the order of creation, etc.).[103] Ben Elᶜazar concludes the chapter with a couplet:

> The allegory of the Intellect has been completed, conveyed through
> [a story of] love.
> Consider its positive [aspect], my friend, but let not your soul bear
> anything blemished.

It is clear that such a story emanates from the same intellectual world as *Le Roman de la rose.* One might compare the speaker's tumultuous quest for the Rose in the *Roman* with the soul's quest for the Intellect as well as general devices such as dream narration and personification. There is a significant parallel between the soul's instruction in Neoplatonic philosophy toward the end of Ben Elᶜazar's tale and the teachings of Natura and Genius toward the end of the *Roman.* Also, the admonition in Ben Elᶜazar's final couplet reminds the reader of the God of Love's advice in the *Roman:* "Take care not to utter dirty words or anything bawdy. You should never open your mouth to name anything base."[104]

Still, the style of allegory is executed differently in the two texts. In the *Roman,* the narrator enters a world of personified vices, virtues, emotions, gods, and goddesses (characters bear names such as Envy, Jealousy, Resistance, Hope, Chastity, the God of Love, Natura) who interact with him and with one another. In *Sefer ha-meshalim,* the first-person speaker describes events that take place within him but does not interact with the characters in the same manner. Although the heart and Intellect may act with jealousy or passion, the characters are always concrete parts of the narrator's self and not personifications of emotional abstractions. In the *Roman,* one is never told exactly what the Rose signifies or what the narrator's union with it means. Even Genius's explanation of the garden and the spring (with obvious Christological overtones) toward the end of the *Roman* does not provide a solution for the text as a whole. The reader is left to decipher the mystifying text with little hope of working out all of its intricacies. Ben Elᶜazar's chapter, although extremely complex in its narrative structure and ontological status, clearly identifies all of its characters, providing the reader with an interpretive map. Finally, whereas the Intellect is the goal of the soul's pursuit in *Sefer ha-meshalim,* Reason is maligned in the *Roman,* for it is she who strives to dissuade the speaker from following the advice of the God of Love.

In any case, at least this one chapter of *Sefer ha-meshalim* may be called an allegory in the proper sense. The question, then, is whether the rest of the book should be read as philosophical allegory. Some chapters are understood best as exempla that resist interpretation in light of philosophical ideas. For example, in chapter 10 the narrator departs his hometown of ᶜAdᶜadah because sin and violence had grown rampant. He wanders until he reaches Qedesh, where he encounters a pack of wolves and takes one of the newborn cubs to raise as his own. At the same time, he happens upon a youth who has strayed from his parents, whom he also takes home to raise. For some time, the wolf grows up to be trustworthy and the boy to be wise and humble, but ultimately each reverts to his original nature. The boy surrounds himself with scoundrels (*nevalim*), apparently the people of his original stock, and leaves his adoptive father. Similarly, the wolf happens upon a flock of sheep and goats and leaves his master to pursue the flock. When the wolf's master asks him, "Will you repay my kindness with cruelty?," the wolf replies in his own defense, "I can only act in accordance with my lineage for I am no better than my ancestors!"[105] The narrator responds with resignation, "I raised and exalted sons but they transgressed against me. From that day forward, I knew that the branch followed its root and sprig and that the son followed his people and seed."[106] Just as the wolf remains a wolf, even when raised in captivity, so the son of a scoundrel remains a scoundrel, even when raised in good culture. The story, which has clear parallels in Arabic and European sources, is a straightforward parable with a clear moral and does not refer to any philosophical reality beyond what is presented.[107] If all the stories of *Sefer ha-meshalim* are, in fact, *meshalim*, then the term is being used in several senses and does not fit neatly into modern categories of reading.

The most pressing question is whether the so-called love stories should be read as philosophical allegories, parables of the mundane, or as love stories in the plain sense only. Has Ben Elᶜazar, in the first chapter, the "Allegory of the Intellect," spoken through the language of love, offered the reader a hermeneutic guide for interpreting the love stories? Schirmann writes that "in [the love stories], the border between reality, legend and allegory [*mashal*] is blurred."[108] The use of character names signifying gems (Sapir, Peninah), beauty (Shapir, Yefefiyah), intelligence (Maskil), and celestial bodies (Sahar, Kimah) make allegorical readings tempting. Is it significant, for example, that the names Sapir (sapphire) and Shapir (handsome), lovers in chapter 5, are also words used by the soul to describe herself in chapter 1?[109] Perhaps significantly, the last part of the narrator's name, Rav Peᶜalim me-Qavṣ'el, is also the name of a character in Don Vidal Benveniste's (late fourteenth–early fifteenth century) allegorical love story "Meliṣat ᶜefer ve-dinah."[110] In the second part of Benveniste's text, the author specifically identifies each character with a philosophical counterpart, Rav Peᶜalim signifying the Active Intellect (*ha-sekhel ha-poᶜel*), linked through the shared root *pᶜl*.[111] Although it would be anachronistic to impose the same meaning upon Ben Elᶜazar's narrator, it is possible that the author does use names to signify ideas outside of the text.

Raymond Scheindlin does not see the love stories as philosophical allegories but as "worldly allegories" (what others might call parables or exempla) relating to human impulses, impulses that form the focal tension of much Romance literature: the desire for love on one hand and the duty of social responsibility on the other. Regarding the love story of Sapir and Shapir, Scheindlin writes:

> It would seem that the scene is nothing but allegorical [*alegori*] and that the two lovers possessing nearly identical names are nothing but two inner inclinations within a single personality. The subject of the story is thus the balance of two contrary impulses in man: the admiration of beauty, the passive impulse, represented by Sapir; and participation in society, the active impulse, represented by Shapir.[112]

Similarly, Scheindlin sees Yoshfeh's two loves in chapter 7 as opposing forces: Yefefiyah represents beauty while Yemimah represents social responsibility.[113] For Scheindlin, the messages of the love stories do extend beyond their plain meanings but are still mundane. Characters signify real inclinations that people interested in social and moral development face in the course of their lives.

Whether the love stories contain hidden messages of philosophical significance is difficult to evaluate. If we try to match up characters in stories with specific concepts, the alignment is never as neat as in chapter 1. However, as Matti Huss points out, allegory need not provide a one-to-one correspondence between a figure in the story and an external concept. Some of the most famous allegories in European literature (e.g., *Le Roman de la rose*) vigorously resist neat analysis, a point that has led to a bewildering number of interpretations. Allegory's very appeal is often tied to its ambiguity. The final verdict on the meaning of the love stories, insofar as there can ever be one, seems far off. Unfortunately, we do not know how the stories were interpreted by medieval readers. The one surviving manuscript of *Sefer ha-meshalim* is bound together with Berekhia ha-Naqdan's *Mishlei shuᶜalim*

(Fox fables), which does not present philosophical material.[114] Perhaps more light will be shed through the study of Ben Elʿazar's still-unpublished philosophical works.

Structure

AUTHORIAL VOICE

Sefer ha-meshalim appears on the surface to be among the most classical Hebrew rhymed prose narratives, with only al-Ḥarīzī's and perhaps Ibn Ṣaqbel's works adhering more closely to the classical style. The book consists of several episodes, not one, and each episode is introduced with the fixed phrase *Neʾum Lemuʾel Ben Ittiʾel* (Lemuʾel Ben Ittiʾel spoke), as is typical of what Huss calls the Andalusian Hebrew *maqāmāt.*[115] Still, numerous aspects of *Sefer ha-meshalim* separate it from the classical *maqāma* tradition. Lemuʾel Ben Ittiʾel does not stand in opposition to a single protagonist who resurfaces in each story; he is not a foil, the victim of a scoundrel's pranks, or an accomplice in a trickster's ruses. In fact, he only appears as an active character in half of the episodes (1, 2, 3, 8, 10). In the four chapters published by Schirmann as "love stories," Lemuʾel narrates discrete tales that involve their own protagonists and does not participate at all. Lemuʾel is primarily a relater of events (an extradiegetic narrator) and an occasional actor in rhetorical and moralistic episodes (an intradiegetic narrator). When he does act, he is the protagonist himself, one who is morally upright and not mendacious.

Like al-Ḥarīzī, Ben Elʿazar occasionally inserts himself into the text, here identifying with the perspective of the narrator. In chapter 1, when the narrator awakes at the end of a long dream sequence placed in the mouth of Lemuʾel Ben Ittiʾel, it is written: "And *Jacob* awoke from his sleep" (Gen. 28:16),[116] which is self-referential. Most conspicuously, the author writes quite plainly in the introduction (as mentioned also above): "I did not mention my name in my stories, but I altered it and changed it to Lemuʾel Ben Ittiʾel."[117] Whereas authorial voice in the *Taḥkemoni* exists in the interplay among characters' speech, it is more centralized in *Sefer ha-meshalim* in the voice of the narrator. Still, one can never assume complete identity between the author and his narrator (even in examples wherein the narrator bears the name, or a nickname, of the author).[118]

At times, Ben Elʿazar plays with the fictitious status of his narratives and references characters from one chapter within the fictional world of another chapter. At the beginning of chapter 3, the poet Yeḥiʾel Ben Yeraḥmeʾel asks his literary companions, "Have you seen the poetry of Yemimah the beloved of Yoshfeh [a character from chapter 7]?" and praises the imagery contained in a specific verse.[119] This feature might be compared with Cervantes's metafictional practice of referencing his own works within the fictional worlds of his other works, as when Don Quixote's niece finds (and burns) books by Cervantes standing on the bookshelf of her uncle, who is also Cervantes's creation.[120] Such metafictional devices lay bare the mechanics of creating fiction and humorously remind the reader that the author is just behind the curtain. A broad study of such phenomena across literary traditions is in order.

PLOT, CHARACTER DEVELOPMENT

The patterns of plot development in the love stories of *Sefer ha-meshalim* are quite distinct from those of the classical *maqāma* and the Andalusian *maqāmāt*. Although a structural comparison between these stories and all Arabic and European literary forms is impossible, some basic points of comparison with the *maqāma*, Arabic romance, and French Romance are made below.

Whereas plot resolution in the classical *maqāma* materializes through anagnorisis, resolution in the love stories depends on character evolution and the tying up of diverse narrative threads. Episodes usually present some sort of tension, which is resolved through the course of the narrative, often through a test endured by the protagonist. Characters are far from static; they face challenges, disappointments, fall in love, and mature. The episodes of the *Taḥkemoni*, in contrast, always begin and end the same way, with the narrator and the protagonist traveling on their separate paths and ready for an encounter. The narrator never grows wiser, and the protagonist never departs from his picaro lifestyle. In contrast, the episodes of *Sefer ha-meshalim* exhibit a great diversity of developments.

In chapter 5, the bird hunter Sapir pursues his beloved Shapir (both lover and beloved are male), though Shapir is lured away by the wicked pederast Birshᶜa from Sodom, whom he mistakes for a righteous judge. Sapir wanders in search of his beloved until he finds Shapir by a spring with Birshᶜa. Shapir is grateful that Sapir has come to his rescue. Rather than fighting over the youth, Birshᶜa and Sapir agree to stand before a judge, who sentences Birshᶜa to death.[121]

In chapter 6, Maskil and Peninah exchange love poems, fall in love, and enjoy each other by the "River of Love," until a gigantic black horseman disrupts their tryst by threatening Maskil. Maskil mounts his horse and overcomes his adversary in battle; the lovers marry and spend "all of their days in tranquillity and favor, enjoying their days in peace and their years in sweetness."[122]

In chapter 7, Yoshfeh leaves his parents' home in a time of political crisis and descends with a band of hooligans to Cairo, where he has an adventure with two beloveds. After being kidnapped by Yemimah and witnessing Yemimah and Yefefiyah battling over him in the guise of men, he comes to enjoy the love of both. When a third horseman approaches, Yoshfeh valiantly mounts a horse with spear in hand and vaunts an attack. The horseman, it turns out, is only Yoshfeh's servant Masos, who has come to announce the restoration of peace in Yoshfeh's hometown. Still, Yoshfeh's display of valor represents a sign of maturation through a sort of test. Yoshfeh returns home with his two beloveds and his servant, who is ultimately married to Yoshfeh's sister.

In chapter 9, Sahar arrives a stranger in Aleppo and, through a rather unchivalrous adventure in the king's palace, is taught the practice of courtly love by the princess Kimah. The two are married, and Sahar ascends the royal throne after Kimah's father's death. This episode is discussed further below.

In these examples, the unfolding of the plot involves a transformation of the main character. The protagonists usually begin naïve, immature, ineloquent, and unworldly and undergo some transformative experience through a test such as being initiated into battle or learning the importance of poetic improvisation for romantic courtship. Shapir matures beyond his youthful naïveté, and Sapir, through an arduous pursuit, wins his beloved back from the wicked pederast. Yoshfeh leaves his home a foolish and passive youth and returns a capable and chivalrous lover. Sahar comes to Aleppo ignorant of sophisticated behavior, learns the art of courtly love from Kimah, and later to balance his duties as a married man and political ruler. Maskil falls in love and fights valiantly to protect his affair from a rival.

TIME

Sefer ha-meshalim cannot be said to take place in any singular time. Because the narrator relates a number of first-person events and the author professes identification with the narrator, the reader might assume that some events take place during the lifetime of the author. However, we should not understand Ben Elᶜazar's identification with his narrator in a stringent sense; the stories are not autobiographical. The stories in which the narrator appears as a bearer of tales are not set at any particular time.[123]

Relative to the lives of the stories' central characters, the episodes do not take place in biographical time (i.e., connecting episodes from birth until the present, or until death, within some explanatory narrative) but fit well with the "adventure-time" chronotope of chivalric Romance, which Bakhtin describes as exhibiting a "*subjective playing with time,* an emotional and lyrical stretching and compressing of it."[124] In French Romance, the romances of *The Thousand and One Nights,* and in *Sefer ha-meshalim,* we are shown neither short snippets of experience nor full spans of life.[125] Instead, the stories narrate limited episodes in the lives of characters that are somehow transformative.[126] The chronotope is obviously quite different from that of the classical *maqāma,* which shows only brief moments of unchanging characters' lives.

Other techniques of narrative time distinguish *Sefer ha-meshalim* from classical *maqāma* structure. One feature is the attempt to narrate events taking place in more than one location simultaneously. In chapter 7, Yoshfeh buys Yefefiyah at the slave market and takes her to a palace to consummate their relationship. Following the description of these events, the narrator whisks the reader back to the slave market, where the embittered Yemimah is plotting to kidnap Yoshfeh:

> The two [Yoshfeh and Yefefiyah] were grasping ears, touching cheeks, kissing lips, winking eyes, battling with eyelids. And in the market of maidens there was a lovely maiden adorned with crystals. When she saw that Yoshfeh had left her behind and did not take her, she grew angry. Her name was Yemimah.[127]

Yemimah acquires arms and a horse and sets off in pursuit of the lovers. We know that the events are simultaneous because Yoshfeh and Yefefiyah are still in bed when Yemimah reaches the palace. Although this device for portraying simultaneous events is the most simple one possible, its very existence distinguishes the narrative needs of al-Ḥarīzī and Ben Elᶜazar.

DEVICES OF CONCLUSION

Whereas classical *maqāmāt* always end as they begin, with the narrator and protagonist continuing on their respective journeys, the love stories in *Sefer ha-meshalim* always offer a definitive sense of conclusion. In chapter 5, the wicked pederast Birshᶜa is sentenced to death and Sapir and Shapir are reunited. In chapter 6, after the death of their adversary Kushan, Maskil and Peninah erect a heap of stones over him, just as Joshua and the Israelites erected a heap of stones over their enemy Akhan Ben Zeraḥ (Joshua 7). In chapter 8, which is discussed at length in the next chapter of this book, the villain Akhbor is murdered and cast into a pit while his maidservants seek a new life beyond his control.[128] In chapter 9, Sahar marries Kimah and inherits her father's throne (further below).

In some instances, the conclusion is conveyed through an epilogue, a glimpse of the future (relative to the story's main events, still past relative to the narrator's place in history). Concluding sections of stories are introduced with "It happened days later" or "It happened thereafter";[129] although the stories might have ended before this point, the inclusion of the epilogue allows for a conclusion with an even greater sense of resolution or a final unexpected twist. Again, this feature reveals a change in narrative technique between the works of al-Ḥarīzī and Ben Elᶜazar.

MINOR CHARACTERS

Whereas minor characters are seldom found in the classical *maqāmāt,* Ben Elᶜazar works with several characters at a time and concludes his narratives without leaving loose ends. At the conclusion of the story of Yoshfeh and his two loves, for example, Yoshfeh returns to his hometown not only with Yefefiyah and Yemimah, but also with Masos, who had been his servant in Egypt.[130] Masos is married to Yoshfeh's sister Ṣipur, whom Yefefiyah and Yemimah teach courtly manners and love poetry. As is common in Arabic romance and in French Romance (and also in Shakespearean comedy), even minor characters find new fates by intertwining their lives with those of the protagonists. In Chrétien de Troyes' practice of *conjointure,* the "putting together" of the poem, several narrative strains involving minor and major characters are woven together to form a coherent whole.[131] Ben Elᶜazar's practice more closely resembles examples from *The Thousand and One Nights,* as when the Persian physician in the story of Niᶜma and Nuᶜm is appointed vizier by the caliph for having demonstrated acumen and skill in helping the couple reunify.

From *Maqāma* to romance

The view that *Sefer ha-meshalim* follows the structure of the classical *maqāma* is only true with respect to the book's most superficial qualities—prosody and the use of certain fixed phrases (So-and-so son of So-and-so spoke, etc.). Although he was indebted to the *maqāma* tradition, Ben Elᶜazar applied new narrative ideals involving complex plots with protagonists who overcome flaws, mature, and undergo transformations. Sahar, Yoshfeh, Maskil, and Sapir all fit the model of a lover who endures some test to be unified with his beloved. Sahar learns to adhere to the proper code of love and thereby becomes fit for marriage and political leadership. Yoshfeh's flaw is his passivity, which he overcomes through his adventure with Yefefiyah and Yemimah, both model knights. Once he has learned chivalry, he returns home with his beloveds as a mature member of society. Maskil thwarts a foe in battle to be unified with his beloved. Sapir allows his relationship with Shapir to be disrupted by a rival until he strives for reunification. The stories fit best within the genre of romance, though it remains a question as to whether they are identified best with Arabic romances or French Romances.

A closer examination of chapter 9 will help elucidate Ben Elᶜazar's narrative ideals, especially since this episode may be compared with the earliest text from the Hebrew rhymed prose corpus, Ibn Ṣaqbel's "Neᵓum asher ben yehudah," and has clear Arabic and French parallels.[132] Ben Elᶜazar's episode begins in the season of spring, when a youth of royal blood named Sahar, "whose cheek was clothed in light and splendor," leaves his home of Gat Rimon. He is traveling by boat when he is caught in a storm that leaves him shipwrecked on the "shores of Aleppo."[133] While he is reciting a poem about God's might, a maiden spots him and beholds his beauty. She tells the news to her mother, who relates it to another woman, until all the maidens of the city descend to the seashore to behold the handsome youth. Sahar inquires about a booming voice he hears coming from the "house of prayer." Two armed black men (*kushim*) approach Sahar and capture him in a net. Sahar recites an eloquent poem about his misfortune, leaving the women astounded. They are awed equally by his physical beauty and by the beauty of his words. From behind a wall, a lovely "gazelle" named Kimah tosses Sahar an apple inscribed with a short love poem. Sahar beholds Kimah's beauty, and she blows him a kiss. One of the king's eunuchs chastises her for her forward behavior and shuts the palace doors before Sahar. Sahar and Kimah are both left brokenhearted, full of longing and desire.

Sahar weeps desperately in the streets until a young woman bearing a love poem, one of Kimah's messengers, informs him that the maiden who had sent him the apple was named Kimah and that she was a princess. Sahar exclaims, "Draw me after you, let us run!"[134] and the envoy leads him to the palace. In the courtyard, where Sahar is left alone, two beautiful maidens approach and lead him to a bed to rest. Sahar is then led to another chamber, where there are four maidens. Sahar prostrates himself at their feet and asks naïvely, "Which of you is my mistress Kimah?" They order him to lift up his eyes and behold a curtain upon which is written, "Read this poem before you enter the room," followed by a poem with advice for courting Kimah. To win his beloved, Sahar will have to speak eloquently and compose love songs. Sahar desperately continues hoping for his beloved to appear and asks the maidens for assistance. They tease him a bit before bringing him to the entrance of an inner court, which is covered with another curtain inscribed with a poem:

Before you enter the room, love, lift up your eyes and read the curtain's writing.
Come in humility to its inner court, then you will be given passage in the fawn's house.
Choose brief words on a sweet matter, and then your soul will be drawn after the heart of a lover.
Rejoice in a fawn, then your soul will find pleasure and possess all that it desires.

Sahar enters the chamber and behold, there are now eight maidens. He inquires after his beloved, but they chide him by twisting biblical quotations out of context: "Your question is too profound for us! It is deep, deep, who can find it out? [Eccles. 7:24]. How can you seek Kimah on the earth?[135] Do you not quake, do you not tremble? Who has [ever] ascended to the heavens and descended?"[136] Sahar responds with a clever poem about "Kimah of the earth" (i.e., not of the heavens) and then shouts aloud, begging the women to help him. He is told to read yet another poem inscribed upon a curtain before entering the next chamber, where Sahar meets another group of women, who hand him a scroll with a poem to read.

Finally, after much frustration and exhaustion, Sahar is surrounded by a crowd that regales him with much pomp and leads him to Kimah. He exclaims, "Would that I could see my beloved Kimah! Come what may! Alas, my roaring has poured forth like water!" Sahar has thus displayed essential signs of the courtly lover: the outward display of his lovesickness and the bold pronouncement of his feelings. Hearing his words, Kimah responds sweetly, "My heart has wandered twice as much as yours, as the reed wanders in water. My heart has gone out from within me for it is burnt by the flame of separation from you." She recites a love poem, approaches him, prostrates herself before him, and allows him to kiss her upon the hand but not upon the lips.[137] Disappointed and confused, Sahar's face falls. Kimah assures him, "Why has your face fallen? Is it our desire to kiss and embrace? Such is not done in our place. Rather, our desire and the desire of nobility is to purify and whiten hearts."

The two exchange sweet words, and Kimah leads Sahar inside a chamber made of glass, surrounded on all sides by water. Thinking naïvely that he will drown, Sahar undresses in order to swim. Kimah explains the construction of the chamber, and there the two take delight in each other, exchanging love poems without touching each other all night long. In the morning, a maiden comes and informs Kimah that her father, the king, is approaching and that she should hide Sahar. The king walks in just as Sahar is concealing himself and strikes him, threatening to throw him in prison. Kimah convinces her father that their love is pure, and the two are allowed to marry.

A great feast lasting an entire year is made for the couple.[138] Ultimately, the king falls ill and dies. Sahar gets up from the feast, buries the king, and inherits the throne. In an epilogue, we learn that Sahar and Kimah went back and forth between quarreling and renewing their love for many years: "And so Sahar and Kimah argued from time to time. Hence they renewed their love and led it [forward], whetting the swords of their desire. But enmity never arose between them, and the soul of one longed and pined for the other."[139]

The story of Sahar and Kimah shares many points of commonality with the earliest Hebrew rhymed prose narrative, "Neʾum asher ben yehudah," by Ibn Ṣaqbel. In both stories, the desire of the lover is aroused when a maiden behind a wall tosses him an apple inscribed with a love poem. In both stories, the lovers' meeting is prolonged through the protagonist's encounters with other maidens. Both stories present the motif of an older man, the "master of the house" or the "king," interfering with the tryst and threatening the lover. However, *Sefer ha-meshalim* diverges from its parent text in many respects. Throughout Sahar's frustrating attempts to reach his beloved through her maidservants, he reads many poems that simultaneously assure him of Kimah's love for him and instruct him in the practice of courtly love. Asher, on the other hand, is given no such instruction. The texts diverge most significantly from the moment of encounter between the lovers. Whereas the beloved in "Neʾum asher ben yehudah" is revealed to be a man in disguise, retaining the *maqāma*'s resolution through ruse and anagnorisis, Sahar and Kimah are ultimately united. This conversion of the parent text highlights the narrative's focus on the love ideal, a love that is chaste and pure and that leads to a lasting union.

Raymond Scheindlin sees Asher in "Neʾum asher ben yehudah" as a ridiculous parody of a courtly lover who misses every opportunity to prove himself capable of sophisticated behavior. Asher never learns to recite poetry, as is demanded of the lover. Sahar, on the other hand, undergoes a process of maturation, largely through the instruction of his wiser and more sophisticated beloved. Sahar arrives in Aleppo a stranger, unfamiliar with the ways of the land. He is confused by the booming voice coming from the "house of prayer," undoubtedly a mosque, and does not know to comply with the local sexual code of limiting kisses to the hand.[140] He is baffled by the glass chamber, believing that he would drown in the surrounding water. Although endowed with beauty and an eloquent tongue, Sahar does not understand the code of courtly behavior—specifically, how to woo his beloved through refined poetry.

Sahar is an extremely passive, even feminized, character. He is shipwrecked, captured in a net, and led from chamber to chamber without making any of his own choices. When Kimah's envoy invites him to the palace, he responds with the words of the *female* speaker in the Song of Songs: "Draw me after you, let us run!" He blunders many times in his pursuit of Kimah. Standing before four of Kimah's servants, he crudely and naïvely asks which is his beloved. Without rebuking him, the maidens direct him to read a poem, his first lesson. Entering chambers deeper within the palace, he continues to err until he learns to recite poetry in praise of his beloved. A turning point is certainly Sahar's clever poem about the earthly, rather than the celestial, Kimah. Another is his bold proclamation that actually causes Kimah to respond. However, once united with Kimah, Sahar continues to display his lack of refinement until the lovers become entwined in a mutual game of exchanging verses, the key to a cultured affair. Sahar continues to take two steps forward and one step back until he finally reaches a point of maturity in marriage. Not only is he a capable lover, but he is also fit to rule. He ascends the throne after the death of the king and sustains his marriage with Kimah. By getting up from his wedding feast and ascending the throne, Sahar succeeds in balancing his duty for social responsibility with his love.[141]

Although "Neʾum asher ben yehudah" and the story of Sahar and Kimah both conclude with the marriage of the protagonist, the institution of marriage bears a different connotation in each text. As Scheindlin suggests, Asher's marriage to the daughter of the man who duped him is a further sign of his uncourtliness. Sahar's marriage, in contrast, is attained through the consummation of a real pursuit, one through which the protagonist matures and learns the ways of the world and of love.

Apart from "Neʾum asher ben yehudah," other sources and parallels can be identified in works by Jewish and Muslim authors. Sahar's fear of drowning upon beholding the glass chamber evokes a legend concerning King Solomon and the Queen of Sheba in the Aramaic *Targum sheni.* When the queen is brought into the king's presence, he is seated in a glass chamber. Thinking that his throne is situated in a pool of water, she lifts her skirts (revealing her hairy legs). As Jacob Lassner has shown, this story also has important allusions in the Qurʾān and parallels in later Islamic texts that preserve the details of the water-like glass chamber and the queen's reaction. (Interestingly, the Queen of Sheba legend and the story of Sahar and Kimah both hinge on gender reversal; Sahar is feminized by behaving like the queen, just as the queen is made masculine through the attribution of hairy legs.)[142] Other elements call to mind motifs from *The Thousand and One Nights.* In the story of Masrūr and Zayn al-Mawāsif, poems are inscribed on jewelry, clothing, and on curtains. In the story of ᶜAzīz and ᶜAzīza, the uncourtly ᶜAzīz, who was beckoned by a fetching woman from behind a lattice, is given instructions on courtship by his cousin ᶜAzīza (who is really in love with him and dies of lovesickness).[143]

The final scenes, wherein Sahar and Kimah spend the night in conversation and convince her father of the purity of their love, call to mind a story from the *Kitāb al-aghānī* that relates the affair of al-Aḥwaṣ, the lover of Salāma, a servant (and sexual possession) of the caliph Yazīd. The lovers meet secretly within the palace while Yazīd observes them from a hiding place. The lovers weep on account of their passion and "did not stop conversing until dawn," exchanging sweet words and verses of poetry. As al-Aḥwaṣ is skulking off, Yazīd seizes him and demands that they reveal the truth about the night's events. "They told him and recited the verses they had recited without omitting a letter or changing anything from what [Yazīd] had heard." Satisfied with their honesty, Yazīd asks them if they love each other, to which they both respond in the affirmative (and in verse), and he ultimately gives Salāma to al-Aḥwaṣ in marriage.[144]

Ben Elᶜazar seems to draw upon an established topos of Arabic writing involving a lover's successful pursuit of a beloved (who is associated with a powerful male figure) through a palace adventure. Such themes are also prominent in *The Thousand and One Nights,* as in the story of Niᶜma and Nuᶜm.[145] Like Sahar, the suitor Niᶜma is rather uncourtly and feminized (he sneaks into the palace disguised as a slave girl, loses his way, and nearly passes out). Again, the story concludes with the caliph bestowing his favor upon the lovers, who had met clandestinely. By the twelfth century, the "love in the palace" topos had also penetrated French literature, as evidenced in *Le Conte de Floire et Blanchefleur.*

It is thus obvious that Ben Elᶜazar modified Ibn Ṣaqbel's story quite significantly to fit a different set of narrative ideals. Anagnorisis, the ruse, and the narrator-protagonist relationship are all abandoned in favor of adventure, character maturation, sanctioned love, and union. In using "Neʾum asher ben yehudah" as the point of departure for the story of Sahar and Kimah, Ben Elᶜazar does not merely imitate the parent text; rather, the new story conspicuously inverts the literary and cultural ideals of the text produced in al-Andalus. By keeping the parent text just beneath the surface, the author plays on the reader's expectations and highlights the freshness of his material. The practice of inverting *maqāma* plotlines in *Sefer ha-meshalim* is treated further in chapter 6 of this book.

Between romance and Romance

For the story of Sahar and Kimah, Ben Elᶜazar did not need to look far beyond plotlines and motifs that were present or emerging in the Arabic tradition. The pith of Ben Elᶜazar's story can be related plausibly to the skeletal presentation of the "love in the palace" adventure in the story of al-Aḥwaṣ and Salāma from the *Kitāb al-aghānī;* Sahar and Kimah would largely be at home in the world of *The Thousand and One Nights,* especially when we consider the comparable blundering of Niᶜma and Sahar and the general narrative flow of the two stories. The main differences between the stories of Niᶜma and Nuᶜm and of Sahar and Kimah (apart from such obvious points as Nuᶜm's being the caliph's slave rather than his daughter) are the active role played by Kimah in pursuing her beloved and the process of maturation that Sahar successfully undergoes. As Heath mentions, characters in the romances of *The Thousand and One Nights* are largely passive (Niᶜma's only active role is his sneaking into the palace, which he does by covering his masculinity and with the help of a physician); although the reader witnesses the protagonists' maturation, in the *Nights* it is Fate that brings couples together or cuts them asunder, not their own perseverance or inaction. The ultimate unification of Niᶜma and Nuᶜm derives from the socially sanctioned form of their relationship (being husband and concubine), whereas Kimah transforms Sahar into a courtly lover deserving of her love. For his part, Sahar learns to adhere to the courtly code, which makes him deserving of the love and power he comes to enjoy.

The protagonists of *Sefer ha-meshalim* are thus conspicuously more active than their counterparts in *The Thousand and One Nights.* This is even more pronounced in the other stories of *Sefer ha-meshalim,* wherein lovers assume risks and take up arms in battle. These stories also do not present Arabic parallels as readily as the story of Sahar and Kimah. To be sure, Arabic epics present heroes who thwart their enemies in battle, but they do not undergo internal transformations; these protagonists are presented as brave and chivalrous from childhood until their heroic deaths. The active role of the protagonists in controlling their destinies in *Sefer ha-meshalim* may reveal an affinity with narrative ideals of the French tradition, wherein scholars have understood plot development as a transformation between two states of being for the protagonist. In many Romance examples, the protagonist is granted worldly success, then realizes that his existence is flawed (that he is not sufficiently chivalrous or is so consumed with love that he neglects social responsibility), and finally embarks on an adventure through which the flaw is resolved.[146] In Chrétien's *Yvain,* for example, the protagonist rejects who he is, a knight whose preoccupation with honor is a detriment to his marriage, to become a chivalrous knight who can balance the quest for honor with mature love (even abandoning his name to adopt the epithet "the Knight of the Lion").[147]

Of course, Sahar is no Yvain, nor is Maskil, Yoshfeh, or Sapir. Ben Elᶜazar does not create protagonists who embark upon chivalrous forest adventures or engage in tournaments to earn love and prestige. Yet his characters do embody the internal transformations characteristic of Romance protagonists. They fall somewhere between characters such as Niᶜma and Asher, who are essentially incompetents, and the masculine and self-reliant heroes of Romance. Ben Elᶜazar's protagonists are not chivalrous by nature; they are flawed but ultimately rise to challenging occasions. Chrétien de Troyes' protagonists usually possess admirable qualities innately but still must undergo tests to balance love and social responsibility. Although Ben Elᶜazar's stories are never as complex as Chrétien's lengthy Romances, there are notable parallels at the most basic level of character development and the use of a test as a narrative device.

There is no reason to assume that Ben Elᶜazar drew solely upon Arabic or French sources to the exclusion of the other. Many elements of *Sefer ha-meshalim* seem closely related to Arabic romances while others—especially the love topos, the tests of chivalry, and the fundamental position of character development as a structural device—place the book comfortably within the Romance environment. Ben Elᶜazar seems to mix traditions with a fairly liberal yet artful hand. The author appears particularly fond of elements that were popular in *both* the Arabic and Romance sources.

Sefer ha-meshalim is important both for the literary models it emulates and for those it rejects. The love stories embody a clear shift away from the literary values of the classical *maqāma* and a movement toward the romance genre that was gaining momentum in Christian Europe and in the Near East. *Sefer ha-meshalim* reveals the hybrid literary and cultural environment in which it was forged, although the precise contours of the book's hybridity remain obscured by the limits of our knowledge concerning the interpenetration of Arabic and French sources. One might view the book primarily as a part of the trend of transferring Arabic knowledge to Christian Europe, a trend in which Jews and Christians participated alike. At the same time, the book can be viewed as a product of the confluence of Arabic and European traditions in Iberia, the dynamic crossroads where the Islamic and Christian worlds met.

Six

Voice

Maqāma and Morality

> Instead of the virginal fullness of an inexhaustible object, the prose writer is faced with a multiplicity of routes, roads, and paths that have been laid down in the object by social consciousness. Along with the internal contradictions of the object itself, the prose writer comes to discover as well the social heteroglossia that surrounds the object, the Tower of Babel confusion of languages that goes on around any object. The dialectics of the object are interwoven with the social dialogue surrounding it. For the prose writer, the object is a condensation of heterological voices among which his own voice must also resound; these voices create the background necessary for his own voice, without which his literary nuances would not be perceived, and without which they "do not sound."
>
> —Mikhail Bakhtin[1]

In the previous chapter, voice was introduced as a topic within the framework of narrative structure. It was shown that voice is not centered within the speech of any one character of the *Taḥkemoni,* whereas it is more concentrated in the speech of the narrator in *Sefer ha-meshalim.* Also, the *Taḥkemoni* utilizes an intradiegetic narrator throughout, whereas *Sefer ha-meshalim* alternates between an intradiegetic and an extradiegetic narrator. The present chapter considers the implications of these strategies for understanding how the *Taḥkemoni* and *Sefer ha-meshalim* relate to social issues of thirteenth-century Jewish life. As discussed elsewhere in this book, the relationship between literature and reality is exceedingly complex. The aim here is not to determine the medieval Hebrew mechanics of representing reality (hence the chapter is not a part of the project initiated by Erich Auerbach's *Mimesis*).[2] Nor is the aim to evaluate on a philosophical level whether reality can be represented by literature at all (Paul De Man was undoubtedly right, to an extent, when he wrote that "it is not *a priori* certain that literature is a reliable source of information about anything but its own language").[3] Rather, the purpose is to study how some topics of "real life" exist within and are refracted by the texts; we are interested less in how the *Taḥkemoni* and *Sefer ha-meshalim* create a sense of reality than in how they

Taḥkemoni and *Sefer ha-meshalim* create a sense of reality than in how they simultaneously reveal it and conceal it. Central to the discussion is the significance of narrative structure and the role of narrative voice.

Authorial Screens in the *Taḥkemoni*

From its beginnings, scholarship on the *Taḥkemoni* has concerned itself with the reconstruction of the author's biography and the realia of the thirteenth century. From the places Ḥever ha-Qeni visits and the individuals he encounters, positivists have used the *Taḥkemoni* as an almost documentary source by assuming an identity between author and protagonist. Judith Dishon argues that the *Taḥkemoni* faithfully represents thirteenth-century realia such as architectural details and professions: "Al-Ḥarizi was one of the Jewish travelers of the Middle Ages who wrote about his adventures in a poetical yet nonetheless realistic and descriptive way."[4] Ross Brann critiques Dishon's surface-level approach:

> The *Taḥkemoni* undoubtedly reflects certain realia of the places al-Ḥarīzī visited and possibly refers to his experiences or incidents he witnessed on his travels. But to completely separate the realistic from the imaginative is to ignore the way in which these elements are intertwined in the text and to seriously misunderstand the literary character of the *Taḥkemoni*.[5]

Brann's study concentrates on literary representations of Muslim characters in the *Taḥkemoni*. He concludes that *maqāma* 22, wherein Jewish youths (including Ḥever ha-Qeni) test a Muslim astrologer and suffer abuse at the hands of a Muslim mob but then are redeemed by a just Muslim magistrate, is ultimately an expression of Jewish powerlessness in Muslim society and Jewish ambivalence toward life under Islam.[6] This reading is determined through analyzing the episode's unique literary structure wherein expected conventions are manipulated. Ḥever ha-Qeni does not appear in disguise but speaks to the narrator plainly; he is not an invincible trickster but the victim of his own plan that backfires. The role of public rhetorician usually played by Ḥever ha-Qeni is occupied by a *real* astrologer, who creates a spectacle and speaks with remarkable eloquence (in Hebrew, of course). When he enters the public domain that is clearly Muslim, the seemingly insuperable Ḥever ha-Qeni is rendered powerless, which testifies to Jewish insecurity. This is not to say that the event "happened" but rather that the author made literary adjustments to the reader's expectations in order to signal a social and political message.[7]

The *Taḥkemoni* certainly touches on other thirteenth-century realia. It is possible that *maqāma* 7, the "Battle of Two Warriors," is not only a rhetorically sophisticated battle description but also an allusion to the Muslim-Christian battles of the Reconquista or the Crusades; as a native of Iberia and traveler in Palestine and Syria, al-Ḥarīzī would have been familiar with both. Ḥever ha-Qeni appears before Heman ha-Ezraḥi undisguised and relates that he traveled in his youth with a band of valorous men from Persia to the lands of Meshekh and Tiras until they reached the "Land of Qedar" (Islamdom), which was caught in the throes of war. The travelers witnessed a great battle. On one side, the children of Savtaʾ and Raʿma were arrayed; the children of Togarmah stood opposite them. Tracing the lineages of the warring parties, we find that Savtaʾ and Raʿma are sons of Kush son of Ḥam son of Noaḥ (Gen. 10:7; 1 Chron. 1:9) while Togarmah is the son of Gomer son of Yefet son of Noaḥ (Gen. 10:3). People from Kush (or *kushim*) are sometimes associated with Muslims in Hebrew literature,[8] and one of Kush's brothers is Miṣrayim, identified, of course, with Egypt. One of Togarmah's brothers is Ashkenaz, and one of his uncles is Yavan, domains associated with Christendom (territories of modern Germany and Greece, respectively). Meshekh and Tiras, toward which the protagonist is traveling, are also names of brothers of Togarmah.[9] Thus, Ḥever ha-Qeni and his friends were traveling when they halted in Islamdom to witness a battle between Muslims and Christians. The travelers were trapped in the midst of the battle: "We were caught between them, as if they were lions and we were prey between their teeth." Rather than taking sides, the travelers tried to remain neutral: "and between them we dwelt in silence."[10]

This episode may be an allusion to the Jewish predicament between the warring parties of Christianity and Islam during the thirteenth century. Beneath the *maqāma*'s entertaining style and rhetorical brilliance is a kernel of reality. Still, although the battle description has elements of realism (weaponry, blood, etc.), it also refrains from referring directly to place and time. The episode both reveals reality and conceals it. Like *maqāma* 22, the episode begins with Ḥever ha-Qeni undisguised and speaking to the narrator plainly. The portrayal is not meant to present a specific event that the author witnessed; the protagonist should not be mistaken as the author's mouthpiece. The author selects a discursive strategy that encodes and alludes to reality in such a way that the narrative draws on the real world without offering specifics.

It is questionable whether a reader can uncover an author's real attitudes in any literary work. Such an endeavor is particularly precarious with the *maqāma*, given its penchant for deception and misrepresentation.[11] As shown in the previous chapter, the author occasionally surfaces in each of his two main characters but cannot be identified wholly with either. At times, the author seems closely associated with his protagonist; at other times, a great chasm divides them. The speech of a character can be ontologically removed from the author by several degrees. Statements placed in the mouth of the protagonist are often unreliable and, despite their convincing presentation, might be the opposite of what the author truly believes.

At times, however, even the duplicitous Ḥever ha-Qeni makes arguments that al-Ḥarīzī likely supported himself. In *maqāma* 17, for example, Ḥever ha-Qeni offers a diatribe against the schismatic Karaites and recounts (or fabricates) a debate wherein a Rabbanite interlocutor trounces a Karaite defender. Because the author was certainly a Rabbanite, we can assume that the arguments against the Karaites (many of which derive from polemical tracts) are in conformity with his true beliefs and are intended to be sound (at the very least, the arguments conform to the dominant beliefs of al-Ḥarīzī's audience). The same is true of *maqāmāt* in which the learned protagonist details the history of Hebrew poetry and prescribes rules for its composition (*maqāmāt* 3 and 18). Certainly not all of the protagonist's speech is meant to mislead.

In other cases, the protagonist's mendacity is transparent and seems absolutely reprehensible, as when Ḥever swindles the pious out of their money through a deceitful sermon or some other dissimulation. In such cases, the protagonist is a model of impiety, of what one should not do (even if his *speech* appears to be moral). Despite the occasional rebuke with which the narrator reproves the protagonist, Heman ha-Ezraḥi's actions cannot be identified with the author's moral stance; his condemnation is tepid at best, since he praises Ḥever's eloquence and cunning more than he questions the propriety of his actions. Al-Ḥarīzī creates tension around moral subjects without investing his own voice wholly in either main character; in most instances, his real voice is located outside the text.

The *Taḥkemoni* thrives on the tension between truth and falsehood, which is created among the speech acts of the various characters and within the contradictions of the protagonist's speech. Ḥever ha-Qeni is a liar who sometimes relates truths. Heman ha-Ezraḥi is a truth teller who reports lies and might even fabricate stories occasionally as well.[12] Al-Ḥarīzī, as an author of fiction, is by definition a liar;[13] he relates the speech of a truth teller and a liar who sometimes tells the truth. When the reader applies to the *maqāmāt* the binary choice of "true/false," he finds himself locked in a nonsensical paradox, just as the viewer of an Escher drawing cannot reconcile the image before him with binaries such as "above/below" or "in front/behind." The reader feels that he knows what subject al-Ḥarīzī is writing about but may feel less certain as to what exactly the author is saying about it.

It is in some of the debate-centered *maqāmāt* that the author's views are most deeply buried. Such episodes are generally built around a topic, which might be quite jejune, and pit opposing views about the topic against one another. Their forms, which derive from Arabic *jadal* (debate literature, as found in many genres), are rather simple. The narrator arrives at a place and hears a debate wherein the protagonist plays one of the interlocutors. When the subject entails two opposing perspectives—such as the debate over the ant vs. the flea, man vs. woman, or day vs. night—there are two parties. When the subject requires more voices—such as the debate over the twelve months of the year or the seven virtues—there is a matching number of speakers. In some episodes, Ḥever ha-Qeni presents both sides of a case in order to entertain listeners and to earn some coin. In general, no side of a debate is clearly victorious over another. Not every dispute resolves as neatly as the one between Rabbanite and Karaite.[14] Even in the debate over the benefits and hardships of travel (*maqāma* 26), a topic we might assume was decided in a book so consumed with wanderlust, the reader is left without an answer. The *maqāmāt* juxtapose contrasting opinions on topics and give prominence to the "social heteroglossia" around such topics. As a genre that mixes different kinds of speech, the *maqāma* creates a forum for opposing positions to confront one another and to hang in tension. We do not learn al-Ḥarīzī's real views per se, but rather that certain topics were of social relevance.

Although it is difficult to imagine that anyone was deeply invested in the ant vs. flea debate, some subjects were certainly of greater importance. Let us consider the *Taḥkemoni*'s treatment of wine drinking. So idealized in Andalusian poetry, (non-sacramental) wine drinking remained a symbol of refined culture for some but became a sign of decadence for others. Like their counterparts in the classical Arabic *maqāmāt*, characters in the *Taḥkemoni* seek out drink in popular taverns, perhaps even more than in aristocratic gardens. *Maqāma* 27 is a rhetorical episode that contains a discourse concerning the benefits and harms of wine drinking. Heman ha-Ezraḥi reports that, during his youth, he wished to separate himself from drunkards and follow the path of the abstemious (whom he calls the "Nazirites"). After fulfilling his vow for a year, he returned to the tavern and encountered a group of youths drinking and praising wine. One recited, "The earth is like a beautiful girl, and wine is the juice of her mouth," and another replied, "Wine is joy's envoy, and the dissipater of misery," and so on. Among the drinkers was an elderly man whose "eye was always on the cup, the goblet continuously going around in his right hand." The old man disparaged the others' rhetoric and then delivered his own lengthy discourse about the praiseworthy qualities of wine. Dumbfounded by the skill of his rhetoric, the listeners asked the old man to make the opposite argument, contra wine and concerning its ill effects. The second discourse was equally as impressive as the first. Wine pains the head and confounds the soul; it makes the wise foolish and is the foundation of evil. Convinced by this argument, many of the listeners swore off wine and took vows of abstemiousness. The old man, of course, turned out to be Ḥever ha-Qeni, who departed after conversing with the narrator.

While the protagonist gives equal time to arguments for and against wine, one wonders whether the two sides of the discourse are truly equal (i.e., from the protagonist's perspective). The structure of the narrative suggests otherwise. What does it mean for a drunkard in a tavern to deliver a discourse on the harmful effects of wine that causes others to take vows of abstemiousness? As we know, there is no real argument against wine, since the protagonist's speech is unreliable. He only argues against wine to display his rhetorical skill; clearly, if he believed the arguments he made against wine, he would not have been found drinking in the tavern in the first place. The drinkers who abandon drink are more easily convinced than they are virtuous. Heman ha-Ezraḥi takes a vow of abstemiousness only to renounce it and encounter drinkers who adopt the vow he had abandoned. He does not seem to renounce wine again.

The point of the episode is certainly not to convey a moral message but rather to entertain through the verbal duel. But can we say anything about al-Ḥarīzī's stance toward wine drinking? In addition to this episode, Ḥever ha-Qeni is often portrayed as fond of the cup; we can safely say that the protagonist, at least, likes to drink. However, given Ḥever ha-Qeni's status as a social outsider, his endorsement (or habit) cannot be considered evidence of the author's view. But Heman ha-Ezraḥi drinks with the protagonist in other episodes, and associates drink with refined culture.[15] Many poems throughout the *Taḥkemoni,* placed in the mouths of the narrator, the protagonist, and other speakers, sing the praises of the fruit of the vine without a hint of opprobrium. As will be shown in the following chapter, wine drinking is intimately associated by al-Ḥarīzī with garden settings, which are idealized in the *Taḥkemoni.* Still, al-Ḥarīzī's real opinion, if it can be discerned at all, is obscured behind several layers of narrative speech and an intricate weave of truth and falsehood.

Most importantly, the episode highlights wine drinking as a topic of social discourse. Without discussion surrounding the topic of wine drinking, the text would "not sound" in the world of its medieval readers. Again, the *Taḥkemoni* is primarily about representing different types of speech, including the speech of drunkards and the abstemious; more than the book contains a clear argument about wine drinking, it represents competing voices surrounding the topic in medieval Jewish culture (and, more broadly, Arab-Islamic culture). The sophisticated placement of realia in the text is accomplished through playful voice games such that the author stands at several steps of remove from his characters' speech.

The narrator/protagonist dichotomy in the *Taḥkemoni* sometimes serves to create ambivalence surrounding objects; such is the case with the topic of aristocracy. Ideal men in the *Taḥkemoni,* as they are described in *maqāma* 46, generally adhere to a typology of Andalusian leadership. They are men of wealth and power who generously patronize Jewish learning and are themselves sometimes accomplished in the disciplines of halakhah, the sciences, and poetry.[16] Bernard Septimus has identified the "princes" (*nesiʾim*) of Barcelona, whom al-Ḥarīzī praises, with an aristocracy sympathetic to Andalusian cultural ideals.[17] However, some episodes reflect greater ambivalence. In *maqāma* 3, when the narrator is traveling through a city of the Islamic East, he is invited by an aristocrat to join a feast. Inside the palace, which is of ornate Islamic design, aristocrats are feasting on delicacies and wine. Believing that he has found refined culture and a group of fellow literati, Heman ha-Ezraḥi rejoices and recites a wine poem in the Andalusian style appropriate for the occasion. Later in the episode, Ḥever ha-Qeni, the true intellectual (appearing in the guise of a glutton), rebukes the aristocrats for their ignorance in matters of poetry and storms out of the feast.[18] The narrator desires aristocracy while the protagonist disdains it.

Is al-Ḥarīzī pro-aristocratic or anti-aristocratic? Can we identify him with either of the main characters? It is likely that al-Ḥarīzī identifies with both positions. Like Heman ha-Ezraḥi, the author traveled the East in search of sophisticated culture similar to the lost culture of al-Andalus; Ḥever ha-Qeni's disdain may signal disappointment. The subject of al-Ḥarīzī's attitude toward the East is discussed further in the following chapter of this book, in the section treating geography. By diffusing his own voice among the speakers in the *Taḥkemoni,* al-Ḥarīzī is able to allude to topics of cultural relevance while distancing himself from specific positions. More than the *Taḥkemoni* makes cogent arguments concerning topics such as wine drinking or aristocracy, it creates a forum for contrary voices to confront one another.

Imitation and Exploitation: A New Reading of the Eighth Chapter of *Sefer ha-Meshalim*

> Know that all men in the world, apart from wine merchants [*sov'im*], are scoundrels [*nevalim*],
> For [the wine merchants] take a bit of silver and order wineskins [*nevalim*] to be filled with golden waters.
>
> —Moses Ibn Ezra

> Boors became great and numerous in the nation, and the mightiest among them were the imbibers of wine [*sov'ei yayin*].
>
> —Jacob Ben Elʿazar

The episode of *Sefer ha-meshalim* that scholarship has associated most closely with Arabic literature is chapter 8, which Schirmann titled "The Story of a Hypocritical Old Man."[19] The story employs familiar motifs such as the hypocritical preacher of the *maqāma* and a scene of debauchery similar to scenarios in *The Thousand and One Nights.* Scholars have generally read the episode as an artifact of a lingering Judeo-Arabic symbiosis without situating the Arabic elements within the narrative as a whole. The following discussion offers a new reading of this episode that draws together a number of analytic methods treated in this book, including the significance of authorial voice, the place of *maqāma* motifs within the story's overall structure, and the relationship between the story and social realia of thirteenth-century Jewish culture. The end of the discussion argues that Ben Elʿazar repudiated certain Andalusian social values and preferred a courtly model more closely associated with Christendom than Islamdom. This is one of the few examples in the book wherein the author structures Arabic and European motifs in a pattern of contrast. Let us begin with a plot summary.

Lemu'el Ben Itti'el relates that in the days of his youth, he used to travel from nation to nation, "now sleeping in deserts and forests, now in village houses, as is the custom of travelers on the road." Upon arrival at an unnamed city "whose inhabitants were wealthy and whose merchants were princes [*sarim*]," Lemu'el decides to stay. The following morning, he awakes to find that the people are really "treacherous people, children of wrongdoing . . . their judges, judges of deceit, wolves of the steppe who leave no bone until morning" (Zeph. 3:3).

Contemplating leaving, Lemu'el hears the booming voice of an old man leaning on his staff, whom he takes to be a righteous and virtuous man. The man, named Akhbor from Mount Tabor, has an outstanding physical characteristic: his enormous and unruly beard, which Lemu'el perceives as a "beard of truth." The people gather around Akhbor, who proceeds to deliver an eloquent sermon in poetry and prose. He urges the people to lead a simple life, perform pious deeds, and give to charity:

> I adjure you by the Shelter of the Most High [Ps. 91:1] that you show mercy to the poor and unfortunate. Do not despise the Shelter of God when a petitioner adjures you. The parable of a poor man who begged at a door for morsels of food and the occupant gave him a crumb: He [the poor man] adjured him by the Shelter of the Most High, saying, "Add for me a little wheat for I have young children who dwell in hunger and thirst!" Then the owner of the house transgressed, lied, and acted heretically[20] in his home and said, "How can you adjure me by the Shelter of the Most High? Do you not see that I myself am poor and unfortunate?" Before he even finished speaking, pangs and crushing seized him, and his Creator struck him with blindness, madness, and ruin. A voice came: "Such will happen to those who despise the Shelter of the Most High!" Accept discipline, my brothers, and perhaps on the Day of Anger and Rage you will be sheltered in the Shelter of the Most High!

This is followed by another parable of a poor man who goes out to seek livelihood after a three-day fast, relying upon God alone (this idea is similar to the Islamic theme of *tawakkul*).[21] He asks a wealthy merchant for assistance, but the merchant, who was "shaking off wine," rebukes him.[22] God ultimately changes the merchant's heart so that he decides to write the poor man a promissory note in the amount of four shekels, but his hand errs so that he writes the note in the amount of four hundred shekels. Having lost his wealth, the merchant recognizes that it was God who caused his hand to err and piously accepts that it is "God alone who makes one man wealthy and another poor" (this expression is also very Islamic in tone).

Captivated by the sermon, the people open their purses and contribute generously to Akhbor's cause. Had this been a *maqāma* by al-Ḥarīzī, the expected scene of recognition and separation would now occur. The narrator would recognize the mendicant as his old friend Ḥever ha-Qeni; he would be astounded at his eloquence and would laud his cunning. Instead, Lemuʾel Ben Ittiʾel follows Akhbor to a palatial home, observing him from a place of hiding. Lemuʾel describes the opulent setting of the "preacher's" home:

> His house had ten entrances like the mansions of military generals. I would recount its ramparts,[23] courtyards, and rows of masonry[24] were my tongue sufficient to report what my eyes beheld.[25] Who could speak of the fountain and its waters, the birds and the latticework, the many species of trees and roses and buds, the fire pans and vessels, vessels for drinking wine, all types of finery for dress and vessels of copper, silver, and gold?[26]

From his hiding place, Lemu'el declares in his heart that Akhbor is a "scoundrel [*mi-benei ha-nevalim*], a man of nefarious deeds." While Akhbor is reclining in his courtyard, four maidservants enter, help him undress, and kiss his hand. They set before him delicacies to eat and old wine to drink. Each of the maidservants sings a different wine song, replete with the clichés of Andalusian poetry. For example:

Wine like the color of lightning or the color of flame,
 it lights the heart of its drinker with its spark.
It is bitter, yet sweeter than honey.
 Its scent gives life for its vigor is like myrrh.
If there is distress in any man's heart,
 it sends out a troop of joy to annihilate it.
It makes the heart of the stingy like the heart of the generous,
 on account of it the tightfisted opens his hand.[27]

Pleased with the poems, Akhbor recites his own poem about drinking and sexual desire. Drunk with wine, Akhbor sports with the maidens, passing from one bosom to the next until he falls asleep in a blissful state (this scene of debauchery bears a resemblance with some episodes from *The Thousand and One Nights*).[28] Finally, a fifth maidservant enters, this time a *kushit*, "a worn-out black woman, her lips like a firebrand[29] plucked from burning, her eyes like flames."[30] Watching Akhbor carouse with the black maidservant, Lemu'el can no longer control his anger, and shouts: "This is all licentiousness!" He darts out from his hiding place, assaults the couple, and strips them bare. Akhbor recites verses in his defense, explaining that he prefers a black woman over a "pure" one (i.e., a white one). The narrator answers with his own verse:

What is wrong with the black woman that she has a stench,
 while a [white] maiden is spiced with myrrh?
Pure like a lily in the hand of the desirer,
 the praise and majesty of every eye.
Every black woman is without a mind;
 she is silly, noisy, and wayward.[31]
I give every black woman counsel:
 "Return, go back to where you were created!"[32]

The four maidservants return to the scene and join in the attack against Akhbor. They curse him and mock him, chiding his unruly beard and his desire for the black woman. Each takes a turn reciting a poem ridiculing her lord, just as they had recited wine poems earlier. The first recites a poem mocking Akhbor's beard, a symbol of false piety:

Akhbor's beard is the beard of a foolish shepherd,
    its branches go in every direction.
Its length reaches down to Sheol
    with such might that all strength is spent.
Little animals pass through it.
    I asked: "Are there monkeys hidden there?"[33]
I saw the likeness of birds flying in it
    and fleas inherited it as a nest.
They answered me: "Akhbor's beard is like a forest
    where there are wildcats and little foxes.
There the escaping arrow-snake nests;
    it is a covering even for the rock-badger.
There they dwell, tranquil and secure.
    Also a man [can dwell there] beneath a grapevine of security.
Each man beneath his fig tree,[34] in the shade of
    Akhbor's beard, full of sap and freshness."[35]

The second maidservant mocks his beard and his desire for the black woman, playing on numerous biblical verses: "He made his bed in a dark place [cf. Job 17:13]. He had intercourse with the daughters of Ḥam,[36] and works over coal" (cf. Isa. 44:12). After each takes her turn spurning Akhbor, the four together yank at his beard and beat him to death. They bind the corpse in ropes and cast it into a pit, pronouncing (playing on Gen. 34:14): "A polluted man shall never dwell with us, for it would be a disgrace for us!"[37]

By now, it would seem that Lemuʾel has left the scene or returned to a hiding place; he does not appear again for the rest of the episode. After his brief yet poignant intrusion into the narrative, he retreats to become an extradiegetic and omniscient narrator. One wonders exactly where Lemuʾel is supposed to be during the story's concluding epilogue, in which the four maidens leave Akhbor's mansion and engage in their own love story:

> They went out to the vineyards to browse in the gardens and to pick roses, strolling through orchards, meandering through the myrtles. They wore chequered robes and told parables, riddles, and precious songs by the grape-blossoms and vines and by all kinds of buds. They spoke by[38] the trees, the roses, and the buds. At noon, they lay beside the pools of water, sitting beneath the shade, playing harps and lutes. Four young men were listening to the sound of their song, hearing their dancing and playing, enjoying the sound of the music, peering through the lattice. [The maid-

ens] became aware of this and said, "Who is it who listens to our voices, standing behind our wall? Are you friend or foe?"[39]

The suitors flirt with the maidens and seek their hands in marriage but are refused for lack of chivalrous grace. One of the maidens recites a poem, concluding the episode and giving the plot a final twist:

Lovers who knocked at the doors of fawns have done wrong.
Alas! They have been brutish, barbarous, and dull-hearted!
For lovers cannot come to a fawn unless they have been oppressed
[by her].
It is not for the oppressed to oppress unless they are flattering.
If they are lovers, let them give a sign, some proof that[40] their cause
is just!
If they are lovers, why have they not restrained themselves?[41]
For pure lovers[42] are fainthearted, kindled flames,
They murmur and act like madmen for they are crying out in anguish.
If you are lovers, then where are the tears flowing upon your cheeks?
Where are the pleas of lovers? Where are the sweet words?
Where are the constant lovers who are stronger than fawns,
Who pronounce[43] their passion upon the tablet of their heart that they
engraved?
[. . .] if they prosper and grow wealthy?
Lovers, with this will you be tested, not through quarreling may you
contend.
Get up, quick, and hurry to tear off the bands of wandering!
Let each man take possession of a companion, each portion shall be
assigned by lot![44]
Hence a man leaves his father and mother and clings to a graceful
gazelle.[45]
[The suitors] quickly understood and each man took hold of his woman,
They renewed their youth and [the women] leaned upon their lovers.

Schirmann adduced the motif of the hypocritical preacher, the wine poems, the garden setting, and the link with *The Thousand and One Nights* as evidence for the influence of Arabic literature.[46] Indeed, the opening segment of the episode closely mimics a standard *maqāma* plot. The closest parallel from Arabic literature is the first *maqāma* of al-Ḥarīrī's collection,[47] in which the protagonist swindles a mosque congregation with an eloquent sermon. The narrator follows the protagonist back to a cave and finds him luxuriating and drinking wine. The narrator mildly rebukes the protagonist, but the protagonist defends himself by blaming necessity and the cruelty of Fate for his behavior. The narrator does not counter the protagonist's defense.

Ben Elᶜazar's story differs from the precedent in numerous ways. From the moment that Lemuʾel jumps out of his hiding place and physically assaults Akhbor and the black maidservant, the narrative goes in a direction unprecedented in Hebrew literature; the poems on Akhbor's beard, Akhbor's violent murder, and the epilogue of the four suitors are all unique. The episode may be divided into two main parts, with Lemuʾel's assault on Akhbor and the black maidservant providing a line of division:

I.
  A. Lemuʾel arrives at the unnamed city of sinners
  B. Akhbor recites the sermon and collects money
  C. Akhbor returns to his mansion
  D. The four (white) maidservants recite wine poems
  E. Akhbor sports with the black maidservant

II.
  F. Lemuʾel comes out of hiding to attack Akhbor and the black maidservant
  G. The four (white) maidservants mock Akhbor with poems and kill him
  H. The maidservants leave the mansion and retreat to the vineyards
  I. Epilogue of the four suitors

The two sections are counterpoints to each other. Motifs in one part mirror and contrast motifs in the other. The motif of the preacher's beard, thought to be a beard of piety and truth in part I (B), is revealed to be a beard of impiety and mendacity in part II (G). The four wine songs sung by the maidservants in the garden (D) are paralleled by the four poems they recite to mock Akhbor (G). The women's status as Akhbor's servants and objects of desire (D) stands in contrast with their role in the epilogue as women unowned who take delight in one another's company and control the courtship with their suitors (I). The garden setting in Akhbor's mansion (C) mirrors and contrasts the garden in which the suitors court the maidens (I).[48] This pattern of contrast between the two parts questions whether the Arabic motifs may be called "influences." While Ben Elᶜazar draws these motifs from Arabic literature, he enframes them within a complex structure that inverts the values of the parent literature.

Scenes D and I represent two models of the lover-beloved relationship that are diametrically opposed to each other. The former is easily identified with the values of Arabic and Andalusian Hebrew love poetry: a socially superior male is served and entertained by maidservants who are skilled in the arts of song and coquettish flirtation. The setting of the scene is familiar:

a courtyard with fountains, various species of trees and flowers, vessels for drinking wine, and other wares. It is the standard *hortus conclusus* so celebrated in Andalusian poetry, a point highlighted by the type of entertainment and the content of the wine poems. The conspicuous absence of wine drinking in the garden in scene I links *Sefer ha-meshalim* with the European tradition (it is not a common theme in the troubadour lyric).[49] The lover-beloved relationship presented in scene I closely mimics the model presented in troubadour poetry, Romance narrative, and other episodes of *Sefer ha-meshalim*. The men are not the maidens' social superiors but are their equals or, more likely, their inferiors. The suitors are not capable lovers who have mastered the arts of flirtation and seduction but learn through the instruction of their female counterparts. According to the women's instructions, the men must woo them through flattery, clever conversation, and manifest signs of lovesickness; they must act in accordance with an established set of rules. Of course, some motifs may have roots in the Andalusian courtly lyric or the ᶜUdhrī tradition, such as the call for outward signs of lovesickness, including weeping and acting like a madman. Still, several elements make the topos here rather distinct, such as the social positions of the women and their suitors, the men's proposal of marriage, and the active role that the women play in the courtship.

Ben Elᶜazar places the two models of love in stark contrast with each other, highlighting the preference for the latter over the former. Again, this is one of the few instances in the book in which Ben Elᶜazar presents Arabic and European motifs in a pattern of contrast. Of course, if one maintains the thesis that troubadour and hence Romance love ideals ultimately stem from the court culture of al-Andalus, then in a sense the idealized topos can be viewed as a continuation of past values. However, the author hones in on the most prominent aspect that separates the types of "courtly love" idealized in al-Andalus and Provence: the status of the beloved as inferior or superior, as maidservant or lady. The episode is ultimately about transition from one social model to another, from one identified with the Arabic culture of al-Andalus to one identified with the courtly culture of the Christian north.

Apart from the shift in the love ideal, numerous aspects of the episode echo other social issues of the thirteenth century, such as aristocracy, wine drinking, and possibly concubinage. At the beginning of the story, Lemuʾel arrives at a nameless city, giving only the detail of the inhabitants' wealth—"its merchants were princes [*sarim*]"—and he later identifies the inhabitants as lewd and treacherous. The reader of the *Taḥkemoni* will recall that al-Ḥarīzī identifies Barcelona as a "city of princes" (*nesiʾim*) and Toledo as a city with many princes as well.[50] This is not to say that Ben Elʿazar is identifying the fictional locus with a specific city or Akhbor with a specific leader but rather that he is hinting at the subject of Jewish social models current in his day. As discussed in chapter 4, debates over aristocratic leadership were central in thirteenth-century Iberian Jewish culture. Anti-aristocrats characterized the Andalusian-style ruling elite as decadent while the aristocrats sought to secure their position and quell voices of rebellion. It is well documented that some aristocratic Jews kept concubines, particularly Muslim concubines, in Christian Iberia; the practice was hotly debated among jurists such as Naḥmanides and Ibn Adret in the thirteenth century.[51] As Jonathan Ray points out, in a fourteenth-century manual for Jewish courtiers, Menaḥem Ben Aharon Ibn Zeraḥ critiques "those who walk in the court of our master the king" for flouting "laws concerning women and wine," among other infractions, because of their desire for luxuries.[52] These subjects underlie the depiction of Akhbor, who is a hybrid of the *maqāma* protagonist and an aristocrat with Andalusian tastes for wine, luxurious courtyards, and women; the black maidservant in particular may be meant to be a Muslim. Chapter 7 of *Sefer ha-meshalim* also touches on the theme of corrupt leadership; Yoshfeh leaves his parents' house during a period of political crisis during which "Time established sons of iniquity" (*benei beliyaʿal*) over "the nobility" (*benei ha-nedivim*); the usurpers are described as scoundrels (*nevalim*) and evildoers (*reshaʿim*).[53] Here, too, it is possible that Ben Elʿazar is hinting at some social reality.

Sefer ha-meshalim presents a sustained critique against wine drinking. In his mendacious sermon, Akhbor chastises the uncharitable, particularly the wealthy man "shaking off wine" who rebukes the beggar on his doorstep (B). As is common in the *maqāma*, moral pronouncements are inverted when Akhbor turns out to be a wealthy wine drinker himself (D). Unlike the classical *maqāma*, however, *Sefer ha-meshalim* inverts the moral message a second time through the narrator's critique, which Akhbor does not succeed in deflecting. Lemuʾel pronounces Akhbor one of the *benei ha-nevalim*, a "son of the scoundrels"; this formulation and the repeating references to *nevalim* in other episodes make it sound as though the "scoundrels" constitute a specific group. Perhaps significantly, the word *naval* is a homograph that also means "wineskin." It is likely that the two meanings of *naval* were closely associated in the author's mind (especially since Andalusian Hebrew authors had frequently played with this double entendre).[54] Once an inspiration for poets, wine is now a cause of cultural decay. Lemuʾel laments in chapter 4: "The generation of foolishness had grown mighty, poetry was lost and hidden, it died or was broken or taken captive. . . . Boors became great and numerous in the nation, and the mightiest among them were the imbibers of wine."[55] Other characters in the book are labeled *nevalim* and are marked by their taste for wine.[56] The wine poems of chapter 8 are the only wine poems in the book. They are not simply a product of the "influence" of Arabic and Andalusian literature in the post-Andalusian environment. Rather, the author enframes this Andalusian subject within a complex narrative structure in order to critique the opulence and decadence that wine poems signify.

While Ben Elᶜazar was certainly familiar with the *maqāma* and Arabic poetic genres, he inverts their structures and themes in favor of a new mood and symbolic vocabulary. The predictable pattern of the deceitful mendicant is recast in a new narrative frame, stressing not continuity but a break with the past. The two-part structure of the narrative allows contrasting motifs to stand out in bold relief. It is true but insufficient to hold that Ben Elᶜazar is influenced by the *maqāma* genre or Andalusian wine poetry; rather, he comments upon these models through a calculated intertextual game. Akhbor is a caricature of the Andalusian-style aristocrat. His home is a palace; his taste for wine, wine poetry, and subservient women is that of a despised elite. Casting Akhbor's corpse into a pit is a fantasy of revolution against an Andalusian-style aristocracy.[57]

Ben Elᶜazar has not only juxtaposed two models of love in this story but also two models of storytelling. Lemuʾel is both an intradiegetic and an extradiegetic narrator. He first functions like a narrator in a classical *maqāma;* he hears the sermon of a preacher, whom he comes to recognize as a trickster. After functioning as a bold protagonist, Lemuʾel withdraws entirely and relates events as an omniscient narrator outside of the story; he narrates the epilogue as though he were not present, just as he narrates all the other love stories in the book. One imagines that Ben Elᶜazar could have written chapter 8 using an extradiegetic narrator throughout. Akhbor could have duped the people out of their money and pleasured himself in his garden and the maidservants could have overthrown Akhbor, left the garden, and been courted by their suitors, all without the intervention of the narrator. The practice of textual manipulation that began with the *maqāma* (in that it cast existing genres in a new literary structure) has been taken to a new level through the manipulation of the *maqāma* genre itself.

Ben Elᶜazar probably used an intradiegetic narrator not only to signal an affinity with the classical *maqāma* but also to define a clear moral stance concerning the content of the story. While we can never assume a complete identity between author and narrator, the action of the narrator here—atypical for the classical *maqāma*—is extremely significant. By having Lemuʾel pronounce judgment on Akhbor and instigate his actual murder, Ben Elʿazar leaves little room for multiple interpretations of the story. The reader must identify with Lemuʾel's moralizing position and renounce aristocratic sumptuousness as a decadent cultural model.

The narrator's very name recalls the anti-indulgent admonition of King Lemuʾel's mother in Proverbs 31:

> The words of Lemuʾel, king of Massa, with which his mother[58] admonished him: Do not give your strength to women, your vigor to those who destroy kings. Wine is not for kings, O Lemuʾel, not for kings to drink, nor any strong drink for princes, lest they drink and forget what has been ordained. . . . Speak up for the dumb, for the rights of all the unfortunate. Speak up, judge righteously, champion the poor and the needy.

The moral message of chapter 8 of *Sefer ha-meshalim* fits this admonition precisely, touching upon leadership, sexual propriety, wine drinking, and the needs of the poor. Although the narrator's name pays tribute to al-Ḥarīzī and al-Ḥarīrī, its associations with moral imperatives also indicate a different intention. The social values extolled in Andalusian literature and embraced by the Andalusian-style aristocracy are treated only with scorn. Although Ben Elʿazar was heir to the intellectual traditions of al-Andalus (grammar, philosophy, Arabic, and Hebrew), he clearly renounced the established cultural posture of Andalusian leadership. This is not to say that the author was "anti-courtly"; if the epilogue of episode 8 is meant to be exemplary, then the social model being advocated is still courtly. However, it is the court of Christendom rather than the court of Islamdom.

The Hebrew rhymed prose literature of the thirteenth century functioned as a theater wherein divisive cultural debates could be played out. Like the *Taḥkemoni, Sefer ha-meshalim* allows contrasting social voices to collide; both texts sound against realia of thirteenth-century Jewish life. But there is also a great deal that separates the two texts. Discourse in the *Taḥkemoni* revels in the degrees of separation between characters' speech and the actual author, to such an extent that the author's own voice is difficult to discern. Although there are also degrees of separation in *Sefer ha-meshalim* (Ben Elʿazar represents Lemuʾel, who represents Akhbor, who misrepresents himself), a firmer bond is drawn between the author and his narrator than in the *Taḥkemoni.* The author associates himself with only one character in his book, not two. Although multiple voices collide in *Sefer ha-meshalim,* the moralizing voice is allowed to prevail. Neither al-Ḥarīzī nor Ben Elʿazar composed a manifesto on the place of Andalusian values in post-Andalusian Jewish culture. However, the topic of cultural transition was never far beneath the surface of their writings. Realia of the day were placed within their texts in sophisticated ways through the manipulation of narrative structure and authorial voice.

Seven

Space

Landscape, Geography, and Transition

In chapter 1, it was shown that the Andalusian Hebrew poetics of estrangement and nostalgia was grounded in a lingering memory of the garden landscape and its counterpoints in the desert and forest. The first part of this chapter continues this discussion by considering aspects of landscape in Hebrew narrative fiction by focusing on the role of idyllic landscapes in al-Ḥarīzī and Ben Elʿazar.[1] The discussion explores the significance of authors' idealizations of given landscapes as a gauge for measuring the degree of their identification with the Andalusian literary tradition and Andalusian social values. The second half of this chapter considers the representation of geography, another dimension of narrative space, again focusing on the cultural outlooks of al-Ḥarīzī and Ben Elʿazar. Neither author imagines geography in exactly the same way as his Muslim or Christian contemporaries. Al-Ḥarīzī's presentation of geography reflects his own journey from Iberia to Provence and the Islamic East and a concern for the transmission of knowledge from West to East. As is common in Arabic and European literatures of conquest and expansion, *Sefer ha-meshalim* includes love stories wherein characters cross the border between Christian and Islamic territories. Ben Elʿazar largely shares the perspective of an author of Christian European literature who sends characters from Christendom to an unfamiliar and exotic Islamic world, though his narratives do not convey a similar ideology of religious expansionism.

Landscape: Idyllic Places

Arabic and Hebrew *maqāmāt* make use of a variety of landscapes, ranging from desert wastelands to oases, open meadows, mountain passes, natural rivers, and palace gardens, sometimes existing in real geography and sometimes in generic or imaginary places. The various authors of *maqāmāt* identify certain landscapes as idyllic places over others by building upon the associations that are culturally inscribed within those landscapes. The following discussion focuses on the preferred landscapes of al-Ḥarīzī and Ben Elʿazar by situating their ideal spaces vis-à-vis the Arabic and European traditions. Al-Ḥarīzī diverges from the Arabic *maqāma* tradition by identifying the garden over the desert as the font of literary culture. The Hebrew author remembers the Andalusian-style *hortus conclusus* as the source from which Hebrew poetry sprang, just as Arabic authors identify the Arabian desert as the birthplace of Arabic verse. Ben Elʿazar idealizes neither the desert nor the Andalusian garden but chooses other landscapes in which to set his idyllic scenes. Chapter 8 of *Sefer ha-meshalim,* the only chapter to present an enclosed garden, presents two variations on the *hortus conclusus,* one of which may be associated with the Andalusian garden while the other supplants this model with a new ideal. Ben Elʿazar's versions of the *locus amoenus* reveal similarities with some Arabic texts but suggest a greater affinity for landscape trends emerging in Christian Europe.

Landscape in the Arabic Maqāma *and in al-Ḥarīzī*

In modern scholarship, the Arabic and Hebrew *maqāma* episodes that have been the least valued from a narrative perspective are the so-called rhetorical *maqāmāt.* Very little happens in these episodes with respect to action, humor, or plot development.[2] Although the narrative frame seems merely a pretext for rhetorical pyrotechnics, the significance of these episodes should not be overlooked. Because the characters of *maqāmāt* are ultimately in search of fine rhetoric, it is worth noting where they actually find it. Rhetorical episodes sometimes contain subtle elements that create the feeling of having arrived at an idyllic place: the protagonist might appear undisguised, the ubiquitous ruse might be absent, discourse might be more honest than deceitful, and departure scenes might be altered or omitted.

In *maqāma* 27 of al-Hamadhānī, ʿIsā Ibn Hishām travels through the desert and finds rest in the shade of a Bedouin tent.[3] By the tent pegs are several Arab youths, one of whom is improvising poetry of a superlative quality. The Bedouin youth assures the narrator that he has arrived at the "house of security, the land of hospitable reception" as one might expect of the Bedouin, famed for their generosity. In fact, the narrator has arrived at the house of al-Aswad Ibn Qinān, a famous Bedouin sheikh (long dead by al-Hamadhānī's day).[4] The narrator is ultimately brought to a house where others are also enjoying hospitality, Abū al-Fatḥ among them. The protagonist tells the narrator that they have been enjoying hospitality at the house of al-Aswad for some time, and that he should do the same. The two continue to reside together for a stint (*zaman*) before departing. Of course, the story is one variety of a ruse wherein the protagonist—and ultimately, the narrator—takes advantage of Bedouin hospitality, freeloading to enjoy extended comfort. Still, the Bedouin themselves appear as blameless. This is a rare instance wherein the narrator and protagonist remain together for a period of time, suggesting that they are actually enjoying this "land of hospitable reception" where generosity reigns and poetry is pure. This is not to say that al-Hamadhānī necessarily longed for the desert in a real sense or that he rejected the urban culture of his time. Rather, the story demonstrates that the Bedouin desert had resonance for him as a place of hospitality and elevated poetry.

Absent from al-Hamadhānī's narratives is any idealization of aristocratic garden culture. As in the *Taḥkemoni*, the social mores of aristocrats are sometimes mocked. In *maqāma* 22, the protagonist reports that he was brought to a bourgeois mansion with the promise of being fed. His hunger is prolonged as the wealthy proprietor takes him on an endless tour of the palace's luxuries, bragging ostentatiously all the while. In *maqāma* 15, the narrator is invited to a banquet in a luxurious home

> whose carpets were spread and whose coverings were unfolded and whose table was laid, and we found ourselves among a company who were passing their time amid bunches of myrtle twigs, and bouquets of roses, broached wine vats and the sound of the flute and the lute . . . a table whose vessels were filled, whose gardens were in flower and whose dishes were arranged in rows with viands of various hues.[5]

The company is busy praising the writings of al-Jāḥiẓ when a gluttonous rhetorician rebukes them for their literary ignorance and points out the famous author's blunders.[6] Rather than constituting any ideal space, the aristocratic palace is the site of exposing the lack of *adab* (refined culture and manners) of the ruling class. As in al-Ḥarīzī's writings, the aristocracy is approached with ambivalence, since the narrator desires it while the protagonist disdains it.

The aristocratic garden fares slightly better in al-Ḥarīrī. Most of al-Ḥarīrī's *maqāmāt* are rhetorical and take place in settings of all kinds. Only one episode, *maqāma* 24, is set in a garden; the garden is described briefly, evoking the description of paradise in the Qurʾān. The narrator is with a group of youths in the environs of Baghdad in springtime:

> [We agreed to amuse ourselves by] going forth to one of the meadows, to cast our eyes on the verdant gardens, and refine our thoughts by watching for rains. We set out, like the months in number [i.e., twelve] and like the two drinking companions of Jadīma[7] in affection, to a garden that had claimed its ornamentation and adorned itself [Qurʾān 10:25],[8] whose flow-

> ers were diverse and colored. With us was headstrong ruddy [wine] and cupbearers like suns, the singer who sings and amuses the listener.[9]

Even if this setting is outside, beyond the palace and city, the furnishings and social activities are what would be expected of the palace garden soirée—flowers, wine drinkers, a singer. The protagonist approaches the scene and a grammatical debate ensues, ending with the presentation of twelve grammatical riddles (corresponding to the twelve companions). Abū Zayd refuses to give solutions until he is given a gift from each of the twelve. Although the protagonist ultimately shows his superior wit, as he did in al-Hamadhānī's *maqāma* 15, the garden is not a subject of disdain in itself. Rather, it appears as a pleasant location for rhetorical exchange.

The ideal landscape in al-Saraqusṭī's *maqāmāt* is certainly the desert. The author sometimes refers to specific deserts but also to unidentifiable desert landscapes. Although one might expect the Andalusian author to have had some interest in the garden, this landscape is lacking in his collection. The desert is far more idealized than it is in the *maqāmāt* of al-Hamadhānī or al-Ḥarīrī. In *maqāma* 47, al-Sāʾib Ibn Tammām reports that during the days of his youth, he was fond of the company of "pure-blooded, Bedouin Arabs, people endowed with reliable genealogies," and so he "marched over their winding dunes and sandy hillocks." In the desert of Banū Asad, in the Arabian Peninsula, the narrator and his fellow travelers hunt oryx and retire by oasis pools. Abū Ḥabīb arrives undisguised and shares eloquent anecdotes with the Bedouin. Finally, they come to the subject of love poetry and erotic verse and Abū Ḥabīb calls upon seven youths to recite love poems. The youths recite poems in the ʿUdhrī style, their discourse continuing through the night, until Abū Ḥabīb's expected departure.

Similarly, al-Saraqusṭī's *maqāma* of the poets (*maqāma* 30), in which Abū Ḥabīb lavishes praise upon Jāhiliyya, Umayyad, and ʿAbbasid poets (Andalusian poets are conspicuously absent), is set in a "tractless wilderness, in the company of emaciated travelers, deeply engaged in conversation, handling the reins, and stroking the manes of horses." When the noonday heat becomes too intense, the desert travelers pitch tents in the bend of a valley. There they encounter Abū Ḥabīb, who shares his knowledge of poets with the travelers and finally departs.[10] There is no ruse in either of these episodes; the narrator is able to recognize the protagonist with minimal scrutinizing, and the discourse is all quite honest. Living in a politically tumultuous time, al-Saraqusṭī looked eastward and backward to the font of Arab culture, fantasizing about a distant place and time characterized by generosity, valor, and precious discourse. It is possible that the author viewed the garden, which so often represented Andalusian aristocracy, as a symbol of decadence and cultural demise.

A related idyllic landscape of al-Saraqusṭī's *maqāmāt* is the desert oasis. In *maqāma* 44, al-Sā'ib is traveling with a "brave youth who was descended from royalty . . . enjoying the wilderness of wastelands and deserts." They reach a "fertile valley, and were seated under the still branches of a tree . . . beneath an outstretched shade, next to a meandering river, and beside some plants of which the fruit was ripe for picking." This place reminds the travelers of the mountain pass of Bawwān that was memorialized by the ʿAbbasid poet al-Mutanabbī and is the home of al-Sā'ib's companion. Ultimately, Abū Ḥabīb appears and congratulates the youth for finding such a worthy friend as al-Sā'ib. The *maqāma* is also atypical in that there is no ruse. Al-Sā'ib asks Abū Ḥabīb to stay with them, but the protagonist declines and departs.[11]

Al-Ḥarīzī never idealized the untamed desert as al-Saraqusṭī did.[12] The most idealized landscape for al-Ḥarīzī is clearly the courtly garden, the landscape most closely associated with the culture of Andalusian aristocracy. For al-Ḥarīzī, the garden is the locus of high Jewish culture, just as the desert is the locus of high Arab culture for al-Saraqusṭī. As mentioned, al-Ḥarīrī includes a garden description comprising only a few lines in a rhetorical *maqāma*.[13] In his translation of the episode, al-Ḥarīzī takes this small window of opportunity to compose an extensive garden description:

> We went out to a garden bed surrounded with lilies, dressed in standards, dripping with calamus and cassia. The eyes of its buds were like the eyes of a cloistered woman; the pomegranates of its lilies like the breasts of a maiden. Its breezes hovered throughout its four quarters and blew the scents of its spices. The hands of the rains opened from their locked storehouses and let out the stores of its spices. Before us were fruit-bearing trees of every kind with their seeds [Gen. 1:12]. With us there was a lovesick woman rousing love song; she is the daughter of grapes [i.e., wine], circling by way of attractive wine pourers banded with silver [cups]. With us were poets teaching instruction to murmurers. First came singers and then musicians [Ps. 68:26], pleasing the hearts of listeners and bringing them joy.[14]

As an author in the Hebrew Andalusian tradition, al-Ḥarīzī was probably eager to utilize a genre popular in his literary world yet largely neglected by al-Ḥarīrī.[15] In his rewriting of this episode, al-Ḥarīzī allows the garden tradition, and hence the Andalusian culture for which the garden was a synecdoche, to live.[16]

In the *Taḥkemoni,* rhetoric can be found in a market square, a synagogue, a house of study, a garden, a court, or along the road. Still, these places are not given equal weight in the book. The Andalusian-style garden serves as the setting of two rhetorical *maqāmāt* in the *Taḥkemoni.* Although rhetorical *maqāmāt* also take place in other settings, these garden episodes are distinguishable from the others because of their subtle departures in narrative structure. *Maqāma* 5 is set in a garden in spring. Heman ha-Ezraḥi witnesses a tournament of twelve poets, each charged to improvise a poem on a month of the year. Ḥever ha-Qeni stands among them as teacher and prince:

> It was the season of spring, the beloved and cherished month of Nisan. Rain was formed from the tears of dew on the rose's cheek. The garden, with its embroidery of roses, was a mouth encircled by lips. The earth wore embroidered garments of buds. She decked herself with her earrings and jewels. The rose illuminated her eyes like a flame, illuminating the front of her face, her gardens, her flowers and buds. Upon her gardens were buds and blossoms; her lilies were upon her Sharon. Herbs were verdant upon her face. The garden's spices were drawn to our nostrils, going wherever the wind blew.[17]

In this description (which is only partly quoted here), al-Ḥarīzī captures many aspects of the Andalusian garden poem, from the flowers and garden beds to the thunderstorm that brings water to the garden and the wine that brings joy. The subsequent poems on months of the year likewise include much garden description. Ḥever ha-Qeni is the prince of this culture, master of its social order and rhetorical forms. Significantly, this garden is not set in or near any city in real geography. It is utopian in the true sense of the word—it exists "nowhere." Like the gardens of the estranged Andalusian author Moses Ibn Ezra, al-Ḥarīzī's gardens are *poetic* gardens; they derive from garden poems primarily and from actual gardens only secondarily. The *maqāma* makes a transition from placelessness to real geography in its atypical conclusion, wherein the poems reach Damascus and become as dear to the community as the *Shemʿa* prayer. There is no standard departure scene; rather, the utopian garden of rhetoric gives way to a scene of revelry and celebration. By omitting a departure scene and by altering the standard *maqāma* formula, al-Ḥarīzī distinguishes between the garden and other landscapes, making it stand out as an ideal place.

Maqāma 49 also diverges from the standard *maqāma* conclusion. A Zephyr of Dawn (*ruaḥ sheḥarim*) brings the narrator to a garden in order to utter secrets to him:

> She brought me to a garden, lush and refreshing, its bushes entangled, its plants intertwined. The bounteous crop of its moons, its bulbs and flowers, the tenderness of its blossoms were like the cheek of her youth, inlaid with embroidered designs. The garden bed was decorated with the garment of her delight and her scarlet settings.[18]

Throughout the rest of the *maqāma,* the narrator continues to describe (in poetry and prose) the many elements of the "embroidered" garden: trees, grapes, garden beds, watercourses, wine goblets, wine, a single female musician, and beautiful male youths. At the end of the episode, Heman approaches the handsome youths, who greet him and ask him his place of origin:

> They greeted me in peace, saying, "Peace upon you, what is your place of origin?" I said, "Sefarad is my land, and the Land of Israel[19] is my destination." They said to me, "May your sky not grow dark, may your place not be lacking!" They set me a place among those summoned. Behold! Most of them were prophets! Among them was the father of wondrous poetry, Ḥever ha-Qeni. When he recognized me, he ran to embrace me. He embraced me around my neck and kissed me, and said to his companions, "Now your happiness and rejoicing are complete, for until now you have not come to your resting place and inheritance." I stayed a month to delight in them and to pluck delicacies from the fruit of their mouths, until Time inclined the whip of separation upon us and pretended not to know us, and painted our eyes with the mascara of wandering and separated us.[20]

Just as Heman is the poets' "resting place and inheritance," this garden is the destination of the narrator's journey. The garden exists nowhere in real geography. Even if it is outdoors and not adjacent to a palace, the garden is strongly associated with the accoutrements and appearance of the Andalusian garden. The idea of a wandering intellectual from Iberia finding his place of repose in a placeless garden is suggestive of nostalgia for a lost culture. Whereas Mosul is the setting for a *maqāma* about an incompetent cantor and the poets of Damascus are all said to be inept, the Andalusian-style garden where Ḥever ha-Qeni teaches the poetry of old is suspended beyond any conventional space. The personified Zephyr of Dawn leads the narrator to a secret garden where culture and rhetoric survive. As in the poetry of Moses Ibn Ezra, the garden is a place remembered that evokes Andalusian culture. Again, there is no abrupt separation of narrator and protagonist; Heman and Ḥever, who usually repel each other quickly, stay together for an entire month![21] The idyllic and fantastic sense that pervades this garden episode is created by the suspension of narrative space and the slowing of narrative time.

As discussed in chapter 1, in the post-Andalusian environment the garden becomes an icon of Andalusian culture in the minds of Muslim and Jewish poets. Poets long for al-Andalus of the past by remembering it as a garden and describe places of their own day as new gardens. These garden descriptions are mediated by a fixed poetic garden tradition far more than they are inspired by actual gardens. Al-Ḥarīzī remembers the Iberia of his youth as a garden and portrays Alexandria and Damascus in similar terms. The connection between the Andalusian garden of the past, current-day gardens, and the fantasy gardens of rhetoric is significant. The garden remains a symbolic place of origin, a cultural spring that is partially realized in other geographical locations but is also an unattainable chimera. The persistence of the garden as an ideal place in al-Ḥarīzī's oeuvre points to cultural remembering and longing. As stated concisely in the *Taḥkemoni*'s opening poem:

> . . . In his land his might and glory rose on high,
> but with wandering he is brought low, humbled . . .
> His land was the garden of God,
> But he was exiled from its comeliness, driven out . . .
> His name is well-known, Judah Ben Solomon,
> and the name of his land and birthplace is Sefarad.[22]

Water over Stones: Landscape in Sefer ha-meshalim

Sefer ha-meshalim does not make extensive use of landscape in its rhetorical episodes. Chapter 2, a debate over the respective virtues of poetry and prose, is not set in a garden, meadow, or desert but rather in a *beit midrash,* a house of study. Chapter 3, a tournament among poets, takes place in a generic council of intellectuals.[23] Ideal landscapes are simply not to be found in the book's rhetorical episodes.

The feeling of having arrived at an idyllic place is experienced in the love stories, particularly at moments when lovers are united. In chapter 6, the story of Maskil and Peninah, the pure and innocent youths are sporting with each other when she suggests to him:

> "Come, my love, we will go out to the field and repose in the villages [cf. Song of Songs 7:12], for such is the custom of fawns" [i.e., lovers]. He hastened to rise from his seat and readied his chariot. Male and female youths went out and strolled along the rivers and alighted upon the river of love, the place of the nobility's delight. There were stones like sapphires, water flowing over them; sweet, pleasant trees surrounded [the river], their branches long, their boughs many, species of birds of flight upon them,

> leaping and twittering. The valleys were covered with spice beds, spread over with them. They fondled the breasts of delight and covered themselves with the garment[24] of pleasure. They sat beneath the shade of tranquility, delighting in joy and mirth.[25]

Certainly, the vocabulary of this landscape description is very similar to that found in Andalusian garden poems. Still, this landscape seems rather distinct. First, the setting is outdoors and not connected to a palace. This is not the planned landscape of a courtyard interior. It shares elements with the desert oasis occasionally encountered in *maqāma* literature (trees, a river, etc.), though it does not seem to be situated within a desert. The association with the delight of nobility also distinguishes the landscape. At the "river of love," there is ample space for lovers to stroll at leisure. Unlike the rivulets in a man-made garden, the water of the river flows over stones, which seem like radiant gems. Around the river are trees with chirping birds, and beyond the foreground are valleys. There is no sense that the landscape has been planned by an engineer or an artist, nor is the description made to impose a sense of the artificial upon the natural. Activities associated with the Andalusian garden, such as wine drinking and the entertainment of singers, are also absent.

A similar landscape is present in chapter 5, in which the young lovers Sapir and Shapir are separated when Shapir is lured away by the nefarious Birshᶜa of Sodom.[26] Sapir wallows to the point of self-destruction, until he is led to his lover and finds him with Birshᶜa at *ᶜein rogel.*[27] After Birshᶜa is imprisoned and Shapir repents for the folly of his temptation, the lovers retire to a spring:

> [Sapir's] heart rejoiced in his beloved, and his soul[28] was glad. He beheld the spring, that it was broad with sweet waters, watering plains and valleys. Pleasant[29] trees were planted along banks that watered them constantly so that they might send forth branches. All of the birds upon them were chirping. The spring was pure like the face of a gazelle. Its stones were white, [its] rubies were large and small, redder than the color of coral.[30]

Again the landscape seems natural, not planned. Again there are trees planted by water, birds chirping, and stones like gems beneath the water.[31]

What is this place to which the lovers have retreated? What is the landscape's significance and whence its origin? Tracing sources for landscape descriptions is a difficult endeavor, especially since most world literatures include descriptions of gardens and natural refuges. The natural, outdoor settings of *Sefer ha-meshalim* bear a striking resemblance with a *locus amoenus* of the classical tradition that becomes prominent in European vernacular literature and is also present in several Arabic texts. Ernst Robert Curtius describes this "pleasance" as a "beautiful, shaded natural site. Its minimum ingredients comprise a tree (or several trees), a meadow, and a spring or brook. Birdsong and flowers may be added. The most elaborate examples also add a breeze."[32] Curtius gives an example from late Latin poetry, from a poem by Tiberianus, a poet of the Constantine period:

> Through the fields there went a river; down the airy glen it wound,
> Smiling mid its radiant pebbles, decked with flowery plants around.
> Dark-hued laurels waved above it close by myrtle greeneries,
> Gently swaying to the whispers and caresses of the breeze.[33]

Even earlier, in Greek traditions of Arcadia, we find the following description in an idyll of Theocritus (third century BCE):

> Then went Castor of the nimble coursers and Polydeuces ruddy as the wine together wandering afield from the rest, for to see the wild woodland of all manner of trees among the hill. Now beneath a certain slabby rock they did find a freshet brimming ever with water pure and clear. The pebbles at the bottom of it were like to silver and crystal, and long and tall there grew beside it, as well firs and poplars and planes and spiry cypresses, as all fragrant flowers which abound in the meadows of outgoing spring to be loved and laboured of the shag bee. In that place there sat taking the air a man both huge and terrible.[34]

Castor and Polydeuces' encounter with the "huge and terrible" man certainly reminds one of the disruption of Maskil and Peninah's tranquil moment at the "river of love" by the giant black horseman.

Romance literature adopts this *locus amoenus* of classical verse and puts it to various uses. The twelfth-century French *Le Conte de Floire et Blanchefleur,* most of which is set in Babylon, includes a description of the Euphrates: "Precious stones lie within the stream: no man ever saw gems with gleam so bright: sapphire, chalcedony, jacinth, sardonyx." Beside the river is a garden including trees, birds, fruits, spices, and a freshwater spring, which also ripples over "emerald and gravel." Above the spring grows the "Tree of Love" where the emir chooses his brides (whom he ultimately puts to death).[35] Other European vernacular texts transform the *locus amoenus* into a place pregnant with allegorical suggestion. The allegorical garden of *Le Roman de la rose,* a work roughly contemporary with *Sefer ha-meshalim,* bears many elements of its predecessors.[36] Apart from the paintings of the seven vices on the four walls, the garden consists of a few basic objects: birds, trees, a lawn, and the marble Fountain of Narcissus, which contains luminous crystals at its bottom.[37] Although the garden is clearly artificial, secluded within walls and furnished with a marble fountain, the organization of space is relatively haphazard. The trees are spaced widely around the fountain, held together loosely by a green lawn. In Romance, even landscapes that are artificially planned lack the careful ordering of space associated with the Andalusian garden.

Striking in all of the excerpts—from Theocritus, to Tiberianus, to *Floire et Blanchefleur,* to Guillaume de Lorris and Jacob Ben Elᶜazar—is the place of water as the site for love and the inclusion of radiant stones beneath the water of the river or spring.[38] This might make a model of influence from classical idylls, to medieval Romance, to *Sefer ha-meshalim* seem attractive.[39]

However, as Jaroslav Stetkevych has shown, idyllic landscapes exist in various imaginative Arabic texts—including Ibn Ṭufayl's *Ḥayy ibn yaqẓān,* al-Maᶜarrī's *Risālat al-ghufrān,* and *The Thousand and One Nights*—which must also be considered. Such texts bear a generic and possibly a genetic relationship to the idylls of the classical tradition. Ben Elᶜazar's nature descriptions call to mind the gardens where lovers meet in *The Thousand and One Nights.* In the story of ᶜAlī Ibn Bakkār and Shams al-Nahār, the slave girl of Harūn al-Rashīd, the caliph's "Palace of Paradise" includes a pond beside which maidservants sit on couches singing and strumming on lutes; here ᶜAlī Ibn Bakkār and Shams al-Nahār exchange verses of love (sung by the maidservants).[40] Yet this and all the other gardens in the *Nights*—including those in the stories of Shahriyār and his brother, Masrūr and Zayn al-Mawāsif, ᶜAzīz and ᶜAzīza, and Ibrāhīm and Jamīla—are man-made constructions; they feature domed pavilions, sculptures in gold and silver, jeweled staircases, and so on, and usually refer to the social practice of wine drinking.[41]

Water sources are commonly found in other Arabic texts at key narrative moments. In Ibn Sīnā's allegorical tale *Ḥayy ibn yaqẓān,* the narrator is immersed in the Spring of Life, situated at the border of the celestial Occident and Orient, the symbolic threshold of Matter and Form.[42] Al-Maᶜarrī's description of paradise in *Risālat al-ghufrān* depicts male and female singers in a garden flowing with rivers.[43] In the second journey of Sindbad the Sailor, a tale of medieval origin that was later incorporated into *The Thousand and One Nights,* the protagonist sits (alone) by a "spring of pure water" on a "beautiful island abounding with trees, ripe fruits, fragrant flowers, singing birds, and clear streams."[44] The theme of luminous stones shining beneath water seems rare in Arabic literature but is found in the sixth voyage of Sindbad the Sailor; the protagonist narrowly escapes a shipwreck, to find himself by a mountain stream: "I saw in that stream a great many rubies and royal pearls and all kinds of jewels and precious stones, which covered the bed of the stream like gravel, so that all the channels, which ran through the fields, glittered from their profusion."[45]

Once again, it is difficult to link the motif from *Sefer ha-meshalim* exclusively to an Arabic or European source. It is possible that the author was drawing, either through written or oral transmission, upon traditions that were Arabic, European, or both. Although Ben Elʿazar likely drew upon some Arabic prototypes, the combination of elements—the setting's remove from civilization, its lack of artificiality, the association of the landscape with love, and the seclusion of the lovers—seems more closely related to the classical and Romance model. Even if one maintains that the topos in Ben Elʿazar's work can be explained sufficiently by cobbling together Arabic precedents, the question remains as to why the author selected this idyllic landscape over others. The landscape is quite distinct from the Andalusian style garden that was so beloved by al-Ḥarīzī.

The Andalusian-style garden is generally not idealized in *Sefer ha-meshalim*. Instead, the locus associated with wine drinking and the entertainment of aristocrats by maidens is the object of scorn and disdain. As discussed in the final section of chapter 6, the narrator Lemuʾel Ben Ittiʾel becomes morally enraged upon witnessing the indulgent practices of an aristocrat in his palace garden. The identification of the garden in chapter 8 of *Sefer ha-meshalim* with the Andalusian-style *hortus conclusus* is unmistakable. Such a garden would be Heman ha-Ezraḥi's and Ḥever ha-Qeni's finest refuge but is a decadent bastion of immorality in Lemuʾel Ben Ittiʾel's view.[46]

At the end of the episode, the four maidservants leave the palace garden after murdering their lord Akhbor and enter another setting, where they are approached by the four suitors (also quoted in chapter 6 of this book):

> They went out to the vineyards to browse in the gardens and to pick roses, strolling through orchards, meandering through the myrtles. They wore checkered robes and told parables, riddles, and precious songs by the grape-blossoms and vines and by all kinds of buds. They spoke by[47] the trees, the roses and the buds. At noon, they lay beside the pools of water, sitting beneath the shade, playing harps and lutes. Four young men were listening to the sound of their song, hearing their dancing and playing, enjoying the sound of the music, peering through the lattice. [The maidens] became aware of this and said, "Who is it who listens to our voices, standing behind our wall? Are you friend or foe?"[48]

The space is clearly surrounded with walls, yet this *hortus conclusus* could not be more distinct from the Andalusian garden; indeed, the author has juxtaposed two versions of the *hortus conclusus,* one of which is readily associated with the Islamic world and the other with Christendom. The garden of Akhbor and his servants offers ornate architectural elements, fire pans, wine vessels, and wine. The garden of the four ladies and their suitors lack these accoutrements.

Sefer ha-meshalim's enclosed garden of virtuous ladies and suitors more closely resembles the aristocratic garden of Romance literature—which has been called the *hortus ludi*, so called because of its association with play (*ludus*) and leisure—than the Andalusian garden.[49] As Elizabeth Augspach has shown, the garden in twelfth- and thirteenth-century Romance is a "social space, a place of recreation and relaxation, and ladies are naturally associated with pleasure."[50] The *hortus ludi* is removed from (but adjacent to) the noise, stench, and gloom of the castle. It is a playground for knights and ladies, the scene of dining, dancing, conversing, courting, frolicking, and music making.

Additionally, the *hortus ludi* serves as a place of refuge for lovers, especially those whose forbidden love makes them flee beyond society's gaze; in Chrétien de Troyes' *Cligès*, the protagonist and his beloved Fenice meet in a garden:

> [Fenice] then entered a pleasant and agreeable orchard. In the center of the orchard was a grafted tree that spread out at the top and was covered with many leaves and flowers. All the branches were trained to hang down so that they almost touched the ground, all, that is, except the trunk from which they grew. The trunk rose straight up. Fenice desired no other location. The small lawn beneath the grafted tree was most delightful and beautiful. . . . *It was there that Fenice went to play*, and made her bed beneath the grafted tree. It was there that the pair knew their joy and delight. And a high wall connected to the tower surrounded the entire orchard so that no one might come there without climbing first through the tower. Now Fenice was happy. There was nothing that displeased her. Lying on the flowers and the leaves, she had all she desired: she was free to embrace her lover.[51]

Although one might find walls, music, rhetoric, and flirtation in both the Romance garden and in the Andalusian garden, the assumed social dynamic is different in each. In the Andalusian garden (as in the garden of Akhbor and his maidservants), one is always aware of a man or an elite company of men being entertained by a singer, dancer, or flirtatious wine pourer. The men are usually seated and served, a sign of their social superiority over the servant. In the *hortus ludi*, social equals entertain one another by playing on instruments, reciting poems, and by making flirtatious conversation.

Never in Andalusian literature do four women go out to a garden to enjoy one another's company and to be courted by an equal number of suitors. The women appear as the men's social superiors rather than their trained and subservient wine pourers. As Augspach has shown for Christian literature, the garden is a space under a woman's control; this topos may be considered an extension of the power afforded the lady, the *dame,* in the Romance courtship.[52] The sharp dichotomy between social models in the eighth chapter of *Sefer ha-meshalim* is expressed succinctly through the language of landscape as the four maidservants leave the *hortus conclusus* of Akhbor and enter a new *hortus conclusus,* a *hortus ludi,* that is very much their own.

Geography

One feature common to all Hebrew poetry of the Andalusian period is a confined conception of space. The poet's gaze is generally fixed within strict borders, focusing on the limits of the garden, perhaps looking up to the sky, but almost never beyond his immediate surroundings. Mention is seldom made of places outside of al-Andalus, and when they are mentioned, those places appear as extremely distant. In the days of Ḥasdai Ibn Shapruṭ, Khazaria was a remote, quasi-mythic kingdom that the Jewish patron could "explore" through epistles and emissaries only.[53] When Samuel the Nagid claimed victory in the battle of Alfuente, he urged his coreligionists to regale him as far as Palestine, Egypt, and the academies of Babylonia.[54] The Land of Israel, which naturally merited much attention in devotional verse, also appeared as distant, almost unattainable. Beginning in the mid-twelfth century, this narrow purview began to open up, with Moses Ibn Ezra's poems of estrangement from Castile and Navarre and Judah Halevi's poems from his journey to Palestine. Still, throughout the writings of these wandering poets, the distances from al-Andalus to Navarre, Palestine, and Iraq continued to appear vast.

The Hebrew rhymed prose narratives are consistent in depicting a different conception of space. Although the precise formulation of narrative space differs from one text to another, places suddenly appear much closer together. Characters are constantly on the move, jumping from city to city—and to nonexistent utopian places—in the blink of an eye. Following the decline of Andalusian Jewry, Hebrew authors became very concerned with places, now casting an eye toward a broad world that individuals (especially fictional characters) could traverse with ease. Here is a point where history and literature converge; the geopolitical shifts of the post-Andalusian period brought about a literary transformation in which the very layout of the world was reimagined.[55]

Interestingly, R. W. Southern has noted a similar phenomenon concerning a shift in European literature from epic to Romance in the wake of the Crusades. Comparing the *Song of Roland* with the Romances of Chrétien de Troyes, he writes of the former, "We are in a limited world, the boundaries of which are clearly marked. It is for the most part . . . France from Mont St. Michel to the Rhine and from Boulogne to the Loire, with the coast road to the Pyrenees well mapped. Beyond the Pyrenees lies an unknown Moslem world, a wonder-world of fantasy and evil—a kind of parody of the Christian world."[56] In Romance, however, "we take a bird's-eye view of earth from above, where all unevennesses are leveled out, and from where it seems that men can go anywhere without difficulty. . . . The world is a wide one and we can move effortlessly from Winchester to Regensburg or Constantinople."[57] Similarly, in the post-Andalusian period, Hispano-Jewish literature looked beyond the Duero, the Pyrenees, and the Straits of Gibraltar to set its stories in Palestine, Egypt, the Maghreb, Provence, Syria, and Iraq, all closer together than ever before.

Scholars of literature have emphasized that the strict dichotomy assumed to exist between fiction and travel writing is false. Percy Adams has written, concerning the modern novel: "[W]riters who invented characters and sent them on journeys—and that means the great majority of authors of epics, romances, historic and other long narratives—satirized the details of travelers, employed such details imaginatively, perhaps fantastically, or actually transferred real ones from travel books."[58] Just as fictional writing draws upon a world that is factual, so travel writing, often assumed to be strictly documentary, employs something of the imaginative, and sometimes in heavy doses.

Maqāma literature, as an amalgam of many genres of writing, draws on the world described by travel writers by using the "facticity" of travel accounts to lend movement, familiarity, and sometimes irony to texts. There are, of course, great differences between the typical *maqāma* and the travel narrative. The *maqāma* usually reflects little interest in relating detailed information about a place (population size, economic matters, etc.) and generally lacks the travel narrative's sequential progression through a series of locations (a single *maqāma* episode usually entails one or two places at most, though we will see that the *Taḥkemoni*'s forty-sixth chapter is an exception). Still, the *maqāma* does retain the most essential element of the travel narrative: narrating the movement of a protagonist through space. In selecting an array of places in which to set their stories, and by ordering those places in a specific way, the authors of travel narratives and *maqāmāt* reveal a great deal about how they perceive the world. Narratives, fictional and factual alike, not only produce a rough sketch of the places within an author's purview but also give those places unequal weight, distorting their distances and presenting them in a kind of hierarchy.

The discussion that follows investigates the topic of geography in the works of three Iberian Jewish authors (with a brief excursus on the Arabic *maqāma*), including Benjamin of Tudela, who wrote a Hebrew itinerary of his journey from Christian Iberia through parts of Europe, North Africa, and the Islamic East; and the now-familiar authors al-Ḥarīzī and Ben Elʿazar. The discussion notes structural affinities and differences among the works and emphasizes that each work reveals a unique perspective on geography and the author's orientation between the realms of Christendom and Islamdom.

The Itinerary of Benjamin of Tudela *(Twelfth Century)*

The Itinerary of Benjamin of Tudela has been an essential text for reconstructing the Jewish communities of the twelfth century. Scholars have generally been interested in using Benjamin's data to paint a picture of the medieval Jewish world in a positivist fashion.[59] In contrast, we are interested in the literary dimensions of Benjamin's itinerary and in the construction of the world that emerges from his representation of geography. Benjamin begins his journey from his birthplace, Tudela in Christian Iberia, writing in the first person:

> I journeyed first from my native town to the city of Saragossa, and thence by way of the River Ebro to Tortosa. From there I went a journey of two days to the ancient city of Tarragona with its Cyclopean and Greek buildings, the like thereof is not found among any of the buildings in the country of Sefarad. It is situated by the sea, and two days' journey from the city of Barcelona, where there is a holy congregation, including sages, wise and illustrious men, such as R. Sheshet, R. Shealtiel and R. Solomon, and R. Abraham, son of Chisdai. This is a small and beautiful city lying upon the sea-coast. Merchants come thither from all quarters with their wares, from Greece, from Pisa, Genoa, Sicily, Alexandria in Egypt, Palestine, Africa and all its coasts. Thence it is a day and a half to Gerona, in which there is a small congregation of Jews. A three days' journey takes one to Narbonne.[60]

By the time he leaves Barcelona, Benjamin changes voice from the first-person "I journeyed" to the impersonal "It is an *x*-day journey to destination *y*," a voice he sustains throughout the rest of the narrative. For this reason, the text is understood best as an "itinerary" rather than a first-person travelogue. The use of this formula makes it difficult to know whether the author journeyed from place to place in the order related, and sometimes whether he journeyed to those places at all.[61]

Benjamin offers relatively sparse information about the first cities he encounters, most notably his hometown of Tudela, for which no information is offered whatsoever. Tortosa is equally generic. The architecture of Tarragona is mentioned only because it is anomalous in Iberia. It is a common characteristic of the travelogue to be reticent about places that are the most familiar to the author, both because the author imagines an audience with a perspective similar to his own and because the familiar seldom seems worthy of documentation. Despite the sparing amount of detail, we can already detect hints of the subject categories that will concern Benjamin throughout the itinerary: distances, geography, architecture, beauty, mercantile activity, trade routes, Jewish communities, and illustrious men. Barcelona merits some detail, being beautiful and an important mercantile center. Nearby Gerona has a small community of Jews. Not represented in this passage is Benjamin's penchant for ancient sites of religious and historical significance, which he details abundantly for the communities of the East.

The amount of detail Benjamin offers increases the farther he strays from his place of origin. His descriptions of the communities of the East have a certain "wonders of the East" feel about them. Baghdad, apart from its topography, architecture, wise men, and philosophers, also houses "magicians, masters in all types of witchcraft." In Persia, we read of the "people who worship the wind and live in the wilderness, and who do not eat bread, nor drink wine, but live on raw uncooked meat. They have no noses, and in lieu thereof, they have two small holes, through which they breathe."[62] We also read about Chinese helmsmen who, when thrown from their ship in a storm, cleverly cover themselves in ox hide in order to be seized by a griffin (*grifo*); intending to devour the sailor, the griffin brings him to a mountaintop but is then slain by the clever helmsman.[63] The theme of the griffin recalls the legendary *rukhkh* bird from *The Thousand and One Nights;* Ḥasan al-Baṣri wraps himself in camel skin to be carried to a mountaintop by the *rukhkh,* and Sindbad is also carried by a *rukhkh* in his second journey.[64]

The order of the itinerary is roughly as follows: Iberia—Provence—Italy—Constantinople—Greece—Levant—Iraq—Yemen—Persia—India—China—Aden—Libya—Ethiopia—Egypt—Sicily—Italy (again)—Germany—France (again). Marcus Nathan Adler notes that the order of Benjamin's travels seems somewhat "circuitous."[65] Why would one journey from Iraq to Persia via Yemen? Why not reach Yemen from Egypt? Why travel as far east as China and then return to Egypt, which was so close to Palestine early in the narrative? Why the repetition of Italy and France, even mentioning specific cities twice? Adler describes the erratic pattern as "understandable," given the turbulent political situation of Benjamin's time.[66]

As much as the curious order of the text might reflect medieval trade routes, it also helps illustrate Benjamin's worldview. The world is roughly divided into Christian and Muslim kingdoms. Benjamin begins in Christendom, where he is from, and ultimately comes to Palestine, a disputed territory in his day. From there, he embarks upon the Muslim world, beginning with three Arabic-speaking countries (Syria, Iraq, Yemen), and then explores more remote territories of Muslim influence (Persia, China, India). He then backtracks to more of the Arabic-speaking Islamic world in North Africa, Egypt, and Sicily. From Sicily, he returns to the Christian world for his final sections on Italy, Germany, and finally France, bringing the text back to the border of where it began. Thus, Christian Iberia would seem to contact the Christian world only; Benjamin ignores the Muslim kingdom in al-Andalus and makes North Africa seem more distant than it is in reality. The Iberian Peninsula appears as a part of Christian Europe. Thus, Benjamin's perspective is very much one of an author from the Christian world who sees the Islamic world as distant, foreign, and exotic. This is not to say, however, that he was untouched by Arabic literary or cultural trends. As mentioned, some of the exoticism of Benjamin's tales is reminiscent of similar scenes from *The Thousand and One Nights,* and, more generally, his style calls to mind the works of Muslim travelers. Still, his manner of framing the world identifies Christendom as his home.

Geography in the Arabic Maqāma

It is more difficult to find spatial order in the *maqāmāt* than in travel narratives, since episodes seldom follow one another in a consistent way and time is anything but chronological.[67] Still, much can be learned about an author's conception of geographic space, especially when we contrast one author with another. Al-Hamadhānī's stories are set exclusively in the Islamic world, with a heavy emphasis on the cities of Iraq and Persia, although Syria, Egypt, and the Arabian Peninsula also appear with some frequency. Al-Ḥarīrī's map of the world looks very much the same. Both authors largely refer to that part of the world most familiar to them. Interestingly, al-Saraquṣṭī's *maqāmāt,* although composed in al-Andalus by an author who may have never traveled to the East, are set almost exclusively in the East, focusing especially on the Arabian Peninsula. As James Monroe has shown, there is "a deliberate attempt to downplay the presence of al-Andalus in the work."[68] Al-Saraqusṭī does not dwell on cities in his immediate sphere of reference, nor does he simply reuse the geographical scheme of al-Hamadhānī and al-Ḥarīrī. Writing soon after the Almoravid takeover of al-Andalus, al-Saraqusṭī turned to the East as a more appropriate location for the realization of literary scenarios. Although idealizing the East as the font of high culture was not uncommon in the Arabic literature of the Islamic West, al-Saraqusṭī's preoccupation, precisely at a time when displaced Andalusian authors were memorializing their homeland, is striking.

Geography in al-Ḥarīzī

In his Hebrew translation of al-Ḥarīrī's *maqāmāt,* al-Ḥarīzī transplants almost all stories to Palestine and its environs, both because he wished to maintain the purity of his lexicon by selecting biblical place names only and because he wished to re-create the significance of Arabic place names in Hebrew discourse. The most obvious example is the resetting of al-Ḥarīrī's *maqāma* of Mecca, the destination of Muslim pilgrims, in Jerusalem, the destination of Jewish pilgrims.[69] In *maqāma* 19, the narrator departs from Iraq because of a drought and travels in the direction of Naṣībīn, a place praised by geographers for its beauty and plenty. In al-Ḥarīzī's rendition, the narrator begins in the drought-ridden land of Maratayim (Jer. 50:21, in Babylonia) and descends into Egypt, hearing that "there are rations in Egypt" (Gen. 42:2). Al-Ḥarīzī replaces a land of plenty recognized in Arabic geography with a Hebrew equivalent, mediated through the Joseph story in the Bible. Al-Ḥarīrī's twenty-fourth *maqāma* is set in Qaṭīᶜat al-rabīᶜa, which, according to al-Sharīshī, was an estate in Baghdad consisting of two fiefs on either side of a river. Al-Ḥarīzī sets the story in Miṣpeh gilᶜad, which was also constructed on two sides of a river (the Jordan), the eastern part being allotted to the Gadites and Reubenites (Numbers 32) and the western part to Menasseh (Joshua 17).[70] More important to al-Ḥarīzī than actual locations is the meaning associated with places within their respective cultural discourses.[71] In some instances, al-Ḥarīzī manages to preserve the approximate location of a place while invigorating the text with a biblical reference, as when he translates Alexandria in *maqāma* 9 with the biblical On, the residence of Potiphera, father-in-law of Joseph.[72] Although al-Ḥarīzī includes places from Egypt to Palestine and Iraq, covering much of the same geography as al-Ḥarīrī (excluding the Maghreb, Azerbaijan, and Persia), the weight of the narratives has surely shifted to Palestine and its environs, producing a "Hebraized" or "Judaized" text.

In composing the *Taḥkemoni,* al-Ḥarīzī had complete freedom to set stories wherever he chose. However, the author de-emphasized Palestine and included a broader vision of geography. The stomping ground of Heman ha-Ezraḥi and Ḥever ha-Qeni ranges from the Maghreb to al-Andalus, Christian Iberia, Provence, Palestine, Egypt, Syria, and Iraq (i.e., most of the world where there were Jewish communities). Place names in the *Taḥkemoni* are a complex topic, since they are sometimes selected for semantic and intertextual associations and do not refer to specific places as such. For example, *maqāma* 6, wherein Ḥever ha-Qeni relates to the narrator how he was duped into marriage with a hideous woman through the deceit of an old hag, is set in Teveṣ (Judg. 9:50), recalling the story of Abimelech's failed siege of a tower, when a woman dropped a millstone on his head.[73] In fact, it is not the protagonist who sets his story in Teveṣ but rather the narrator (who does not yet know the protagonist's story!), who opens, "I alighted in Teveṣ." The reader is tipped off that a story about the wiles of women is coming even before the protagonist appears.[74] Similarly, *maqāma* 36 is set in the land of Sevaʾim (the Sabaites, Isa. 45:14), where the protagonist proceeds to a tavern to find Ḥever ha-Qeni and a group of youths drinking wine.[75] Of course, Sevaʾim also calls to mind its homonym "drunkards, wine imbibers" (Ezek. 23:42), rendering the place name "the land of the wine drinkers," which is fitting for the scene that follows.

In many other cases, however, place names are selected from concrete locations in al-Ḥarīzī's world, offering some representation of reality. Stories are set in Damascus, Jerusalem, Tiberias, Mosul, Antioch, Baghdad, and other places, many of which the author himself is believed to have visited. In some cases, places are identified by their names in the Bible while in other cases they are simply transliterated into Hebrew characters. Al-Ḥarīzī sometimes offers glimpses of his attitudes toward specific communities. His ludicrous portrayal of the boorish Jewish community of Mosul, with its unlettered cantor who botches the morning prayers into a blasphemous garble, undoubtedly contains a kernel of truth for the author.[76] Complaints about the distortion and plagiarism of Andalusian poetry in Damascus taverns likely has some basis in reality as well.[77]

Apart from giving the names of cities that make up the author's world, the *maqāmāt* seldom offer much in the way of *ordering* space. Unlike the narration in most travel narratives, *maqāma* narration is not continuous but rather purposefully fragmented. Moving from one chapter to the next, the reader senses that the order of cities is almost random. The chapter of the *Taḥkemoni* that offers the most insight into al-Ḥarīzī's conception of geography is *maqāma* 46, in which Ḥever ha-Qeni, appearing undisguised from the beginning of the chapter, recounts all the lands he has visited and the laudable and blameworthy qualities of the cities' inhabitants. This chapter has been useful for historians who have strived to reconstruct the communities described, taking al-Ḥarīzī's narrative as an eyewitness account. In contrast, the following analysis considers how al-Ḥarīzī represents and orders space in the narrative. Although the account is based on al-Ḥarīzī's observations, it also bears the earmarks of having been written in hindsight. Ḥever ha-Qeni begins his discourse:

> I was told in the days of my youth that Sefarad was a delight to the eyes, its light like the sun in the midst of the heavens, the spice of its dust myrrh to the nose, the flavor of its delicacies like honey to the jaws, its air the life of souls, its soil the choicest of soils, the splendor of souls, the joy of God and men, the flowers of its garden like the stars in the heavens, its land the crocus of the Sharon, the lily of the valley. The spirit of desire caused me to ascend furrows and to traverse lakes and seas, so I journeyed through deserts and cleft open breakers and traveled through passages. I made Sefarad my destination from my own land. And when I arrived there and encamped within its borders, I inhaled the myrrh and aloes among its tents. Praises seemed insufficient for her goodness, tongues inadequate for her attributes. I roamed through it from one end to the other, from city to city, and I passed through the land of Ishmaelites and from there I left for the land of the uncircumcised, where the Israelites dwell. I came to the princely city, Toledo, city of the kingdom whose garment is the grace of dominion and whose ornament is refined culture, to show the nations and princes its beauty, for there the tribes of God ascended.[78]

After describing several cities of Castile and Aragon (Toledo, Calatayud, Lérida, Barcelona), their inhabitants, intellectuals, poets and patrons, the protagonist goes on to describe several communities of Provence (Narbonne, Beaucaire, Marseille) and their dignitaries. From there, the protagonist journeys "by sea to the lands of the East," first to Alexandria and then to Cairo and Jerusalem. From Jerusalem, he continues to several cities within the borders of the Land of Israel (Ashkelon, Acre, Safed), and then to Damascus, which occupies a long section of the narrative. From Damascus he journeys to Mount Zemarayim,[79] Ḥoms, and Aleppo, which also occupies a long section of the narrative. After Aleppo, the protagonist visits a few other cities of the East (Maraghah, Sarūj, Aram-Naharayim, Harran, and Mosul), finally arriving in Baghdad, where the narrative ends.[80] There is no final exchange between the narrator and protagonist and no departure scene.

There is nothing illogical or inconsistent in the arrangement of geographical space. One might complete such a journey without backtracking or crisscrossing one's route; this itinerary may have approximated al-Ḥarīzī's own, though it is undoubtedly an idealized version.[81] Interestingly, al-Ḥarīzī's

Judeo-Arabic *maqāma, al-Rawḍa al-ʾanīqa* (The Elegant Garden), also recounts an Eastern journey with many of the same details but follows a slightly different itinerary.[82] For example, Fusṭāṭ and Cairo are the first cities mentioned in Egypt, rather than Alexandria. A likely explanation for this is that the two texts are ordered according to different logical principles. The Arabic version, which is later, presents the most major cities in the region first, whereas the Hebrew is ordered according to the route a traveler arriving from the Mediterranean might actually take; naturally, one would come to the port city of Alexandria before traveling up the Nile to Cairo.

In any case, the *Taḥkemoni* offers virtually no topographical description, which places it in contrast with Benjamin of Tudela's *Itinerary.* Accounts of city layout, landscape, and architectural and engineering achievements are likewise absent for the most part. Instead, al-Ḥarīzī writes almost exclusively about individual leaders and men of learning, using the narrative as an opportunity to praise individuals of his age and lampoon others: "I mention their names in my book and engrave them in it with a pen of iron, so that the last generation will behold their deeds."[83]

Naturally, not every city gains the same amount of attention in the narrative. The general flow of the narrative involves a movement from West to East, from al-Andalus, to Christian Iberia, southern France, the "proximate" East (Egypt, Palestine, Syria), and ultimately the "distant" East (Iraq). Movement flows from city to city, addressing small settlements briefly and giving extensive treatment to the largest communities of the day. There is almost no mention of any space except a city; nothing is said of the terrain between any two points apart from the sea traversed between Provence and Palestine, and the Nile river that joins Alexandria and Cairo.

Like any narrative, the travelogue, or a semi-fictitious travelogue such as the *Taḥkemoni*'s forty-sixth chapter, is created by an author who orders space, structuring it and infusing it with a unique perspective. The arrangement of space in this narrative corresponds to the perspective one might expect of al-Ḥarīzī himself. Even if Ḥever ha-Qeni's journey is not identical with al-Ḥarīzī's own personal itinerary, it is a schematic, idealized version of his general movement. Still, the author and the protagonist should not be confused. Unlike al-Ḥarīzī, Ḥever ha-Qeni was not born in Sefarad but began his journey from his "own land," the Land of Wandering (*elon be-ṣaʿananim*), and came to Sefarad upon learning of its distinguished reputation.

One of the most interesting points of the narrative is the protagonist's brief visit in Iberia to "the Land of the Ishmaelites," for which there is no mention of specific cities or individuals (unlike for every other region in the narrative). In al-Ḥarīzī's day, of course, there were virtually no Jews in the cities of Islamic al-Andalus. But if there were no Jews to speak of, then why include Islamic Iberia in the narrative, and why as the starting point of the journey (that is, after *elon be-ṣaᶜananim*)? The author himself was not born in Islamic Iberia and, for all we know, never even visited there. All we are told of Islamic Iberia is what the protagonist learned in the days of his youth—that it was a delight to the eyes, the life of souls, a garden. In the *Taḥkemoni,* Islamic Iberia exists as a place of memory that is condensed and abridged, evoked but not described. Perhaps because of his own nostalgic longing or perhaps out of respect for the Andalusian tradition, al-Ḥarīzī considered al-Andalus important to include in his geographical representation.[84]

The overall conception of space in this chapter of the *Taḥkemoni* is quite distinct from *The Itinerary of Benjamin of Tudela.* In the *Itinerary,* the narrative begins and ends in Christendom, thus enframing the Islamic world within the Christian world, the author's point of reference. Christian Iberia somehow seems to border the Christian world only, even though a Muslim kingdom lay just to the south of Benjamin's point of origin. Ḥever ha-Qeni's itinerary, in contrast, is a unidirectional journey from Islamdom (al-Andalus) through Christendom (Christian Iberia and Provence) and back to Islamdom (the East). If the representation of geography in the *Taḥkemoni* stubbornly resists a center, it does have a vanishing point in the East.

In fact, the movement from West to East is a repeating motif in the *Taḥkemoni* and is helpful in understanding al-Ḥarīzī's perspective on cultural transition in the centuries following the decline of Andalusian Jewry. Although al-Ḥarīzī was born in Christendom, his cultural identity remained bound to al-Andalus. Throughout his writings, one gains the sense that al-Ḥarīzī sought to re-create what was lost with the demise of Andalusian Jewry. The Islamic East provided the most viable site for cultural revitalization. When al-Ḥarīzī praises the Jews of Aleppo, *before* mentioning any of the indigenous dignitaries, he mentions Rabbi Joseph Ibn ᶜAqnin, a leading figure in Maghrebi Judeo-Arabic thought, who left the Maghreb for Aleppo: "Apart from the pleasant qualities of [Aleppo's] community and the precious deeds of its leaders, the savior and master, the sage Rabbi Joseph the Maghrebi came to it some thirty years ago. His wisdom is as Ecclesiastes', his mind is like burning coal, his tongue a consuming flame."[85] Here, a comparison between al-Ḥarīzī and al-Saraquṣṭī is poignant; whereas al-Saraquṣṭī identified with the East but remained in al-Andalus, al-Ḥarīzī identified with al-Andalus and migrated to the East.

The movement of knowledge from West to East also underscores several chapters of the *Taḥkemoni.* In *maqāma* 5, the *maqāma* of the months of the year, Heman ha-Ezraḥi witnesses a tournament of twelve poets, each charged to improvise a poem on a month of the year. The setting is a palace garden in spring, the description of which includes endless clichés borrowed from Andalusian poetry.[86] The poets recite poems about the garden, its wine and watercourses, its lovely maidens and youths. Instead of concluding with a departure scene, the episode ends with the poems reaching Damascus:

> And when these words were heard in Damascus, its congregation learned them as they learned the recitation of the *Shemᶜa* [prayer]; they kept their commandments and were meticulous about their very letters, learning their laws by heart. Every day they rise early to recite them in their palace gardens, before one can distinguish between blue and violet.[87] They utter them in the morning service before their prayers and at night.[88] Their sleep cannot be sweet until they recite them in bed. Everyone one of them learned them, from the meek to the mighty—they, their children, and their children's children forever and ever.[89]

This is a clear expression concerning the arrival of Andalusian knowledge in the East and the zealousness with which the Easterners cultivated that knowledge. Al-Andalus is not mentioned explicitly, but the identity of the poetry's contents as Andalusian in origin is unmistakable.[90] Of course, the scene is meant to be humorous and perhaps even a bit critical; the song that so enthralled the people of Damascus also became the song of drunkards. However, the movement of knowledge from West to East remains at the core of the narrative.

Regarding the status of culture in the Islamic East, al-Ḥarīzī offers mixed messages. On the one hand, wisdom is as great in the East as it is in Iberia, attributable to astronomical and geographical phenomena:

> The border of Sefarad corresponds directly to the middle of the heavens, beneath the line of latitude.[91] The children of Babylonia are on the latitudinal line in the East while the children of Sefarad are on the line in the West. For this reason, wisdom disseminated in both of these extremes, for they are on opposite sides of the sphere; they are the pillars upon which the house is fixed. In both of these places, the world became wondrous and mighty.[92]

On the other hand, the quality of Eastern poetry (along with the poetry of France, Germany, and Greece), is held in low esteem:

> There is no wisdom that [the inhabitants of these countries] did not inherit, and there is no good quality that they did not conquer; only the land of poetry did they behold from afar but not enter. They thought that they

> learned the art of rhyme, and held that they observed it, but poetry remained distant from them and did not approach as the East is distant from the West.[93]

In *maqāma* 3, the *maqāma* of the poets, Ḥever ha-Qeni appears at an Eastern aristocratic feast disguised as a gluttonous old man in tattered clothes. Throughout a semi-cultured conversation concerning the Andalusian poets, the protagonist sits silently, feigning ignorance. Ultimately, he interrupts the aristocrats' banter and rebukes their ignorance: "As for the poets you have mentioned, I was there when they fought their battles; I am come from the battlefield. My heart is a scroll for their themes, I am a book of remembrance for their poems."[94] After speaking eloquently about the poetry of the bygone age, Ḥever storms out of the feast, frustrated at his company of epigones. Ḥever ha-Qeni is a relic from a past era, now condemned to wander the earth without an equal. He is the conduit of a lost, idyllic culture to the present. The present, however, is lacking a refined circle of luminaries as once existed in al-Andalus. Al-Ḥarīzī portrays the East as a place where the Andalusian heritage is esteemed, perhaps the only place where an intellectual can find culture, even if it is ultimately unsatisfying.

Studying the representation of space in the *Taḥkemoni* is essential for understanding al-Ḥarīzī's orientation in the thirteenth-century culture of transition. Although born in Christian Iberia, al-Ḥarīzī portrays al-Andalus as the cultural spring from which all creativity, including his own, flows. It is a quasi-mythic place of origin that is remembered and idealized. In his representation of geography, al-Ḥarīzī only includes places in Christendom that are culturally continuous with al-Andalus (Christian Iberia and Provence are thus included, and northern France and Germany are excluded); the focus of the text remains fixed on the Islamic world and issues arising with the transplanting of culture from West to East.

Geography in Ben Elᶜazar

Sefer ha-meshalim does not contain a travelogue that may be associated with the author's experience even though several characters are sent on journeys, usually to places in the Islamic world. In chapter 7, the protagonist Yoshfeh journeys from his hometown of Ḥaṣar Susa to Cairo, where he encounters two women in a slave market, both of whom become his lovers. In chapter 9, the youth Sahar from Gat Rimon is shipwrecked in the city of Ṣova, probably Aleppo, "on the seashore,"[95] where he falls in love with the princess Kimah. One might imagine that Ben Elᶜazar's sources were Arabic because of the story settings. However, the *Chansons de geste* and Romances such as *Le*

Conte de Floire et Blanchefleur and *Aucassin et Nicolette* also send characters on journeys to the Islamic world, which makes the trail of influence more difficult to trace. The question to consider is whether Islamic cities exist within the author's world of experience or whether they are imagined as part of a distant world "over the border."[96] This is best approached by considering the manner of city description and the author's frame of reference.

The only places described in *Sefer ha-meshalim* that can be identified with specific cities are in the Islamic world. Ben Elᶜazar's city descriptions are reminiscent of writings of travelers and other authors of imaginative fiction. Let us consider his description of Cairo. After arriving in Cairo, Yoshfeh

> dwelt between the two walls[97] and saw that its walls were whiter than limestone, that its stones were redder than coral, their forms like sapphire,[98] their tips like yellow jasper, stone that is black, red, and hail-colored, possessing all precious ornaments.[99] One stone seemed to be two, and each stone had seven eyes.[100] The building was made wondrous with stones to such an extent that it seemed inlaid with jewels. He picked up his poem and said:
>
> Cairo is praised,
> elect among her sisters,
> Fortified on all sides,
> her towers are lofty,
> With a wall of checkered craftsmanship,
> its plated settings are beautiful.
> Its stones are the color of sapphire;
> its edges are like jasper.
> She is like a mother to provinces,
> and the cities are her daughters.
> Among them she is like a queen-consort,
> her handmaidens all around.
> The ornaments of her ring and necklace
> are the Nile around her throat.
> She does not fear the coming of heat
> for her rivers are her rain.
> How lovely are her dwellings,
> how goodly her habitations![101]

After leaving his place "between the two walls," we move directly to the "market of sweet young women"; Ben Elᶜazar's employment of the slave market as a literary topos is certainly reminiscent of several scenarios in *The Thousand and One Nights.*[102] From the slave market, Yoshfeh and Yefefiyah come to an oriental palace:

> The house had twelve entrances and lacked no beautiful thing. In the courtyard were planted lovely trees of every species, high and lofty; within it were pools of water and all sorts of birds and winged creatures. Surrounding the pools and springs were meshes of latticework, long and beautiful boughs, birds flying, murmuring, and chirping. The structure of the house was comely, a house grand in appearance. Four buildings, windows facing one another, grasped the courtyard. [The buildings'] construction was strong and firm. Upon their surfaces were columns and a beam. When he came and saw it, he picked up his poem and said:
>
> A broad palace of lofty construction,
> forms of lions engraved upon it.
> The buildings of its mansions bear inscriptions;
> its upper chambers are lovely and spacious.
> From the mouths of lions water pours forth
> upon numerous stones like bdellium.[103]
> Trees are planted along a pool of water,
> their branches extend to the tank.[104]
> They are verdant in the summer and fall;
> in cold and in heat they remain succulent.
> Turtledoves chirp on branches
> and doves cry out among shrubs;
> They declared their pedigrees among buds and lilies
> and brought forth eggs and chicks.[105]
>
> Masos brought him every ornament, a bed of carpets, and gave him a treasure from every precious vessel in the guarded house.[106]

The descriptions of the gate and the oriental palace inspire wonder but are also generic; they are likely extracted from a conglomeration of reports of Cairo that Ben Elᶜazar had read or heard. Medieval Muslim and Christian travelers left ample descriptions of the Egyptian capital, which is also depicted repeatedly in *The Thousand and One Nights.*[107] There is no source that corresponds with Ben Elᶜazar's description precisely, though elements of the description can be found in various travel writings. Many gates in the Islamic world were double-walled, such as those in Baghdad or Bab Zuwaylah in Cairo. The famous pilgrim Ibn Jubayr, who visited Cairo in 1183, describes the fortifications of Cairo's famous encompassing citadel, which corresponds with Ben Elᶜazar's praise for Cairo as "fortified on all sides."[108] Arab travelers such as al-Baghdādī (1160–1231) and Ibn Saᶜīd (1213–86) comment upon the extraordinary height of buildings in Cairo (corresponding with Ben Elᶜazar's "lofty towers") but refrain from likening the appearance of facades with multicolored stones.[109] In fact, Ibn Saᶜīd, who was Ben Elᶜazar's contemporary, writes that the mosques of Cairo are less ornate than those of Seville and Marrakech and that the general appearance of the city is dilapidated and without a "single white wall" (which contradicts Ben Elᶜazar's "walls whiter than limestone").[110] Although some travelers describe mosaics on certain buildings, particularly mausoleums, the *gates* of Cairo are never depicted as fancifully as they are in *Sefer ha-meshalim.* In many ways, the description is of the generic variety one might encounter in *The Thousand and One Nights.*

Elaborate descriptions of Cairo were not solely the domain of Muslim travelers. A Latin description (also translated into French) of a Cairo palace was penned by William, archbishop of Tyre, a crusader of the twelfth century:

> Since the palace of that monarch is unique and after a fashion quite unfamiliar to our world, I have deemed it well to set down in detail what I have learned from the trustworthy accounts of those who visited that great prince, to describe its grandeur, his vast riches, and exceeding magnificence. . . . Hugh of Caesarea, accompanied by Geoffrey Fulcher, a knight of the Temple, entered Cairo under the escort of the sultan, as chief of the embassy which was sent thither. On arriving at the palace, which in the Egyptian language is called *Cascare.* . . . they were conducted into a large and spacious court open to the sky which freely admitted the sun's rays. There, supported by columns of marble covered with designs in relief were promenades with fretted and gilded ceilings and pavements of various colored stones. . . . So elegant was both material and workmanship that involuntarily the eyes of all who saw it were ravished by the rare beauty and never wearied of the sight. There were marble fish pools filled with limpid waters; there were birds of many kinds, unknown to our part of the world.[111]

Ben Elᶜazar's and William of Tyre's descriptions share a number of details, including columns, engravings, pools, exotic trees, and birds. Like Ben Elᶜazar's description and those found in *The Thousand and One Nights,* William of Tyre's representation of Cairo is idealized and inclines toward the wondrous and the exotic.

For Ben Elᶜazar, Cairo was an appropriate backdrop for a tale of the erotic and the exotic.[112] We will probably never know exactly which sources Ben Elᶜazar employed in creating his literary representation of Cairo. His depiction was constructed out of images of the Islamic world reaching Christian Iberia through Arabic written sources and popular tales and possibly through the reports of Christian crusaders and pilgrims. In any case, the description of the Egyptian capital is a product of the imagination of an author who never visited Cairo and who wished to design an exotic place for the entertainment of his readers.

Another city description is found in chapter 9, when Sahar comes to Ṣova, which is likely meant to be Aleppo. As in the case of Cairo, the description of the city focuses on marvelous and exotic elements. Moving from one palace chamber to another and gradually approaching his beloved, Sahar is finally united with Kimah in an inner chamber:

> They came into the palace and its doors were cypress inlaid with yellow jasper, the work of magicians. Its floor, walls, and ceiling were made entirely of glass; the water formed a wall for them on their right and on their left.[113] When [he][114] came at first to [the palace] and [marveled] at its wondrous construction, he stripped off his clothing and shoes in order to swim, for he thought [the glass chamber] to be watercourses and rivulets. When he saw the water flowing beneath the floor, he thought that he would be in the water and drown.

As mentioned in chapter 5, the entire scene is reminiscent of the legend of Solomon and the Queen of Sheba as recounted in the Aramaic *Targum sheni* and in several Islamic texts. Ben Elᶜazar may have set this story in Aleppo since, according to the travelogue of Ibn Jubayr, the city's citadel contained an indoor spring of freshwater such that the water was kept in two cisterns behind a strong double wall.[115] For the details of the construction, Ben Elᶜazar may have also drawn upon the descriptions of ingenious water-carrying machines for which Arab engineers were renowned.[116] Benjamin of Tudela's description of the water clock at Bab Jayrūn in Damascus could also have been a source of inspiration:

> There is a glass wall made with the workmanship of magicians, apertures all around corresponding to the counting of days of the year. As the sun enters each of [the apertures] on its [proper] day, it strikes it on twelve gradations corresponding to the hours of the day. In the palace are houses built of gold and glass such that when people walk around the wall they see one another whether one is inside or outside even though the wall is between them. There are pillars plated with gold and silver, pillars of marble of all colors.[117]

Benjamin and Ben Elᶜazar share the impression that the workmanship is that of magicians and the detail of completely transparent glass walls. Interestingly, remarkable water-carrying devices are also mentioned in French narratives about the Islamic world; the "Tower of Maidens" (in Babylon) as described in *Le Conte de Floire et Blanchefleur* presents an indoor spring and a hydraulic lift.[118]

It is possible that Ben El^cazar's sources were Arabic and/or French works since Islamic cities are portrayed similarly in both. In either case, Ben Elᶜazar does not seem particularly familiar with the places in which his stories unfold, which explains why the city of Ṣova is incorrectly located "on the seashore." The point here is not to demonstrate that Ben Elᶜazar failed to do his geography homework. Rather, it is to show that the Islamic world in *Sefer ha-meshalim* is a wonder world of exotic adventure, a place imagined, perhaps known through literature, but not truly known. It is a place of wondrous architecture, ingenious devices, and slave markets.

The geographical frame of reference in *Sefer ha-meshalim* is suggestive of an author who considered Christendom home and looked outward at the world of Islam. Characters that arrive at cities of the Islamic world generally begin their journeys in Christendom. Chapter 6, which never refers to a specific city in real geography, is instructive. The story opens with the "king of beauty" charging his ministers to "find a male or female fawn" (a beautiful boy or girl) "in all the territories of Shefer."[119] The ministers quickly produce the thirteen-year-old boy Maskil, who is appointed royalty and seated upon a throne. At this point, Maskil's advisers declare, "Behold, we have heard that there are lovers in the land of the Arabs!" Maskil hitches his chariot, assembles his entourage of soldiers and lovers, and journeys all night *derekh ha-ᶜarava,*[120] which may be translated "in the direction [literally, "the way"] of the Arabs." In the land of the Arabs, Maskil encounters the lovely Peninah, who is immediately entranced by her suitor. Recognizing his origins in Christendom, she recites a verse: "The face of the lover is ruddy [*admu*]. Because of this, they are called Edomites" (*adomiyyim,* i.e., "Christians").[121] This is a love story that unfolds across the border of the Christian and Islamic worlds, with Christendom serving as the starting point of reference.[122] Such a perspective is generally shared in the *Chansons de geste*—wherein knights venture forth from Christian territories to make forays against the Muslim enemy—and in Romance. In *Aucassin et Nicolette,* the protagonists journey from Beaucaire, to Provence, to Carthage (the Muslim city where Nicolette was born), and ultimately back to Beaucaire, where they are married.[123] In contrast, Arabic romances such as the stories of ᶜUmar Ibn al-Nuᶜmān or ᶜAlī Nūr al-Dīn and Maryam the Girdle-Girl from *The Thousand and One Nights* use Islamdom as the starting point of reference and allow protagonists to journey to Christendom.[124]

As mentioned, in chapter 7 the handsome youth Yoshfeh sets out on a journey to Cairo after his hometown, Ḥaṣar Susa, falls into decline following the political ascent of *nevalim,* scoundrels. Of course, it is difficult to know exactly where Ḥaṣar Susa is supposed to be; it is mentioned in Josh. 19:5 as part of Simeonite territory, although it seems unlikely that Ben El^cazar had Palestine in mind. The town name literally means "village of the horse," which is probably meant as a counterpoint to Cairo later in the story, where the mode of transportation is the mule.[125] Yoshfeh joins a band of reckless brutes, wine drinkers, and scoundrels and journeys with them through rivers and over mountains. Ultimately, he traverses the following places, which are transliterated here because of the striking phonetic effect:

> *va-yelekh el ereṣ meratayim / el shaʿarayim ve-ʿaditayim / el aram naharayim / be-ereṣ talʾuvot u-mabuʿei mayim / ʿad boʾo el ereṣ miṣrayim / meqom ye-ʾorim raḥavei yadayim / ve-ʿimo ha-alpayim ve-ha-maʾatayim / va-yeshev bein ha-ḥomotayim /*[126]
>
> He went to the land of Maratayim,[127] to Shaʿarayim[128] and ʿAditayim[129] and to Aram Naharayim,[130] [through] a land of drought[131] and [a land of] springs of water until he came to the land of Egypt, the place of the broad rivers, thousands[132] accompanying him. He dwelt between the two walls.

If we interpret all of the place names according to their known locations, then Yoshfeh would have journeyed from Palestine to Iraq, back to Palestine, and then back to Iraq before descending into Egypt. It seems unlikely that Ben Elʿazar actually meant all of these place names literally. Instead, they appear to be assembled here because of their shared phonetic quality of ending with the sound pattern of the dual form, *-ayim,* the rhyming sound of the passage. Because of the hammering effect of this sound repetition, the reader is constantly thinking of the number "two." Thinking grammatically, *maratayim* might be understood as a dual form derived from *marat* or *marʾa,* meaning "woman" in Aramaic and Arabic, respectively. Thus, the land of Maratayim might be rendered "the land of two ladies," appropriately foreshadowing the encounter of Yoshfeh and his two loves. Moreover, it might be a way of distinguishing between religio-cultural regions, between the land of one lady and the land of two ladies, between the land of monogamy and the land of polygamy, between the domains of Christianity and Islam. Through this long string of dual sounds, Yoshfeh journeys across a great border between his home in Christendom and the new and exotic Islamic world, where one can win the love of multiple slave girls. Egypt is the site of Yoshfeh's maturation process, wherein he learns to love and to act bravely. At the end of the narrative, Yoshfeh returns home a great adventurer, having mastered the distant terrain.

It is not clear whether other journeys in the book begin in Christendom or in Islamdom. In chapter 9, Sahar leaves his hometown of Gat Rimon (literally, "pomegranate press," a place name in Josh. 21:24) to travel by sea, when he is carried by a great storm to the "Sea of ᶜArava" (2 Kings 14:25) and to the city Ṣova, which, again, is likely meant to be Aleppo. We do not know that Gat Rimon is in Christendom; place names involving *rimon* (pomegranate) in earlier Hebrew texts refer to Granada, which was still under Muslim control in Ben Elᶜazar's day. On the other hand, reaching the Sea of ᶜArava may signify coming to Arab territory, just as journeying *derekh ha-ᶜarava* signified "in the direction of the Arabs" in chapter 6.[133] If the starting point is in Christendom, then this furthers the argument that the author's point of view is similar to that of his Christian contemporaries. If Gat Rimon is Granada, then Sahar's journey would be an adventure within Islamdom, suggesting that Ben Elᶜazar mixed points of view in his book.

In any case, Ben Elᶜazar's tales cannot simply be considered Hebrew versions of the interreligious love stories from the *Chansons de geste,* French Romances, or Arabic romances in that they omit the essential element of religious *conversion.* Christian authors consistently depict the conversion of Muslim characters, and vice versa; their stories embody the spirit of religious expansion and conquest particular to their age. Not surprisingly, the Jewish author avoids the conversion motif altogether. Although Ben Elᶜazar clearly adopts the theme of love between religious Others, he does not use it to support broader religious and political ideologies as Christian and Muslim storytellers do. Thus, although the book largely reveals an author who considered Christendom home, his cultural outlook and his narrative art are not identical to those of his Christian contemporaries.

Conclusion
Out of the Garden

One title that I considered for this book was *Out of the Garden: Cultural Transition in Iberian Jewish Literature.* The provocative phrase before the colon would have alluded to the nostalgia-laden associations of expulsion from paradise and also the discursive practice of figuring al-Andalus as a lost garden in Hebrew and Arabic letters. The title would have also signified going out of the garden in another sense that forefronts the contested place of Andalusian courtly values in Christian Iberia. Leaving the garden—at least the Andalusian-style *hortus conclusus*—could also mean leaving it behind and with good riddance, as suggested by the eighth chapter of Jacob Ben El^cazar's *Sefer ha-meshalim,* when four maidservants leave the world of Andalusian-style aristocracy for a new world, also courtly, to become ladies.

As discussed in the introduction, this book has treated two intertwined topics: "literature in transition" and "transition in literature." The destabilization of Andalusian Jewish society and the relocation of Jewish centers to Christian Iberia instigated several literary trends, such as the development of a Hebrew poetics of estrangement and the emergence of the Hebrew rhymed prose narrative. Whereas previous scholarship has understood these trends as imitative—one a product of Muslim-Jewish symbiosis in al-Andalus and the other an aftereffect of this symbiosis in Christian Iberia—this book has viewed cultural transition as a formative element in Hebrew literature. Cultural decay and migration were at the root of Moses Ibn Ezra's thoroughly Arabized nostalgic poems. The invasions of the Almoravids, the Reconquista, and the Almohads gave rise to a diverse range of poetic responses to catastrophe. The changing cultural context of the twelfth and thirteenth centuries called for a literary form that was more flexible than poetry, that allowed for a broader representation of the world and social types, and that allowed for existing elements of the Hebrew corpus to be refashioned and commented upon.

The variety of Hebrew rhymed prose narratives attests to the rich and complex literary world of Christian Iberia and to the cultural hybridity of

Jews within that environment. Judah al-Ḥarīzī remained a champion of the classical *maqāma* form, although the *Taḥkemoni* presents occasional thematic elements that are informed by trends in Christian literature. Jacob Ben Elʿazar's *Sefer ha-meshalim* testifies simultaneously to the transfer of Arabic literary values to Christian Europe and to the Europeanization of Iberian Hebrew literature. Some Arabic literary motifs, especially stock motifs of the classical *maqāma,* are evoked by Ben Elʿazar only in order to be lampooned. Although most elements of the book can be traced to Arabic precedents (or at least parallels, some of which postdate *Sefer ha-meshalim*), some motifs are more fully identifiable with aspects of European vernacular literature (landscape, courtly social practices, the love ideal). On the level of narrative structure, Ben Elʿazar embraced new ideals associated with the romance genre that was sweeping the Islamic world, primarily in popular literature, and also the Christian world. The book therefore bears witness to the complex interplay of literary currents in Christian Iberia, although the precise dynamics of this interplay remain obscure because relatively little is known about the circulation of Arabic popular literature and European vernacular literature in the thirteenth century.

Regarding "transition in literature," this book has treated a number of interrelated topics: the poetics of estrangement, forms of lamentation over catastrophe, and the representation of al-Andalus and its social norms. The Hebrew poetics of estrangement was shown to draw upon the repertoire of themes and motifs conveyed in the Arabic corpus; it might even be the case that authors' very experience of displacement was shaped by the discourse on estrangement and longing in Arabic literature. Moses Ibn Ezra's selection of the *qaṣīda* form to express estrangement and nostalgia for al-Andalus was fitting for an author with thoroughly Arabized values. Although he cast his voice in the language of the Bible, the Arabic character of his poetry also identified him as a speaker within the Arabic tradition addressing a dispersed circle of Jews with similar Arabized values. Judah Halevi sometimes joined in Ibn Ezra's Arabic-style musings over the past (especially when writing to Ibn Ezra). But when portraying the fall of communities during the Reconquista, Halevi imposed a dimension of theology on historical events that Ibn Ezra never did for the Almoravid invasion (or the Reconquista). Halevi interpreted Jewish suffering as compensation for Israel's waywardness and as God's just decree. Halevi's *petiḥa*s drew upon the sound of mourning firmly established in public Jewish lamentation rituals and were intended to offer consolation and evoke sympathy across the Jewish community. Interestingly, Arabic motifs of estrangement are more ensconced in Halevi's poems of pilgrimage to the Land of Israel; only through an experience of *ightirāb*—estrangement—could one atone for sin and attain the desired spiritual state of the devout. Abraham Ibn Ezra, who lamented the decline of Andalusian Jewry from afar, did so by conflating the local experience of Andalusian and Maghrebi Jewry with traditional tropes of Israel's exile and by memorializing fallen cities with their actual names. At the same time, the tone of his strophic poem remained highly personal.

Judah al-Ḥarīzī turned to the Arabic genre of wandering rogues and itinerant rhetoricians to create a literary world of movement and instability that mirrored his own experience. For all of its obsession with rhetorical display, the *Taḥkemoni* conveyed a kind of poetics of nostalgia insofar as its vagabond protagonist was gravely dissatisfied with the age in which he lived and yearned for the past, much like his counterparts in classical Arabic *maqāmāt*. Al-Ḥarīzī's own movement to the Islamic East was probably motivated by a search for satisfying culture, which meant finding a class of Arabized Jews versed in Hebrew literature and an Arabic Muslim court that would patronize a Jewish poet. Indeed, concern for Jewish cultural renewal in the East based on an Andalusian model lay at the heart of the *Taḥkemoni*.

Jacob Ben Elʿazar was dedicated to central pursuits of the Jewish Andalusian intellectual project, including the study of Arabic literature and philosophy and experimentation with Hebrew as a literary language. Yet he also portrayed select Andalusian social values as decadent and immoral, particularly those most readily associated with the courtier lifestyle. For Ben Elʿazar, the past could be preserved selectively. He replaced Andalusian social values with those of the Christian north while importing intellectual traditions from Islamdom to Christendom, which, after all, was also a pursuit of his Christian contemporaries.

Throughout the period of transition, al-Andalus was signified by the garden, the *hortus conclusus*, a favored subject of Andalusian Hebrew verse that came to stand for al-Andalus itself and its social mores. Authors who migrated out of al-Andalus carried with them memories of a courtier culture that was epitomized by its favorite setting, the garden. Most authors used the garden, over against other landscapes, to convey longing and nostalgia. From Christian Iberia, Moses Ibn Ezra re-created gardens whose existence was entirely poetic. Judah al-Ḥarīzī, who knew the garden primarily through poetic representations, set idyllic episodes of the *Taḥkemoni* in utopian gardens—replete with singers, wine pourers, and wine vessels—that stood as fonts of refined rhetoric and elegant discourse. Among authors treated in this study, only Jacob Ben Elʿazar satirized the garden and its associated social practices in order to pronounce the arrival of a new age and social code.

This book makes contributions to several areas of scholarship. It offers new interpretive lenses for the field of medieval Hebrew literature. I have combined traditional philological scholarship with a measured employment of modern literary theory while remaining mindful of the literary concerns of medieval readers. Although the medieval authors did not indicate why they selected specific motifs, poetic forms, or narrative strategies, these literary choices undoubtedly had significance for them, at least on an intuitive level. The poetics of nostalgia was firmly grounded in the evocation of specific themes—weeping over ruins, gazing at the night sky, wandering deserts—whose valences were culturally determined. Writing a poem in *qaṣīda, petiḥa,* or strophic form added a layer of meaning beyond the words of a poem and affected the way in which a poem would be received through associations with existing conventions. Creating figurative images was not merely a gratuitous exercise in revealing similitude among disparate objects but served as a vehicle for creating poetic meaning. Manipulating narrative voice allowed authors to refract cultural themes within their literary representations.

Studying the writings of Jews in twelfth- and thirteenth-century Iberia allows for a unique perspective on the paradox of cultural division and cohesion in medieval Iberia, especially since Jews were not religious insiders in either the Muslim or Christian domains. Does Hebrew literature represent Islamic and Christian Iberia as culturally continuous? Does it lend credence to modern perspectives that emphasize intellectual and cultural cross-pollination across the political and religious divide? Like Muslims and Christians, Jews generally portrayed al-Andalus and Christian Iberia as very different places. At the beginning of the twelfth century, Moses Ibn Ezra saw Christian Iberia as a foreign territory distinguished from al-Andalus by language, cultural practices, and landscape. In the second half of the twelfth century, Abraham Ibn Daud saw the flight of Jews "barefoot on the mountains of twilight" after the Almohad revolt as migration from one place to another. Judah al-Ḥarīzī divided the peninsula neatly into Muslim and Christian territories.

At the same time, the Hebrew literature of the thirteenth century reveals a high degree of hybridity, confirming that intellectual trends and popular storytelling techniques were not blocked by language or political barriers. Al-Ḥarīzī's *Taḥkemoni* and Ben Elᶜazar's *Sefer ha-meshalim* both betray that the authors were touched by Arabic and European literary currents. In several instances, motifs of Hebrew literature can be linked with parallels that were shared by Arabic and European vernacular literatures themselves. None of this is to say, however, that al-Ḥarīzī or Ben Elᶜazar thought of the Iberian Peninsula as unified, either politically or culturally. Ben Elᶜazar, in particular, presented some Arabic and European motifs in a pattern of contrast. Whether or not Provençal court culture was originally derivative of the Andalusian, Ben Elᶜazar found the two models sufficiently distinct to merit juxtaposition.

As an imaginary construct, Jewish Iberia—that is, Sefarad—underwent a physical transformation as al-Andalus became a memory. Having once been a Hebrew term that functioned discursively as the equivalent of al-Andalus, Sefarad came to designate a region with no real political boundaries that existed wherever Jews imagined it to be. Its borders were defined variously by different authors who restricted it to areas wherein Jews cherished select cultural values. Moses Ibn Ezra considered Sefarad to be al-Andalus only. Al-Andalus and also Castile (but notably not Aragon) were within Abraham Ibn Daud's Sefarad; for him, the borders of the imagined Jewish territory were determined by continuities in intellectual pursuits and the social values of a courtier class. In the thirteenth century, Judah al-Ḥarīzī stressed continuities in cultural and intellectual tastes among Jews in Christian Iberia, Provence, and the Islamic East. His Sefarad comprised Islamic and Christian domains, including cities in Aragon; al-Andalus remained Sefarad even though it had lost its Jewish population. Still, it is unlikely that al-Ḥarīzī's Sefarad extended to all corners of the peninsula. In essence, it was the extension of a Sefardi cultural model that determined the physical borders of Sefarad, and not vice versa.[1]

Most generally, this book has approached the problem of reading literature and history in light of each another. How can we avoid the circularity of reading texts in light of historical narratives that are, after all, constructed out of other texts? Undoubtedly, the circularity cannot be avoided altogether. My reading of chapter 8 of *Sefer ha-meshalim,* for example, is predicated on the interpretive lens provided by the Jewish class struggles of the thirteenth century. One might argue that the reading is designed to confirm a preconceived narrative. However, we must also ask what the price would be of *not* using historical data as a tool in literary interpretation. Certain texts (political cartoons are a good example) lose their meanings when severed from the world outside the text. Character portrayal means something very different when it involves a caricature of a known social type. Failure to recognize political divisions and social concerns would result in misreading. One must approach the dialectical process of reading judiciously but not imagine that texts are unrelated to their contexts as though time and provenance do not matter.

The analysis of literary texts can also change existing scholarly narratives. This book has challenged dominant theses within the fields of medieval Hebrew literature and Jewish history more broadly. Rather than viewing Hebrew literature as merely descriptive and imitative, this book has shown that literature functioned as an efficient vehicle for conveying a discourse about cultural transition. Rather than viewing the Hebrew literature of Christian Iberia as epigonic, this book has revealed that Jews in Christian Iberia enframed and recast the Andalusian literary heritage with great awareness, sometimes for ironic and even subversive purposes. Another thesis with which this book has engaged is the generalization that the Jews of Islamdom were deeply ingrained in their host culture while the Jews of Christendom were insular. Literary authors in Christian Iberia engaged with Arabic literature down to its most recent developments and were also affected by the literary trends of Christendom.

Was movement from the domain of "Ishmael" to the domain of "Edom" seen by Jews as a positive or a negative development? During the twelfth and thirteenth centuries, Iberian Jews stood with one foot in the Islamic world and one foot in the Christian world and could fix their gaze toward either horizon. Moses Ibn Ezra clearly viewed movement as decline, since Christendom appeared as a cultural and intellectual desert. Judah Halevi portrayed Christian Iberia as a place where Jewish culture had the potential to thrive, although his numerous poems from the unrest of the Reconquista reveal disappointment with the instability of Jewish existence under Christian rule. Halevi did not, however, couple this disillusionment with yearning for the past under Islam. Rather than seeking a revitalized Jewish court culture within Islamdom, Halevi set his sights on Jerusalem as a spiritual destination. Still, one is struck by how smoothly and enthusiastically he integrated into Jewish society in Alexandria and Cairo, which he called a Garden of Eden along the Nile. Abraham Ibn Ezra complained about the intellectual sterility of Christendom but, rather than returning to the Arabic-speaking world, where he may have found intellectual soul mates and greater possibilities for patronage, he traveled deeper into Christian Europe. It is difficult to reconcile his "preference" for the climate of Islamdom with his actual choice to reside in Christendom.

Judah al-Ḥarīzī left Christian Iberia, where he was active primarily as a translator, for the Islamic East, where he found patronage and prestige as an author of original Hebrew works and as an author of Arabic poetry. His notion of a successful cultural model was formed by his impression of Jewish court culture in al-Andalus. Jacob Ben El^cazar remained at home in Christian Iberia and adopted values of the Andalusian heritage selectively. The positions of these authors, taken together with those of other intellectuals, testify that the question of where life was better, under Christianity or Islam, was very much contested. Only with the help of literary texts read with careful attention to devices, conventions, tropes, and techniques can we discern this period of transition in all its complexity.

Notes

Introduction

1. Judah Halevi, *Kitāb al-radd wa al-dalīl fī al-dīn al-dhalīl* (*al-kitāb al-khazarī*), ed. David H. Baneth and Haggai Ben-Shammai (Jerusalem: Magnes, 1977), 169 (Book 4:17). Judah Ibn Tibbon translates *al-taghārrub* as *gerut*. At first glance, one might think that the translator has transformed Abraham's action from "emigration" to "conversion"; however, *gerut* appropriately captures the connotation of accepting the burden of becoming a stranger.

2. Ibid., 228 (Book 5:23).

3. I refrain from translating the Hebrew term *Sefarad* with "Spain," "Iberia," or "al-Andalus." This is explained further below.

4. Also, in a letter to David of Narbonne, Halevi states: "All I ask of God . . . [is] that He proclaim my freedom from slavery, find me a place of rest, and *exile* [or *estrange*] *me* to the place of living waters" (emphasis mine), *Dīwān,* 1:225.

5. Jefim Schirmann, *Ha-shirah ha-ᶜivrit bi-sefarad u-be-provans,* 2 vols. (Tel Aviv: Dvir; Jerusalem: Mosad Bialik, 1954–60), 1:489. (These volumes are herein abbreviated *HHSP.*)

6. See Franz Rosenthal, "The Stranger in Medieval Islam," *Arabica* 44 (1997): 35–75; the treatise attributed to al-Jāḥiẓ, "Risāla fī al-ḥanīn ilā al-awṭān," in *Rasāʾil al-Jāḥiẓ,* ed. ᶜA. S. Hārūn (Cairo: Maktabat al-khānjī, 1964–79), 2:380–412; Abū al-Faraj al-Iṣfahānī's *Adab al-ghurabāʾ,* ed. Ṣ. D. al-Munajjid (Beirut: Dār al-kitāb al-jadīd, 1972), this book has been translated into English by Patricia Crone and Shmuel Moreh, *The Book of Strangers: Medieval Arabic Graffiti on the Theme of Nostalgia* (Princeton, N.J.: Markus Wiener, 2000); Wadad Qadi, "Dislocation and Nostalgia: *Al-ḥanīn ilā l-awṭān,* Expressions of Alienation in Early Arabic Literature," in *Myths, Historical Archetypes and Symbolic Figures in Arabic Literature,* ed. Angelika Neuwirth et al. (Stuttgart: Steiner [in Komm], 1999), 3–31; Mark R. Cohen reflects upon the use of the term *gharīb* in connection with the "foreign poor" in Genizah letters, *Poverty and Charity in the Jewish Community of Medieval Egypt* (Princeton, N.J.: Princeton University Press, 2005), 72–77.

7. Moses Ibn Ezra, *Kitāb al-muḥāḍara wa al-mudhākara,* ed. A. S. Halkin (Jerusalem: Mekize Nirdamim, 1975), 2, 4.

8. Ibid., 66.

9. Dates of Islamic history in Iberia generally follow Mahmoud Makki, "The Political History of al-Andalus (92/711–897/1492)," in *The Legacy of Muslim Spain,* ed. Salma Khadra Jayyusi (Leiden: E. J. Brill, 1992), 3–87; some of these dates are marked slightly differently in other scholarly works.

10. Jews and Muslims remained highly integrated, most often in business but also, as some *fatwas* indicate, in residential areas; see Ibrāhīm al-Qādirī Būtshīsh, *Mabāḥith fī al-tārīkh al-ijtimāᶜī li-l-maghrib wa al-andalus khilāl ᶜaṣr al-murābiṭīn* (Beirut: Dār al-ṭalīᶜa li-l-ṭibāᶜa wa al-nashr, 1998), 95. Although Jewish merchants remained active during the first half of the twelfth century, the arrival of the Al-

moravids seems to have reduced their commercial opportunities; see Olivia Remie Constable, *Trade and Traders in Muslim Spain* (Cambridge: Cambridge University Press, 1994), 93. On the interpenetration of Muslims and Jews in urban society amid a growing segregationist ideology, see the well-known market regulations of Ibn ᶜAbdūn (Seville, early twelfth century): English translation by Bernard Lewis in Olivia Remie Constable, ed., *Medieval Iberia: Readings from Christian, Muslim and Jewish Sources* (Philadelphia: University of Pennsylvania Press, 1997), 175–79. The only evidence for the physical persecution of Jews during the Almoravid period recounts the storming of Jewish homes in Cordoba in 1134–35, leading to a number of deaths and the seizure of property; a similar attack may have affected the Jews of Granada twenty days later. Jewish safety was thus no more compromised than during the Tāʾifa period, which witnessed the more extreme massacre of Granadan Jewry in 1066. The Cordoba attack is mentioned by Mark R. Cohen, "Persecution, Response, and Collective Memory: The Jews of Islam in the Classical Period," in *The Jews of Medieval Islam: Community, Society, and Identity,* ed. Daniel Frank (Leiden: E. J. Brill, 1992), 147 n. 6. Būtshīsh, *Mabāḥīth fī al-tārīkh,* 101, mentions the Cordoba attack and also the incident in Granada, relying upon an anonymous source.

11. There was no noteworthy decline in intellectual activity during the Almoravid period; Isaac Alfāsi, Judah Halevi, Joseph Ibn Ṣaddīq, Solomon Ibn Ṣaqbel, Abraham Ibn Ezra, and Moses Maimonides were all active (or at least educated) in Almoravid al-Andalus.

12. Eliahu Ashtor, *The Jews of Moslem Spain,* 3 vols. in 2 with a new introduction and bibliography by D. J. Wasserstein (Philadelphia: Jewish Publication Society, 1992). Ashtor's narrative oddly concludes in the year 1085 with the Christian conquest of Toledo, at least seventy-five years before the Jewish presence in Islamic al-Andalus ceases to be detectable.

13. Yitzḥak Baer, *A History of the Jews in Christian Spain,* trans. Louis Schiffman, 2 vols. (Philadelphia: Jewish Publication Society, 1961–66). See his discussion "Intellectual Currents during the Reconquest," 64ff. For Ashtor and Baer, it would seem that Almoravid al-Andalus is already the era of the Jews of Christian Spain.

14. A recent contribution to the study of this period is a book on Judah Halevi and his circle of confidants; see Moshe Gil and Ezra Fleischer, *Yehudah halevi u-venei ḥugo* (Jerusalem: Ha-igud ha-ᶜolami le-madaᶜei ha-yahadut, 2001). This work depicts a transnational community of learned merchants whose correspondence reflects concerns for Jewish learning and communal advocacy. Of particular interest for our purposes are letters such as that of Ḥalfon Halevi ben Natanel, a merchant who visited al-Andalus for a period of two years, who wrote to Isaac, son of Abraham Ibn Ezra, in the year 1130 concerning his regrets after leaving al-Andalus to return to Egypt. See Gil and Fleischer, 332–37.

15. Valuable information about Jewish courtier culture during the Tāʾifa and Almoravid periods can be found in David Wasserstein's study of the Tāʾifa period, *The Rise and Fall of the Party-Kings* (Princeton, N.J.: Princeton University Press, 1985); see the discussion of the diminished yet extant Jewish courtier activity under the centralized Almoravid system, 99, 192.

16. Although some believe that they fled as a result of Almohad violence and persecution; see below.

17. The precise effects of the Almohad takeover of al-Andalus, with the first troops crossing the Straits of Gibraltar in 1125 though not securing power until 1147, remain recondite. Halkin and Munk believe that the invasion suddenly snuffed out Jewish life in al-Andalus, whereas Corcos-Abulafia believes that the decline was more gradual. Abraham Halkin, "Le-toledot ha-shemad bi-yemei ha-almoḥadin," in *Joshua Starr Memorial Volume* (New York: Conference on Jewish Relations, 1953), 101–10; D. Corcos-Abulafia, "Le-ofi yaḥasam shel shelitei ha-al-muwaḥḥadūn li-yehudim," *Zion* 32 (1967): 137–60. Halkin and Munk attribute an (undocumented) violent persecution to the reign of Ibn Tūmart (d. 1130) that forced Jews to accept conversion, flight, or martyrdom. Corcos-Abulafia argues that the status of Jews deteriorated only in 1165 following the execution of a Jewish notable, initiating a short period of unrest and forced conversion. For a summary of responses to this theory, see Constable, *Trade and Traders,* 95 n. 58.

18. Although we know of no Jewish intellectual life from the Almohad period, al-Andalus does not appear as devoid of Jews. The presence of Jews in al-Andalus is suggested by a writ issued by Alfonso X to Joseph Shabbetai in 1255. Following the conquest of Almohad Seville, the monarch confirmed that the Jew would retain the property rights that "he had enjoyed under the Moors . . . behind the stalls of the Jewish money-changers." See Baer, *A History of the Jews in Christian Spain,* 1:113.

19. Bulliet estimates that by 961, only half of the population of al-Andalus had adopted Islam, reaching perhaps 80 percent by 1100; see Richard W. Bulliet, *Conversion to Islam in the Medieval Period: An Essay in Quantitative History* (Cambridge, Mass.: Harvard University Press, 1979); for some revisions and an account of "Arabisation" in addition to "Islamisation," see Thomas F. Glick, *From Muslim Fortress to Christian Castle: Social and Cultural Change in Medieval Spain* (Manchester, England: Manchester University Press, 1995), 51–63. Islamic historical narratives and jurisprudence reveal that Muslim officials sometimes spoke a local, Latin-derived vernacular and that the Qurʾānic story of Joseph was recited in al-Andalus in Romance as late as 1120; see Consuelo López-Morillas, "Language," in *The Literature of al-Andalus,* ed. María Rosa Menocal, Raymond P. Scheindlin, and Michael Sells (Cambridge: Cambridge University Press, 2000), 33–59.

20. López-Morillas, "Language"; Joseph Yahalom, "New Clues from an Encounter with Old Spanish," in *Jewish Studies at the Turn of the Twentieth Century,* ed. Judit Targarona Borrás and Angel Sáenz-Badillos (Leiden: E. J. Brill, 1999), 1:561–67; David J. Wasserstein, "The Language Situation in al-Andalus," in *Studies on the Muwaššaḥ and the Kharja (Proceedings of the Exeter International Colloquium),* ed. Alan Jones and Richard Hitchcock (Reading, England: Ithaca, 1991), 1–15; S. M. Stern, "Les Vers finaux en espagnol dans les muwaššaḥs hispano-hebraïques: Une contribution à l'étude du vieux dialecte espagnol 'mozarabe,'" *Al-Andalus* 13 (1948): 299–346.

21. Edomese—"Christian-speak," based on a nickname for Esau, progenitor of Christianity, in Gen. 24:30; probably some Latin-derived vernacular. Qedar—a descendant of Ishmael, hence Arabic. Jefim Schirmann, *Toledot ha-shirah ha-ʿivrit bi-sefarad ha-muslemit,* edited, supplemented, and annotated by Ezra Fleischer (Jerusalem: Magnes, 1995), 25. When Ibn Gabirol identified Arabic as the language of Muslims and Romance as the language of Christians, he was probably referring to

the languages' communities of origin, since Muslims, Christians, and Jews spoke both languages in eleventh-century al-Andalus.

22. María Rosa Menocal, *The Ornament of the World: How Muslims, Jews, and Christians Created a Culture of Tolerance in Medieval Spain* (Boston: Little Brown, 2002).

23. For example, see María Rosa Menocal, *The Arabic Role in Medieval Literary History: A Forgotten Heritage* (Philadelphia: University of Pennsylvania Press, 1987); Jerrilynn Dodds, "The Mudejar Tradition in Architecture," in *The Legacy of Muslim Spain,* 592–97; Luis M. Girón-Negrón, *Alfonso de la Torre's* Visión Deleytable: *Philosophical Rationalism and the Religious Imagination in Fifteenth Century Spain* (Leiden: E. J. Brill, 2001).

24. Quoted in Franz Kobler, *A Treasury of Jewish Letters: Letters from the Famous and the Humble* (New York: Farrar, Straus and Young, 1952), 98–99.

25. Unfortunately, we do not know whether Jews living in Christian Iberia in the early part of the Middle Ages referred to themselves as Sefardim. The term does not appear, for example, in the tenth-century responsa of R. Amram Gaon to the community of Barcelona.

26. Washington Irving, *The Alhambra,* with an introduction by Elizabeth Robins Pennell, illustrated by Joseph Pennell (London: Macmillan, 1931).

27. Jorge Luis Borges, *Labyrinths: Selected Stories and Other Writings,* ed. Donald A. Yates and James E. Irby (New York: New Directions, 1964), 153–54.

28. L. P. Harvey, "The Political, Social and Cultural History of the Moriscos," in *The Legacy of Muslim Spain,* 201; on the nostalgic legacy of al-Andalus, see the review essay of Jayyusi's volume by Robert Irwin, "Andalusia of the Mind," *Times Literary Supplement,* August 13, 1993, 8.

29. S. D. Goitein sees the Hebrew poetry of Spain as the absolute acme of Jewish-Arab "symbiosis": *Jews and Arabs: Their Contact Through the Ages* (New York: Schocken, 1964), 155ff. Further on the term "symbiosis," see Steven M. Wasserstrom, *Between Muslim and Jew: The Problem of Symbiosis Under Early Islam* (Princeton, N.J.: Princeton University Press, 1995).

30. See, for example, Isadore Twersky's discussion of Maimonides' choice to write the *Mishne Torah* in Mishnaic Hebrew: *Introduction to the Code of Maimonides* (*Mishne Torah*) (New Haven, Conn.: Yale University Press, 1980), 324–36.

31. Bernard Septimus, "Hispano-Jewish Views of Christendom and Islam," in *In Iberia and Beyond: Hispanic Jews Between Cultures, Proceedings of a Symposium to Mark the 500th Anniversary of the Expulsion of Spanish Jewry,* ed. Bernard Dov Cooperman (Newark, Del., and London: University of Delaware Press and Associated University Presses, 1998), 43–65.

32. Bernard Septimus, *Hispano-Jewish Culture in Transition: The Career and Controversies of Ramah* (Cambridge, Mass.: Harvard University Press, 1982); idem, "'Open Rebuke and Concealed Love': Naḥmanides and the Andalusian Tradition," in *Rabbi Moses Naḥmanides (Ramban): Explorations in His Religious and Literary Virtuosity,* ed. Isadore Twersky (Cambridge, Mass.: Harvard University Press, 1983), 11–34. For a recent treatment of Iberian Jewish culture from the perspective of book art, see Katrin Kogman-Appel, *Jewish Book Art Between Islam and Christianity: The Decoration of Hebrew Bibles in Medieval Spain,* trans. Judith Davidson (Leiden: E. J. Brill, 2004).

33. Yom Tov Assis, "Sexual Behavior in Medieval Hispano-Jewish Society," in *Jewish History: Essays in Honour of Chimen Abramsky,* ed. Ada Rapaport-Albert and Steven J. Zipperstein (London: P. Halban, 1988), 25–59; idem, *The Golden Age of Aragonese Jewry* (London and Portland, Ore.: Littman Library of Jewish Civilization, 1997), chapter 5.

34. Bernard Septimus, "Piety and Power in Thirteenth-Century Catalonia," in *Studies in Medieval Jewish History and Literature,* ed. Isadore Twersky (Cambridge, Mass.: Harvard University Press, 1979), 197–230.

35. The need for such a study is already suggested by Baer; see *A History of the Jews in Christian Spain,* 95.

36. For a recent book on the post-Andalusian period that cuts across textual genres, see Gil Anidjar, *"Our Place in al-Andalus": Kabbalah, Philosophy, Literature in Arab Jewish Letters* (Stanford, Calif.: Stanford University Press, 2002). From a deconstructionist perspective, the author analyzes the modern project to represent the twelfth and thirteenth centuries as the "end" of al-Andalus, one of several "ends" of Jewish life in the Iberian Peninsula, culminating with the Expulsion in 1492. Noting that scholarship uses such ends to delimit hermetic boundaries between periods—that periods and places such as al-Andalus only "appear as they disappear"—Anidjar studies texts belonging to different genres (located by scholarship as philosophical, mystical, and literary), sharing only the feature of their context: that al-Andalus is disappearing or has already disappeared.

37. See, for example, Hayden White, *Metahistory: The Historical Imagination in Nineteenth-Century Europe* (Baltimore: Johns Hopkins University Press, 1973); Gabrielle M. Spiegel, *The Past as Text: The Theory and Practice of Medieval Historiography* (Baltimore: Johns Hopkins University Press, 1997).

38. Robert Chazan, "The Facticity of Medieval Narrative: A Case Study of the Hebrew First Crusade Narratives," *Association for Jewish Studies Review* 16 (1991): 31–56.

39. Ivan Marcus, "From Politics to Martyrdom: Shifting Paradigms in the Hebrew Narratives of the 1096 Crusade Riots," *Prooftexts* 2 (1982): 40–52; idem, "The Representation of Reality in the Narratives of 1096," *Jewish History* 13 (1999): 37–48.

40. Haim Beinart, *Conversos on Trial: The Inquisition in Ciudad Real,* trans. Yael Guiladi (Jerusalem: Magnes, 1981).

41. Benzion Netanyahu, *The Marranos of Spain: From the Late XIVth to the Early XVIth Century According to Contemporary Hebrew Sources,* 2nd ed. (New York: American Academy for Jewish Research, 1973); idem, *The Origins of the Inquisition in Fifteenth Century Spain,* 2nd ed. (New York: New York Review of Books, 2001). See also Carlo Ginzburg, *The Cheese and the Worms: The Cosmos of a Sixteenth-Century Miller* (New York: Penguin, 1982); idem, *Ecstasies: Deciphering the Witches' Sabbath* (New York: Pantheon, 1991).

42. Norman Roth, "'Deal Gently with the Young Man': Love of Boys in Medieval Hebrew Poetry in Spain," *Speculum* 57 (1982): 20–51.

43. Neḥemiah Allony, "Ha-ṣevi ve-ha-gamal be-shirat sefarad," *Oṣar yehudei sefarad* 4 (1961): 16–42.

44. For example, the poetry of Samuel the Nagid has been treated much more in the context of reconstructing the poet's (fascinating) biography and eleventh-

century Andalusian culture than in the context of literary study. See, however, Tova Rosen-Moked and Eddy M. Zemaḥ, *Yeṣirah meḥukamah: ʿIyyun be-shirei shmuel ha-nagid* (Jerusalem: Keter, 1983).

45. For an introduction to key terms of literary theory, see Frank Lentricchia and Thomas McLaughlin, eds., *Critical Terms for Literary Study*, 2nd ed. (Chicago: University of Chicago Press, 1995); Terry Eagleton, *Literary Theory: An Introduction* (Minneapolis: University of Minnesota Press, 1996).

46. Seth Schwartz, *Imperialism and Jewish Society: 200 B.C.E. to 640 C.E.* (Princeton, N.J.: Princeton University Press, 2001), 2.

47. Constructions of exile are also the subject of an article by Esperanza Alfonso, "Tefisat ha-galut u-teḥushat shayyakhut ba-sifrut ha-ʿivrit bi-yemei ha-beinayim," *Mikan* 1 (2000): 85–96. The article treats conceptions of national exile in texts by Ḥasdai Ibn Shapruṭ, Baḥya Ibn Paquda, and Solomon Ibn Gabirol.

48. Mark Cohen, "Persecution, Response, and Collective Memory."

49. In much of nineteenth- and early-twentieth-century scholarship, it became common to refer to the period of Jewish life in al-Andalus as the "Golden Age," a grandiose term betraying a fantasy of coexistence whereby Muslim rulers recognized Jews not only as subjects but as equals. This vision is now considered a myth debunked, originally constructed to serve the exigencies of European Jewish scholars who found precedent for their own acculturation by romanticizing the period of Muslim-Jewish coexistence. See Ismar Schorsch, "The Myth of Sephardic Supremacy," *Leo Baeck Institute Year Book* 34 (1989): 47–66. Within works of literary history, where the term may be more useful, the parameters of the "Golden Age" have not been completely stable. The Protestant scholar Franz Delitzsch, apparently the first scholar to use the term, divides the Hebrew poetry of Spain into three periods: the "Golden Age" (940–1040), the "Silver Age" (1040–1140), and the "Age of Roses Among the Thorns" (1140–1240); in this schema, made according to subjective aesthetic criteria, the "Golden Age" ends even before the death of Samuel the Nagid, while Solomon Ibn Gabirol, Moses Ibn Ezra, and Judah Halevi fall into the "Silver Age." See Franz Delitzsch, *Zur Geschichte der jüdischen Poesie* (Leipzig: K. Tauchnitz, 1836). Ashtor's chapter, "The Golden Age of Hebrew Literature," concludes with Solomon Ibn Gabirol and Baḥya Ibn Paquda, both authors of the eleventh century, and does not include such luminaries as Judah Halevi, Moses Ibn Ezra, or Abraham Ibn Ezra. In the introduction to his anthology of Hebrew poetry in Spain and Provence, Jefim Schirmann, using terms more descriptive than "golden" or "silver," offers the following division of periods: "beginnings of Hebrew poetry in Spain" (c. 950–1020), "classical period" (c. 1020–1150), "postclassical period in Spain" (c. 1150–1300), and "decline" (c. 1300–1492). Schirmann measures classicism and quality as functions of adherence to Arabic models; see *HHSP*, 1:lv. The value of the "Golden Age" has usually been measured as a function of acculturation with classical Arabic culture, a standard that has led many scholars to consider Jewish life in Islamic lands as superior to life in Christian lands, where Jews were less acculturated. For a critique of this tendency, see Ivan Marcus, *Rituals of Childhood: Jewish Acculturation in Medieval Europe* (New Haven, Conn.: Yale University Press, 1996), 9; idem, "Beyond the Sephardic Mystique," *Orim: A Jewish Journal at Yale* 1, 1 (autumn 1985): 35–53.

50. In general, see Schirmann, *Toledot ha-shirah . . . muslemit;* Raymond P. Scheindlin, *Wine, Women, and Death: Medieval Hebrew Poems on the Good Life* (Philadelphia: Jewish Publication Society, 1986); idem, *The Gazelle: Medieval Hebrew Poems on God, Israel, and the Soul* (Philadelphia: Jewish Publication Society, 1991); Ross Brann, *The Compunctious Poet: Cultural Ambiguity and Hebrew Poetry in Muslim Spain* (Baltimore: Johns Hopkins University Press, 1991).

51. Poets of this postclassical period such as Todros Halevi Abulafia (1247–d. after 1298) and Meshullam Dapierra have been characterized as "epigonic" or even "pathetic"; see Ezra Fleischer, "The 'Gerona School' of Hebrew Poetry," in *Rabbi Moses Naḥmanides (Ramban),* 35–49. Some have begun to study the intrinsic merits of this poetry; Ross Brann and Angel Sáenz-Badillos, "The Poetic Universe of Samuel Ibn Sasson, Hebrew Poet of Fourteenth-Century Castile," *Prooftexts* 16 (1996): 75–103; Angel Sáenz-Badillos, "Metrica romance y metrica hebrea," *Congreso Internacional "Encuentro de las Tres Culturas"* 3 (1988): 143–54; Aviva Doron, *Meshorer be-ḥaṣar ha-melekh: Ṭodros halevi abulᶜafiah—shirah ᶜivrit bi-sefarad ha-noṣrit* (Tel Aviv: Dvir, 1989); Angel Sáenz-Badillos, "Hebrew Invective Poetry: The Debate between Todros Abulafia and Phinehas Halevi," *Prooftexts* 16 (1996): 49–73.

52. The earliest example, by Solomon Ibn Ṣaqbel, was actually composed in al-Andalus. Authors from Christian Iberia include Joseph Ibn Zabāra (born c. 1140), Judah Ibn Shabbetai (1168–1225), Judah al-Ḥarīzī (c. 1166–1235), Jacob Ben Elᶜazar (mid-thirteenth century), and others. Further, see chapter 4.

53. Both his Bible commentaries and his poetry were introduced to Jewish intellectuals in Europe; Ibn Ezra's correspondence with Rabbenu Tam even reveals that the French rabbi learned to compose poetry in the prosodic style of the Andalusian school.

54. As expressed in his famous poem "Aha yarad ᶜal sefarad"; for a translation and analysis of this poem, see chapter 2 of this book; see also Ross Brann, "Tavniyot shel galut be-qinot ᶜivriyot ve-ᶜaraviyot bi-sefarad," in *Sefer yisraᵓel levin,* ed. Reuven Tsur and Tova Rosen (Tel Aviv: Tel Aviv University, 1994), 1:45–61.

55. Israel Levin, *Avraham ibn ᶜezra: Ḥayyav ve-shirato* (Tel Aviv: Ha-Qibbuṣ ha-Meᵓuḥad, 1966), 22.

56. Where he does not exactly fit, either, since the author also spent much time in Italy and England. See *HHSP,* 1:569–623; and Schirmann, *Toledot ha-shirah ha-ᶜivrit bi-sefarad ha-noṣrit u-bedarom ṣarfat,* edited, supplemented, and annotated by Ezra Fleischer (Jerusalem: Magnes, 1997), 13–92.

57. Fine examples for Hebrew poetry include Brody's masterful verse-by-verse commentary to the poetry of Moses Ibn Ezra, *Shirei ha-ḥol,* ed. Heinrich Brody (vol. 1, Berlin: Schocken, 1935; vol. 2, Jerusalem: Schocken, 1941) and David Yellin's *Torat ha-shirah ha-sefardit,* 3rd ed. (Jerusalem: Magnes, 1978), which methodically introduces the student to the critical topics most central to medieval critics—quantitative meter, rhyme, types of wordplay, and conventional themes.

58. Dan Pagis, *Shirat ha-ḥol ve-torat ha-shir le-moshe ibn ᶜezra u-venei doro* (Jerusalem: Mosad Bialik, 1970). See also Pagis's review essay "Trends in the Study of Medieval Hebrew Literature," *Association for Jewish Studies Review* 4 (1979): 125–41. Despite some exceptions, Pagis's observations remain true for the most part.

59. G. J. H. van Gelder, *Beyond the Line: Classical Arabic Literary Critics on the*

Coherence and Unity of the Poem (Leiden: E. J. Brill, 1982), 208. See also the review by Suzanne Pinckney Stetkevych, *Journal of Near Eastern Studies* 47, 1 (1988): 63–64.

60. Wolfhart Heinrichs, "Literary Theory: The Problem of Its Efficiency," in *Arabic Poetry: Theory and Development,* ed. Gustave von Grunebaum (Wiesbaden: Harrassowitz, 1973), 19–69. Similarly, Raymond Scheindlin notes medieval critics' reluctance to look at clusters of lines or whole poems and concludes that "we must go beyond the native critics"; see his *Form and Structure in the Poetry of al-Muʿatamid ibn ʿAbbād* (Leiden: E. J. Brill, 1974), 23. Joseph Sadan attempts to solve the problem by focusing on topics that are marginal in, but not absent from, medieval criticism; see his "Maiden's Hair and Starry Skies: Imagery Systems and *Maʿānī* Guides; the Practical Side of Arabic Poetics as Demonstrated in Two Manuscripts," *Israel Oriental Studies* 11 (1991): 57–88.

61. Kamal Abu-Deeb, "Toward a Structural Analysis of Pre-Islamic Poetry," *International Journal of Middle East Studies* 6 (1975): 148–84; Stefan Sperl, *Mannerism in Arabic Poetry* (Cambridge: Cambridge University Press, 1989); Suzanne Pinckney Stetkevych, "Structuralist Interpretations of Pre-Islamic Poetry: Critique and New Directions," *Journal of Near Eastern Studies* 42, 2 (1983): 85–107; idem, *The Mute Immortals Speak: Pre-Islamic Poetry and the Poetics of Ritual* (Ithaca, N.Y.: Cornell University Press, 1993); idem, *The Poetics of Islamic Legitimacy: Myth, Gender, and Ceremony in the Classical Arabic Ode* (Bloomington: Indiana University Press, 2002).

62. It is rare, in fact, for poets themselves to be critics or vice versa. The Jewish poet-critics Moses Ibn Ezra and Elʿazar Bar Yaʿaqov are exceptional. See also the review of van Gelder's book by James E. Montgomery, "On the Unity and Disunity of the *Qaṣīdah*," *Journal of Arabic Literature* 24 (1993): 271–77.

63. Israel Levin, *Meʿil tashbeṣ,* 3 vols. (Tel Aviv: Tel Aviv University Press, 1995).

64. Tova Rosen-Moked, *Le-ʾezor shir: ʿAl shirat ha-ʾezor ha-ʿivrit bi-yemei ha-beinayim* (Haifa: Haifa University Press, 1985); this book is a literary history of the Hebrew girdle poem (*muwashshaḥ*) more than a work of form criticism per se. Yael Feldman's *Bein ha-qeṭavim le-qav ha-meshaveh—shirat yemei ha-beinayim: Tavniyot semanṭiyot ba-shir ha-murkav* (Tel Aviv: Papyrus, 1987) is a study of the Hebrew *qaṣīda* that focuses on the topic of poetic unity.

65. Arie Schippers, *Spanish Hebrew Poetry and the Arabic Literary Tradition: Arabic Themes in Hebrew Andalusian Poetry* (Leiden: E. J. Brill, 1994).

66. One of the finest studies remains Pagis's *Shirat ha-ḥol ve-torat ha-shir le-moshe ibn ʿezra u-venei doro,* which details the literary qualities of Moses Ibn Ezra's poetry in light of medieval but also contemporary literary theory. Note, however, that Pagis retained reservations about adopting modern methods too liberally, which he found to be the case with the New Criticism–style readings in Eddy Zemaḥ, *Ke-shoresh eṣ: Qeriah ḥadashah be-11 shirei ḥol shel shelomoh ben gevirol* (Jerusalem: Akhshav, 1962). Other examples of close readings of individual poems that have received more positive critical acclaim include Scheindlin, *Wine, Women, and Death;* idem, *The Gazelle;* Rosen-Moked and Zemaḥ, *Yeṣirah meḥukamah.* Studies of rhymed prose narratives will be addressed in part 2 of this book.

67. An important recent contribution on gender is Tova Rosen, *Unveiling Eve: Reading Gender in Medieval Hebrew Literature* (Philadelphia: University of Pennsyl-

vania Press, 2003). See also idem and Eli Yassif, "The Study of Hebrew Literature in the Middle Ages: Major Trends and Goals," in *The Oxford Handbook of Jewish Studies,* ed. Martin Goodman et al. (Oxford: Oxford University Press, 2002), 241–94.

1. Space

1. On the landscape tradition in classical and European literature, see Ernst Robert Curtius, *European Literature and the Latin Middle Ages* (Princeton, N.J.: Princeton University Press, 1953), 183–202.

2. Schippers, *Spanish Hebrew Poetry and the Arabic Literary Tradition,* 181–216; Masha Itzḥaki, *Elei ginat ᶜarugot: Shirat ha-gan ve-ha-peraḥim ha-ᶜivrit bi-sefarad* (Tel Aviv: Makhon Katz, 1988); much information on garden poems is included in the sections on wine poetry and love poetry in Levin, *Meᶜil tashbeṣ,* 2:147–434.

3. Simon Schama, *Landscape and Memory* (New York: Knopf, 1995), 83, 98.

4. On the so-called *shuᶜubiyya* poetry, see Julia Ashtiany et al., eds., *ᶜAbbasid Belles-Lettres,* The Cambridge History of Arabic Literature (Cambridge: Cambridge University Press, 1990), 187.

5. Corinne Saunders, *The Forest of Medieval Romance: Avernus, Broceliande, Arden* (Rochester, N.Y.: Brewer, 1993).

6. Aḥmad Ibn Muḥammad al-Maqqarī al-Tilimsānī, *Nafḥ al-ṭīb min ghuṣn al-andalus al-raṭīb,* ed. Iḥsān ᶜAbbās (Beirut: Dār al-ṣadir, 1968), 1:129. All translations are my own unless otherwise noted.

7. Thomas F. Glick, *Islamic and Christian Spain in the Early Middle Ages* (Princeton, N.J.: Princeton University Press, 1979), 54. Useful articles on landscape in Islamic Iberia include idem, "Tribal Landscapes of Islamic Spain: History and Archaeology," in *Inventing Medieval Landscapes: Senses of Place in Western Europe,* ed. John Howe and Michael Wolfe (Gainesville: University Press of Florida, 2002), 113–35; Janina M. Safran, "From Alien Terrain to the Abode of Islam: Landscapes in the Conquest of al-Andalus," in *Inventing Medieval Landscapes,* 136–49.

8. Quoted in Kobler, *A Treasury of Jewish Letters,* 99. This same insect, the *kermes* (*qirmīz*) in Arabic, is also mentioned as a valued commodity in al-Maqqarī, *Nafḥ al-ṭīb,* 1:154.

9. Al-Maqqarī, *Nafḥ al-ṭīb,* 1:176.

10. Arabic text in Fāṭima Ṭaḥṭaḥ, *Al-ghurba wa al-ḥanīn fi al-shiᶜr al-andalusī* (Rabat, Morocco: Al-mamlakah al-maghribīyah, 1993), 53.

11. Glick, *Islamic and Christian Spain,* 55.

12. E.g., Abū ᶜĀmar al-Sālamī and Abū ᶜUbayd al-Bakrī. See al-Maqqarī, *Nafḥ al-ṭīb,* 1:126.

13. E.g., al-Shaqindī: "As for Granada, it is the Damascus of the cities of al-Andalus." See al-Maqqarī, *Nafḥ al-ṭīb,* 1:147.

14. Glick, *Islamic and Christian Spain,* 63.

15. The Jewish author Judah al-Ḥarīzī describes Damascus in such terms in an Arabic *maqāma;* text in Joshua Blau and Joseph Yahalom, *Masᶜei yehudah: Ḥamishah pirqei masᶜa meḥuzarim le-al-ḥarīzī* (Jerusalem: Ben-Zvi Institute, 2002), 116. See also the descriptions of Alexandria by al-Ḥarīzī in the *Taḥkemoni,* ed. Y. Toporovsky (Tel Aviv: Mosad Harav Kook, 1952), 89, and by the Karaite Moses Darᶜi, in Israel Davidson, "Maḥberet no amon u-miṣrayim," *Madaᶜei ha-yahadut* 2 (1927): 300–

301. In the seventeenth century, al-Maqqarī described Damascus in a similar style; see *Nafḥ al-ṭīb,* 1:58.

16. Irving, *The Alhambra,* 1.

17. Ibid. (my italics).

18. Ibid., 6.

19. Glick, *Islamic and Christian Spain,* 103.

20. Schama, *Landscape and Memory,* 61.

21. On Hebrew garden poetry, see Scheindlin, *Wine, Women, and Death.* Arabic examples may be found in James T. Monroe, *Hispano-Arabic Poetry: A Student Primer* (Berkeley: University of California Press, 1974). See also the works in the following note.

22. See Fairchild Ruggles, "The Gardens of the Alhambra and the Concept of the Garden in Islamic Spain," in *Al-Andalus: The Art of Islamic Spain,* ed. Jerrilynn D. Dodds (New York: Metropolitan Museum of Art, 1992), 163–71; James Dickie, "The Hispano-Arabic Garden: Its Philosophy and Function," *Bulletin of the School of Oriental Studies* 31 (1968): 237–48.

23. On the use of Qurʾānic imagery in Arabic garden poetry, see Suzanne Pinckney Stetkevych, "Intoxication and Immortality: Wine and Associated Imagery in al-Maʿarrī's Garden," in *Homoeroticism in Classical Arabic Literature,* ed. J. W. Wright and Everett K. Rowson (New York: Columbia University Press, 1997), 210–32. Similar effects are found in Hebrew verse with biblical allusions.

24. On "iconic representation" as a mimetic form of representation, see Frank Lentricchia, "Representation," in *Critical Terms for Literary Study,* 14–15.

25. Moses Ibn Ezra, *Shirei ha-ḥol,* 7, poem [5]. This poem is discussed in greater depth in chapter 3; see also the poetic translation and discussion of this poem by Scheindlin, *Wine, Women, and Death,* 34–39.

26. An anthology of these poems has been compiled and studied by ʿAbd Allah Muḥammad al-Zayyāt, *Rithāʾ al-mudun fī al-shiʿr al-ʿarabī* (Bengasi, Libya: Qāryūnis Jāmiʿat, 1990). The city lament is also the subject of a Ph.D. dissertation by Ibrāhīm al-Sinjilāwī, "The Lament for Fallen Cities: A Study of the Development of the Elegiac Genre in Classical Arabic Poetry" (University of Chicago, 1983).

27. Arabic text in Muḥammad al-Zayyāt, *Rithāʾ al-mudun,* 657ff. This poem is quoted more fully in chapter 2. For a similar nostalgic musing over Cordoba in Arabic prose and poetry, see Ibn Ḥazm, *The Ring of the Dove,* trans. A. J. Arberry (London: Luzac Oriental, 1953), 180–82. See also Jaroslav Stetkevych's discussion of Ibn Khafāja's poem of longing for Valencia in *The Zephyrs of Najd: The Poetics of Nostalgia in the Classical Arabic Nasīb* (Chicago: University of Chicago Press, 1993), 189.

28. Samuel the Nagid, *Dīwān (Ben Tehillim),* ed. Dov Jarden (Jerusalem: Hebrew Union College, 1966), 209 [67], lines 13–20; the Judeo-Arabic superscription reads: *wa-lahu fī al-ṣabā ʿind intiqālihi min qurṭuba.*

29. *Qeluʿah:* according to the Arabic cognate *qilʿ/qulūʿ,* meaning "sail." Ibn Janāḥ understands the word *qelaʿim* in Exod. 27:9 (i.e., the hangings on the Tabernacle) to be a metaphorical usage of the word "sails"; see Adolf Neubauer, *The Book of Hebrew Roots by Abū al-Walīd Marwān Ibn Janāḥ* (Oxford: Clarendon, 1875), 636. Otherwise, it may be translated "tossed about."

30. On Ibn Ezra in general, see, most recently, Raymond P. Scheindlin, "Moses

Ibn Ezra," in *The Literature of al-Andalus,* 252–64. On Halevi, see Joseph Yahalom, "Judah Halevi: Records of a Visitor from Spain," in *The Cambridge Genizah Collections: Their Contents and Significance,* ed. Stefan C. Reif (Cambridge: Cambridge University Press, 2002), 123–35; and Ross Brann, "Judah Halevi," in *The Literature of al-Andalus,* 265–81.

31. Judah Halevi, *Dīwān des Abū-l-Ḥasan Jehuda ha-Levi,* ed. Ḥayyim Brody, 4 vols. (Berlin: Schriften des Vereins Mekize Nirdamim, 1894–1930), 1:154 [101], lines 35–38.

32. Halevi, *Dīwān,* 1:56 [41]. The excerpts below are taken from lines 1–12. "Flourishing plantings" = *Naʿaman:* Isa. 17:10. Although it is probably the name of a specific plant, perhaps the Adonis plant or the poppy, Abraham Ibn Ezra understands this as "fast growing," based on the Arabic cognate *nʿm,* "to be tender, green." There is also a red flower called *shaqāʾiq al-naʿamān* in Arabic, which is probably the poppy; see Edward William Lane, *Arabic-English Lexicon,* 8 vols. (London: Williams and Norgate, 1863–1893), 1578.

33. Halevi, *Dīwān,* 1:112 [78], lines 1–6. See also the partial translation and discussion in Brann, *The Compunctious Poet,* 98.

34. *Shiddah ve-shiddot,* occurring only once in the Bible (Eccles. 2:8); the meaning is uncertain. Halevi's usage is consistent with Ibn Janāḥ's definition, *ʿazīza, ʿazāʾiz / karīma, karāʾim* (precious, high-minded / virtuous, generous women); see Neubauer, *The Book of Hebrew Roots,* 703.

35. "Gedudei leil nedod" (The troops of a night of wandering), Moses Ibn Ezra, *Shirei ha-ḥol,* 185, poem [185]; this important poem is translated and discussed in chapter 3.

36. Further on the time sequence of the *qaṣīda,* see chapter 2.

37. The medieval scribe introduces this poem, which is a long panegyric in *qaṣīda* form, with the following Arabic superscription: "And by him belonging to the art of description [*funūn al-awṣāf*] and he appended to it the praise of Abū al-Ḥasan al-Battāt; he said it while settled in Castile." Modern scholars have done little to go beyond this medieval notion of reading, which imagines the art of writing to be interested solely in description while ignoring the poetics of nostalgia so essential to reading the poem.

38. Moses Ibn Ezra, *Kitāb al-muḥāḍara,* 2.

39. *lima hamma ʿalaihi akthar ahl waqtina min al-istithqāl liʿl-adab.*

40. Reading *ikhtiyāb,* not *iktiyāb.*

41. Moses Ibn Ezra, *Kitāb al-muḥāḍara,* 2, 4. This passage is partly discussed in the introduction to this book.

42. The same quotation from the Qurʾān is mentioned in a similar context in *Rasāʾil al-Jāḥiẓ,* ed. ʿA. S. Hārūn, 2:389. Halkin traces the sources of several of the proverbs in his footnotes to the passage.

43. The same quotation is found in an almost identical form in *Rasāʾil al-Jāḥiẓ,* 2:387. See below on the image in Ibn Ezra's poetry.

44. I.e., the outposts and hinterlands distant from Muslim power centers, a term common in Arabic texts from the period of the Reconquista.

45. Moses Ibn Ezra, *Maqālat al-ḥadīqa fī maʿnā al-majāz wa al-ḥaqīqa,* MS Oxford 1430, folio 11a.

46. Moses Ibn Ezra, *Shirei ha-ḥol,* 125 [120], lines 59–60.

47. Also, in a highly nostalgic *qaṣīda* written from Castile in response to a poem received from a friend in the "West," Ibn Ezra begins, "Is it the myrtle of a letter's greeting that brings me scent or is it the scent of spice gardens [itself]?" (Moses Ibn Ezra, *Shirei ha-ḥol,* 134 [131], line 1).

48. Ibid., 193 [193], lines 3, 8.

49. Ibid., line 31.

50. *Eṣ hadar,* "goodly tree," understood in rabbinic tradition as the citron tree.

51. Unlike the Arabic poetry of nostalgia for al-Andalus, Hebrew expressions of loss seldom make mention of specific cities. Aviva Doron has taken the general absence of place names as a sign that Jews did not relate to the geopolitical reality of al-Andalus in the same manner as did non-Jews; see her "ʿArim ba-shira ha-ʿivrit bi-sefarad," in *Sefer yisraʾel levin,* 1:69–78. This raises important questions concerning the specific valence of garden imagery in nostalgic Hebrew poetry. Does the garden in this retrospective corpus stand specifically for al-Andalus and its cities, or is it evoked more generally as a way of memorializing a way of life? While the Hebrew poets occasionally refer to specific place names (usually Granada, in the form *beit rimon*), their longing seems to be more culturally based.

52. On the *ẓuʿun* motif, see Ezz El-Din Hassan El-Banna, "'No Solace for the Heart': The Motif of the Departing Women in the Pre-Islamic Battle Ode," in *Reorientations: Arabic and Persian Poetry,* ed. Suzanne Pinckney Stetkevych (Bloomington: Indiana University Press, 1994), 165–79.

53. Early Umayyad period. See A. F. L. Beeston et al., eds., *Arabic Literature to the End of the Umayyad Period* (Cambridge: Cambridge University Press, 1983), 419ff.

54. Ibid.

55. See n. 4 above.

56. J. Stetkevych, *The Zephyrs of Najd,* chapter 3.

57. See also the classic article by Israel Levin, "Ha-bekhi ʿal ḥorvot ha-meʿonot ve-ha-demut ha-lailit ha-meshoṭeṭet," *Tarbiṣ* 36 (1966): 278–96.

58. Samuel the Nagid, *Dīwān,* 288 [141].

59. Ibid., 216 [72], line 6.

60. Although this example is not mentioned, see Allony, "Ha-ṣevi ve-ha-gamal be-shirat sefarad."

61. Schirmann, *HHSP,* 1:172 [54], lines 1–2.

62. Solomon Ibn Gabirol, *Shirei ha-qodesh le-rabi shelomo ibn gabirol,* ed. Dov Jarden, 2 vols. (Jerusalem: Dov Jarden and the American Academy for Jewish Research, 1971–72), 45 [23], line 11.

63. For an early example, see Ignaz Goldziher, "Bemerkungen zur neuhebräischen Poesie," *Jewish Quarterly Review* 14 (1902): 734–36.

64. Levin, "Ha-bekhi ʿal ḥorvot ha-meʿonot," 287–88.

65. Schippers, *Spanish Hebrew Poetry,* 159.

66. Raymond P. Scheindlin, "The Hebrew Qasida in Spain," in *Qasida Poetry in Islamic Asia and Africa,* ed. Stefan Sperl and Christopher Shackle (Leiden: E. J. Brill, 1996), 125–26.

67. Moses Ibn Ezra, *Shirei ha-ḥol,* 90 [91], lines 1–6.

68. Ibid., 9 [7], lines 1–4.

69. "They lie on ivory beds, lolling on their couches, feeding on lambs from the flock and on calves from the stalls. They hum snatches of song to the tune of the lute. They account themselves musicians like David. They drink [straight] from the wine bowls and anoint themselves with the choicest oils. They shall head the column of exiles; they shall loll no more at festive meals" (Amos 6:5–7; translation, *Tanakh,* Jewish Publication Society).

70. A related usage may be intended by Abraham Ibn Daud with reference to the sons of R. Joseph Halevi, who fled Lucena at the "Head of Exiles" to settle in Toledo. See Gerson D. Cohen, *Sefer haqabbalah: The Book of Tradition by Abraham Ibn Daud; A Critical Edition with Translation and Notes* (Philadelphia: Jewish Publication Society, 1967), Hebrew section, 66.

71. I.e., "departed," not "died."

72. Moses Ibn Ezra, *Shirei ha-ḥol,* 18 [13], lines 16–22.

73. Ibid., lines 23–27. This "dry wind" is also a reference to the desert landscape, Jer. 4:11, "dry wind of the hills in the wilderness."

74. Ibid., lines 28–29.

75. Or, alternatively, the culture of Jews of the Christian north.

76. Moses Ibn Ezra, *Shirei ha-ḥol,* 26 [20], line 37. This poem is already pointed out by Baer, *A History of the Jews in Christian Spain,* 1:63–64 (emphasis mine).

77. Glick, *Islamic and Christian Spain,* 57.

78. Al-Maqqarī, *Nafḥ al-ṭīb,* 1:154.

79. Ibid., 1:201. Interestingly, the same insect is mentioned in Ḥasdai Ibn Shaprūṭ's famous letter to the king of the Khazars, "In the mountains and woods of our country, cochineal is gathered in great quantity."

80. Ibid., 4:140.

81. See also Moisés Orfali, "Ecología y estrategias sociales en la jurisprudencia hispano-hebrea," in *Creencias y culturas: Cristianos, judíos y musulmanes en la España medieval,* ed. Carlos Carrete Parrondo and Alisa Meyuhas Gimio (Salamanca: Universidad Pontificia de Salamanca, 1998), 181–202.

82. Glick, *Islamic and Christian Spain,* 78.

83. Ibid., 103.

84. Trans. Thomas N. Bisson, in Constable, *Medieval Iberia,* 125–26.

85. *Las siete partidas* (7.15.28); see Glick, *Islamic and Christian Spain,* 74.

86. Usually in *tarḍiyyāt,* hunting poems. An example is the *ayk,* "thicket" mentioned in a hunting poem of Ibn Khafājah; see Al-Maqqarī, *Nafḥ al-ṭīb,* 1:683. See also Jaroslav Stetkevych, "The Hunt in the Arabic *Qaṣīdah:* The Antecedents of the *Ṭardiyyah,*" in *Tradition and Modernity in Arabic Language and Literature,* ed. J. R. Smart (Richmond, England: Curzon, 1996), 102–18.

87. Saunders, *The Forest of Medieval Romance.*

88. *El Poema de Mío Cid* (*The Poem of the Cid*), trans. Rita Hamilton and Janet Perry (London: Penguin, 1975), 24–25.

89. Ibid., 163–65.

90. Neubauer, *The Book of Hebrew Roots,* 290. See also Saᶜadia Gaon's translation of Ps. 29:9.

91. Halevi, *Dīwān,* 4:67–69 [24]. See also Israel Levin, "Ha-sevel be-mishbar ha-reqonqisṭa be-shirato shel yehudah halevi," *Oṣar yehudei sefarad* 7 (1964): 52. The forest is also associated with estrangement in a famous tale of *The Thousand*

and One Nights. In the story "Gharīb and His Brother ʿAjīb," ʿAjīb orders his servants to execute his father's pregnant concubine, who, ʿAjīb had been warned through a dream, would give birth to a son who would usurp ʿAjīb's right to the throne. The executioners spare her but abandon her in the forest, where she gives birth. She names the child Gharīb, "Stranger," on account of her estrangement. See Richard F. Burton, *The Book of the Thousand Nights and a Night,* 8 vols. (New York: Heritage, 1934), 6:257–95, 7:1–90.

92. Moses Ibn Ezra, *Shirei ha-ḥol,* 74 [72], lines 48–51.

93. Ibid., 175 [176], lines 4–8.

94. Ibid., 113–14 [112], lines 14, 31 (emphasis mine).

95. The foreignness of the myrtle in Christian Iberia is confirmed by a reference in the *Stupor Mundi* of Alfonso X (1221–84). In the story of Joseph, Phutiphar builds palaces in honor of Pharaoh Nicrao and plants "many very valuable trees that smelled very good, and much myrtle, which is a very noble and exotic tree." Quoted in Michael McGaha, *Coat of Many Cultures: The Story of Joseph in Spanish Literature 1200–1492* (Philadelphia: Jewish Publication Society, 1997), 342.

96. *Qiryat yeʿarim,* playing on a place name in the Bible, Josh. 9:17 and elsewhere.

97. Todros Abulafia, *Gan ha-meshalim ve-ha-ḥidot,* ed. David Yellin, 2 vols. (Jerusalem: Weiss, 1934), 2:66 [571].

2. Form

1. On the history of the division between the two disciplines, see Rosen and Yassif, "The Study of Hebrew Literature of the Middle Ages," 257–58.

2. Rather than mascara.

3. Lit., "distant from joining together."

4. Lit., "its hand," i.e., its span.

5. I.e., the speaker is chastising himself for not concealing his emotions.

6. Cf. Job 38:37.

7. I.e., "departed," not "died."

8. Moses Ibn Ezra, *Shirei ha-ḥol,* 18–19 [13].

9. The broadest history of the *qaṣīda* in various languages is Stefan Sperl and Christopher Shackle, eds., *Qasida Poetry in Islamic Asia and Africa* (Leiden: E. J. Brill, 1996).

10. Renate Jacobi, "The Origins of the Qasida Form," in *Qasida Poetry in Islamic Asia and Africa,* 21–34.

11. The literature is quite extensive. In general, see Renate Jacobi, "Qaṣīda," in *Encyclopedia of Arabic Literature,* ed. Julie Scott Meisami and Paul Starkey (London and New York: Routledge, 1998), 630–33; and Andras Hamori, *On the Art of Medieval Arabic Literature* (Princeton, N.J.: Princeton University Press, 1974). A select bibliography by period: Pre-Islamic: Renate Jacobi, *Studien zur Poetik der altarabischen Qaṣīde* (Wiesbaden: Steiner, 1971); James E. Montgomery, *The Vagaries of the Qaṣīdah: The Tradition and Practice of Early Arabic Poetry* (Cambridge: E. J. W. Gibb Memorial Trust, 1997); S. Stetkevych, *The Mute Immortals Speak.* Early Islamic: Sperl, *Mannerism in Arabic Poetry.* ʿAbbasid: Suzanne P. Stetkevych, *Abū Tammām and the Poetics of the ʿAbbasid Age* (Leiden: E. J. Brill, 1991); Beatrice Gruendler,

Medieval Arabic Praise Poetry: Ibn al-Rūmī and the Patron's Redemption (London: Routledge Curzon, 2003). Andalusian: J. Stetkevych, *The Zephyrs of Najd;* Beatrice Gruendler, "The Qasida," in *The Literature of al-Andalus,* 211–31.

12. James T. Monroe, "Oral Composition in Pre-Islamic Poetry," *Journal of Arabic Literature* 3 (1972): 1–53; Michael Zwettler, *The Oral Tradition of Classical Arabic Poetry* (Columbus: Ohio University Press, 1978).

13. See Sperl, *Mannerism in Arabic Poetry.*

14. S. Stetkevych, "Structuralist Interpretations of Pre-Islamic Poetry."

15. Ṭaḥṭaḥ, *Al-ghurba wa al-ḥanīn fī al-shiʿr al-andalusī;* al-Zayyāt, *Rithāʾ al-mudun fī al-shiʿr al-ʿarabi;* J. Stetkevych, *The Zephyrs of Najd;* see also Crone and Moreh, *The Book of Strangers;* Rosenthal, "The Stranger in Medieval Islam"; Teresa Garulo, "La nostalgia de al-Andalus: Génesis de un tema literario," *Qurtuba* 3 (1998): 47–63; William Granara, "Remaking Muslim Sicily: Ibn Ḥamdīs and the Poetics of Exile," *Edebiyāt* 9 (1998): 167–98.

16. Quoted in J. Stetkevych, *The Zephyrs of Najd,* 51–52.

17. Goldziher, "Bemerkungen zur neuhebräischen Poesie," 734–36; discussed in J. Stetkevych, *The Zephyrs of Najd,* 146.

18. J. Stetkevych, *The Zephyrs of Najd,* 147, 151.

19. *Ḥanīn* is a short form of *al-ḥanīn ilā al-waṭan,* "longing for the homeland" (the title of a treatise by al-Jāhiẓ) and is the Arabic word closest to the English "nostalgia."

20. Who lamented the fall of Sicily; see also Granara, "Remaking Muslim Sicily."

21. Ṭaḥṭaḥ also includes authors of the Naṣrid kingdom of Granada and a section on religious yearning.

22. Arabic text, al-Zayyāt, *Rithāʾ al-mudun,* 657ff. Part of this poem is discussed above in chapter 1.

23. Earlier Hebrew *qaṣīda*s treating non-nostalgic themes include Dunash Ben Labraṭ's "Deʿeh libi ḥokhmah" (*HHSP,* 1:35–40), which combines inward ethical exhortation with panegyric; and Isaac Ibn Khalfūn's "Ḥoli libi ve-gam marbīt yegonav," which opens with a love poem and makes a transition to panegyric: Isaac Ibn Khalfūn, *Shirei rav yiṣḥaq ibn khalfūn,* ed. A. Mirsky (Jerusalem: Mosad Bialik, 1961), 92 [20].

24. E.g., Samuel the Nagid, *Dīwān,* ed. Jarden, 155 [48], 206 [66].

25. Ibid., 206–208 [66], lines 7–26.

26. Lit., "the daughters of my eyes."

27. I.e., the Pleiades, which was awake all night teaching her young, can testify to the poet's weeping and insomnia.

28. As grains have shriveled, cf. Job 1:17.

29. I.e., Lamekh, a murderer in Gen. 4:23.

30. Based on Lev. 25:47: "If a resident alien among you has prospered, and your kinsman being in straits, comes under his authority and gives himself over to the resident alien among you, or to a *member of an alien's family,* he shall have the right of redemption."

31. When Benjamin, accused of stealing a goblet from Joseph's house, is taken as a slave by Joseph, Judah petitions Joseph for Benjamin's freedom and offers himself as a slave in Benjamin's place (Genesis 44).

32. On the *ṣuʿlūk,* see Suzanne Pinckney Stetkevych, "The Ṣuʿlūk and His Poem:

A Paradigm of Passage Manqué," *Journal of the American Oriental Society* 104, 4 (1984): 661–78.

33. Samuel the Nagid, *Dīwān,* ed. Jarden, 155–56 [48].

34. Contra Jarden, who comments that it is the Pleiades, and not the poet, that is naked and bare. The nakedness of the poet wandering through the desert is more in line with Arabic poetry, particularly that of the *ṣaᶜālīk,* or brigand poets.

35. *Yeshimon, shamot, masha'on, ṣima'on, ṣiyya.*

36. Between Samuel the Nagid and Moses Ibn Ezra, nostalgic themes are also expanded upon by Solomon Ibn Gabirol. This poet does not use the themes to commemorate political upheaval but rather to express his loneliness and social isolation. See, for example, Ibn Gabirol, *Shirei ha-ḥol,* ed. Jarden, 45–47 [23]. See also Levin, "Ha-bekhi ᶜal ḥorvot ha-meᶜonot." See also Miriam Goldstein, "Adaptations of the Arabic *Qaṣīda* in Andalusian Hebrew Poetry," *Ben ᶜever la-ᶜarav* 3 (2004): vii–xxxviii.

37. Moses Ibn Ezra, *Shirei ha-ḥol,* 90–91 [91].

38. The contrast is emphasized with a *tajnīs* (paranomasia) between "nested" (*qonenu*) and "to lament" (*le-qonen*).

39. The Arabic cognate, *ḥnn,* conveys "commiseration" and also "longing, yearning"; the use of the Hebrew here may also imply "yearning."

40. Lit., "at their feet," as in Judg. 4:10.

41. Further on the significance of the desert, see chapter 1.

42. *ᶜAmdu*—used like the Arabic root *wqf.*

43. *Rosh golim,* Amos 6:7; the significance of this sobriquet as a signifier of aristocratic culture is discussed in chapter 1.

44. *Ṣaᶜanu*—evoking the Arabic cognate *ẓᶜn,* the root associated with the departure of tribes motif in pre-Islamic poetry.

45. Lit., "in the shade of organs."

46. Brody points out that such impossibilities are designated in Arabic *mazj al-shakk wa al-yaqīn,* a blending of doubt and certainty, or *tajāhul al-ᶜārif,* feigned ignorance. The impossibility is a kind of hyperbole used to emphasize the stars' role as agents of distress and estrangement.

47. *Beqiᶜeihem*—lit., "fissures" (of houses).

48. Cf. Judg. 18:4.

49. *Ḥamasi*—lit., "the wrong done to me"; cf. Gen. 16:5.

50. The relationship between the drip of tears and the destruction of dwellings is emphasized by a full *tajnīs* between "drip," *ᶜaraf,* and "destroy," *ᶜaraf.*

51. The contrast also contains an effective *tajnīs* between "gazelles," *ṣeva'im,* and ostriches' "gathering as a host," *niṣba'u.*

52. Moses Ibn Ezra, *Shirei ha-ḥol,* 9 [7].

53. The same time sequence may be seen in "Gedudei leil nedod'" (translated and discussed in chapter 3). Observe also the similar time sequence in another poem by Ibn Ezra (*Shirei ha-ḥol,* 123 [120]), in which the speaker laments "dwellings whose inhabitants have departed [*ṣaᶜanu*], ruined by tears" and promises to ransom himself for the "nights that gleamed with [friends]" and "days that passed like a shadow and seem to my thoughts but dreams dreamt." Following classical *qaṣīda* form, the poem opens in a lamentable present and evokes memories of past companionship and pleasure, returning to the present and the *mamdūḥ.*

54. See chapter 1 and Doron, "ᶜArim ba-shirah ha-ᶜivrit."

55. He addresses his exegetical treatise *Maqālat al-ḥadīqa fī maᶜnā al-majāz wa al-ḥaqīqa* to "remaining notables from among the loved ones and vanquished [*fulūl*—scattered remnants of an army], . . . pure fugitives among the people of refined culture," inviting them to participate in a "council of learned people of the distant frontiers [*al-thughūr al-nāʾiya*] and refined people of these remote parts" who can demonstrate their "fine lineage [*ḥasab*]" and "culture [*adab*]." See MS Oxford 1430 f. 11a. Ibn Ezra even dedicated a treatise (now lost) specifically to the subject of lineage, *Maqāla fī faḍāʾil ahl al-ādāb wa al-aḥsāb* (Treatise on the Excellence of the Men of Culture and Lineage), undoubtedly treating the superiority of Jews of Andalusian stock over their coreligionists in Christian Iberia. On this work, see also Pagis, *Shirat ha-ḥol ve-torat ha-shir,* 16 n. 8.

56. I.e., Israel, a refugee from the Land of Israel.

57. The Land of Israel.

58. Hab. 1:6, where the nation is the Chaldean nation.

59. *Periddati;* Fleischer suggests "at evening."

60. I.e., Israel.

61. As Fleischer suggests, this might be "my."

62. I.e., the Lord turned the Christians' hearts to hate Israel for Israel's sin.

63. I.e., Israel.

64. Following Fleischer's emendation.

65. Following Fleischer's emendation.

66. Based on Ezek. 4:21. The four punishments are sword, famine, wild beasts, and pestilence.

67. I.e., when God will arouse His wrath and shake out the earth, the righteous (the pebbles) will not be destroyed along with the wicked.

68. Ezra Fleischer, "Ḥomerim ve-ᶜiyyunim li-qerat mahadurah ᶜatidit shel shirei rabi yehudah halevi," *Asufot* 5 (1991): 122–24.

69. Schirmann, *Toledot ha-shirah ha-ᶜivrit . . . muslemit,* 439 n. 83. On this unrest, see Pilar León Tello, *Los Judíos de Toledo* (Madrid: Consejo Superior de Investigaciones Cientificas Instituto "B. Arias Montano," 1979), 1:30. León Tello also mentions anti-Jewish activities in earlier years.

70. Gerson D. Cohen, "Esau as Symbol in Early Medieval Thought," in *Jewish Medieval and Renaissance Studies,* ed. Alexander Altmann (Cambridge, Mass.: Harvard University Press, 1967), 19–48; reprinted in Gerson D. Cohen, *Studies in the Variety of Rabbinic Cultures* (Philadelphia: Jewish Publication Society, 1991), 243–69. For the Crusades, see examples in Abrahm Meir Habermann, *Sefer gezerot ashkenaz ve-ṣarfat* (Jerusalem: Ofir, 1971), 61–71. See also Alan Mintz, *Ḥurban: Responses to Catastrophe in Hebrew Literature* (New York: Columbia University Press, 1984).

71. For examples of *qaṣīda*s over friends, see "Demᶜa ᶜasher hayta ke-ṭal ḥermon" (Halevi, *Dīwān,* 2:278–80 [55]) and "ᶜAyin ᶜasher tashuṭ ke-soḥeret" (ibid., 1:137–41 [94] = Schirmann, *HHSP,* 1:449–54 [182]).

72. According to the rules of much Andalusian Hebrew devotional poetry. For this system, see Ezra Fleischer, *Shirat ha-qodesh ha-ᶜivrit bi-yemei ha-beinayim* (Jerusalem: Keter, 1975), 349ff.

73. "Lo aleikhem shomᶜei shimᶜi," Judah Halevi, *Shirei ha-qodesh le-rabi yehudah*

halevi, ed. Dov Jarden (Jerusalem, 1978–85), 893–94 [395]. Lines 1–15 were also published by Neḥemiah Allony, "Shirim ḥadashim le-rabi yehudah halevi," in *Meḥqarei lashon ve-sifrut* (Jerusalem: Reuven Mas, 1991), 4:419–21; lines 16–32 were published by Yehudah Ratzaby, "Qinot ḥadashot le-rav yehudah halevi," *Sinai* 114 (1994): 5–7. The poem is mentioned in passing in Fleischer, "Ḥomerim ve-ᶜiyyunim," 121.

74. Lam. 1:12. This reference is most effective, "May it never befall you, all who pass along the road. Look about and see: Is there any agony like mine which was dealt out to me when the Lord afflicted me on His day of wrath?" (translation, *Tanakh,* Jewish Publication Society).

75. I.e., Christendom, based on Gen. 32:4, "the land of Seᶜir, the country of Edom."

76. Although the biblical source (Deut. 33:12) refers to resting between God's shoulders, the reference here seems to be to Seᶜir.

77. Lit., "was with me."

78. Cf. Prov. 4:18.

79. Lit., "measured"; cf. 1 Sam. 2:3, "For the Lord is an all-knowing God, by Him actions are measured."

80. Lam. 5:16.

81. Dung (*domen*), always associated with carcasses, as in 2 Kings 9:37 and elsewhere.

82. Cf. Isa. 13:16.

83. Cf. Lam. 5:12.

84. Cf. Gen. 50:20.

85. Cf. Ps. 68:20.

86. Cf. Exod. 14:13.

87. See the note by Ratzaby in "Qinot ḥadashot le-rav yehudah halevi."

88. Cf. Deut. 28:32.

89. Cf. Lam. 2:16.

90. Ratzaby comments that they used the spoils in their churches.

91. Based on several verses from the prophetic books of the Bible; see Jarden's notes for exact references.

92. See Fleischer, *Shirat ha-qodesh ha-ᶜivrit,* 412.

93. "ᶜAqonen ᶜal mar telaʾotai," in Halevi, *Dīwān,* 4:131 [55]. There are three stichs per line, seven syllables per stich, with stichs 1 and 2 rhyming and stich 3 (a biblical verse) ending with the word *yisraʾel:* a/a/*yisraʾel,* b/b/*yisraʾel,* etc. It is unknown which community this poem addresses. However, Halevi refers specifically to being caught between the troops of Seᶜir and Qedar (Christendom and Islamdom), making Toledo a likely candidate. In addition to these poems, "Gerushim mi-beit taᶜanugim" is associated with the fall of Majorca (in MS Firkovitch, II, 208.1, 9a); further, see the note by Fleischer in Schirmann, *Toledot ha-shirah . . . sefarad,* 447 n. 119. The poem was originally published in *HHSP,* ascribed to Isaac Ibn Ghiyāt, 1:135. The attribution to Halevi is discussed by Jefim Schirmann, *Shirim ḥadashim min ha-genizah* (Jerusalem: Ha-akademiya ha-leʾumit ha-yisraʾelit le-madaᶜim, 1965), 235, 244. For other Halevi poems from the time of the Reconquista, see Levin, "Ha-sevel be-mishbar ha-reqonqisṭa. be-shirato shel yehudah halevi."

94. Brody considers "Aqonen ᶜal mar telaʾotai" to be among Halevi's "sacred"

poems. Similarly, Jarden identifies "Lo aleikhem shomᶜei shimᶜi" (above) as "sacred" verse. Halevi's *petiḥas* on individuals are all included in volume 2 of *Dīwān,* ed. Brody, on secular verse.

95. See Halevi, *Dīwān,* 2:69–92 [poems 1–10]. All these examples use syllabic meter (usually six or seven syllables), the final stich of each line being a biblical verse concluding with a constant word. Some of the poems contain four stichs instead of three. Several of the poems are introduced as *petiḥas*. The form is also used by Joseph Ibn Ṣaddīq, *Shirei yosef ibn saddīq,* ed. Jonah David (New York: American Academy for Jewish Research, 1982), 76–78 [30].

96. E.g., Halevi, *Dīwān,* 2:69 [1], lines 1–6; 75 [3], line 6.

97. Ibid., 2:73 [2], line 36: "He [the deceased] fell like a bird into a trap on the land" resembles "Lo ᶜaleikhem ḥokhei teshuᶜa," line 18.

98. For the formal features of the strophic form, see the discussion of Abraham Ibn Ezra below.

99. Schirmann, *Shirim ḥadashim,* 244 [109]; 245 [110]; 247 [111]. See also laments over Jerusalem by Halevi in strophic form: "Sheʾar yashuv" is in quantitative meter, Schirmann, *Shirim ḥadashim,* 248–49 [112]; "Eikh ᶜam gadol" is published by Ratzaby, "Qinot ḥadashot le-rav yehudah halevi," 7–9 (correcting a version published by Jarden).

100. Schirmann, *Shirim ḥadashim,* 247, lines 3–4.

101. Ibid., 244, lines 1–3.

102. Ibid., poem 110, lines 1, 4.

103. For example, in "Ma laᶜam ki huᶜam," Halevi mourns a prominent figure named Judah (possibly Judah Ben Jacob Ibn Ezra, the brother of Abraham Ibn Ezra) and bemoans the loss for his family and all Israel. See Ratzaby, "Qinot ḥadashot le-rav yehudah halevi," 20–23.

104. Schirmann suggests that this "orchard" is a group of students, which is logical given the following lines.

105. Cf. Isa. 42:8. By "idols," he means "unworthy people."

106. Lit., "shrubs."

107. "Bark"—and possibly the images in the previous line—is probably a reference to the scent of the wood from which the boat was built.

108. Lit., "going on hand and nose."

109. I.e., the Temple; cf. Lam. 2:1.

110. Ps. 118:6.

111. "Heṣiqatni teshuqati le-ʾel ḥai" (Halevi, *Dīwān,* ed. Brody, 2:172–74 = Schirmann, *HHSP,* 1:501–502 [214a]).

112. On liminality, see Arnold van Gennep, *The Rites of Passage,* trans. Monika B. Vizedom and Gabrielle L. Caffee (Chicago: University of Chicago Press, 1960).

113. See the introduction to this book.

114. Raymond Scheindlin links the religious dimensions of Halevi's pilgrimage with the Sufi ideal of *tawakkul,* reliance upon God alone. See his "Mid-Life Repentance in a Poem by Judah Halevi," *Maghreb Review* 29 (2004): 40–52; "*Tawakkul* in the Poetry of Judah Halevi," in *Sasson Somekh Festschrift* (forthcoming).

115. I.e., tears; Lam. 1:16.

116. The desert ostrich is a symbol of lament in Lam. 4:3.

117. Job 3:7; and see Abraham Ibn Ezra's comment on this verse.

118. Lit., "yearning."

119. I.e., a mosque.

120. A sign of distress; Ezek. 21:19.

121. Jer. 8:23, i.e., so that I could weep sufficiently.

122. Lit., "make bald."

123. I.e., in labor.

124. Mortally wounded, as in Jer. 51:4.

125. 1 Sam. 25:17.

126. I.e., Hagar, an epithet for Islam.

127. Israel Levin, *Yalquṭ avraham ibn ᶜezra* (New York: Keren Yisraʾel Maṣ, 1985), 101–103.

128. Schirmann, *Toledot ha-shirah ha-ᶜivrit . . . ṣarfat,* 19 n. 26.

129. Ibid., 27.

130. Levin, *Avraham ibn ᶜezra,* 26.

131. Ibid., 22.

132. On Arabic strophic poetry, see James T. Monroe, "*Zajal* and *Muwashshaḥa:* Hispano-Arabic Poetry and the Romance Tradition," in *The Legacy of Muslim Spain,* 1:398–419.

133. As Ezra Fleischer has noted, the absorption was facilitated by the enthusiasm for strophic forms in Hebrew poetry outside of al-Andalus; see his *Shirat ha-qodesh ha-ᶜivrit bi-yemei ha-beinayim,* 344–49.

134. On this poem, see also the in-depth analysis by Brann, "Tavniyot shel galut." None of Halevi's strophic poems from the Reconquista follows this form exactly, either. The closest is "Golah asher haglatah," in Schirmann, *Shirim ḥadashim,* 109–10, which consists of four strophes of seven or eight lines each and begins with a three-line *maṭlaᶜ*. Halevi's name does not appear in the acrostic.

135. See examples in Schirmann, *HHSP,* 1:581–85 [259]; 1:588–90 [260]; 1:596–98 [262]; and 1:601–602 [266].

136. Ibid., 1:580–81 [257]. Interestingly, the poet's name appears in the form *Avram* instead of *Avraham,* which might be a sign of loss, inverting the theme of name change in the Bible, since the biblical patriarch was first "Avram" but became "Avraham" when he was promised that he would become a "father of many nations" (Gen. 17:5).

137. This point is also noted by Levin in his classic study of Abraham Ibn Ezra, *Avraham ibn ᶜezra,* 222–23.

138. E.g., Levin's *Yalquṭ avraham ibn ᶜezra,* where the poem is included in the section on secular verse. This point has been observed by Brann, "Tavniyot shel galut," 51 n. 28.

139. Schirmann, *Toledot ha-shirah ha-ᶜivrit . . . ṣarfat,* 20. For such an example, see "Mi yiten roᶜshi mayim," in Habermann, *Sefer gezerot ashkenaz,* 66ff.

140. During this period, the Maghreb and al-Andalus constituted a single political unit. The poet is known to have visited the Maghreb.

141. Moses Ibn Ezra, "Aha yarad": line 2, Lam. 1:16; line 3, Lam. 4:3; line 11, Ezek. 21:19; line 12, Jer. 8:23; etc.

142. Brann, "Tavniyot shel galut," 53.

143. E.g., line 12 (She could not find peace), line 14 (They divided my clothing), and several other places.

144. This is also true in one of Halevi's laments during the Reconquista writ-

ten in strophic form; see Schirmann, *Shirim ḥadashim,* 244 [109], 1–2, "Exile who was exiled in Sefarad and France, have you heard of the plunder that has come to the wondrous community?" The poems on 245–46 [110] and 247–48 [111] do not include second-person addresses to the community and are not as personal as "Aha yarad."

145. The poem is published in Jefim Schirmann, "Qinot ʿal gezerot be-ereṣ yisraʾel, afriqa, sefarad, ashkenaz, ve-ṣarfat," *Koveṣ ʿal yad* 3, 13 (1939): 31–35. The second line of the poem is the opening line of "Aha yarad" and the poem retains the *-ayim* rhyme at the end of each strophe. The poem does not, however, make reference to cities in Iberia. Schirmann notes that "Aha yarad" circulated in forms expanded upon by scribes or other poets and suggests that "Eikh neḥerav maʿarav" may be a type of expansion. This suggestion is backed by the great length and irregularity of the stanzas. Levin, *Avraham ibn ʿezra,* 19, attributes the poem to Ibn Ezra himself.

3. Imagery

1. Joseph Weiss, "Tarbut ḥaṣranit ve-shirah ḥaṣranit," *World Congress of Jewish Studies* 1 (1947), 8–9; Pagis, *Shirat ha-ḥol ve-torat ha-shir,* 257.

2. For some of the shifting definitions, see: Cecil Day Lewis, *The Poetic Image* (New York: Oxford University Press, 1947), 18; John A. Cuddon, *A Dictionary of Literary Terms and Literary Theory,* 4th ed. (Oxford: Blackwell, 1998), s.v. "imagery"; Gary Carey and Mary Ellen Snodgrass, *A Multicultural Dictionary of Literary Terms* (Jefferson, N.C.: McFarland, 1999), 76; Chris Baldick, *The Concise Oxford Dictionary of Literary Terms* (Oxford: Oxford University Press, 1990), 106–107; Norman Friedman, "Imagery," in *The New Princeton Encyclopedia of Poetry and Poetics,* ed. Alex Preminger and T. V. F. Brogan (Princeton, N.J.: Princeton University Press, 1993), 559–66.

3. See, for example, Philip N. Furbank, *Reflections on the Word Image* (London: Secker & Warburg, 1970); and Roger Fowler, ed., *A Dictionary of Modern Critical Terms* (London and New York: Routledge and Kegan Paul, 1987), 19–20.

4. On the New Criticism, see Eagleton, *Literary Theory,* chapter 3.

5. The Russian formalist/structuralist Roman Jakobson took issue with this narrow view of poetry and dedicated an article to analyzing a poem that involved no imagery (in the sense of tropes) but made use instead of "grammatical imagery." See Roman Jakobson and Peter Colaclides, "Grammatical Imagery in Cavafy's Poem 'Remember Body,'" *Linguistics: An International Review* 20 (1966): 51–59. The authors write: "W. H. Auden asserts that simile and metaphor were never used by this poet [Cavafy], whose lines give plain factual descriptions deprived of any ornamentation whatsoever, so that one cannot speak of Cavafy's imagery. Yet *grammatical* imagery . . . is the artist's most powerful device . . . based on a wide range of morphological and syntactic similarities and contrasts, various facets of contiguity and remoteness, rigorous selection and dense aggregation, dazzling symmetries and their licentious transgressions" (59).

6. What in Arabic criticism is called *al-mushabba bihi,* "that to which something is likened."

7. See, for example, Caroline F. E. Spurgeon, *Shakespeare's Imagery and What It Tells Us* (Cambridge: Cambridge University Press, 1935); Theodore H. Banks,

Milton's Imagery (New York: Columbia University Press, 1950). Spurgeon aims to use imagery to throw light on Shakespeare's "personality, temperament and thought," assuming that through images, the author "to some extent unconsciously, 'gives himself away'" (4). Banks similarly writes, "Aesthetic considerations are largely irrelevant. We are concerned not with the various types of images, the degree of their elaboration, or their literary quality or function, but only with the manner in which they reveal the writer's fields of interest: his preoccupations and beliefs, his likes and dislikes, his knowledge and ignorance, his experience or lack of it, in short, his personality" (xii).

8. René Wellek and Austin Warren, *Theory of Literature* (New York: Harcourt, Brace, 1949), 198.

9. Henry Treece, *Dylan Thomas, "Dog Among the Fairies"* (London: L. Drummond, 1949), 47 n. 1.

10. Kenneth Burke, *Language as Symbolic Action* (Berkeley: University of California Press, 1966).

11. Northrop Frye, *Anatomy of Criticism* (New York: Atheneum, 1957).

12. For example, Robert Weimann's study of Shakespearean metaphor situates the very relation between tenor and vehicle within the social context of Elizabethan England: *The Structure and Society of Literary History: Studies in the History and Theory of Historical Criticism* (Charlottesville: University Press of Virginia, 1976). Images such as "the foul body of th'infected world" or "sun-like majesty" are said to stem from "the system of correspondences between the human body and the body politic or between the macrocosm and contemporary society" (229–30).

13. See, for example, Jonathan Culler, *Structuralist Poetics* (Ithaca, N.Y.: Cornell University Press, 1975), 178–83 and also n. 5 above, concerning the possibility of poetry without tropes.

14. E.g., *istiʿāra,* metaphor; *tashbīh,* simile based on physical attributes; *tamthīl,* nonphysical simile. These translations are approximate; the terms shift within the corpus of classical Arabic criticism. On the transformation of the term *istiʿāra* from a specialized sense of metaphor distinctive of early Arabic criticism to a more generalized usage in the Aristotelian sense, see Wolfhart Heinrichs, *The Hand of the Northwind: Opinions on Metaphor and the Early Meaning of Istiʿāra in Arabic Poetics* (Wiesbaden: Steiner [in Komm], 1977); see also Mordechai Z. Cohen, "Moses Ibn Ezra vs. Maimonides: Argument for a Poetic Definition of Metaphor (*Istiʿāra*)," *Edebiyāt* 11 (2000): 1–28.

15. Sadan, "Maiden's Hair and Starry Skies."

16. Kamal Abu-Deeb, *Al-Jurjānī's Theory of Poetic Imagery* (Warminster, England: Aris and Phillips, 1979). For the purposes of his study, Abu-Deeb understands imagery in its figurative manifestation only; i.e., "She is a rose" would constitute an image whereas "Red roses covered the white wall" would not. Al-Jurjānī focuses on the nature of relation between an object and the comparate used in describing it.

17. Ibid., 274ff.

18. Ibid., 291.

19. Ibid., 285–86.

20. The Arabic superscription reads, *wa-lahu fī al-hilāl,* "and by him concerning

the crescent moon." Solomon Ibn Gabirol, *Shirei ha-ḥol le-rabi-shelomo ibn gabirol,* ed. Dov Jarden (Jerusalem: Hebrew Union College, 1975), 347, poem [192].

21. Such is Jarden's reading, based on Judg. 5:28. Alternatively, *nishqafa* could mean "shining," as in Song of Songs 6:10: "Who is this shining like the dawn?"

22. Lit., "violet." See other examples in Yehudah Ratzaby, "ʿIyyunim be-darkhei shirateinu ha-sefardit," in *Baruch Kurzweil Memorial Volume,* ed. M. Z. Kaddari et al. (Tel Aviv: Schocken, 1975), 325.

23. I.e., it stuck out its lip but quickly retracted once it realized it was going to be kissed by "your" lip.

24. A type of metaphor (*istiʿāra*) constructed by endowing an object with an attribute that it cannot possess by nature. See Heinrichs, *The Hand of the Northwind;* Mordechai Cohen, "Moses Ibn Ezra vs. Maimonides."

25. See, for example, Yehudah Ratzaby, "Ḥolyo u-bediduto shel ibn gabirol le-or shirato," *Sinai* 84 (1979): 1–8.

26. See comments in the introduction to this book.

27. Moses Ibn Ezra, *Kitāb al-muḥādara wa al-mudhākara,* 142.

28. Yellin, *Torat ha-shirah ha-sefardit,* 152–87.

29. Dan Pagis, "Ṣiburei dimuyyim," in his *Ha-shir davur ʿal ofnav* (Jerusalem: Magnes, 1993), 109–23 (originally printed in *Meḥqarei yerushalayim be-sifrut ʿivrit* 1 (1981): 196–210); "Play and Substance: Aspects of Hebrew-Spanish Imagery," in his *Hebrew Poetry of the Middle Ages and the Renaissance* (Berkeley: University of California Press, 1991), 25–43.

30. Pagis, "Play and Substance," 42; the Hebrew poem is found in Solomon Ibn Gabirol, *Shirei ha-ḥol,* 211ff., poem [102].

31. E.g., Scheindlin, *Wine, Women, and Death,* introduction and chapter 1. Schippers, *Spanish Hebrew Poetry,* 181–216, treats the garden as one among several subjects under the heading "Nature Poetry"; the chapter is divided according to various conventional motifs—the description of the garden as a woman, the wind as a transmitter of greetings, birds, descriptions of the heavens, rains, night, stars, etc.—adducing examples of each from the Hebrew and Arabic traditions. See also Schippers's comments in the conclusion, 321–33. Much information can also be found in the discussions on "wine" and "love" in Levin, *Meʿil tashbeṣ,* 2:147–434.

32. See discussions in Weiss, "Tarbut haṣranit"; Jefim Schirmann, "The Function of the Hebrew Poet in Medieval Spain," *Jewish Social Studies* 16 (1954): 235–52; G. Cohen, *Sefer ha-qabbalah,* 269ff.; and Scheindlin, *Wine, Women, and Death,* 3–33. For the minority view that medieval Hebrew poems were not intended for the elite only but also for the populous, see Norman Roth, *Jews, Visigoths and Muslims in Medieval Spain: Cooperation and Conflict* (Leiden: E. J. Brill, 1994), 85–106.

33. Itzḥaki, *Elei ginat ʿarugot.*

34. *Nitʿei naʿamanim;* see chapter 1, n. 32.

35. Schirmann, *HHSP,* 1:34–35.

36. Perhaps a sign of poor manners. Hence Scheindlin's translation, "like giants at their meat." The word *ʿanaqim* might also suggest "those with long necks" (related to the alternate meaning of *ʿnq,* "necklace"), enabling them to drink from bowls.

37. Jarden understands this verse to mean "we sat *as if* in a palace," suggesting that the shade of the pomegranate and plane trees created an enclosure similar to a

palace, generally constructed out of terebinth and oak. Although there is a certain logic to this, supplying the absent "as if" seems forced. Given that such gardens are generally found in the courtyards of large houses and palaces, the more literal reading seems preferable and does not detract from the effect of contrasting trees.

38. *Ḥatulah*—"swaddling band," i.e., a covering, as in Job 38:9: "I made cloud its garment, and thick darkness its swaddling-band."

39. As in Ezek. 1:24, the sound made by the movement of the heavenly beasts, associated with the sound of a military camp.

40. Samuel the Nagid, *Dīwān,* ed. Jarden, 283, poem [132].

41. As in *kikar leḥem,* a (round) loaf of bread; see Brown, Driver, and Briggs, *A Hebrew and English Lexicon of the Old Testament* (Peabody, Mass.: Hendrickson, 1979), 502–503.

42. On the significance of roundness in poetry, see the enlightening discussion by Gaston Bachelard, *The Poetics of Space,* trans. Maria Jolas (New York: Orion, 1964), chapter 10. See also the comments of J. Stetkevych, *The Zephyrs of Najd,* 180–81.

43. While the word should not be confused with the usage in modern Hebrew, associated with the cuddling of infants (and also "Pampers"), it does suggest wrapping and enclosure.

44. On the wine pourer, see, for example, Scheindlin, *Wine, Women, and Death,* 19–20, 83–84; and Schippers, *Spanish Hebrew Poetry,* 120–25, 145–80.

45. Cf. Exod. 15:8.

46. The hooks on the edges of the curtain in the Tabernacle (Exod. 26:6), probably the bulbs or petals.

47. *Ṣiṣ*—cf. Jer. 48:9; Ibn Janāḥ translates *janāḥ,* "wings."

48. Jarden, *Shirei ha-ḥol,* 338, poem [181] = Brody-Schirmann 84 [138].

49. See, among others, Schirmann, *Toledot ha-shirah . . . muslemit,* 264ff. and 265 n. 56 for further references. See, especially, Ratzaby, "Ḥolyo u-bediduto."

50. Jarden, *Shirei ha-ḥol,* 336, lines 5–9.

51. Cf. Lev. 17:6: "And the priest shall sprinkle the blood upon the altar of the Lord."

52. Lev. 19:28: "You shall not make gashes in your flesh for the dead, or *incise any marks* on yourselves," i.e., tattoo. The idea of nature tattooing a design on the earth is also found in the pre-Islamic Arabic poet Labīd: "The torrents exposed the ruins as if they were books whose pens renewed their texts, or the repetitive motion of a tattoo artist dripping antimony on palms, their tattoos appearing upon them." Arabic text in Abū Bakr Muḥammad Ibn al-Qāsim al-Anbār, *Sharḥ al-qaṣāʾid al-sabʿ al-ṭiwāl al-jāhiliyyāt,* ed. ʿAbd al-Salām Muḥammad Hārūn, 2d ed. (Cairo: Dār al-maʿārif, 1969), 526–27 (lines 8–9).

53. Referring to the design of the high priest's breastplate; Exod. 28:11.

54. *Qiṭṭer*—this verb is especially associated with offering sacrificial smoke, as in 1 Kings 22:24: "The people still sacrificed and offered [*mezabḥim u-meqaṭrim*] at the shrines."

55. I.e., afflicted, stricken.

56. Afflictions listed in Deut. 28:22, probably suggesting the colors red and green.

57. See e.g., Pagis, "Play and Substance," 43.

58. Jarden, *Shirei ha-ḥol,* 73, poem [40], line 4.

59. Moses Ibn Ezra, *Shirei ha-ḥol,* 7, poem [5]; see also the discussion of this poem by Scheindlin, *Wine, Women, and Death,* 34–39.

60. E.g., the poem discussed above (The garden wears an ornamented coat) is difficult to date. One might imagine that the poet is describing a garden that is actually before him and that the imagery derives from a living court culture. However, it is also possible that the garden exists in the poet's memory only.

61. Schirmann, *Toledot ha-shirah . . . ṣarfat,* 89–90. The entire section on Isaac Ben Abraham Ibn Ezra is written by Ezra Fleischer.

62. Although some of Isaac Ben Abraham Ibn Ezra's poems suggest a life of comfort and ease while others emphasize the vicissitudes of time and distress, it would be a priori reasoning to associate the former type with al-Andalus and the latter type with Egypt and Iraq only. Isaac Ben Abraham Ibn Ezra's "Boᶜarah ba-lev" (Schirmann, *HHSP,* 1:622 [285] = Isaac Ben Abraham Ibn Ezra, *Yiṣḥaq ben avraham ibn ᶜezra: Shirim,* ed. Menahem H. Schmelzer [New York: Jewish Theological Seminary, 1980], 141), one of the poet's *muwashshaḥs* that suggest desire for a young woman or man, illustrates this problem. The poetic speaker is isolated and depressed when a "lovely [female] gazelle" approaches and reveals the secret of his despair: he is distressed on account of "Isaac's" departure, an event that also caused Orion to withhold its light. Through her beauty and the cup in her hand, the woman brings the speaker to rejoice and forget separation. Fleischer assumes that this poem was written while the author was still in al-Andalus because there was no "market" for such poems in Egypt or Iraq (Schirmann, *Toledot ha-shirah . . . ṣarfat,* 90). Fleischer's assumption, although reasonable, is arbitrary. It is just as likely that the poet was situated beyond the borders of al-Andalus and composed a personal poem in an Andalusian style, just as Judah Halevi and Moses Ibn Ezra did. It might even be that the departed "Isaac" in the poem is self-referential, that Isaac Ibn Ezra is lamenting his own wandering, and that passion and drinking are his only comforts. In short, a range of interpretations seems possible, and we must not conclude that every poem evoking Andalusian themes necessarily emanates from the Andalusian context.

63. They have been discussed in scholarship, though not from the perspective of shifting cultural contexts. See Feldman, *Bein ha-qeṭavim le-qav ha-meshaveh,* 24–50. Feldman is primarily interested in the relationship between the garden and panegyric sections of the poem, focusing on the topic of poetic unity. The topic of imagery is not discussed with specific reference to cultural context.

64. Moses Ibn Ezra, *Shirei haḥol,* 170, poem [172].

65. I.e., to a wine party.

66. *Reᶜav*—Ibn Janāḥ (root *rᶜh*) includes the definition for some instances (Ps. 139:2, Eccles. 2:22, Dan. 2:29, where the quotation is Aramaic) "thought, examination, attention" (*al-fikr, al-tafaqqud wa al-riᶜāya*). Note that the last term is a cognate of the Hebrew term being explained. Thus Ibn Janāḥ sees common meaning for the root in Hebrew, Aramaic, and Arabic. Abraham Ibn Ezra sometimes explains the meaning similarly; see Brody.

67. "Variegated": cf. Judg. 5:30.

68. *Gapei*—Ibn Janāḥ understands the word according to an Aramaic cognate meaning "wings," though he understands it figuratively as meaning the "extreme part of something."

69. "Wine": cf. Exod. 22:28.

70. Cf. Isa. 34:15.

71. Lit., "occurrences, events" but clearly in a negative sense (as in 1 Kings 5:18). Also, perhaps, influenced by the Arabic cognate *fajīʿa,* "misfortune, calamity, disaster."

72. *La-ʿut*—meaning uncertain. Brody prefers "to satiate, give drink." According to Brody, some interpreters understand the derivation to be from *ʿet,* time, thus "to say something at its proper time." Ibn Janāḥ explains "to give understanding." The translation "to satiate at the proper time" incorporates the two main interpretations.

73. Lit., "its departures and alighting."

74. Moses Ibn Ezra, *Shirei haḥol,* 185, poem [185].

75. Or, perhaps, "containing various kinds of description."

76. Alternatively, "tired from running," though "too tired to run" seems preferable.

77. See 1 Kings 6:4 and Rashi's commentary.

78. Accepting Brody's emendation, reading *sof* instead of *ṣuf,* honey. Brody's emendation is supported by the reading in a manuscript to which he did not have access; see the note by Pagis in volume 3 of Moses Ibn Ezra, *Shirei haḥol,* 225.

79. "Weak" or "languid" (as in line 11). I translate "weak" here to contrast "powerful."

80. Cf. Ps. 40:13.

81. *Saṭṭim*—probably thinking of the Arabic *ḍāllīn,* "those who turn from the path, go astray," as in Qurʾān 1:7 and many other places.

82. Brody suggests that these droplets are beauty marks.

83. Num. 21:6, or "fiery serpents"; i.e., locks of hair, curls.

84. *Sitrei*—"veils" or "coverings." "Veils" is reinforced by the Arabic cognate *sitār,* "veil, drape, screen."

85. *Neʿeṭafim*—or "faint, weary." "Bent over" is based on the Arabic cognate *ʿaṭf,* "to incline, bend," as suggested in numerous biblical verses cited by Ibn Janāḥ.

86. Further, see chapters 1 and 2.

87. See Israel Levin, "Zeman ve-tevel be-shirat ha-ḥol ha-ʿivrit bi-sefarad bi-yemei ha-beinayim," *Oṣar yehudei sefarad* 5 (1962): 68–79.

88. There is an interesting parallel to this portrayal of Time in the wedding poem by Moses Ibn Ezra, "Ha-reaḥ mor meʾaḥez ha-afasim" (The scent of myrrh grasps the ends [of the earth]), in Moses Ibn Ezra, *Shirei haḥol,* 159–61 [160]: "Know that Time is a slave to your [the groom's] will and its sons are assembled for your every whim; they hurry to draw your requests near and to drive off whatever vexes your heart."

89. Further on this topos, see chapters 1 and 2 of this book.

4. Context

1. *Ridicule,* directed by Patrice Leconte (Miramax, 1996).

2. For "Mac Flecknoe," see *John Dryden,* ed. Keith Walker (Oxford: Oxford University Press, 1994), 1–6; on Shadwell, see M. F. McBride, *Folklore of Dryden's England: Gleanings from the Plays of Mac Flecknoe* (Washington, D.C.: University Press of America, 1982), especially chapter 8, "Wit and Wits." See also E. N.

Hooker, "Pope on Wit: The Essay on Criticism," in *The Seventeenth Century: Studies in the History of English Thought and Literature from Bacon to Pope,* ed. Richard Foster Jones et al. (Stanford, Calif.: Stanford University Press, 1951), 225–46.

3. The fact that wit also played a role in seventeenth-century English poetry makes the medieval and early-modern cases more parallel.

4. I am using the word "European" to designate parts of Europe dominated by Christianity; of course, al-Andalus was also a part of the European continent.

5. See the discussion by G. Cohen, *Sefer ha-qabbalah,* 293–302.

6. Ibid., 53 [Hebrew section]. Although Ibn Daud would probably not object to the sentiment of Gerson Cohen's translation, "where their descendants have retained their identity down to the present," it is a bit exaggerated.

7. Ibid., 65–66 [Hebrew section].

8. Ibid., 70–71 [Hebrew section].

9. On this and the following information, see Baer, *A History of the Jews in Christian Spain,* vol. 1, chaps. 1 and 2; Septimus, *Hispano-Jewish Culture in Transition,* introduction; Assis, *The Golden Age of Aragonese Jewry;* most recently, see Jonathan Ray, *The Sephardic Frontier: The Reconquista and the Jewish Community in Medieval Iberia* (Ithaca, N.Y.: Cornell University Press, 2006).

10. Septimus, "Piety and Power in Thirteenth-Century Catalonia."

11. Assis, "Sexual Behavior in Medieval Hispano-Jewish Society"; Ray, *The Sephardic Frontier,* 165–75.

12. Bernard Septimus, "Ha-shilton ha-ṣiburi be-barṣalonah bi-tequfat ha-polmos ʿal sifrei ha-rambam," *Tarbiṣ* 42 (1973): 389–97.

13. Septimus, "Piety and Power," 213.

14. Baer, *A History of the Jews in Christian Spain,* 1:90–96.

15. In general, see Steven Harvey, "Arabic into Hebrew: The Hebrew Translation Movement and the Influence of Averroes Upon Medieval Jewish Thought," in *The Cambridge Companion to Medieval Jewish Philosophy,* ed. Daniel H. Frank and Oliver Leaman (Cambridge: Cambridge University Press, 2003), 258–80; Alfred Ivry, "Philosophical Translations from the Arabic in Hebrew During the Middle Ages," in *Recontres de cultures dans la philosophie médiévale,* ed. J. Hamesse and M. Fattori (Louvain-la-Neuve, Belgium, 1990), 167–86; Jonathan P. Decter, "The Rendering of Qurʾānic Quotations in Hebrew Translations of Islamic Texts," *Jewish Quarterly Review* 96 (2006): 336–58.

16. See Septimus, *Hispano-Jewish Culture in Transition,* 35ff.

17. E.g., Rabbi Meir Abulafiah; see Septimus, *Hispano-Jewish Culture in Transition.* See also Septimus, "Open Rebuke and Concealed Love," regarding Naḥmanides.

18. Rhymed prose is found in the *siluq* section of the classical *qedushta* (an ancient liturgical form) and is obviously without Arabic influence. The historical text from Italy *Megilat aḥimaʿaṣ* (c. 1054) is likely influenced by Arabic literary values. On the *siluq* and *Megilat aḥimaʿaṣ,* see Schirmann, *Toledot ha-shirah ha-ʿivrit. . . . ṣarfat,* 55 n. 174 and 93 n. 4. Hebrew epistles and Hebrew introductions to Judeo-Arabic epistles are also frequently written in rhymed prose and should be understood as being influenced by the Arabic epistolary style; for some examples (from the twelfth century), see Simḥa Assaf, "Qoveṣ shel iggerot r. shmuʾel ben ʿeli u-venei doro," *Tarbiṣ* 1, 1 (1929): 102–30; 1, 2 (1929): 43–84.

19. Schirmann, *HHSP,* 1:554–65; for an English translation, see Raymond P.

Scheindlin, trans., "Asher in the Harem," in *Rabbinic Fantasies: Imaginative Narratives from Classical Hebrew Literature,* ed. David Stern and Mark J. Mirsky (New Haven, Conn.: Yale University Press, 1990), 253–67.

20. Joseph Ben Meʾir Zabarra, *Sefer shaʿashuʿim,* ed. Israel Davidson (Berlin, 1925); English translation: *The Book of Delight by Joseph Ben Meir Ibn Zabara,* trans. Moses Hadas, intro. Merriam Sherwood (New York: Columbia University Press, 1932).

21. Matti Huss, "Minḥat yehudah, ʿEzrat ha-nashim, ve-ʿEin mishpaṭ—mahadurot madaʿiyot bi-leviyat mavoʾ, ḥilufei girsaʾot, meqorot u-ferushim" (Ph.D. diss., Hebrew University, 1991); see also the partial English translation by Raymond P. Scheindlin, "The Misogynist," in *Rabbinic Fantasies,* 269–94. For an analysis of this text, see Rosen, *Unveiling Eve,* 103–23.

22. Concerning the status of misogyny and misogamy in the text and their treatment in modern scholarship, see Rosen, *Unveiling Eve.* Rosen argues that the misogamic parts of the text are undermined while the misogynistic parts remain unreversed.

23. Abū Muḥammad al-Qāsim Ibn ʿAli al-Ḥarīrī, *Maḥberot ittiʾel,* trans. Judah al-Ḥarīzī, ed. Yiṣḥaq Pereṣ (Tel Aviv: Moledet, 1951).

24. Al-Ḥarīzī, *Taḥkemoni,* ed. Y. Toporovsky. For an English translation in rhymed prose, see Judah al-Ḥarīzī, *The Book of Taḥkemoni: Jewish Tales from Medieval Spain,* translated, explicated, and annotated by David Simha Segal (London: Littman Library of Jewish Civilization, 2001).

25. Yaʿaqov Ben Elʿazar, *Sipurei ahavah shel yaʿaqov ben elʿazar,* ed. Jonah David (Tel Aviv: Tel Aviv University, 1993).

26. Zvi Malakhi, "Megilat ha-ʿofer le-rav elihu ha-kohen, maqāma alegorit mi-sefarad," in *Be-oreaḥ madʿa, meḥqarim be-tarbut yisraʾel mugashim le-aharon mirski,* ed. Zvi Malakhi (Lod: Makhon habermann le-meḥqarei sifrut, 1986), 317–52; see also Israel Levin, "Ha-ʿofer ve-ha-ṣipurim: ʿAl megilat ha-ʿofer le-rav eliyahu ha-kohen ve-iggeret ha-ṣipurim le-ibn sina," *Meḥqarei yerushalayim be-sifrut ʿivrit* 10–11 (1987–88): 577–611.

27. For a critical Hebrew text and English translation, see Isaac Ibn Sahula, *Meshal ha-qadmoni: Fables from the Distant Past,* ed. Raphael Loewe (Oxford: Littman Library of Jewish Civilization, 2004). An older edition of the Hebrew is also available: Isaac Ibn Sahula, *Meshal ha-qadmoni,* ed. Yisrael Zamora (Tel Aviv: Mosad Bialik, 1952).

28. Matti Huss, ed., *Meliṣat ʿefer ve-dinah le-don vidal benveniste: Pirqei ʿiyyun u-mahadurah biqortit* (Jerusalem: Magnes, 2003).

29. For samples of other texts, see Yehudah Ratzaby, *Yalquṭ ha-maqāma ha-ʿivrit* (Jerusalem: Mosad Bialik, 1974). For an Egyptian example from the second half of the thirteenth century, see Yosef Ben Tanḥum ha-Yerushalmi's "Neʾum aḥituv ben ḥakhamoni," published in Joseph Yahalom, "Tafqido shel sipur ha-misgeret be-ʿibudim ʿivriyim shel maqamot," in *Sefer yisraʾel levin,* ed. Tsur and Rosen, 1: 136–54.

30. Dan Pagis, "Variety in Medieval Rhymed Narratives," *Scripta Hierosolymitana* 27 (1978): 79.

31. On this terminology, see S. D. Goitein, "Ha-maqāma ve-ha-maḥberet: Pereq be-toledot ha-sifrut ve-ha-ḥevrah ba-mizraḥ," *Maḥbarot le-sifrut* 5 (1951): 26–40.

32. E.g., Menocal, *The Arabic Role in Literary History;* Americo Castro, *The Structure of Spanish History* (Princeton, N.J.: Princeton University Press, 1954); and further discussion below.

33. On the reading of Arabic texts by Jews, see E. Gutwirth, "Hispano-Jewish Attitudes to the Moors in the Fifteenth Century," *Sefarad* 49, 2 (1989): 237–62.

34. María Rosa Menocal, *Shards of Love: Exile and the Origins of the Lyric* (Durham, N.C.: Duke University Press, 1994), 39.

35. Badīʿ al-Zamān al-Hamadhānī, *Maqāmāt,* ed. Muḥammad ʿAbduh (Beirut: Al-maṭbaʿah al-kathūlikiyah li-al-ābāʾ al-yasūīyīn, 1889); English translation: *The Maqāmāt of Badiʿ al-Zamān al-Hamadhānī,* trans. W. J. Prendergast (London: Curzon, 1915). In general, see A. F. L. Beeston, "Al-Hamadhānī, al-Ḥarīrī and the *Maqāmāt* Genre," in *ʿAbbasid Belles-Lettres,* 125–35; James T. Monroe, *The Art of Badīʿ Az-Zamān al-Hamadhānī as Picaresque Narrative* (Beirut: American University of Beirut, 1983).

36. On the reuse of materials such as sermons, epistles, *ḥadīth,* and poetic genres, see Abdalfattah Kilito, *Les Séances* (Paris: Sindbad, 1983) and the earlier article by idem, "Le Genre séance: Une introduction," *Studia Islamica* 43 (1976): 25–51.

37. Medieval testimonies concerning the number of episodes al-Hamadhānī invented range from twenty, to forty, to four hundred. Fifty-two have been preserved in manuscripts. On the number of *maqāmāt* and textual problems, see Jaakko Hämeen-Anttila, *Maqama: A History of a Genre* (Wiesbaden: Harrassowitz, 2002), 39–40.

38. On the types of *maqāma* plots in al-Hamadhānī, see Hämeen-Anttila, *Maqama,* 55–61.

39. Rina Drory, "The Maqama," in *The Literature of al-Andalus,* 193. This is not to say, however, that al-Hamadhānī had no imitators before al-Ḥarīrī. See, for example, Stefan Wild, "Die zehnte Maqāma des Ibn Nāqiyā: Eine Burleske aus Baghdad," in *Festschrift Ewald Wagner zum 65. Geburtstag, Band 2: Studien zur Arabischen Dichtung,* ed. W. Heinrichs and G. Schoeler (Beirut: Steiner, Stuttgart [in Komm], 1994), 427–38; Philip Kennedy, "Reason and Revelation or a Philosopher's Squib (The Sixth Maqāma of Ibn Nāqiyā)," *Journal of Arabic and Islamic Studies* 3 (2000): 84–113; Hämeen-Anttila, *Maqama,* 126–47.

40. English translation: *The Assemblies of al-Ḥarīrī,* ed. and trans. Thomas Chenery and F. Steingass, 2 vols. (London: Williams and Norgate, 1867–98 [rpt. 1969]).

41. For a convenient list of plot types in al-Ḥarīrī's *maqāmāt,* see ʿAbdal Raḥman Marʿī, "Hashpaʿat maqamot al-ḥarīrī ʿal maḥbarot taḥkemoni" (Ph.D. diss., Bar-Ilan University, 1995), 66.

42. Pierre Mackay, *Certificates of Transmission on a Manuscript of the Maqamas of Ḥarīrī. Ms. Cairo, Adab 105* (Philadelphia: American Philosophical Society, 1971).

43. Abū al-Ṭāhir Muḥammad Ibn Yūsuf al-Saraqusṭī, *Al-maqāmāt al-luzūmiyya,* ed. Aḥmad Badr Ḍayf (Alexandria, Egypt: Al-Hayʾah al-Miṣrīyah al-ʿĀmmah li-l-kitāb, 1982); idem, *Al-maqāmāt al-luzūmiyya,* trans. James T. Monroe (Leiden: E. J. Brill, 2002). (I wish to thank James Monroe for sharing with me his translation of al-Saraqusṭī prior to publication.) James T. Monroe, "Al-Saraqusṭī Ibn al-Ashtarkūwī: Andalusī Lexicographer, Poet, and Author of *al-Maqāmāt al-Luzūmiyya,*" *Journal of Arabic Literature* 28, 1 (1997): 1–37; idem, "Al-Saraqusṭī

Ibn al-Ashtarkūwī (Part II)," *Journal of Arabic Literature* 29 (1998): 31–58. See also Alexander E. Elinson, "Tears Shed over the Poetic Past: The Prosification of *Rithā᾽ al-Mudun* in al-Saraqusṭī's *Maqāma Qayrawāniyya*," *Journal of Arabic Literature* 36 (2005): 1–27.

44. In some narratives, the discourse is opened by a second narrator, al-Mundhir Ibn Ḥummām, apparently to begin the text on a different rhyme.

45. Requiring a two-consonant rhyme, over and above the usual single consonant required by al-Ḥarīrī; this rhyme scheme was first applied to poetry by the Syrian poet Abū ᶜAlā᾽ al-Maᶜārri in his collection *Luzūm mā lā yalzam.*

46. Although the final episode of al-Ḥarīrī's *maqāmāt* details the protagonist's Sufi conversion, it is not as definitively conclusive as al-Saraqusṭī's ending.

47. For more extensive discussions of the Andalusian *maqāma,* see Drory, "The Maqama"; H. Nemah, "Andalusian *Maqāmāt*," *Journal of Arabic Literature* 5 (1974): 83–92; Fernando de la Granja, *Maqāmas y risālas Andaluzas* (Madrid: Instituto Hispano-Árabe de Cultura, 1976); Iḥsān ᶜAbbās, *Tārīkh al-adab al-andalusī: ᶜAṣr al-ṭawā᾽if wa al-murābiṭīn* (Beirut: Dār al-thaqāfa, 1997), 243ff.; Yūsuf Nūr ᶜAwaḍ, *Fann al-maqāmāt bayna al-mashriq wa al-maghrib* (Beirut: Dār al-qalam, 1979); Hämeen-Anttila, *Maqama,* 206–53; Ismāᶜīl El-Outmani, "La Maqāma en al-Andalus," in *La sociedad Andalusí y sus tradiciones literarias* (special issue of *Foro Hispánico*), ed. Otto Zwartjes (Amsterdam and Atlanta: Rodopi, 1994), 105–25.

48. Drory, "The Maqama," 196.

49. ᶜAbbās, *Tārīkh al-adab al-andalusī,* 247.

50. Nemah, "Andalusian *Maqāmāt*." The *maqāma* form is used for eulogy, invective, love poetry, town description, pedagogy, and as a medium for discussing the administration of justice.

51. Nemah calls him the first *maqāma* author of al-Andalus; he dies only a few years after al-Saraqusṭī, so it seems difficult to know which author composed his collection first. The earliest Andalusian *maqāmāt* mentioned by Drory date from the reign of the Almerían governor al-Muᶜtaṣim ibn Ṣumādiḥ, who reigned from 1051 until 1091: "The Maqama," 196.

52. The narrator, who shares the name of al-Ḥarīrī's narrator al-Ḥarīth, is wandering the countryside (described in detail) and comes upon a sheikh collecting money from the poor through his impressive eloquence. The narrator invites the sheikh to stay at his home with the intention of stealing his money. The sheikh only pretends to sleep and is nowhere to be found when the narrator awakes; his only trace is a series of poems left in the narrator's house. The sheikh has taken leave for the tavern, where he has spent all his money and is in debt to the tavern-keeper (the narrative includes a detailed description of the tavern, customers, and servants). Finally, the narrator finds the sheikh and petitions him to compose verses in his honor; the sheikh obliges him with a poem of eighteen lines.

53. Nemah, "Andalusian *Maqāmāt*," 85.

54. Monroe, *The Art of Badīᶜ Az-Zamān,* 103.

55. Because al-Hamadhānī locates Alexandria as a city at the "Umayyad Frontier," Muḥammad ᶜAbduh, the editor of the *maqāmāt,* argues that this is not Alexandria in Egypt but the lesser known Alexandria in al-Andalus (64 n. 4). ᶜAbduh's suggestion seems unlikely since Alexandria in Egypt was often referred to as *al-thaghr* (the frontier) in Fāṭimid times and later.

56. The character is said to be based on an actual person of the same name, who came to a mosque of Basra in worn garments and eloquently begged for alms after his home in Sarūj was destroyed by the Franks in 1101. See the introduction to al-Ḥarīrī's *maqāmāt* by Chenery, *The Assemblies of al-Ḥarīrī,* 21.

57. Quoted in Monroe, "Al-Saraqusṭī" (Part I), 4 n. 8. See also chapter 7 below.

58. For a convenient selection of comments of scholars such as Chenery, Nicholson, Prendergast, Gibb, von Grunebaum, and others, see Monroe, *The Art of Badīᶜ Az-Zamān,* 87–89.

59. E.g., Hämeen-Anttila, *Maqāma;* Monroe, *The Art of Badīᶜ Az-Zamān;* Daniel Beaumont, "The Trickster and Rhetoric in the *Maqāmāt,*" *Edebiyāt* 5 (1994): 1–14.

60. See the collection of essays edited by Stefan Leder, *Story-telling in the Framework of Non-fictional Arabic Literature* (Wiesbaden: Harrassowitz, 1998).

61. The most inclusive publication on the popular epic to date is M. C. Lyons, *The Arabian Epic: Heroic and Oral Storytelling,* 3 vols. (Cambridge: Cambridge University Press, 1995), which includes an analytic introduction, synopses of the major epics, a narrative motif index, and a comparative index. The book is valuable for its breadth, although many problems, such as the dates of specific texts and the genetic relationship among texts, are left unresolved. Good starting points on *The Thousand and One Nights* are Robert Irwin, *The Arabian Nights: A Companion* (London: Allen Lane, 1994); and *The Arabian Nights Encyclopedia,* ed. Ulrich Marzolph and Richard van Leeuwen, 2 vols. (Santa Barbara, Calif.: ABC-CLIO, 2004), which contains essays on the manuscript tradition and various themes.

62. See Hilary Kilpatrick, *Making the Great Book of Songs: Compilation and the Author's Craft in Abū al-Faraj al-Iṣbahānī's* Kitāb al-aghānī (London: Routledge Curzon, 2003), 106.

63. See Remke Kruk, "The *Arabian Nights* and the Popular Epics," in *The Arabian Nights Encyclopedia,* 1:34–38; G. Canova, "*Sīra* Literature," in *Encyclopedia of Arabic Literature,* 726–27 and the related articles on ᶜAntara, Banī Hilāl, Dhāt al-Himma, and others.

64. In one premodern edition of the text, which numbers some 5,600 pages, the story begins with the generation of Noah and traces genealogical history leading up to the unusual birth of ᶜAntara. See the structuralist study by Peter Heath, *The Thirsty Sword: Sīrat ᶜAntar and the Arabic Popular Epic* (Salt Lake City: University of Utah Press, 1996).

65. Kruk, "The *Arabian Nights* and the Popular Epics," 36.

66. See Heath, *The Thirsty Sword,* 27–28.

67. See the entry "Romances of Chivalry," in Marzolph, ed., *The Arabian Nights Encyclopedia,* 2:691–93.

68. Peter Heath, "Romance as Genre in *The Thousand and One Nights,*" *Journal of Arabic Literature* 18 (1987): 1–21; 19 (1988): 3–26.

69. Ibid., 18:10–11.

70. S. D. Goitein, "The Oldest Documentary Evidence for the Title *Alf Laila wa Laila,*" *Journal of the American Oriental Society* 78 (1958): 301–302.

71. Heinz Grotzfeld, "The Manuscript Tradition of the *Arabian Nights,*" in *The Arabian Nights Encyclopedia,* 1:17–21.

72. Menéndez Pidal dates the text to 1140. Others date the text later, to the late

twelfth or early thirteenth century, e.g., Alan D. Deyermond, *A Literary History of Spain*, The Middle Ages (London: Benn, 1971), 45.

73. Regarding Arabic influence, the most obvious sign is the hero's epithet *Cid,* from the Arabic *sayyid,* "master, lord."

74. Richard E. Chandler and Kessel Schwartz, *A New History of the Spanish Language* (Baton Rouge: Louisiana State University Press, 1961). See 44ff. on the epic and 155ff. on Spanish prose fiction. It should be noted that a "narrative-lyric" also emerged in the late twelfth and early thirteenth century. Noteworthy examples include the *Disputa del alma y el cuerpo,* a debate between the body and the soul; *Denuestos del agua y el vino,* a debate between water and wine; and *Elena y María,* in which two girls debate the qualities of their lovers, one a knight and the other a cleric. See 55–56. Such debates, of course, share much with rhetorical *maqāmāt,* though Chandler associates them with French precedents.

75. Curtius, *European Literature and the Latin Middle Ages.*

76. Compare, for example, the first chapter of *Sefer ha-meshalim,* in which Intellect (*sekhel*), Wisdom's companion, rides a chariot toward the narrator's soul, with Alan of Lille's (d. 1202) *Anticlaudianus, or the Good and Perfect Man,* trans. James J. Sheridan (Toronto: Pontifical Institute of Mediaeval Studies, 1973), in which Reason drives a chariot constructed by the seven Liberal Arts, drawn by the five Senses, to request God's assistance in constructing a perfect human being (per the request of Nature). While the aims of the two texts are quite different, the parallel is striking. Of course, it is possible that both texts share classical antecedents.

77. The so-called *mixtum sive compositum;* see Curtius, *European Literature and the Latin Middle Ages,* 147–48. As in the case of Arabic, there are Latin discussions regarding the respective merits of poetry and prose.

78. Further details on specific texts will be given later in this chapter and in subsequent chapters. Most of the discussion is adapted from Michel Zink, *Medieval French Literature: An Introduction,* trans. Jeff Rider (Binghamton, N.Y.: Center for Medieval and Renaissance Texts and Studies, 1995); and Denis Hollier et al., *A New History of French Literature* (Cambridge, Mass.: Harvard University Press, 1994).

79. See Norman Daniel, *Heroes and Saracens: An Interpretation of the Chansons de Geste* (Edinburgh: Edinburgh University Press, 1984).

80. See Zink, *Medieval French Literature,* chapter 4.

81. For the sui generis position, see the literature review in Menocal, *The Arabic Role in Medieval Literary History* (Menocal is critical of this view). A proponent of the Latin influence model is Peter Dronke, *Medieval Latin and the Rise of the European Love-Lyric,* 2nd ed. (Oxford: Oxford University Press, 1968). A case can be made that the troubadour lyric and Provençal court culture as a whole have roots in the literature and courtly tradition of al-Andalus, though the issue has not been settled. See Menocal, *The Arabic Role in Medieval Literary History;* Cynthia Robinson, *In Praise of Song: The Making of Courtly Culture in al-Andalus and Provence, 1005–1134 A.D.* (Leiden: E. J. Brill, 2002); Gustave E. von Grunebaum, "The Arabic Contribution to Troubadour Poetry," *Bulletin of the Iranian Institute* 7 (1946): 138–51. See also the critique of this thesis by J. A. Abu-Haidar, *Hispano-Arabic Literature and the Early Provençal Lyrics* (Richmond, England: Curzon, 2001).

82. Although the actual social status of the lady has been the object of some debate, there is no doubt concerning the lover's submissiveness (or at least the affectation thereof) before her. In Andreas Cappelanus's treatise on love, courtship is considered appropriate only when the suitor is of a status beneath his lady's. See his *The Art of Courtly Love,* trans. John Jay Parry (New York: Columbia University Press, 1941).

83. Zink, *Medieval French Literature,* 37–40; A. J. Demony, "Courtly Love and Courtliness," *Speculum* 28 (1953): 44–63; Linda Paterson, "*Fin'amor* and the Development of the Courtly *Canso,*" in *The Troubadours: An Introduction,* ed. Simon Gaunt and Sarah Kay (Cambridge: Cambridge University Press, 1999), 28–46.

84. See William E. Burgwinkle, *Love for Sale: Materialist Readings of the Troubadour Razo Corpus* (New York: Garland, 1997); Robinson, *In Praise of Song,* 371–95.

85. In these cases, Pseudo-Calisthenes, Statius's *Thebaid,* and Virgil's *Aeneid,* respectively.

86. Such as Wace's *Roman de Brut,* an adaptation of the *Historia regum Britanniae* (*History of the Kings of Britain*); see Zink, *Medieval French Literature,* 53.

87. Dennis Howard Green, *The Beginnings of Medieval Romance: Fact and Fiction 1150–1220* (Cambridge: Cambridge University Press, 2002).

88. Zink, *Medieval French Literature,* 56.

89. *Le Conte de Floire et Blanchefleur,* ed. Robert d'Orbigny (Paris: Champion, 2003); for an English translation, see *The Romance of Floire and Blanchefleur,* trans. Merton Jerome Hubert (Chapel Hill: University of North Carolina Press, 1966).

90. Patricia A. Grieve, *Floire and Blancheflor and the European Romance* (Cambridge: Cambridge University Press, 1997), 22.

91. See the entry "*Floire and Blanchefleur,*" in Marzolph, ed., *The Arabian Nights Encyclopedia,* 2:551–52.

92. Eugene Mason, trans., *Aucassin and Nicolette and Other Medieval Romances and Legends* (New York: E. P. Dutton, 1910).

93. Clive S. Lewis, *The Allegory of Love* (London: Oxford University Press, 1936), 66.

94. Ibid., 68.

95. Carolynn Van Dyke, *The Fiction of Truth: Structures of Meaning in Narrative and Dramatic Allegory* (Ithaca, N.Y.: Cornell University Press, 1985), 66.

96. David F. Hult, "Jean de Meun's Continuation of *Le Roman de la Rose,*" in *A New History of French Literature,* ed. Denis Hollier et al. (Cambridge, Mass.: Harvard University Press, 1989), 99. This essential text has been translated several times into English. See Guillaume de Lorris and Jean de Meun, *The Romance of the Rose,* 3rd ed., trans. Charles Dahlberg (Princeton, N.J.: Princeton University Press, 1995). There is also a useful bibliography of the *Roman:* Heather M. Arden, *The Roman de la Rose: An Annotated Bibliography* (New York: Garland, 1993).

97. S. M. Stern, "Meqorah ha-ʿaravi shel 'maqāmat ha-ternegol' le-al-ḥarīzī," *Tarbiṣ* 17 (1946): 100–187.

98. Jefim Schirmann, *Die hebräische Übersetzung der Maqamen des Hariri* (Frankfurt am Main, 1930), 71–72. Despite the loose terminology, Schirmann does divide the texts into various types, including collections of fables, novellas, polemical writings, and the classical model of wandering rogues.

99. Israel Levin, *Ḥayy ben meqiṣ le-avraham ibn ʿezra* (Tel Aviv: Makhon Katz, 1983); the medieval manuscript of this text also refers to it as a *maqāma.* On *Ḥayy ibn yaqẓān,* see Henry Corbin, *Avicenna and the Visionary Recital,* trans. Willard R. Trask (London: Routledge and Kegan Paul, 1961). For a discussion and English translation of *Ḥayy ben meqiṣ,* see Aaron Hughes, *The Texture of the Divine: Imagination in Medieval Islamic and Jewish Thought* (Bloomington: Indiana University Press, 2004).

100. Pagis, "Variety in Medieval Rhymed Narratives," 90–91. Pagis distinguishes among three categories of rhymed prose narratives: 1) classical (according to the model of al-Ḥarīrī, exemplified in Hebrew by al-Ḥarīzī); 2) near classical (exemplified by Hebrew authors before al-Ḥarīzī); and 3) rhymed prose narratives of the thirteenth and fourteenth centuries that are influenced by European literature (Dan Pagis, *Ḥidush u-masoret be-shirat ha-ḥol* [Jerusalem: Keter, 1976], 199). Matti Huss further refines Pagis's classification by renaming the second category the "Andalusian Hebrew *Maqāma,*" arguing that such texts as *Sefer shaʿashuʿim, Minḥat yehudah,* and others share basic characteristics despite their diversity. Huss identifies six fundamental qualities that most of these texts share: 1) they are written for the purpose of entertainment; 2) they are composed in rhymed prose with metered poems interspersed; 3) they consist of one continuous story, not several; 4) they make use of fictional characters but without utilizing the narrator/protagonist dichotomy of the classical scheme; 5) they generally use the fixed phrase "he picked up his parable and said" (*va-yisaʾ meshalo va-yomar*) to introduce poems; 6) the narratives are generally introduced with the formula "So-and-So son of So-and-So spoke" (Huss, "Minḥat yehudah," 26–27). In Huss's view, the Andalusian Hebrew *maqāma* is more similar to the Andalusian Arabic *maqāma* than the classical *maqāma,* though his definition of the Hebrew *maqāma* is more rigid than Nemah's conception of the Arabic.

101. Noteworthy studies include: Ross Brann, "Power in the Portrayal: Representations of Muslims and Jews in Judah al-Ḥarīzī's *Taḥkemoni,*" *Princeton Papers in Near Eastern Studies* 1 (1992): 1–22; Matti Huss, "Loʾ haya ve-loʾ nivraʾ: ʿIyyun meshaveh me-maʿamad ha-bidayon ba-maqāmah ha-ʿivrit ve-ha-ʿaravit," *Meḥqarei yerushalayim be-sifrut ʿivrit* 18 (2001): 58–104; idem, "Minḥat yehudah"; Pagis, "Variety in Medieval Rhymed Narratives"; Raymond P. Scheindlin, "Fawns of the Palace and Fawns of the Field," *Prooftexts* 6 (1986): 189–203; Yahalom, "Tafqido shel sipur ha-misgeret"; several chapters of David Segal's commentary to the *Taḥkemoni* discuss structural aspects of the narratives: see al-Ḥarīzī, *The Book of Taḥkemoni;* sections of Rosen, *Unveiling Eve,* deal with gender in Hebrew narratives.

102. See chapter 5 of this book for a fuller bibliography. Also, for a convenient summary of this extensive bibliography, see Marʿī, "Hashpaʿat maqamot al-ḥarīrī," 279–80.

103. See the brief plot summaries at the beginning of this chapter and notes for further information.

104. Scheindlin, "Fawns of the Palace," 200; and "Asher in the Harem," 256.

105. Huss, "Minḥat yehudah," 54ff.; also Rosen, *Unveiling Eve.*

106. See chapter 5.

107. Discussed further in chapter 5.

108. Pagis, *Ḥidush u-masoret,* 199.

109. Zvi Malakhi considers possible Arabic influences on Hebrew allegorical writing in Iberia without considering the possibility of Christian influence, even for texts of the thirteenth and fifteenth centuries, highlighting the assumption of a unidirectional vector of Arabic influence on Hebrew texts. See Zvi Malakhi, "Ha-maqāma ha-ᶜaravit ve-hashpaᶜatah ᶜal ha-alegoriya ha-ᶜivrit," *Maḥanayim* 1 (1992): 176–79. Elsewhere, however, Malakhi suggests the possibility of influence from Christian allegory: "Megilat ha-ᶜofer," 320.

110. Rashi, in his commentary on Amos 4:11, associates the word with blackness.

111. Jefim Schirmann, "Ha-shaᶜar ha-shemini me-'sefer ha-meshalim' li-yaᶜaqov ben elᶜazar," *Qoveṣ ᶜal yad* 8 (1975): 270, lines 259–60.

112. Idem, "Der Neger und die Negerin," *Monatschrift für Geschichte und Wissenschaft des Judentums* 83 (1939): 481–92. On color sensitivity in French narrative, see Jacqueline de Weever, *Sheba's Daughters: Whitening and Demonizing the Saracen Woman in Medieval French Epic* (New York: Garland, 1998).

113. The article is Bernard Lewis, "Raza y color en el Islam," *Al-Andalus* 33 (1968): 1–51.

114. Jefim Schirmann, "Maᶜaseh be-zaqen ṣavuᶜa," in idem, ed., *Le-toledot ha-shirah ve-ha-dramah ha-ᶜivrit* (Jerusalem: Mosad Bialik, 1979), 386.

115. See chapter 5.

116. Goitein, *Jews and Arabs,* 155.

117. For a critique of this tendency, see, for example, Marcus, "Beyond the Sephardic Mystique."

118. Interestingly, María Rosa Menocal has noted the opposite phenomenon in Christian scholarship when tracing the influences upon a figure such as Raymond Llull:

> Urvoy makes explicit the general rejection of the comparison between Llull and Ibn ᶜArabī first posited by Ribera and subsequently by Miguel Asín Palacios—that is, perhaps there are "literary" links of a direct sort that may be accepted, but from a doctrinal perspective the assumption of a direct influence is not warranted because Llull may have drawn inspiration from too many other sources. *In a number of ways this is exactly the kind of highly prejudiced argument made whenever Arabic "sources" are at stake; if any other source can be found, then that source is far likelier, essentially eliminating the Arabic possibility.* (*Shards of Love,* 220–21, italics mine)

119. The problems in imagining the context of Hebrew rhymed prose are not unlike the problems that have surrounded discussions of the *muwashshaḥ*. The *muwashshaḥ* is a strophic form indigenous to al-Andalus, composed mostly in classical Arabic (or Hebrew) but sometimes concluding with a couplet (called the *kharja*) in colloquial Andalusian Arabic or Ibero-Romance. The Romance *kharja*s are the earliest evidence of Romance verse in the Iberian Peninsula. On one hand, scholars, largely Arabists, have explained the strophic form as an outgrowth of an Eastern Arabic strophic form. According to this theory, the *muwashshaḥ* became a popular form that inspired the composition of concluding verses in Romance and may have influenced the rise of the troubadour lyric. Others, often scholars of European lit-

erature, have tended to see the *muwashshaḥ* as a native Iberian form created under the impact of an early, otherwise undocumented, Romance poetry; the Romance *kharjas*, then, have been referred to as the remaining "islands" of what was once a complete "archipelago" of Romance verse. At stake in this debate is much more than our understanding of a literary form but also our conception of vectors of influence between Arabic and European cultures. The bibliography is enormous; see Monroe, "*Zajal* and *Muwashshaḥa*"; Henk Heijkoop and Otto Zwartjes, *Muwaššaḥ, Zajal, Kharja: Bibliography of Strophic Poetry and Music from al-Andalus and Their Influence in East and West* (Leiden: Brill, 2004). On the Hebrew *muwashshaḥ,* see Rosen-Moked, *Le-ʾezor shir.*

120. Leder, "Conventions of Fictional Narration in Learned Literature," 34–60. Joseph Sadan, "Hārūn al-Rashīd and the Brewer: Preliminary Remarks on the *Adab* of the Elite versus *Ḥikāyāt,*" in *Studies in Canonical and Popular Arabic Literature,* ed. S. Ballas and R. Snir (Toronto: York, 1998), 1–22; Muhsin Mahdi, *From History to Fiction: The Tale Told by the King's Steward in the Thousand and One Nights* (Cambridge: Cambridge University Press, 1997); idem, *The Thousand and One Nights (Alf Layla wa Layla): From the Earliest Known Sources* (Leiden: Brill, 1994), 3:164–80.

121. See the brief entry "Floire and Blancheflor," in Marzolph, ed., *The Arabian Nights Encyclopedia,* 2:551–52. On Boccaccio, Chaucer, and others, see Irwin, *The Arabian Nights,* 63–102; Carol F. Heffernan, *The Orient in Chaucer and Medieval Romance* (Woodbridge, England: Brewer, 2003). See also the review essay by Helen Moore on recent titles concerning the origins of medieval Romance: "From the Greek," *Times Literary Supplement,* July 8, 2005, 5–6.

122. See also the comments by Rosen and Yassif, "The Study of Hebrew Literature of the Middle Ages."

123. One fruitful parallel between a section of Ibn Zabarra's *Sefer shaʿashuʿim* and Ibn Buṭlān's *Risālat daʿwat al-aṭibba* (an Eastern Arabic source) has been pointed out by Arie Schippers: "Ibn Zabāra's *Book of Delight* (Barcelona, 1170) and the Transmission of Wisdom from East to West," *Frankfurter Judaistische Beiträge* 26 (1999): 149–61; compare with Jefim Schirmann, "The Harmful Food: A Curious Parallel Between Cervantes and Joseph Zabarra," in *Romanica et Occidentalia,* ed. Moshe Lazar (Jerusalem: Magnes, 1963), 140–42.

5. Structure

1. See Wallace Martin, *Recent Theories of Narrative* (Ithaca, N.Y.: Cornell University Press, 1986).

2. Mikhail Mikhailovich Bakhtin, *The Dialogic Imagination,* ed. Michael Holquist, trans. Caryl Emerson and Michael Holquist (Austin: University of Texas Press, 1981); Viktor Shklovsky, *Theory of Prose,* trans. Benjamin Sher (Elmwood Park, Ill.: Dalkey Archive Press, 1990).

3. See the famous study of folk literature by Vladimir Propp, *Morphology of the Folktale,* trans. Laurence Scott (Bloomington: Indiana University Center in Anthropology, Folklore, and Linguistics, 1958); Roland Barthes, "Introduction to the Structural Analysis of Narrative," in idem, *Image, Music, Text,* trans. Stephen Heath (London: Collins, 1977), 79–124; Tzvetan Todorov, *The Poetics of Prose* (Ithaca, N.Y.: Cornell University Press, 1968); Culler, *Structuralist Poetics.*

4. Wolfgang Iser, *The Act of Reading: A Theory of Aesthetic Response* (Baltimore: Johns Hopkins University Press, 1976); Susan R. Suleiman and Inge Crosman, eds., *The Reader in the Text: Essays on Audience and Interpretation* (Princeton, N.J.: Princeton University Press, 1980); Paul Ricoeur, *Time and Narrative* (Chicago: University of Chicago Press, 1984).

5. In chapter 4, the term "form" was used to designate the "actual shape of a poem." Here, "structure" indicates such narrative devices as the interplay among narrative parts, authorial voice, and the use of time. "Form" and "structure" are slippery terms, especially as the school of structuralism grew out of Russian formalism. The term "form" ultimately fell out of favor, since it was sometimes associated with the Platonic concept of forms, suggesting that literary works (and other artistic expressions) derived from existing ideal forms.

6. See chapter 4.

7. See Joseph Sadan, "Rabi yehudah al-ḥarīzī ke-ṣomet tarbuti: Biografiyah ʿaravit shel yoṣer yehudi be-ʿeinei mizraḥan," *Peʿamim* 68 (1996): 25 n. 21, on the various opinions regarding al-Ḥarīzī's birthplace. This is the best work on al-Ḥarīzī's biography.

8. Ibid., 18–28.

9. For the Arabic text (including the poems), see ibid., 52–61. *Al-Rawḍa al-anīqa* has been in the process of piecemeal publication for many years; the most complete edition (with Hebrew translation) is found in Blau and Yahalom, *Masʿei yehudah,* 91–167.

10. This list has been reiterated several times in scholarship. I am using Rina Drory's "Literary Contacts and Where to Find Them: On Arabic Literary Models in Medieval Jewish Culture," *Poetics Today* 14, 2 (1993): 277–302; here, 285 and appendix.

11. Moshe Idel, "Zehuto shel metargem sefer ʿarugat ha-bosem le-rav moshe ibn ʿezra," *Kiryat sefer* 51 (1975–76): 484–87.

12. Moshe Ben Maimon, *Moreh ha-nevukhim be-tirgumo shel rabi yehudah al-ḥarīzī* (Jerusalem: Mosad Harav Kook, 1953).

13. M. D. Rabinovitz, ed., *Rabeinu moshe ben maimon: Haqdamot le-ferush ha-mishnah* (Jerusalem: Mosad Harav Kook, 1961).

14. According to al-Ḥarīzī's testimony; see *Taḥkemoni,* 406.

15. Moshe Ben Maimon, "Maʾamar teḥiyat ha-metim," trans. Judah al-Ḥarīzī, ed. A. S. Halkin, *Koveṣ ʿal yad* 9 (1989): 129–50.

16. ʿAli Ibn Riḍwān, *Iggeret ʿali ha-ishmaʿeli,* trans. Judah al-Ḥarīzī, ed. M. Grossberg (London, 1900).

17. Ḥunayn Ibn Isḥaq, *Sefer musrei ha-filosofim* (Sinnsprüche der Philosophen), trans. Judah al-Ḥarīzī, ed. A. Loewenthal (Frankfurt am Main: J. Kauffmann, 1896).

18. Galenus, *Dialog über die Seele,* trans. Judah al-Ḥarīzī, ed. A. Jellinek (Leipzig: C. L. Gritzsche, 1852).

19. Al-Ḥarīrī, *Maḥbarot ittiʾel;* Ezra Fleischer, "An Overlooked Fragment of the Translation by Yehudah al-Ḥarīzī of the Maqāmas of al-Ḥarīrī," *Journal of Jewish Studies* 24 (1973): 179–84. Al-Ḥarīzī wrote the translation while still in northern Iberia or Provence, sometime between 1205 and 1216 (see Drory, "Literary Contacts," 285).

20. In addition to this short introduction to the *Taḥkemoni,* one should see some of the numerous fine introductions to the book. See, for example, Schirmann, *Toledot ha-shirah . . . ṣarfat,* 184–221.

21. On the dedications, see A. M. Habermann, "Haqdashot le-sefer *taḥkemoni* ve-reshimat tokhen maqamotav," *Maḥbarot le-sifrut* 5 (1953): 39–46, and Rina Drory, "Al-Ḥarīzī's *Maqāmāt:* A Tricultural Literary Product?" *Medieval Translator* 4 (1994): 66–85.

22. Blau and Yahalom, *Masᶜei yehudah,* 10.

23. Drory, "Literary Contacts"; idem, "Al-Ḥarīzī's *Maqāmāt;* idem, "Ha-heqsher ha-samui min ha-ᶜayin: ᶜAl toṣarim sifrutiyim shel mifgash telat-tarbuti bi-yemei ha-beinayim," *Peᶜamim* 46 (1991): 9–28.

24. Idem, "Literary Contacts," 298.

25. Sadan, "Rabi yehudah al-ḥarīzī ke-ṣomet tarbuti."

26. Jefim Schirmann, "Le-ḥeqer meqorotav shel sefer taḥkemoni li-yehudah al-ḥarīzī," *Tarbiṣ* 23 (1952): 198ff.; Judith Dishon, "Le-meqorah shel ha-maḥberet ha-ᶜesrim ve-eḥat be-sefer taḥkemoni," *Biqoret u-farshanut* 13 (1979): 9ff.; idem, "Neʾum asher ben yehudah li-shelomo ibn ṣaqbel ve-ha-maqāma ha-ᶜesrim be-taḥkemoni li-yehudah al-ḥarīzī," *Biqoret u-farshanut* 6 (1974): 57–65; Y. Danah, "Al-hamadhānī ke-maqor le-rav yehudah al-ḥarīzī," *Dappim le-meḥqar be-sifrut* 1 (1984): 79–89; idem. "Le-meqoro shel sefer taḥkemoni," *Tarbiṣ* 44 (1975): 172ff.; Yehudah Ratzaby, "Le-meqorotav shel taḥkemoni," *Tarbiṣ* 26 (1957): 424ff.; S. M. Stern, "Meqorah ha-ᶜaravi shel 'maqāmat ha-ternegol' le-al-ḥarīzī"; Marᶜī, "Hashpaᶜat maqamot al-ḥarīrī."

27. See Schirmann, *Toledot ha-shirah ha-ᶜivrit . . . ṣarfat,* 153–68 and references therein. See also discussion below in chapter 6.

28. Huss, "Loʾ haya ve-loʾ nivraʾ"; idem, "Ha-bidayon u-maᶜamado ba-maqāmah ha-ᶜivrit: Yehudah al-ḥarīzī ve–immanuʾel ha-romi—hemshekh o temurah?" *Tarbiṣ* 67 (1998): 351–78; and Rosen, *Unveiling Eve.*

29. Blau and Yahalom, *Masᶜei yehudah,* does explicate al-Ḥarīzī's travels, however.

30. See also the thorough discussion of names in David Segal's commentary to his translation: al-Ḥarīzī, *The Book of Taḥkemoni,* 637–45.

31. Actually, here it is written: "He [Solomon] was the wisest of all men: [wiser] than Ethan the Ezrahite, and Heman, Chalkol, and Darda." Heman is the son of Zeraḥ, the son of Judah; by making the narrator a descendant of Judah, al-Ḥarīzī might be making a reference to himself.

32. Al-Ḥarīzī, *Taḥkemoni,* 382.

33. Ibid., 274: "Therefore they call my name 'Ḥever,' because I bring together [*aḥaber*] all precious scattered [poems]."

34. On the association of this root with the Arabic cognate *ẓᶜn,* see chapter 3. Furthermore, the Qenites may be associated with Qayin (Cain) of Genesis, who was condemned by God to become a ceaseless wanderer on earth (Gen. 4:12).

35. The word carries several meanings, including "inexperienced, gullible" but also "generous." The same root (in the third form) also carries another relevant meaning, "to venture, engage in adventures."

36. Of course, al-Ḥarīzī used the name Ḥever ha-Qeni already in *Maḥberot ittiʾel* for al-Ḥarīrī's Abū Zayd. Still, the association between wandering and al-Ḥarīzī's

own biography may be significant, especially as the author identifies with the perspective of his protagonist in some instances.

37. Al-Ḥarīzī, *Taḥkemoni,* 8.

38. Ibid., 13.

39. A recent attempt has been made to link al-Ḥarīzī's satires of members from various classes of society with the medieval "Estate Satire," a didactic form directed toward exposing the flaws of society. See Ayelet Oettinger, "Criticism of the Social Classes in Yehudah al-Harīzī's 'Book of Tahkemoni' and in European Literature of the Thirteenth Century—Affinity and Distinction" (forthcoming); idem, "Ziqato shel sefer taḥkemoni li-yehudah al-ḥarīzī le-satirat ha-maᶜamadot ha-noṣrit" (*Dapim lesifrut,* forthcoming).

40. On Natura, see George D. Economou, *The Goddess Natura in Medieval Literature* (Cambridge, Mass.: Harvard University Press, 1972).

41. Alan of Lille, *The Plaint of Nature,* trans. James J. Sheridan (Toronto: Pontifical Institute of Mediaeval Studies, 1980).

42. Consider also the personification of Philosophia in Boethius, *Consolation of Philosophy,* trans. Joel C. Relihan (Indianapolis: Hacket, 2001).

43. *Musar.* In medieval Hebrew, this term is considered the equivalent of the Arabic word *adab,* which includes morality but also refers to "refined culture."

44. Ramón Menéndez Pidal, ed., *La leyenda de los Infantes de Lara* (Madrid, Impr. de Librería y Casa Editorial Hernando, 1934). Menéndez Pidal dates the text to the second half of the thirteenth century (4). Alan Deyermond, however, dates the text as early as 1000: *A Literary History of Spain,* 39. See also the essay by Curtius, "The 'Chivalric System of the Virtues,'" in *European Literature and the Latin Middle Ages,* 519–37. Curtius mentions that "Islam too developed an ideal of knighthood, which exhibits 'striking coincidences' with that of the Christian West. . . . These indications perhaps suffice to show that we need a new discipline of medieval studies, based on the broadest foundations" (537, and see n. 34).

45. On *manāqib* literature, see Clifford E. Bosworth, "*Manāqib* Literature," in *Encyclopedia of Arabic Literature,* 504–505. While al-Ḥarīzī may have been familiar with *manāqib* literature, the European parallels seems more proximate. Jewish sources on morals such as Solomon Ibn Gabirol's *Mivḥar hapeninim* (Choice of Pearls) or his *Iṣlaḥ al-akhlāq* (Improvement of the Moral Qualities) also lack the seven-part enumeration.

46. Rosen, *Unveiling Eve,* 149–67. See further below in the discussion of Jacob Ben Elᶜazar.

47. Ibid.

48. There are also some minor differences in structure. In the original, the main story is told by ᶜIsa Ibn Hishām, and Abū al-Fatḥ is not recognized until the end of the *maqāma,* and there the anagnorisis seems somewhat forced. In al-Ḥarīzī's version, the story is told by Ḥever ha-Qeni, who is known from the beginning. The change signifies al-Ḥarīzī's tendency to standardize the structure of *maqāmāt,* following al-Ḥarīrī.

49. David S. Segal, "Ha-petiḥa, ha-siyyum ve-ha-sipur ha-ᶜotef be-sefer 'taḥkemoni' li-yehudah al-ḥarīzī," in *Meḥqarim be-sifrut ᶜam yisraᵓel u-be-tarbut teiman: Sefer ha-yuval le-profesor ratzaby,* ed. Judith Dishon and Efrayim Hazan (Tel Aviv:

Bar-Ilan University, 1991), 415–17; Yahalom, "Tafqido shel sipur ha-misgeret." Yahalom argues that al-Ḥarīzī sometimes tempers risqué elements of stories by emphasizing fictionality more than al-Ḥarīrī does.

50. A significant, if somewhat crude, parallel is the structure of the television series *Star Trek.* Fairly predictable yet varied plots unravel within the constraints of an ongoing and repeating narrative form. Every episode begins and ends with the *Enterprise* traveling through space, ready to undertake an adventure, regardless of what takes place during the course of an episode.

51. Brann, "Power in the Portrayal," 8. Brann only includes a few examples for each type; other chapters are added below.

52. 4 (Debate of the Ant and Flea); 5 (*Maqāma* of the Months of the Year); 8 (A Letter Read Forward as Praise, Read Backward as Reproach); 9 (Contest of Poets); 11 (Trilingual Poem, Poems with and without the Letter *Resh*); 13 (Parable of Body and Soul); 15 (On Prayer); 16 (Poets' Boasting Match); 19 (Youths Debate Seven Virtues); 23 (Panegyric for a Man Who Lost His Daughter but Whose Wife Bore a Son); 25 (The Hunt); 26 (Vicissitudes and Benefits of Travel); 27 (In Praise of Wine); 32 (Poetic Repartee between Youth and Sage); 33 (Alphabetical Wordplay on Sinners and Saints); 36 (Homonym Poems); 39 (Poetic Dispute between Day and Night); 40 (Dispute between Pen and Sword); 41 (Dispute between Man and Woman); 42 (Miserliness versus Generosity); 43 (Sea versus Dry Land); 44 (Teacher Who Asks Pupils Questions); 45 (Of Anecdotes, Wise Sayings, and Sealed Enigmas); 49 (In Praise of Fruits and Trees of the Garden); 50 (Scattered Poems).

53. 17 (Against the Karaites); 18 (Origins of Poetry); 46 (Men of the Eastern Cities); 47 (Descriptions of Cities).

54. 6 (The Marriage); 20 (Seven Virgins); 21 (Ḥever Deceives a Country Bumpkin); 29 (The Mendicant Preacher and His Son); 30 (Wandering Physician); 31 (The Captured Robber); 38 (Amulets).

55. 31 (The Horseman's Ruse), 37 (The Snake Charmer); 34 (Tale of the Merchant).

56. Al-Ḥarīzī, *Taḥkemoni, maqāma* 29; al-Hamadhānī, *al-Bukhāriyya, maqāma* 17; al-Ḥarīrī, *al-Ṣanʿaʾiyya, maqāma* 1; and others.

57. On the social reality of poverty and charity for Jews in the medieval Islamic world, see M. R. Cohen, *Poverty and Charity in the Jewish Community of Medieval Egypt.*

58. Hence the name of al-Saraqusṭī's narrator, Abū al-Ghamr, "Possessor of Naïveté."

59. Hämeen-Anttila argues that al-Saraqusṭī's characters are more complex psychologically. Abū Ḥabīb is simultaneously more fallible than Abū Zayd but also more ruthless. See Hämeen-Anttila, *Maqama,* 273–81. Still, one cannot speak of character development.

60. Monroe takes the chronological contradictions of al-Hamadhānī's *maqāmāt* as a sign of the genre's penchant for intentional contradiction: *The Art of Badīʿ Az-Zamān,* 110–13. Hämeen-Anttila critiques Monroe's view since al-Hamadhānī's *maqāmāt* were never meant to be read as a collection; hence, he argues, we should not expect consistency among *maqāmāt* any more than we would among Jūḥa tales (or Mickey Mouse and Donald Duck stories): Hämeen-Anttila, *Maqama,* 100. Al-

though this critique is reasonable with respect to chronology in al-Hamadhānī's *maqāmāt,* we need not discount the significance of contradiction in other authors, especially one who edited his work as a complete whole.

61. Al-Ḥarīzī, *Taḥkemoni,* 15.

62. On the terms "extradiegetic" and "intradiegetic" and other aspects of voice, see Harold F. Mosher, "A New Synthesis of Narratology," *Poetics Today* 1, 3 (1980): 178; Gérard Genette, *Narrative Discourse: An Essay in Method,* trans. Jane E. Lewin (Ithaca, N.Y.: Cornell University Press, 1980), 243–62; Wayne Booth, *The Rhetoric of Fiction* (Chicago: University of Chicago Press, 1961).

63. Al-Ḥarīzī, *Taḥkemoni,* 287. For other examples, see Huss, "Lo᾽ haya ve-lo᾽ nivra᾽," 76 n. 74. The same technique is used by Jacob Ben El[c]azar (further below).

64. Heman invents poems in *Taḥkemoni,* 39, 203, 378–82; Ḥever praises him on 382–83.

65. *Ne᾽um asher ben yehudah* is mentioned in Ḥever ha-Qeni's review of literary history in *maqāma* 3. In *maqāma* 18, al-Ḥarīzī praises another *maḥberet,* entitled *Ne᾽um toviyah ben ṣidqiya,* by Joseph Bar Judah Bar Shim[c]on; see *Taḥkemoni,* 190. It is unclear whether al-Ḥarīzī did not know or did not value the less classical Hebrew rhymed prose narratives.

66. The single manuscript, MS Minken 207, was copied in 1268, thus not long after the author's death. The text is copied in an Ashkenazic script and is bound together with the *Mishlei shu[c]alim* (Fox fables) of Berekhia ha-Naqdan.

67. This is deduced from the fact that the family name Ibn El[c]azar or Abenelezar appears several times in Arabic and Spanish texts from the twelfth and thirteenth centuries in association with a prominent family of Toledo. See Jefim Schirmann, "Sipurei ha-ahavah shel ya[c]aqov ben el[c]azar," *Yedi[c]ot ha-makhon le-ḥeqer ha-shirah ha-[c]ivrit* 5 (1939): 209–66.

68. Abraham Geiger, "Toledot ha-radaq," *Oṣar neḥmad* 2 (1857): 159–62.

69. See Ben El[c]azar, *Sipurei ahavah shel ya[c]aqov ben el[c]azar,* 9 n. 3 The dictionary is MS Leningrad 77.

70. Joseph Derenbourg, *Deux versions hébraïques du livre de Kalīlah et Dimnāh* (Paris: F. Vieweg, 1881), 312–95. The tales originated in India (under the title *Panchatantra*) and are known in Persian, Syriac, Arabic, and other renditions. There are several Arabic versions, the most famous of which is by [c]Abdallah Ibn al-Muqafa[c]. It is unclear which Arabic version Ben El[c]azar had before him when creating his rendition, which is a natural result of his liberal translation method. On *Kalīla wa dimnā* in general, see the article by C. Brockelmann in *Encyclopedia of Islam* (Leiden: Brill, 1960–), 4:503–506. Ben El[c]azar's translation has received relatively little attention, but see Ángeles Navarro Peiro, "La versión hebrea de *Calila y Dimna* de Ya[c]aqob ben El[c]azar," in *Jewish Studies at the Turn of the Twentieth Century,* ed. Judit Targarona Borrás and Angel Sáenz-Badillos (Leiden: E. J. Brill, 1999), 1:468–75. For a comparison of one episode with Arabic and Castilian versions, see Luis Girón-Negrón, "How the Go-Between Cut Her Nose: Two Ibero-Medieval Translations of a *Kalilah Wa Dimnah* Story," in *Under the Influence: Questioning the Comparative in Medieval Castile,* ed. Leila Rouhi and Cynthia Robinson (Leiden: E. J. Brill, 2005), 231–59.

71. Ya[c]aqov Ben El[c]azar, *Kitāb al-kāmil,* ed. Neḥemiah Allony (Jerusalem:

Ha-aqademiyah ha-ameriqanit le-mada^c^ei ha-yahadut, 1977). Recently, see Carlos del Valle Rodríguez, "Nova et vetera in grammaticae hebraicae historia: La obra gramatical de Jacob ben Elazar," *Helmantica* 49 (1998): 139–73.

72. The book consists of twenty-three chapters. Chapters 13–23 were published by Israel Davidson, "Serid me-sefer filosofi le-meḥaber bilti nod^c^a," *Ha-ṣofeh le-ḥokhmat yisra'el* 10 (1926): 94–105 (see also 11 [1927]: 96). Davidson worked from an incomplete manuscript and did not identify the author as Ben El^c^azar. Several complete manuscripts are preserved; see *Sipurei ahavah,* 10 n. 10.

73. The work is dedicated to Shmuel and Ezra, sons of Yehudah Ben Natanel of Beaucaire (in Provence). Further, see Schirmann, "Sipurei ha-ahavah," 212.

74. Jonah David assumes that he "traveled much," but there is really little evidence for this. See Ben El^c^azar, *Sipurei ahavah,* 7.

75. Ibid.

76. Schirmann, "Sipurei ha-ahavah" (author's introduction and chapters 5, 6, 7, and 9); idem, "Ha-sha^c^ar ha-shemini," 259–81 (chapter 8).

77. Ben El^c^azar, *Sipurei ahavah.* Several of the chapters appeared independently prior to the publication of the whole book.

78. Ben El^c^azar, *Kitāb al-kāmil,* 5.

79. Geiger, "Toledot ha-radaq," 161, based on a date given in chapter 4 (*Sipurei ahavah,* 32, lines 23–24): "It was in the year ninety-three when the transgressors completed [their mission] . . . when a king arose and his name was Meliṣ the Seer." Schirmann and David consider this dating likely. However, in the continuation of Geiger's dating, he concludes that Ben El^c^azar was actually of the generation of Moses Ibn Ezra and Judah Halevi and that he was the Rabbi El^c^azar to whom Moses Ibn Ezra dedicated several poems. His second opinion is incorrect.

80. Publications include Schirmann, "Der Neger und die Negerin"; idem, "Les Contes rimés de Jacob ben Éléazar de Toledo," in *Études d'Orientalisme dédiées à la memoire de Lévi-Provençal* (Paris: G.-P. Maisonneuve et Larose, 1962), 1:285–97; idem, "Ha-sha^c^ar ha-shemini"; Pagis, "Ṣiburei dimuyyim"; David S. Segal, "Mishlei ya^c^aqov ben el^c^azar: Le-mahut ha-maḥberet ha-shiv^c^it," in *Be-oreaḥ mad^c^a,* ed. Zvi Malakhi (Jerusalem: Makhon habermann le-meḥqarei sifrut, 1986), 353–63; Joseph Sadan, "Identity and Inimitability: Contexts of Inter-Religious Polemics and Solidarity in Medieval Spain, in the Light of Two Passages by Moshe Ibn ^c^Ezra and Ya^c^aqov ben El^c^azar," *Israel Oriental Studies* 14 (1994): 325–47; Raymond P. Scheindlin, "Sipurei ha-ahavah shel ya^c^aqov ben el^c^azar: Bein sifrut ^c^aravit le-sifrut romans," *Divrei ha-kongres ha-^c^olami ha-eḥad-^c^asar le-mada^c^ei ha-yahadut* 3, 3 (1994): 16ff.; Ángeles Navarro Peiro, "El 'mundus inversus' ('^c^olam hafuj') en el 'Séfer ha-meshalim' de Ya^c^acob ben El^c^azar de Toledo," *Judaísmo hispano* 1 (2002): 209–15; Rosen, *Unveiling Eve,* 95–102, 152–67.

81. The name appears in this extended form only once, at the beginning of chapter 1 (*Sipurei ahavah,* 15). More often, he is simply Lemu'el Ben Itti'el.

82. The name is alluded to one other time in the book. In chapter 3, after Lemu'el wins a poetry competition, his companions compliment him: "Who is like you in great deeds [*rav pe^c^alim*]?"

83. Ben El^c^azar, *Sipurei ahavah,* 14, lines 33–34.

84. In al-Hamadhānī's *Ruṣāfiyya,* Abū al-Fatḥ sodomizes a burglar (the "offending" scene is omitted by ^c^Abduh; see Hämeen-Anttila, *Maqāma,* 44). Homoeroti-

cism is also the subject of al-Hamadhānī's *Shāmiyya* (the entire episode is omitted by ᶜAbduh). In the Islamic West, a *maqāma* by the Tunisian Ibn Sharaf features a pederast who dies of exhaustion after failing to ensnare his beloved (see Hämeen-Anttila, 233). On the theme in the Hebrew *maqāma*, see Jefim Schirmann, "The Ephebe in Medieval Hebrew Poetry," *Sefarad* 15 (1955): 55–68. See also n. 121 below.

85. Schirmann, *Toledot ha-shirah . . . ṣarfat,* 237–38.

86. To these we might add the Andalusian story of *Bayāḍ and Riyāḍ*. Schirmann also recognizes certain thematic parallels with *The Thousand and One Nights.* On *Bayāḍ and Riyāḍ,* see Alois R. Nykl, *Historia de los amores de Bayad y Riyad: Una chantefable oriental en estilo persa* (New York: Printed by order of the trustees, 1941). On love in *The Thousand and One Nights,* see Irwin, *The Arabian Nights,* chapter 7.

87. Schirmann, *Toledot ha-shirah . . . ṣarfat,* 236–38; idem, "L'Amour spirituel dans la poésie hébraïque du moyen âge," *Les Lettres Romanes* 15 (1961): 315–25.

88. These rules are not entirely stable within the troubadour corpus. For Guillaume IX, the characteristics of the lover include "patience, submission to love's demands, an accommodating manner to a great many others, willingness to perform services for them, pleasing actions, and polite speech at court." Paterson, "*Fin'amor* and the Development of the Courtly *Canso,*" 30. For later troubadours, love becomes more ethically oriented.

89. Demony, "Courtly Love and Courtliness."

90. Schirmann, *Toledot ha-shirah . . . ṣarfat,* 236.

91. The arguments of Sahar and Kimah in chapter 9 fortify their love. Compare with the directions in Andreas Capellanus's love treatise, *The Art of Courtly Love,* 158.

92. Scheindlin, "Sipurei ha-ahavah," 17.

93. A Spanish translation of this episode was published by Ángeles Navarro Peiro, "Un cuento de Jacob ben Elazar de Toledo," *El Olivio* 15 (1982): 49–82.

94. Rosen, *Unveiling Eve,* 149–67.

95. Helen Solterer, "Figures of Female Militancy in Medieval France," *Signs* 16, 3 (1991): 522–49; Vern Bullough, "Transvestites in the Middle Ages," *American Journal of Sociology* 79, 6 (1974): 1381–94. See also the discussion above regarding *Taḥkemoni, maqāma* 28.

96. The propriety of women's participation in the Crusades was debated by Christian clerics; see Solterer, "Figures of Female Militancy," 535–37. Consider also the testimony of the Arab historian of the Crusades Imād al-Dīn: "Among the Franks, there were indeed women who rode into battle with cuirasses and helmets, dressed in men's clothes; who rode out into the thick of the fray and acted like brave men although they were but tender women, maintaining that all this was an act of piety, thinking to gain heavenly rewards by it, and making it their way of life." Quoted in Francesco Gabrieli, *Arab Historians of the Crusades* (Berkeley: University of California Press, 1969), 207. It is not impossible that the example in Ben Elᶜazar (and in al-Ḥarīzī above) is based on such Arabic accounts, though the proximity of the European sources also seems likely.

97. See Remke Kruk, "Warrior Women in Arabic Popular Romance," *Journal of Arabic Literature* 24 (1993): 213–40; 25 (1994): 16–33.

98. Abū al-Faraj al-Iṣfahānī, *Kitāb al-aghānī,* 24 vols. (Cairo: Dār al-kutub, 1927), 11:172–73.

99. Although, of course, the title itself is a modern assignment (which is still preferable to Jonah David's title for the collection, *Love Stories of Jacob Ben Elᶜazar,* since several episodes are not love stories at all). The author refers to the stories as his *meshalim;* another possible title would be *Mishlei yaᶜaqov ben elᶜazar.*

100. Joseph Sadan's suggestion; see "Identity and Inimitability," 325.

101. As in Num. 23:7, 18; 24:3, 5.

102. Rosen, *Unveiling Eve,* 95–102.

103. Rosen shows that much of the episode's imagery is drawn from Platonic and Neoplatonic sources. To the sources given there, one should also consider the significant resemblance to Alan of Lille's *Anticlaudianus,* as discussed in chapter 4.

104. Guillaume de Lorris, *The Romance of the Rose,* 60, lines 2109–13.

105. Ben Elᶜazar, *Sipurei ahavah,* lines 84–86.

106. Ibid., lines 90–91.

107. For Arabic precedents, see the anecdote related by al-Jāḥiẓ: "A Bedouin acquired a young wolf and raised it, hoping that he would protect it and domesticate it and that it would become better to him than a dog. When it grew strong, it pounced upon one of his sheep and ate it. The Bedouin said, 'You have eaten my sheep though I raised you among us, / How could you have known that your father was a wolf!'" Al-Jaḥiẓ, *Kitāb al-ḥayawān,* ed. ᶜAbd al-Salām Muḥammad Hārūn, 8 vols., 2nd ed. (Cairo: Maṭbaᶜat Muṣṭafā al-Bābī al-Ḥalabī wa awlādihi, 1966–69), 7:187. See the parallel text on 253 and notes on 187. The theme also surfaces with an interesting variation in Syriac and Spanish sources; a wolf listens to a sermon but loses interest when a flock of sheep passes. See Victor Chauvin, *Bibliographie des ouvrages arabes ou relatifs aux Arabes* (Liège: Vaillant-Carmanne, 1892–1922), 2:125. I have not located another source with Ben Elᶜazar's parallel story about a human child. A comparative study of the motif is in order.

108. Schirmann, *Toledot ha-shirah . . . ṣarfat,* 228.

109. On page 18, the soul speaks to the narrator: "I am cut from crystal [*sapir*], my quarry is precious, awe-inspiring to behold; its brightness is beautiful [*shapir*]."

110. Huss, *Meliṣat ᶜefer ve-dinah le-don vidal benveniste.*

111. See Matti Huss, "Alegoriyah u-bidayon: Sugiyot bi-qeviᶜat meʾafyenav shel ha-modos ha-alegori be-sifrut ha-meḥorezet ha-ᶜivrit." *Sefer yisraʾel levin,* 106.

112. Scheindlin, "Sipurei ha-ahavah," 18.

113. Ibid.

114. See Ben Elᶜazar, *Sipurei ahavah,* 10 n. 13. It is also bound with an anonymous work, *Sefer ḥayyim* (Book of Life).

115. See above, chapter 4 n. 100.

116. Ben Elᶜazar, *Sipurei ahavah,* 17, line 76. See also 20, line 155.

117. Ibid., 14, lines 33–34.

118. In *Sefer shaᶜashuᶜim,* the narrator bears the name of the author. In Ibn Shuhayd's *Risālat al-tawābiᶜ wa al-zawābiᶜ,* the narrator bears the author's *kunya,* Abū ᶜāmir.

119. Ben Elᶜazar, *Sipurei ahavah,* 28, line 13, is a quotation from 66, line 308.

120. On metafiction in Cervantes, see, for example, Elizabeth Sánchez, "From World to Word: Realism and Reflexivity in Don Quijote and La Regenta," *Hispanic Review* 55, 1 (1987): 27–39; Edward Baker, "Breaking the Frame: Don Quixote's

Entertaining Books," *Cervantes: Bulletin of the Cervantes Society of America* 16, 1 (1996): 12–31. I wish to thank Dian Fox of Brandeis University for pointing me to these references.

121. Pederasty and the killing of pederasts surface frequently in the Arabic popular epic. In *Sīrat al-Ẓāhir Baybars* (which postdates *Sefer ha-meshalim*), the killing of pederasts by the protagonist Baybar is a repeating motif. However, the motif of a death sentence issued by a judge is absent. See Lyons, *The Arabian Epic,* 3:304, entry 1. Reckoning justice through a tribunal rather than personal vendetta is notably a central theme at the conclusion of *El Poema de Mío Cid,* in which the Infantes of Carrión receive their due through a court ruling rather than the Cid's unilateral revenge. On homoeroticism, see also n. 84 above.

122. Ben El^cazar, *Sipurei ahavah,* 55, lines 203–204. There is a significant parallel in *Sīrat Sayf al-Tijān,* wherein a king asks the protagonist Sayf's help in protecting his daughter from Haul al-Zamān, a black man who fights with a club and kidnaps princesses. Sayf defeats Haul and marries the princess. See Lyons, *The Arabian Epic,* 2:267, entry 7. Of course, black adversaries are also common in the *Chansons de Geste,* in Romance, and even in the allegorical *Roman de la rose.* In the *Roman,* when the lover is crossing the hedge in pursuit of the Rose, a "base churl" named "Resistance" interferes: "he was large and black, with bristly hair, and his eyes were as red as fire; his nose was flat, his face hideous" (71, lines 2920–25).

123. The only date that occurs in the book relates to "year ninety-three, when the transgressors completed [their mission]" during the reign of "Meliṣ the Seer" (32, lines 23–24). Although Geiger uses this cryptic reference to date the book to 1233, it may not be intended to be specific.

124. Bakhtin, *The Dialogic Imagination,* 151–58 (emphasis mine).

125. Some of the romances in the *sīra* literature are set in biographical time, with protagonists' stories being narrated from birth until death.

126. When childhood is included, it is usually to show that lovers were destined to be together from a young age or since birth.

127. Ben El^cazar, *Sipurei ahavah,* 61, lines 141–46.

128. This chapter is discussed in depth in chapter 6 of this book.

129. Ben El^cazar, *Sipurei ahavah,* chapter 8, 84, line 366; chapter 9, 105, line 522.

130. The idea of the protagonist returning to his place of birth ennobled by his adventure is common in Romance, e.g., *Erec et Enide.* Also, at the conclusion of the *Le Conte de Floire et Blanchefleur,* news reaches Floire (in Babylon) that his father has died, causing him to return home with his beloved. Within Arabic storytelling, Ni^cma and Nu^cm return to their hometown at the end of the story.

131. Norris J. Lacy, *The Craft of Chrétien de Troyes: An Essay on Narrative Art* (Leiden: E. J. Brill, 1980), 341. For a much fuller treatment of *conjointure* and other elements of French narrative, see Douglas Kelly, *The Art of Medieval French Romance* (Madison: University of Wisconsin Press, 1992).

132. Ibn Ṣaqbel's narrative probably also served as the basis for the twentieth chapter of al-Ḥarīzī's *Taḥkemoni.* For a comparison of the two, see Dishon, "Ne^ɔum asher ben yehudah" and comments in Scheindlin, "Fawns of the Palace."

133. On the impossibility of the "shores of Aleppo," see chapter 7.

134. Song of Songs 1:4.

135. Kimah is the name of a constellation (Amos 5:8, Job 9:9).

136. Prov. 30:4.

137. A practice that seems more at home in Christian Europe than in the Islamic world.

138. Long wedding feasts are common in Romance literature and in Arabic popular literature. The wedding feast of Erec and Enide lasts for two weeks; Chrétien de Troyes, *The Complete Romances of Chrétien de Troyes,* trans. and intro. David Staines (Bloomington: Indiana University Press, 1990), 27. For examples from Arabic popular epic, see the references in Lyons, *The Arabian Epic,* 2:318, entry 7.

139. As mentioned above, Scheindlin links the theme of renewing love through quarreling with the Romance tradition. A potentially related theme is found in the *Kitāb al-aghānī* in connection with the ʿUdhrī lovers Jamīl and Buthayna; the lovers separate for a period because of mutual jealousy (Buthayna spoke to another suitor, and Jamīl spoke to another woman) but are later reconciled. See al-Iṣfahānī, *Kitāb al-aghānī,* 8:151–52.

140. As is common in Romance and especially in the *Chansons de Geste,* Muslims are often imagined to possess idealized courtly qualities of Christian society. See Daniel, *Heroes and Saracens,* 72.

141. A protagonist's ascent to the throne at the end of a narrative is known in Romance, in Arabic epic, and in *The Thousand and One Nights.* In Chrétien de Troyes' *Cligès,* the protagonist becomes emperor of Greece. In the *Taghribāt Banī Hilāl,* Naṣr marries the beautiful daughter of the emir al-Ṣāliḥ and succeeds him as ruler of Fes and Meknes (see Lyons, *The Arabian Epic,* 2:146, entry 38). In the *Nights,* Niʿma ascends the throne in the story of Niʿma and Nuʿm.

142. On these sources and other aspects of the Queen of Sheba legend in Judaism and Islam, see Jacob Lassner, *Demonizing the Queen of Sheba: Boundaries of Gender and Culture in Postbiblical Judaism and Medieval Islam* (Chicago: University of Chicago Press, 1993), especially 16, 60.

143. For Masrūr and Zayn al-Mawāsif, see Burton, *The Book of the Thousand Nights and a Night,* 8:205–63; for ʿAzīz and ʿAzīza, see Burton, 2:298–333, 3:1–8.

144. Al-Iṣfahānī, *Kitāb al-aghānī,* 9:133–36. See also Kilpatrick, *Making the Great Book of Songs,* 106.

145. However, Ben Elʿazar does not use *The Thousand and One Nights'* device of nesting stories within frame stories and does not employ fantasy elements such as *jinni,* magic spells, etc. The aesthetic ideal of the *Nights* is achieved through the ongoing postponement of resolution through characters within stories telling stories, often at cliff-hanger moments to save themselves from certain death. Scenarios are nested one within the other (usually by having a character in story *A* relate story *B,* which might contain a character who relates story *C,* etc.) through some logical association such that each story serves as the frame story to the one it introduces. On the *Nights,* see, for example, David Pinault, *Story-Telling Techniques in the Arabian Nights* (Leiden: E. J. Brill, 1992); F. J. Ghazoul, *The Arabian Nights: A Structural Analysis* (Cairo: Cairo Associated Institution for the Study and Presentation of Arab Cultural Values, 1980); Ben Elʿazar does preserve the nesting structure in his translation of *Kalīla wa dimnā.*

146. William Woods, "The Plot Structure in Four Romances of Chréstien de Troyes," *Studies in Philology* 50, 1 (1953): 1–15.

147. Lacy, *The Craft of Chrétien de Troyes,* 10.

6. Voice

1. Quoted in Tzvetan Todorov, *Mikhail Bakhtin: The Dialogical Principle,* trans. Wlad Godzich (Minneapolis: University of Minnesota Press, 1984), 72.

2. Erich Auerbach, *Mimesis: The Representation of Reality in Western Literature,* trans. Willard R. Trask (Princeton, N.J.: Princeton University Press, 1953).

3. Paul De Man, "The Resistance to Theory," *Yale French Studies* 63 (1982): 3–20; the quotation is on 11.

4. Judith Dishon, "Medieval Panorama in the Book of Tahkemoni," *Proceedings of the American Academy of Jewish Religion* 56 (1989): 11–25; the quotation is on 11.

5. Brann, "Power in the Portrayal," 14 n. 2.

6. Also on this *maqāma,* see Raymond P. Scheindlin, "Al-Ḥarīzī's Astrologer: A Document of Jewish-Islamic Relations," *Studies in Muslim-Jewish Relations* 1 (1993): 165–75.

7. This is not to say, however, that the protagonist tells lies whenever he appears disguised or that he tells the truth whenever he is undisguised; in *maqāma* 3, the gluttonous old man tells truths about the history of poetry. In *maqāma* 6, the undisguised protagonist fabricates a story about being tricked into marriage and murdering the bride.

8. See, e.g., Abraham Ibn Ezra in Schirmann, *HHSP,* 1:587, lines 31–32, which is also about a Muslim-Christian battle; Judah Halevi in Schirmann, *Shirim ḥadashim,* 249, line 27. See also the discussion of Jacob Ben Elᶜazar below.

9. Gen. 10:3. Meshekh is identified with Islam by Maimonides, based on Ps. 120:5: "Woe is me, that I sojourn with Meshekh, that I dwell beside the tents of Kedar." See the "Epistle to Yemen," in *Epistles of Maimonides: Crisis and Leadership,* ed. Abraham Halkin and David Hartman (Philadelphia: Jewish Publication Society, 1985), 126.

10. Al-Ḥarīzī, *Taḥkemoni,* 83.

11. James T. Monroe attempts to reveal some of al-Hamadhānī's views in *The Art of Badīᶜ Az-Zamān,* 47–63.

12. Monroe believes that some Arabic *maqāmāt* are intentionally laced with internal contradictions to expose the narrator's speech, like the protagonist's, as mendacious. I have not found Heman ha-Ezraḥi's speech to be disingenuous in this sense. Although we may not have an "unreliable narrator," there are clues that Heman might be spinning tales; for example, he sets stories in places such as Teveṣ or the land of the Sabeans, which turn out to have ironies for events that follow, suggesting that Heman might be inventing stories out of whole cloth for our enjoyment. At the very least, we feel the heavy hand of the author behind the events that Heman narrates.

13. On fiction writers as liars, see Rina Drory, "Three Attempts to Legitimize Fiction in Classical Arabic Literature," *Jerusalem Studies in Arabic and Islam* 18 (1994): 146–64. The idea of poets and fiction writers as liars goes back, of course, to classical works on poetics by Aristotle and Plato.

14. In his structuralist analyses, David Segal often declares one side of a debate the "winner" by comparing the relative merits of competing arguments and noting which side gets the "last word." See, for example, his analyses of gates 4, 39, 40,

41, and 43 in the *Book of Taḥkemoni*. If Segal is right, then al-Ḥarīzī's voice surfaces more frequently. See also the analysis "The Dispute of the Soul with the Body and the Intellect," in Adena Tanenbaum, *The Contemplative Soul: Hebrew Poetry and Philosophical Theory in Medieval Spain* (Leiden: E. J. Brill, 2002), 195–217.

15. He drinks in this episode; *maqāmāt* 3, 23, and 36.

16. Further on this *maqāma*, see chapter 7.

17. Septimus, "Piety and Power."

18. See also *maqāma* 34 (based on al-Hamadhānī's *maqāma* 22), in which an aristocrat who rambles endlessly about his possessions is satirized.

19. Schirmann, "Ma[c]aseh be-zaqen ṣavu[c]a," 1:375–88.

20. Cf. Babylonian Talmud, Baba Batra, 16b.

21. On *tawakkul*, see, for example, Annemarie Schimmel, *Mystical Dimensions of Islam* (Chapel Hill: University of North Carolina Press, 1975), 117–22.

22. Ben El[c]azar, *Sipurei ahavah,* 78, line 175. Cf. Ps. 78:65, which has been understood in numerous ways, including, "a hero *overcome* by wine" (Brown, Driver, and Briggs, *A Hebrew and English Lexicon of the Old Testament*) and "a warrior *shaking off* wine" (Jewish Publication Society). Abraham Ibn Ezra has "as if relying upon his strength."

23. Reading *meṣurotav* instead of *ṣurotav.*

24. Cf. Ezek. 46:23. Otherwise, "encampments."

25. This storytelling technique, wherein the narrator addresses the audience in the second person as though in an oral performance, is common in Romance sources. In *Le Conte de Floire et Blanchefleur,* for example, the narrator describes a long list of precious gems that are said to lie within the Euphrates and adds, "And other [gems] I cannot recall or name, I cannot tell you all." Hubert, *The Romance of Floire and Blanchefleur,* 74, lines 1778–79. The technique is also common in *El Poema de Mío Cid.*

26. Ben El[c]azar, *Sipurei ahavah,* 79, lines 220–224.

27. Ibid., 80, lines 246–250.

28. Schirmann recognized the similarity to the "Porter and the Three Ladies"; see *The Arabian Nights,* trans. Husain Haddawy, based on the text of the fourteenth-century Syrian manuscript ed. Muhsin Mahdi (New York: Everyman's Library, 1992), 66–77. There is actually a greater similarity with "Masrūr and Zayn al-Mawāsif," in which Masrūr is served in a garden by three maidservants who recite wine poetry. See Burton, *The Book of the Thousand Nights and a Night,* 8:205–63.

29. Rashi, in his commentary on Amos 4:11, associates the word with blackness.

30. Schirmann, "Ha-sha[c]ar ha-shemini," 270, lines 259–60.

31. "Noisy and wayward," said of the whore in Prov. 7:11.

32. Ben El[c]azar, *Sipurei ahavah,* 82, lines 301–304.

33. *Sefunim.* Compare Schirmann, *shekhenim,* "Are the inhabitants monkeys?"

34. Beneath his grapevine and fig tree; cf. Micah 4:4.

35. Ben El[c]azar, *Sipurei ahavah,* 83, lines 317–24. Ben El[c]azar also plays with the seemingly pious beard elsewhere in *Sefer ha-meshalim.* In chapter 5, Shapir is impressed by the beard of the nefarious Birsh[c]a, thinking it the beard of a judge, and says, "a belly and a beard are half of being a rabbi." Birsh[c]a, of course, is really a pederast and a scoundrel. Further on beards in medieval and early modern Jewish

culture, see A. Horowitz, "ʿAl mashmaʿuyot ha-zaqan be-qehilot yisraʾel be-mizraḥ u-be-eropa bi-yemei ha-beinayim u-ve-reshit ha-ʿet ha-ḥadashah," *Peʿamim* 59 (1994): 124–48. Al-Hamadhānī also plays with the idea of the beard, though not as extensively as Ben Elʿazar. In *maqāma* 3, Abū al-Fatḥ appears "with a beard that extended so far as to pierce the two arteries attached to the jugular vein." Al-Hamadhānī, *Maqāmāt,* ed. ʿAbduh, 14; trans. Prendergast, 33.

36. One of Ḥam's sons is Kush (Gen. 10:6), hence the association with the *kushit* and blackness. See also David M. Goldenberg, *The Curse of Ham: Race and Slavery in Early Judaism, Christianity, and Islam* (Princeton, N.J.: Princeton University Press, 2004).

37. This inverts the statement of Jacob's sons to Shekhem in Gen. 34:14: "We cannot do this thing, to give our sister to a man who is uncircumcised, for that is a disgrace among us."

38. Or "about."

39. Lit., "Are you one of us or our enemies?" (Josh. 5:13). The entire passage is found in Ben Elʿazar, *Sipurei ahavah,* 84–85, lines 366–75.

40. Following Schirmann's reading *ʿim* rather than David's *yom.*

41. Schirmann indicates that this line is unclear.

42. Following Schirmann's *tamim* rather than David's *tamid.*

43. *Novevim,* following Schirmann's suggestion.

44. Cf. Num. 26:56.

45. Cf. Gen. 2:24.

46. Schirmann, *Toledot ha-shirah . . . ṣarfat,* 234 n. 51.

47. See Chenery, *The Assemblies of al-Harīrī,* 1:108–12.

48. Further, see chapter 7 of this book.

49. Wine drinking is referred to only on occasion in the least courtly of texts and is usually in the context of a meal. For example, in Guillaume IX's "Farai un vers, pos mi somelh," the poetic speaker recounts a meal and subsequent sexual exploit with the wives of En Garin and En Bernard: "To eat they gave me capons and you can be sure I had more than two . . . and the bread was white, and the wine was good, and the pepper was plentiful. . . . I fucked them [the women], you shall hear how many times, one hundred and eighty-eight times." Translation in Frederick Goldin, *Lyrics of the Troubadours and Trouvères: An Anthology and a History* (Garden City, N.Y.: Anchor, 1973), 27–33, lines 43–48, 79–80.

50. Al-Ḥarīzī, *Taḥkemoni,* 346.

51. Assis, *The Golden Age of Aragonese Jewry,* chapter 5.

52. Ray, *The Sephardic Frontier,* 170.

53. Ben Elʿazar, *Sipurei ahavah,* 56, lines 5–12. See also 32, lines 23ff. Also in chapter 10, the youth raised by the narrator becomes attached to a band of *nevalim.*

54. As in the epigraph by Moses Ibn Ezra above, wherein the only ones who are not scoundrels are those who sell wine.

55. Ben Elʿazar, *Sipurei ahavah,* 32, lines 1 and 19.

56. *Nevalim,* "scoundrels," are common objects of scorn in *Sefer ha-meshalim.* In chapter 10, the boy raised by the narrator to be upright reverts to his original people, a band of *nevalim.* In chapter 7, Yoshfeh temporarily joins a band of *nevalim* who lead him down to Egypt; these hooligans are characterized as drinkers of wine.

57. Of course, practices of the "courtier" class were critiqued by Jews already during the Andalusian period. See Bezalel Safran, "Bahya Ibn Paquda's Attitude Toward the Courtier Class," in *Studies in Medieval Jewish History and Literature,* ed. Isadore Twersky (Cambridge, Mass.: Harvard University Press, 1979), 1:154–96.

58. Interestingly, in the Romance *Beaudous,* a young man is instructed in courtly values by his mother before he goes to join King Arthur's court. It is possible that Ben Elʿazar is appealing to a similar sensibility. On *Beaudous,* see Roberta L. Krueger, *Women Readers and the Ideology of Gender in Old French Verse Romance* (Cambridge: Cambridge University Press, 1993), 164.

7. Space

1. I treat the theme of landscape in the medieval Hebrew rhymed prose narrative more comprehensively in my article "Landscape and Culture in the Medieval Hebrew Rhymed Prose Narrative," *Jewish Studies Quarterly* (forthcoming). I wish to thank *JSQ* for allowing me to reprint some of that material here.

2. The narrator usually arrives at a location, beholds the protagonist (either disguised or undisguised, alone or with a group of people), and listens to rhetoric in poetry and prose. The topic of the rhetorical display is often quite jejune (praise of various months of the year or furnishings of the garden, debates over the comparative virtues of ant vs. flea, night vs. day, man vs. woman, etc.). At the conclusion of the rhetorical display, there is usually some kind of departure.

3. Al-Hamadhānī, *Maqāmāt,* ed. ʿAbduh, 138–41; trans. Prendergast, 110–13.

4. Al-Hamadhānī, *Maqāmāt;* see the note by ʿAbduh, 139 n. 9.

5. Prendergast, 71.

6. Both of these episodes are imitated by al-Ḥarīzī, *maqāma* 3 and *maqāma* 34.

7. According to al-Sharīshī, this was Jadīma Ibn Mālik, a king of Iraq recognized for his intelligence. Further, see al-Sharīshī's comments, 2:4.

8. As one can see from al-Sharīshī's note, Qurʾān commentators held various opinions as to the exact meaning of the passage.

9. Al-Ḥarīrī, *Sharḥ maqāmāt al-ḥarīrī al-baṣrī,* with commentary of Abū ʿAbbās al-Sharīshī, 2 vols. (Beirut: Al-maktabah al-thaqāfiyah, 1992), 2:3–13.

10. As mentioned earlier, the absence of Andalusian poets is striking. It should be noted, by the way, that the praise lavished upon poets makes use of extensive wordplay based on the poets' names in the same manner as al-Ḥarīzī (chapter 3). Neither al-Hamadhānī nor al-Ḥarīrī do this in quite the same way.

11. On the mountain pass of Bawwān, see Arthur J. Arberry, *Poems of al-Mutanabbī: A Selection with Introduction, Translations, and Notes* (Cambridge: Cambridge University Press, 1967), 134–40, lines 1–19.

12. A few episodes do take place in the desert, however. *Maqāma* 25, the *maqāma* of the hunt, is set in the desert. In *maqāma* 37, the narrator and his company travel "on the path of the desert and in the steppe" and then happen upon an oasis. In the episode, the protagonist earns some money by charming a snake that had bitten someone. *Maqāma* 31 (the story of the cross-dressed knight) is also set in a desert oasis.

13. Although quoted above, I copy it here for convenience. The narrator and

the youths agree to amuse themselves by "going forth to one of the meadows, to cast our eyes on the verdant gardens, and refine our thoughts by watching for rains. We set out, like the months in number [i.e., twelve] and like the two drinking companions of Jadīma in affection, to a garden that had claimed its ornamentation and adorned itself [Qurʾān 10:25], whose flowers were diverse and colored. With us was headstrong ruddy [wine] and cupbearers like suns, the singer who sings and amuses the listener."

14. Al-Ḥarīrī, *Maḥberot ittiʾel,* trans. al-Ḥarīzī, 201–202.

15. Lavi suggests that al-Ḥarīzī's passage is consistent with his method of translation. Because the verse from the Qurʾān included in al-Ḥarīrī's description is such a pregnant phrase, al-Ḥarīzī had to expand extensively to capture the feeling of the original. See Abraham Lavi, "A Comparative Study of al-Ḥarīrī's Maqamat and Their Hebrew Translation by al-Harīzī" (Ph.D. diss., University of Michigan, 1979–81), 54.

16. The *Taḥkemoni* also makes use of a few other landscapes. In *maqāma* 19, Heman happens upon seven youths by the Euphrates river who are arguing which is the best of the seven virtues. Ḥever ha-Qeni enters the scene and declares them all wrong and that generosity is the greatest of virtues (see above, chapter 5). Episode 20, in which the narrator encounters seven beautiful maidens, is set in a field (*sadeh*); after a flirtatious exchange with the tallest of them, Heman finds that she is actually Ḥever ha-Qeni, long beard and all, disguised behind a veil. Interestingly, al-Ḥarīzī opens an Arabic *qaṣīda* in praise of Abū al-Fatḥ al-Tabrīzī with a nature description but not a garden description; he praises the verdancy and richness of the land in general and makes a transition to the patron who rules over the land; see text in Sadan, "Rabi yehudah al-ḥarīzī," 58–61.

17. Al-Ḥarīzī, *Taḥkemoni,* 59.

18. Ibid., 377.

19. Lit., "the land of the gazelle."

20. Al-Ḥarīzī, *Taḥkemoni,* 382.

21. In *maqāma* 45, in which Ḥever comes to the home of Heman to eat food and drink wine in exchange for some parables, the two stay together for several days. Another ideal place was the inside of an intellectual's home.

22. Al-Ḥarīzī, *Taḥkemoni,* 3.

23. Probably thinking of a *majlis.*

24. Lit., "hair."

25. Ben Elʿazar, *Sipurei ahavah,* 51, lines 61–69.

26. Birshʿa is the name of a Sodomite king in Gen. 14:2.

27. 1 Kings 1:9. This is where Adonijah, trying to muster support in usurping the throne, makes a sacrificial offering in the presence of princes and courtiers. The place name is significant here because it reminds the reader of an incident in which one tries to usurp what rightfully belongs to another, as Birshʿa has "usurped" Shapir.

28. *Kevodo;* cf. Saʿadia Gaon's translation of Ps. 16:9.

29. Following Schirmann's correction of *ʿaṣei noʿam* instead of *ʿaṣei ṭaʿam.*

30. Ben Elʿazar, *Sipurei ahavah,* 46, lines 160–64.

31. The details of a spring and stones beneath the water are also imposed upon

the description of the man-made Cairene garden where Yoshfeh and Yefefiyah delight, "surrounding the pools and springs were meshes of latticework. . . . From the mouths of lions water pours forth upon numerous stones like bdellium." The fact that the entire story takes place within Cairo meant that Ben El[c]azar had to re-create elements of his love refuge within the constraints of an Islamic architectural style. This passage is discussed further below in the section on geography.

32. Curtius, *European Literature and the Latin Middle Ages,* 196.

33. Ibid.

34. Theocritus, *Idylls,* 22:36–42, trans. John M. Edmonds, *The Greek Bucolic Poets* (London: William Heinemann, 1919), 259.

35. Hubert, *The Romance of Floire and Blanchefleur,* lines 1748–1844. As mentioned, the story has been compared with episodes from *The Thousand and One Nights.*

36. The earlier part of this classic book was composed at about the same time as *Sefer ha-meshalim.* Also, in Berceo's *Milagros de nuestra señora,* the author presents a garden for some fourteen stanzas before elucidating it as an allegory for the Virgin Mary (Gonzalo de Berceo, *Milagros de nuestra señora* [London: Tamesis, 1971]).

37. See Guillaume de Lorris, *The Romance of the Rose,* 32–53.

38. The same detail is also found in Ibn Shabbetai's *Minḥat yehudah.* When the fraternity of male youths leaves mixed society, they find a place to rest. It is described as a place with winding rivers, many species of trees and birds, and "springs that fall on stones." See Huss, "Minḥat yehudah," 11, line 268.

39. On the use of the classical landscape tradition in medieval Romance, see Nathaniel B. Smith, "In Search of the Ideal Landscape: From 'Locus Amoenus' to 'Parc du Champ Joli' in the *Roman de la Rose,*" *Viator* 11 (1980): 225–43; James J. Wilhelm, *The Cruelest Month: Spring, Nature, and Love in Classical and Medieval Lyrics* (New Haven, Conn.: Yale University Press, 1965); Kenneth Kee, "Two Chaucerian Gardens," *Mediaeval Studies* 23 (1961): 154–62. For gardens in moral, theological, and literary works, see Durant W. Robertson, Jr., "The Doctrine of Charity in Medieval Literary Gardens: A Topical Approach Through Symbolism and Allegory," *Speculum* 26 (1951): 24–49.

40. *The Arabian Nights,* trans. Haddawy, 298. However, the scene in the Palace of Paradise is distinct from those in *Sefer ha-meshalim* because of the presence of other parties; the lovers' retreat and seclusion is a key theme of *Sefer ha-meshalim*'s love stories. In addition, *The Thousand and One Nights* setting is characterized by the extreme luxury and artificiality of the setting (silk carpets, golden animal sculptures, bejeweled trays of crystal and gold, gold basins, silver couches, etc.). For the image of maidens singing beside pools of water in a Hebrew source, see the opening section of the allegorical "Scroll of the Fawn," by Elijah Ha-Kohen (thirteenth century), in Malakhi, "Megilat ha-[c]ofer"; Malakhi also published an English translation of the text: "Rabbi Elijah Ha-Kohen's Scroll of the Fawn: An Allegorical Maqama from Spain," in *Medieval and Modern Perspectives on Muslim-Jewish Relations,* ed. Ronald L. Nettler (Chur, Switzerland: Harwood, 1993), 127–57.

41. All of these stories are contained in Burton, *The Book of the Thousand Nights and a Night.* Masrūr and Zayn al-Mawāsif, 8:205–63; [c]Azīz and [c]Azīza, 2:298–333, 3:1–8; Ibrāhīm and Jamīla, 9:207–29.

> 42. What aids in gaining this strength [to journey to the different celestial climes] is to immerse oneself in the spring of water that flows near the permanent Spring of Life. When the pilgrim has been guided on the road to that spring, and then purifies himself in it and drinks of that sweet-tasting water, a new strength arises in his limbs, making him able to cross vast deserts. The deserts seem to roll up before him. . . . Whoever bathes in that spring becomes so light that he can walk on water, can climb the highest peaks without weariness, until finally he comes to one of the two circumscriptions [Occident and Orient] by which this world is intersected. (Corbin, *Avicenna and the Visionary Recital,* 141–42)

Also see Corbin's commentary, 159–60. In the Hebrew version by Abraham Ibn Ezra, the narrator describes how immersion in the spring healed his ailments: Levin, *Ḥayy Ben Meqiṣ,* 60. On the *Ḥayy ibn yaqẓān* cycle, see Hughes, *The Texture of the Divine.* See also the use of allegorical landscape in Yosef ben Tanḥum ha-Yerushalmi's *Neʾum aḥituv ben ḥakhamoni,* in Yahalom, "Tafqido shel sipur ha-misgeret," 146.

43. Abū ʿAlāʾ al-Maʿarrī, *Risālat al-ghufrān* (Beirut: Dār al-ṣādir, 1964), 107–108, 118–19, 178.

44. Trans. Husain Haddawy, *The Arabian Nights II: Sindbad and Other Popular Stories* (New York: Everyman's Library, 1995), 12.

45. Ibid., 40.

46. The Cairene garden where Yoshfeh and Yefefiyah delight in each other is not tinged with the same disapproval; even though she is technically his possession, the love between them is mutual. There is no wine drinking in the scene; the only wine they drink is the "wine of their love." The setting of Cairo undoubtedly required that the water source beside which the lovers would enjoy each other would be set in a mansion garden; still, the author takes pains to show that the situation is unlike that in Akhbor's mansion.

47. Or "about."

48. Lit., "Are you one of us or our enemies?" (Josh. 5:13). The entire passage is found in Ben Elʿazar, *Sipurei ahavah,* 84–85, lines 366–75.

49. On the *hortus ludi,* see Rob Aben and Saskia de Wit, *The Enclosed Garden: History and Development of the* Hortus Conclusus *and Its Reintroduction into the Present-Day Urban Landscape,* trans. John Kirkpatrick (Rotterdam: 010 Publishing, 1999), 38ff.

50. Elizabeth A. Augspach, *The Garden as Woman's Space in Twelfth- and Thirteenth-Century Literature* (Lewiston, N.Y.: Edwin Mellen, 2005), 108.

51. See Chrétien de Troyes, *The Complete Romances,* 164–65 (emphasis mine). Although gardens in *The Thousand and One Nights* also appear as domains under a woman's control, they lack the sense of relaxation and play associated with the Romance garden.

52. Gardens can be enchanted places, such as the garden with walls of air and fruit that is ripe year-round in Chrétien's *Erec et Enide.* See Augspach, *The Garden as Woman's Space,* 106–49. Augspach argues that the gardens of medieval Romance present an inversion of the garden from which Adam and Eve were expelled. She also discusses the role of the garden as an allegory for the Virgin Mary in Berceo's

Milagros de nuestra señora; here, too, the Virgin exercises power over men. Although gardens of *The Thousand and One Nights* are sometimes under a woman's control, even then the male (such as Masrūr) can be served wine and entertained.

53. On Ibn Shapruṭ's letter to the Khazar king, see Schirmann, *Toledot ha-shirah . . . muslemit,* 108–10.

54. Schirmann, *HHSP,* 1:85–92 [25], lines 145–46.

55. See also the fine essay by Robert Edwards, "Exile, Self, Society," in *Exile in Literature,* ed. M.I. Lagos-Pope (London: Associated University Presses, 1988), 15–31.

56. Richard W. Southern, *The Making of the Middle Ages* (New Haven, Conn.: Yale University Press, 1966), 242–43.

57. Ibid., 244–45.

58. Percy G. Adams, *Travel Literature and the Evolution of the Novel* (Lexington: University Press of Kentucky, 1983), 112.

59. See, e.g., the introduction by Adler, Benjamin of Tudela, *The Itinerary of Benjamin of Tudela: Critical Text, Translation, and Commentary,* ed. Marcus Nathan Adler (London: Henry Frowde, 1907).

60. Ibid., 3.

61. Even Adler, who generally sees the itinerary as a firsthand account, questions whether Benjamin ever traveled to Yemen. Ibid., 48 n. 2. Adler does not think that Benjamin saw much of Persia or China, either.

62. Hebrew section, 55.

63. Ibid., 61. Al-Saraqusṭī includes a clever reversal of this in *maqāma* 36. The narrator arrives in China and finds the protagonist weaving tales before a Chinese audience about a fantastical phoenix that exists in the Maghreb! Al-Saraqusṭī points to the absurdity of the "wonders of the East" topos by reversing the locations, suggesting that people will believe far-fetched stories about distant places and that the phoenix is no more real in China than it is in the Maghreb. See the commentary by Monroe.

64. Burton, *The Book of the Thousand Nights and a Night,* 8:7–145. For Sindbad, see Haddawy, *The Arabian Nights II,* 13. See also the entry on *al-rukhkh* in Marzolph, *The Arabian Nights Encyclopedia,* 2:694.

65. Benjamin of Tudela, *The Itinerary of Benjamin of Tudela,* ix.

66. Ibid.

67. On the (possibly intentional) temporal contradictions in al-Hamadhānī, see Monroe, *The Art of Badīʿ Az-Zamān,* 109ff.

68. Monroe, "Al-Saraqusṭī . . . (Part II)," 32 n. 6.

69. *Maqāma* 14: al-Ḥarīrī's narrator journeys from Baghdad (*madīnat al-salām*) to al-Khayf, in Mecca. In al-Ḥarīzī's version, he begins in ʿEin rogel (near Jerusalem, 2 Sam. 17:17; 1 Kings 1:19; Josh. 15:7, 18:16; on the border of Judah and Benjamin, literally meaning "spring of treaders," playing on the meaning of *rgl* as "pilgrim") and goes on pilgrimage. Although Jerusalem is not mentioned explicitly, it seems clear that it is the pilgrim's destination.

70. Lavi, "A Comparative Study of al-Ḥarīrī's Maqamat," 27.

71. In other cases, however, al-Ḥarīzī preserves actual locations, as in *maqāma* 22, where he translates *al-furāt,* the Euphrates river, with its Hebrew cognate and equivalent, the river *perat* (Gen. 2:14 and many other places). Only occasionally does

al-Ḥarīzī mimic an Arabic place name when there is no Hebrew cognate; for example, he translates *Ṣanʿa* in Yemen as *Ṣanʿa* (*maqāma* 1).

72. Similarly, al-Ḥarīzī also translates *ḥākim iskandariyya,* "judge of Alexandria" as *kohen on,* "priest of *on*" (Gen. 41:45, 50). Further on the association of Alexandria with *on,* see Jacob Mann, *Jews in Egypt and Palestine Under the Fatimid Caliphs* (London: Oxford University Press, 1920–22), 2:420 (Hebrew index and glossary).

73. Cracking his skull. Abimelech cries out to his attendant to slay him, lest it would be said of him: "A woman killed him!"

74. David Segal notes that the place name prefigures the subject of the chapter, though he does not make this same point exactly. See al-Ḥarīzī, *The Book of Taḥkemoni,* 455.

75. Al-Ḥarīzī, *Taḥkemoni,* 295.

76. *Maqāma* 24.

77. *Maqāma* 18.

78. Al-Ḥarīzī, *Taḥkemoni,* 345.

79. Benjamin of Tudela states that Ḥamṣan (Emesa in Adler's translation) is a city of Zemarites. Emesa is a day's journey from Karjatēn, which is Kiryatayim, and from Hamah. Adler notes that Emesa is now called Ḥoms, 1 (English), 32 (Hebrew). Clearly there is some confusion, since Ḥoms would then appear twice, but the general location is apparent.

80. The ending is logical since the characters are supposed to be somewhere between Baghdad and ʿElam when the story begins.

81. One imagines that the author may have backtracked, taken up residence, been delayed, etc. In the only autographed letter by al-Ḥarīzī, the author apologizes for failing to reach a destination where he had been expected for some time. For a facsimile of the letter with transcription and Hebrew translation, see Blau and Yahalom, *Masʾei yehudah,* 275.

82. For the Judeo-Arabic text of *al-Rawḍa al-anīqa,* see Blau and Yahalom, *Masʿei yehudah,* 91–167.

83. Al-Ḥarīzī, *Taḥkemoni,* 366.

84. As Blau and Yahalom show, a second (probably earlier) version of this chapter omits Iberia and Provence altogether. See their *Masʿei yehudah,* 15. They believe that the western cities were added to give greater background. The western cities are also omitted from *al-Rawḍa al-anīqa,* which is the latest of the versions (though the text is incomplete). From the description of Egyptian cities onward, the three versions follow roughly the same itinerary, including the same major cities, though the Arabic version includes considerably more minor cities and concludes in Baṣra rather than Baghdad.

85. Al-Ḥarīzī, *Taḥkemoni,* 317.

86. This episode was also discussed earlier in this chapter.

87. I.e., the time when one must recite the *Shemʿa.*

88. Also a reference to the times for reciting the *Shemʿa.*

89. Al-Ḥarīzī, *Taḥkemoni,* 72–73.

90. See further below.

91. *Ha-qav ha-shaveh*—lit., "the equator." This is difficult since Iberia clearly does not lie on the equator. The point is that Iberia and Iraq are aligned. Perhaps the term should be translated "equinautical line."

92. Al-Ḥarīzī, *Taḥkemoni,* 182–83.

93. Ibid., 187.

94. Ibid., 43.

95. The city, mentioned several times in the Bible (with slight variations, 2 Sam. 10:6; 2 Sam. 8:3; Ps. 60:2; and elsewhere), is identified with Aleppo in *Taḥkemoni,* 358, and in other geographical writings. If Ben Elᶜazar means Aleppo, then his geography is imprecise since Aleppo is approximately seventy-five miles from the sea. In any case, it is safe to locate Ṣova in Syria by the biblical associations.

96. Although not mentioning the similarity with Romance in this context, Schirmann does suggest,

> The lack of additional hints at Christian countries does not require the conclusion that the sources of *Sefer ha-meshalim* may be sought in Arabic literature only. It is possible, of course, that Ben Elᶜazar moved the scenes to the lands of the East so that his Jewish readers would not be surprised by the strange things that take place. These lands, being far away, could serve as a fitting setting for romantic and imaginative events. (Schirmann, "Maᶜaseh be-zaqen ṣavuᶜa," 378)

97. Between the two walls: The phrase is found many times in the Bible, as in 2 Kings 25:4, where it refers to a gate.

98. Cf. Lam. 4:7, following Schirmann's reading rather than David's: "redder than sapphire."

99. Isa. 2:16. While modern translations have suggested "ships," "vessels," and "standards," Ibn Janāḥ relates the word to *maskit,* which means "ornament, decoration." He probably understands the word as derived from *skhh,* "to look out, gaze," thus "something that attracts a gaze."

100. Zech. 3:9.

101. Lines 49–63.

102. See, for example, the stories of ᶜAlī Nūr al-Dīn and Maryam the Girdle-Girl or Nūr al-Dīn ᶜAli and Anīs al-Jalīs.

103. See n. 31 above.

104. Tank: cf. 1 Kings 7:44.

105. Compare this image with Moses Ibn Ezra, "Qeraᵓani gevir," line 11 (see chapter 3 of this book).

106. Lines 96–107.

107. A nice example is the Tale of the Jewish Doctor; see Burton, *The Book of the Thousand Nights and a Night,* 1:288–300. See also Richard van Leeuwen, "Space as Metaphor in the *Alf Laylah wa laylah:* The Archetypal City," in *Myths, Historical Archetypes and Symbolic Figures in Arabic Literature,* ed. Angelika Neuwirth et al. (Beirut: Deutsche morgenländische, 1999), 493–505.

108. See Abū al-Ḥusain Muḥammad Ibn Jubayr, *Riḥlat Ibn Jubayr,* ed. William Wright; 2nd ed., ed. M. J. De Goeje (Leiden: E. J. Brill, 1907), 51.

109. ᶜAbd al-Laṭīf al-Baghdādī, *The Eastern Key: Kitāb al-ifādah wa al-iᶜtibār,* trans. Kamal Hafuth Zand, John A. Videan, and Ivy E. Videan (London: Allen and Unwin, 1965); al-Baghdādī has a section dedicated to "remarkable things about buildings and ships," which contains no descriptions as wondrous as Ben Elᶜazar's description. The only reference I have found that might be related to Ben Elᶜazar's

description of stones having "seven eyes" are the "disks of glass" on which the pieces of Bab Zuwaylah revolve according to Taqiyy al-Dīn Aḥmad Ibn ʿAlī Ibn ʿAbd al-Qādir al-Maqrīzī, *Al-mawāʿiẓ wa al-iʿtibār fī dhikr al-khiṭaṭ wa al-athār,* ed. Ayman Fuʾād Sayyid (London: Al-Furqān Islamic Heritage Foundation, 2002), 2:270.

110. Note the change in appearance between the eleventh and thirteenth centuries as Cairo became increasingly congested. See also Nezar Alsayyad, "Bayn al-Qasrayn: The Street Between Two Palaces," in *Streets: Critical Perspectives on Public Space,* ed. Zeynep Çelik, Diane Favro, and Richard Ingersoll (Berkeley: University of California Press, 1994), 71–82. An elaborate description is also found in the account of the eleventh-century Persian traveler Nāṣir-i Khusraw, who remarked upon the height of buildings in Cairo (built on five or six levels) and also the walls of a Cairo palace that were "carved with precision . . . [as though it were] carved from a single stone." He also describes the immaculate appearance of homes that seem to be "built out of precious gems and not from gypsum, baked bricks, and stones." See Nāṣir-i Khusraw, *Safarnamah,* trans. into Arabic by Yāḥyā al-Khashshāb (Cairo: Maṭbaʿat Lajnat al-Taʾlīf wa al-Tarjamah wa al-Nashr, 1945), 49.

111. William of Tyre (c. 1130–c. 1190), *A History of Deeds Done Beyond the Sea,* trans. Emily Atwater Babcock and A. C. Krey (New York: Columbia University Press, 1943), 2:319. This is a partial English translation of the Latin *Historia rerum in partibus transmarinis gestarum.* The Latin was also translated into French by Ben Elʿazar's day.

112. Cairo continued to signify a den of debauchery and misconduct in later Hebrew writings, such as Isaac Ibn Sahula's *Meshal ha-qadmoni.* The author reports that he spent time in his youth in Cairo, "a city of trade, with high chambers, [where he, i.e., I] occupied himself with the vanities of the masses in the howling waste of a desert. There he spent many days in turpitude and disgrace." See *Meshal ha-qadmoni: Fables from a Distant Past,* 1:29, lines 68–70 (my translation). Also, on 189, an adulterous woman and her paramour steal the husband's possessions and head off to Egypt, where they will apparently feel at home. Also in *The Thousand and One Nights,* Cairo is associated with the so-called rogue narratives. See the entry on "Cairo" in Marzolph, *The Arabian Nights Encyclopedia,* 2:510–11.

113. Cf. Exod. 14:29.

114. Correcting the text, which has "she."

115. Ibn Jubayr, *Riḥlat Ibn Jubayr,* 251–52.

116. One possible inspiration may have been the water clock (*manjana*) of Bab Jayrūn at the great mosque of Damascus. Ibn Jubayr was the first Muslim to describe the clock, which was constructed out of wood, glass, and yellow brass; there were twelve windowed arches corresponding to the hours of day and night. During the day, mechanical falcons dropped brass balls into brass cups upon the hour. At night, a water-carrying device caused a lamp to be illuminated behind each window every hour. *Riḥlat Ibn Jubayr,* 270. On water clocks in general, see Ibn al-Razzāz al-Jazarī, *The Book of Ingenious Mechanical Devices* (*Kitāb fī maʿrifat al-ḥiyal al-handasiyya*), trans. Donald R. Hill (Dordecht, Holland: D. Reidel, 1974), 17–92.

117. Benjamin of Tudela, *The Itinerary of Benjamin of Tudela,* 30–31 (Hebrew).

118. *The Romance of Floire and Blanchefleur,* trans. Hubert, lines 1656–67.

119. A station in the wilderness (Num. 33:23) and also meaning "beauty."

120. Lit., "the road toward the ʿArava," a place name in Palestine, as in 2 Sam. 2:29.

121. One should consider whether the reader is meant to assume that Maskil is Jewish; *adomiyyim* most often means "Christians" but here might mean "Jews from Christendom." On Muslim-Christian relationships in medieval French literature, see Lynne Tarte Ramey, *Christian, Saracen, and Genre in Medieval French Literature* (New York and London: Routledge, 2001).

122. The theme of capturing Muslim women and leading them to Christian lands occurs seventeen times in the *Chansons de Geste;* see Ramey, *Christian, Saracen, and Genre in Medieval French Literature,* chapter 5. Ben Elʾazar's story warrants comparison with *La Mort aymery* (though here the captor is a Muslim). The Muslim emir seizing Narbonne sends his nephew to the land of *Femenie* to fetch his beloved so that she might enjoy the amenities of Narbonne as soon as the city is captured. The beloved is also to bring along 14,000 of her young girls. The fleet fetches them with song and drum and harp and viol, and so 14,000 girls get ready, "some of the most courtly there were on earth." For synopsis, see Daniel, *Heroes and Saracens,* 72.

123. *Le Conte de Floire et Blanchefleur* provides a variation in that it begins in Galicia with the (yet unborn) heroine Blanchefleur's Christian mother being taken captive by Iberian Muslims led by Floire's father, the king. When news of the Muslim king's death reaches Floire (now in Babylon), he and Blanchefleur return to Islamdom, where Floire accepts baptism and spreads Christianity.

124. For ʿUmar Ibn al-Nuʿmān, see Burton, *The Book of the Thousand Nights and a Night,* 2:77–333, 3:1–114; for ʿAlī Nūr al-Dīn and Maryam the Girdle-Girl, see ibid., 8:264–349.

125. Ibn Saʿīd al-Maghribī expresses surprise that notables in Egypt ride upon mules, which was apparently not the practice in the Maghreb; see Abū al-Ḥasan ʿAlī Ibn Mūsā Ibn Saʿīd, *Al-Mughrib fī ḥulā al-maghrib,* 2 vols., ed. Shawqī Dayf (Cairo: Dār al-maʿārif, 1955), 1:5. Ḥaṣar Susa could thus be in the Islamic West or possibly in Christendom. There is some evidence that it exists in Christendom. There is a reference in chapter 6 that there is no horse like Maskil's in all the lands of Edom. Thus, there is some association between Christendom and horses in the book. The lengthy description of Maskil's horse in chapter 6 (53, lines 139–55) certainly reminds one of the horse description in *Le Conte de Floire et Blanchefleur,* trans. Hubert, lines 968–1009. Arabic poetry, of course, also abounds with horse descriptions.

126. Ben Elʿazar, *Sipurei ahavah,* 57.

127. Jer. 50:21, identified with Babylonia.

128. Either in Judea (Josh. 15:36, 1 Sam. 17:52), or in the Negev (1 Chron. 4:31).

129. Also in Judea (Josh. 15:36).

130. Ps. 60:2, generally identified with "Mesopotamia," between Sarūj and Harran in the *Taḥkemoni,* 364.

131. Hosea 13:5.

132. Lit., "thousands and two hundred"; large numbers of people are sometimes listed as *x* thousand and two hundred in the Bible, e.g., Num. 1:35, 2:21.

133. The "Sea of ʿArava" cannot refer literally to the place name in the Bible

since it is another name for the Dead Sea (Josh. 3:19), which is hardly suitable for a great sea journey. The storm-tossed ship landing in Islamdom is a common motif of medieval French literature; see Ramey, *Christian, Saracen, and Genre in Medieval French Literature*, 71.

Conclusion

1. On the reorientation of Iberian Jewry toward the north, see also Septimus, *Hispano-Jewish Culture in Transition*, 30–32.

Bibliography

ᶜAbbās, Iḥsān. *Tārīkh al-adab al-andalusī: ᶜAṣr al-ṭawāʾif wa al-murābiṭīn.* Beirut: Dār al-thaqāfa, 1997.

Aben, Rob, and Saskia de Wit. *The Enclosed Garden: History and Development of the* Hortus Conclusus *and Its Reintroduction into the Present-Day Urban Landscape.* Trans. John Kirkpatrick. Rotterdam: 010 Publishing, 1999.

Abu-Deeb, Kamal. *Al-Jurjānī's Theory of Poetic Imagery.* Warminster, England: Aris and Phillips, 1979.

———. "Toward a Structural Analysis of Pre-Islamic Poetry." *International Journal of Middle East Studies* 6 (1975): 148–84.

Abu-Haidar, J. A. *Hispano-Arabic Literature and the Early Provençal Lyrics.* Richmond, England: Curzon, 2001.

Abulafia, Todros. *Gan ha-meshalim ve-ha-ḥidot.* Ed. David Yellin. 2 vols. Jerusalem: Weiss, 1934.

Adams, Percy G. *Travel Literature and the Evolution of the Novel.* Lexington: University Press of Kentucky, 1983.

Alan of Lille. *Anticlaudianus, or the Good and Perfect Man.* Trans. James J. Sheridan. Toronto: Pontifical Institute of Mediaeval Studies, 1973.

———. *The Plaint of Nature.* Trans. James J. Sheridan. Toronto: Pontifical Institute of Mediaeval Studies, 1980.

Alfonso, Esperanza. "Tefisat ha-galut u-teḥushat shayyakhut ba-sifrut ha-ᶜivrit bi-yemei ha-beinayim." *Mikan* 1 (2000): 85–96.

Allony, Neḥemiah. "Ha-ṣevi ve-ha-gamal be-shirat sefarad." *Oṣar yehudei sefarad* 4 (1961): 16–42.

———. "Shirim ḥadashim le-rabi yehudah halevi." In *Meḥqarei lashon ve-sifrut,* 4:417–24. Jerusalem: Reuven Mas, 1991.

Alsayyad, Nezar. "Bayn al-Qasrayn: The Street Between Two Palaces." In *Streets: Critical Perspectives on Public Space,* ed. Zeynep Çelik, Diane Favro, and Richard Ingersoll, 71–82. Berkeley: University of California Press, 1994.

al-Anbār, Abū Bakr Muḥammad Ibn al-Qāsim. *Sharḥ al-qaṣāʾid al-sabᶜ al-ṭiwāl al-jāhiliyyāt.* Ed. ᶜAbd al-Salām Muḥammad Hārūn. 2nd ed. Cairo: Dār al-maᶜārif, 1969.

Anidjar, Gil. *"Our Place in al-Andalus": Kabbalah, Philosophy, Literature in Arab Jewish Letters.* Stanford, Calif.: Stanford University Press, 2002.

Arberry, Arthur John. *Poems of al-Mutanabbī: A Selection with Introduction, Translations, and Notes.* Cambridge: Cambridge University Press, 1967.

Arden, Heather M. *The Roman de la Rose: An Annotated Bibliography.* New York: Garland, 1993.

Ashtiany, Julia, et al. *ᶜAbbasid Belles-Lettres.* The Cambridge History of Arabic Literature. Cambridge: Cambridge University Press, 1990.

Ashtor, Eliahu. *The Jews of Moslem Spain.* 3 vols. in 2 with a new introduction and bibliography by D. J. Wasserstein. Philadelphia: Jewish Publication Society, 1992.

Assaf, Simḥa. "Qoveṣ shel iggerot r. shmuʾel ben ʿeli u-venei doro." *Tarbiṣ* 1, 1 (1929): 102–30; 1, 2 (1929): 43–84.

Assis, Yom Tov. *The Golden Age of Aragonese Jewry.* London and Portland, Ore.: Littman Library of Jewish Civilization, 1997.

——. "Sexual Behavior in Medieval Hispano-Jewish Society." In *Jewish History: Essays in Honour of Chimen Abramsky,* ed. Ada Rapaport-Albert and Steven J. Zipperstein, 25–59. London: P. Halban, 1988.

Auerbach, Erich. *Mimesis: The Representation of Reality in Western Literature.* Trans. Willard R. Trask. Princeton, N.J.: Princeton University Press, 1953.

Augspach, Elizabeth A. *The Garden as Woman's Space in Twelfth- and Thirteenth-Century Literature.* Lewiston, N.Y.: Edwin Mellen, 2005.

ʿAwaḍ, Yūsuf Nūr. *Fann al-maqāmāt bayna al-mashriq wa al-maghrib.* Beirut: Dār al-qalam, 1979.

Bachelard, Gaston. *The Poetics of Space.* Trans. Maria Jolas. New York: Orion, 1964.

Baer, Yitzḥak. *A History of the Jews in Christian Spain.* Trans. Louis Schiffman. 2 vols. Philadelphia: Jewish Publication Society, 1961–66.

al-Baghdādī, ʿAbd al-Laṭīf. *The Eastern Key: Kitāb al-ifādah wa al-iʿtibār.* Trans. Kamal Hafuth Zand, John A. Videan, and Ivy E. Videan. London: Allen and Unwin, 1965.

Baker, Edward. "Breaking the Frame: Don Quixote's Entertaining Books." *Cervantes: Bulletin of the Cervantes Society of America* 16, 1 (1996): 12–31.

Bakhtin, Mikhail Mikhailovich. *The Dialogic Imagination.* Ed. Michael Holquist, trans. Caryl Emerson and Michael Holquist. Austin: University of Texas Press, 1981.

Baldick, Chris. *The Concise Oxford Dictionary of Literary Terms.* Oxford: Oxford University Press, 1990.

Banks, Theodore H. *Milton's Imagery.* New York: Columbia University Press, 1950.

Barthes, Roland. "Introduction to the Structural Analysis of Narrative." In *Image, Music, Text,* trans. Stephen Heath, 79–124. London: Collins, 1977.

Beaumont, Daniel. "The Trickster and Rhetoric in the *Maqāmāt.*" *Edebiyāt* 5 (1994): 1–14.

Beeston, Alfred Felix Landon. "Al-Hamadhānī, al-Ḥarīrī and the *Maqāmāt* Genre." In *ʿAbbasid Belles-Lettres.* The Cambridge History of Arabic Literature, ed. Julia Ashtiany et al., 125–35. Cambridge: Cambridge University Press, 1990.

Beeston, Alfred Felix Landon, et al., eds. *Arabic Literature to the End of the Umayyad Period.* Cambridge: Cambridge University Press, 1983.

Beinart, Haim. *Conversos on Trial: The Inquisition in Ciudad Real.* Trans. Yael Guiladi. Jerusalem: Magnes, 1981.

Ben Elʿazar, Yaʿaqov. *Kitāb al-kāmil.* Ed. Neḥemiah Allony. Jerusalem: Ha-aqademiyah ha-ameriqanit le-madaʿei ha-yahadut, 1977.

——. *Sipurei ahavah shel yaʿaqov ben elʿazar.* Critical edition with introduction and commentary by Jonah David. Tel Aviv: Tel Aviv University, 1993.

Ben Maimon, Moshe. "Maʾamar teḥiyat ha-metim." Trans. Judah al-Ḥarīzī, ed. A. S. Halkin. *Koveṣ ʿal yad* 9 (1989): 129–50.

——. *Moreh ha-nevukhim be-tirgumo shel rabi yehudah al-ḥarīzī.* Jerusalem: Mosad Harav Kook, 1953.

Benjamin of Tudela. *The Itinerary of Benjamin of Tudela: Critical Text, Translation, and Commentary.* Ed. Marcus Nathan Adler. London: Henry Frowde, 1907.

Berceo, Gonzalo de. *Milagros de nuestra señora.* London: Tamesis, 1971.

Blau, Joshua, and Joseph Yahalom. *Mas*ᶜ*ei yehudah: Ḥamishah pirqei mas*ᶜ*a meḥuzarim le-al-ḥarīzī.* Jerusalem: Ben-Zvi Institute, 2002.

Boethius. *The Consolation of Philosophy.* Trans. Joel C. Relihan. Indianapolis: Hacket, 2001.

Booth, Wayne. *The Rhetoric of Fiction.* Chicago: University of Chicago Press, 1961.

Borges, Jorge Luis. *Labyrinths: Selected Stories and Other Writings.* Ed. Donald A. Yates and James E. Irby. New York: New Directions, 1964.

Bosworth, Clifford Edmond. "*Manāqib* Literature." In *Encyclopedia of Arabic Literature,* ed. Julie Scott Meisami and Paul Starkey, 504–505. London and New York: Routledge, 1998.

Brann, Ross. *The Compunctious Poet: Cultural Ambiguity and Hebrew Poetry in Muslim Spain.* Baltimore: Johns Hopkins University Press, 1991.

——. "Judah Halevi." In *The Literature of al-Andalus,* ed. María Rosa Menocal, Raymond P. Scheindlin, and Michael Sells, 265–81. Cambridge: Cambridge University Press, 2000.

——. "Power in the Portrayal: Representations of Muslims and Jews in Judah al-Ḥarīzī's *Taḥkemoni.*" *Princeton Papers in Near Eastern Studies* 1 (1992): 1–22.

——. "Tavniyot shel galut be-qinot ᶜivriyot ve-ᶜaraviyot bi-sefarad." In *Sefer yisraʾel levin,* ed. Reuven Tsur and Tova Rosen, 1:45–61. Tel Aviv: Tel Aviv University, 1994.

Brann, Ross, and Angel Sáenz-Badillos. "The Poetic Universe of Samuel Ibn Sasson, Hebrew Poet of Fourteenth-Century Castile." *Prooftexts* 16 (1996): 75–103.

Brown, F., S. R. Driver, and C. A. Briggs. *A Hebrew and English Lexicon of the Old Testament.* Peabody, Mass.: Hendrickson, 1979.

Bulliet, Richard W. *Conversion to Islam in the Medieval Period: An Essay in Quantitative History.* Cambridge, Mass.: Harvard University Press, 1979.

Bullough, Vern. "Transvestites in the Middle Ages." *American Journal of Sociology* 79, 6 (1974): 1381–94.

Burgwinkle, William E. *Love for Sale: Materialist Readings of the Troubadour Razo Corpus.* New York: Garland, 1997.

Burke, Kenneth. *Language as Symbolic Action.* Berkeley: University of California Press, 1966.

Burton, Richard F. *The Book of the Thousand Nights and a Night.* 8 vols. New York: Heritage, 1934.

Būtshīsh, Ibrāhīm al-Qādirī. *Mabāḥith fī al-tārīkh al-ijtimāᶜī li-l-maghrib wa al-andalus khilāl ᶜaṣr al-murābiṭīn.* Beirut: Dār al-ṭalīᶜa li-l-ṭibāᶜa wa al-nashr, 1998.

Canova, G. "*Sīra* Literature." In *Encyclopedia of Arabic Literature,* ed. Julie Scott Meisami and Paul Starkey. London and New York: Routledge, 1998.

Capellanus, Andreas. *The Art of Courtly Love.* Trans. John Jay Parry. New York: Columbia University Press, 1941.

Carey, Gary, and Mary Ellen Snodgrass. *A Multicultural Dictionary of Literary Terms.* Jefferson, N.C.: McFarland, 1999.

Castro, Americo. *The Structure of Spanish History.* Princeton, N.J.: Princeton University Press, 1954.

Chandler, Richard E., and Kessel Schwartz. *A New History of the Spanish Language.* Baton Rouge: Louisiana State University Press, 1961.

Chauvin, Victor. *Bibliographie des ouvrages arabes ou relatifs aux Arabes.* 12 vols. Liège: H. Vaillant-Carmanne, 1892–1922.

Chazan, Robert. "The Facticity of Medieval Narrative: A Case Study of the Hebrew First Crusade Narratives." *Association for Jewish Studies Review* 16 (1991): 31–56.

Chrétien de Troyes. *The Complete Romances of Chrétien de Troyes.* Trans. David Staines. Bloomington: Indiana University Press, 1990.

Cohen, Gerson D. "Esau as Symbol in Early Medieval Thought." In *Jewish Medieval and Renaissance Studies,* ed. Alexander Altmann, 19–48. Cambridge, Mass.: Harvard University Press, 1967. Reprinted in Gerson D. Cohen, *Studies in the Variety of Rabbinic Cultures,* 243–69. Philadelphia: Jewish Publication Society, 1991.

———. *Sefer haqabbalah: The Book of Tradition by Abraham Ibn Daud; A Critical Edition with Translation and Notes.* Philadelphia: Jewish Publication Society, 1967.

———. *Studies in the Variety of Rabbinic Cultures.* Philadelphia and New York: Jewish Publication Society, 1991.

Cohen, Mark R. "Persecution, Response, and Collective Memory: The Jews of Islam in the Classical Period." In *The Jews of Medieval Islam: Community, Society, and Identity,* ed. Daniel Frank, 145–64. Leiden: E. J. Brill, 1992.

———. *Poverty and Charity in the Jewish Community of Medieval Egypt.* Princeton, N.J.: Princeton University Press, 2005.

Cohen, Mordechai Z. "Moses Ibn Ezra vs. Maimonides: Argument for a Poetic Definition of Metaphor (*Istiʿāra*)." *Edebiyāt* 11 (2000): 1–28.

Constable, Olivia Remie. *Trade and Traders in Muslim Spain.* Cambridge: Cambridge University Press, 1994.

Constable, Olivia Remie, ed. *Medieval Iberia: Readings from Christian, Muslim and Jewish Sources.* Philadelphia: University of Pennsylvania Press, 1997.

Corbin, Henry. *Avicenna and the Visionary Recital.* Trans. Willard R. Trask. London: Routledge and Kegan Paul, 1961.

Corcos-Abulafia, D. "Le-ofi yaḥasam shel shelitei ha-al-muwaḥḥadūn li-yehudim." *Zion* 32 (1967): 137–60.

Crone, Patricia, and Shmuel Moreh. *The Book of Strangers: Medieval Arabic Graffiti on the Theme of Nostalgia.* Princeton, N.J.: Markus Wiener, 2000.

Cuddon, John A. *A Dictionary of Literary Terms and Literary Theory.* 4th ed. Oxford: Blackwell, 1998.

Culler, Jonathan. *Structuralist Poetics.* Ithaca, N.Y.: Cornell University Press, 1975.

Curtius, Ernst Robert. *European Literature and the Latin Middle Ages*. Princeton, N.J.: Princeton University Press, 1953.

Danah, Y. "Al-hamadhānī ke-maqor le-rav yehudah al-ḥarīzī." *Dappim le-meḥqar be-sifrut* 1 (1984): 79–89.

———. "Le-meqoro shel sefer taḥkemoni." *Tarbiṣ* 44 (1975): 172ff.

Daniel, Norman. *Heroes and Saracens: An Interpretation of the Chansons de Geste*. Edinburgh: Edinburgh University Press, 1984.

Darʿi, Moses. "Maḥberet no amon u-miṣrayim." In *Madaʿei ha-yahadut*, ed. Israel Davidson, 2:297–308. Jerusalem, 1927.

Davidson, Israel. "Serid me-sefer filosofi le-meḥaber bilti nodʿa." *Ha-ṣofeh le-ḥokhmat yisraʾel* 10 (1926): 94–105 (see also 11 [1927]: 96).

Day Lewis, Cecil. *The Poetic Image*. New York: Oxford University Press, 1947.

De Man, Paul. "The Resistance to Theory." *Yale French Studies* 63 (1982): 3–20.

Decter, Jonathan P. "Judah al-Harizi's Book of Tahkemoni." In *Middle Eastern Literatures and Their Times*, ed. Joyce Moss, 57–64. Santa Monica, Calif.: Moss, 2004.

———. "Landscape and Culture in the Medieval Hebrew Rhymed Prose Narrative." *Jewish Studies Quarterly* (forthcoming).

———. "Literatures of Medieval Sepharad." In *Sephardic and Mizrahi Jewry: From the Golden Age of Spain to Modern Times*, ed. Zion Zohar, 77–100. New York: New York University Press, 2005.

———. "A Myrtle in the Forest: Landscape and Nostalgia in Andalusian Hebrew Poetry." *Prooftexts* 24 (2004): 135–66.

———. "The Rendering of Qurʾānic Quotations in Hebrew Translations of Islamic Texts." *Jewish Quarterly Review* 96 (2006): 336–58.

Delitzsch, Franz. *Zur Geschichte der jüdischen Poesie*. Leipzig: K. Tauchnitz, 1836.

Demony, A. J. "Courtly Love and Courtliness." *Speculum* 28 (1953): 44–63.

Derenbourg, Joseph. *Deux versions hébraïques du livre de Kalīlah et Dimnāh*. Paris: F. Vieweg, 1881.

Deyermond, Alan D. *The Middle Ages*. A Literary History of Spain. New York: Barnes & Noble, 1971.

Dickie, James. "The Hispano-Arabic Garden: Its Philosophy and Function." *Bulletin of the School of Oriental Studies* 31 (1968): 237–48.

Dishon, Judith. "Medieval Panorama in the Book of Tahkemoni." *Proceedings of the American Academy of Jewish Religion* 56 (1989): 11–25.

———. "Le-meqorah shel ha-maḥberet ha-ʿesrim ve-eḥat be-sefer taḥkemoni." *Biqoret u-farshanut* 13 (1979): 9ff.

———. "Neʾum asher ben yehudah li-shelomo ibn ṣaqbel ve-ha-maqāma ha-ʿesrim be-taḥkemoni li-yehudah al-ḥarīzī." *Biqoret u-farshanut* 6 (1974): 57–65.

Dodds, Jerrilynn. "The Mudejar Tradition in Architecture." In *The Legacy of Muslim Spain*, ed. Salma Khadra Jayyusi, 592–97. Leiden: E. J. Brill, 1994.

D'Orbigny, Robert, ed. *Le Conte de Floire et Blanchefleur*. Paris: Champion, 2003.

Doron, Aviva. "ʿArim ba-shira ha-ʿivrit bi-sefarad." In *Sefer yisraʾel Levin*, ed. Reuven Tsur and Tova Rosen, 1:69–78. Tel Aviv: Tel Aviv University, 1994.

———. *Meshorer be-ḥaṣar ha-melekh: Ṭodros halevi abulʿafiah—shirah ʿivrit bi-sefarad ha-noṣrit*. Tel Aviv: Dvir, 1989.

Dronke, Peter. *Medieval Latin and the Rise of the European Love-Lyric.* 2nd ed. Oxford: Oxford University Press, 1968.

Drory, Rina. "Al-Ḥarīzī's *Maqāmāt:* A Tricultural Literary Product?" *Medieval Translator* 4 (1994): 66–85.

——. "Ha-heqsher ha-samui min ha-ʿayin: ʿAl toṣarim sifrutiyim shel mifgash telat-tarbuti bi-yemei ha-beinayim." *Peʿamim* 46 (1991): 9–28.

——. "Literary Contacts and Where to Find Them: On Arabic Literary Models in Medieval Jewish Culture." *Poetics Today* 14, 2 (1993): 277–302.

——. "The Maqama." In *The Literature of al-Andalus,* ed. María Rosa Menocal, Raymond P. Scheindlin, and Michael Sells, 190–210. Cambridge: Cambridge University Press, 2000.

——. "Three Attempts to Legitimize Fiction in Classical Arabic Literature." *Jerusalem Studies in Arabic and Islam* 18 (1994): 146–64.

Eagleton, Terry. *Literary Theory: An Introduction.* Minneapolis: University of Minnesota Press, 1996.

Economou, George D. *The Goddess Natura in Medieval Literature.* Cambridge, Mass.: Harvard University Press, 1972.

Edmonds, John M., trans. *The Greek Bucolic Poets.* London: William Heinemann, 1919.

Edwards, Robert. "Exile, Self, Society." In *Exile in Literature,* ed. M. I. Lagos-Pope, 15–31. London: Associated University Presses, 1988.

El-Banna, Ezz El-Din Hassan. "'No Solace for the Heart': The Motif of the Departing Women in the Pre-Islamic Battle Ode." In *Reorientations: Arabic and Persian Poetry,* ed. Suzanne Pinckney Stetkevych, 165–79. Bloomington: Indiana University Press, 1994.

Elinson, Alexander E. "Tears Shed over the Poetic Past: The Prosification of *Rithāʾ al-Mudun* in al-Saraqusṭī's *Maqāma Qayrawāniyya.*" *Journal of Arabic Literature* 36 (2005): 1–27.

El-Outmani, Ismāʿīl. "La Maqāma en al-Andalus." In *La sociedad Andalusí y sus tradiciones literarias* (special issue of *Foro Hispánico*), ed. Otto Zwartjes, 105–25. Amsterdam and Atlanta: Rodopi, 1994.

Encyclopedia of Islam. Leiden: Brill, 1960–.

Feldman, Yael. *Bein ha-qeṭavim le-qav ha-meshaveh—shirat yemei ha-beinayim: Tavniyot semanṭiyot ba-shir ha-murkav.* Tel Aviv: Papyrus, 1987.

Fleischer, Ezra. "The 'Gerona School' of Hebrew Poetry." In *Rabbi Moses Naḥmanides (Ramban): Explorations in His Religious and Literary Virtuosity,* ed. Isadore Twersky, 35–49. Cambridge, Mass.: Harvard University Press, 1983.

——. "Ḥomerim ve-ʿiyyunim li-qerat mahadurah ʿatidit shel shirei rabi yehudah halevi." *Asufot* 5 (1991): 122–24.

——. "An Overlooked Fragment of the Translation by Yehudah al-Ḥarīzī of the Maqāmas of al-Ḥarīrī." *Journal of Jewish Studies* 24 (1973): 179–84.

——. *Shirat ha-qodesh ha-ʿivrit bi-yemei ha-beinayim.* Jerusalem: Keter, 1975.

Fowler, Roger, ed. *A Dictionary of Modern Critical Terms.* London and New York: Routledge and Kegan Paul, 1987.

Friedman, Norman. "Imagery." In *The New Princeton Encyclopedia of Poetry and Poetics,* ed. Alex Preminger and T. V. F. Brogan, 559–66. Princeton, N.J.: Princeton University Press, 1993.

Frye, Northrop. *Anatomy of Criticism.* New York: Atheneum, 1957.

Furbank, Philip N. *Reflections on the Word Image.* London: Secker & Warburg, 1970.

Gabrieli, Francesco. *Arab Historians of the Crusades.* Berkeley: University of California Press, 1969.

Galenus. *Dialog über die Seele.* Trans. Judah al-Ḥarīzī, ed. A. Jellinek. Leipzig: C. L. Gritzsche, 1852.

Garulo, Teresa. "La nostalgia de al-Andalus: Génesis de un tema literario." *Qurtuba* 3 (1998): 47–63.

Geiger, Abraham. "Toledot ha-radaq." *Oṣar neḥmad* 2 (1857): 159–62.

Gelder, G. J. H. van. *Beyond the Line: Classical Arabic Literary Critics on the Coherence and Unity of the Poem.* Leiden: E. J. Brill, 1982.

Genette, Gérard. *Narrative Discourse: An Essay in Method.* Trans. Jane E. Lewin. Ithaca, N.Y.: Cornell University Press, 1980.

Gennep, Arnold van. *The Rites of Passage.* Trans. Monika B. Vizedom and Gabrielle L. Caffee. Chicago: University of Chicago Press, 1960.

Ghazoul, Ferial Jabourti. *The Arabian Nights: A Structural Analysis.* Cairo: Cairo Associated Institution for the Study and Presentation of Arab Cultural Values, 1980.

Gil, Moshe, and Ezra Fleischer. *Yehudah halevi u-venei ḥugo.* Jerusalem: Ha-igud ha-ʿolami le-madaʿei ha-yahadut, 2001.

Ginzburg, Carlo. *The Cheese and the Worms: The Cosmos of a Sixteenth-Century Miller.* New York: Penguin, 1982.

——. *Ecstasies: Deciphering the Witches' Sabbath.* New York: Pantheon, 1991.

Girón-Negrón, Luis M. *Alfonso de la Torre's* Visión Deleytable: *Philosophical Rationalism and the Religious Imagination in Fifteenth Century Spain.* Leiden: E. J. Brill, 2001.

——. "How the Go-Between Cut Her Nose: Two Ibero-Medieval Translations of a *Kalilah wa Dimnah* Story." In *Under the Influence: Questioning the Comparative in Medieval Castile,* ed. Leila Rouhi and Cynthia Robinson, 231–59. Leiden: E. J. Brill, 2005.

Glick, Thomas F. *From Muslim Fortress to Christian Castle: Social and Cultural Change in Medieval Spain.* Manchester, England: Manchester University Press, 1995.

——. *Islamic and Christian Spain in the Early Middle Ages.* Princeton, N.J.: Princeton University Press, 1979.

——. "Tribal Landscapes of Islamic Spain: History and Archaeology." In *Inventing Medieval Landscapes: Senses of Place in Western Europe,* ed. John Howe and Michael Wolfe, 113–35. Gainesville: University Press of Florida, 2002.

Goitein, S. D. *Jews and Arabs: Their Contacts Through the Ages.* New York: Schocken, 1964.

——. "Ha-maqāma ve-ha-maḥberet: Pereq be-toledot ha-sifrut ve-ha-ḥevrah ba-mizraḥ." *Maḥbarot le-sifrut* 5 (1951): 26–40.

——. "The Oldest Documentary Evidence for the Title *Alf Laila wa Laila.*" *Journal of the American Oriental Society* 78 (1958): 301–302.

Goldenberg, David M. *The Curse of Ham: Race and Slavery in Early Judaism, Christianity, and Islam.* Princeton, N.J.: Princeton University Press, 2004.

Goldin, Frederick. *Lyrics of the Troubadours and Trouvères: An Anthology and a History.* Garden City, N.Y.: Anchor, 1973.

Goldstein, Miriam. "Adaptations of the Arabic *Qaṣīda* in Andalusian Hebrew Poetry." *Ben ᶜever la-ᶜarav* 3 (2004): vii–xxxviii.

Goldziher, Ignaz. "Bemerkungen zur neuhebräischen Poesie." *Jewish Quarterly Review* 14 (1902): 734–36.

Granara, William. "Remaking Muslim Sicily: Ibn Ḥamdīs and the Poetics of Exile." *Edebiyāt* 9 (1998): 167–98.

Granja, Fernando de la. *Maqāmas y risālas Andaluzas.* Madrid: Instituto Hispano-Árabe de Cultura, 1976.

Green, Dennis Howard. *The Beginnings of Medieval Romance: Fact and Fiction 1150–1220.* Cambridge: Cambridge University Press, 2002.

Grieve, Patricia A. *Floire and Blancheflor and the European Romance.* Cambridge: Cambridge University Press, 1997.

Grotzfeld, Heinz. "The Manuscript Tradition of the *Arabian Nights.*" In *The Arabian Nights Encyclopedia,* ed. Ulrich Marzolph and Richard van Leeuwen, 1:17–21. Santa Barbara, Calif.: ABC-CLIO, 2004.

Gruendler, Beatrice. *Medieval Arabic Praise Poetry: Ibn al-Rūmī and the Patron's Redemption.* London: Routledge Curzon, 2003.

——. "The Qasida." In *The Literature of al-Andalus,* ed. Maria Rosa Menocal, Raymond P. Scheindlin, and Michael Sells, 211–31. Cambridge: Cambridge University Press, 2000.

Guillaume de Lorris and Jean de Meun. *The Romance of the Rose.* 3rd ed. Trans. Charles Dahlberg. Princeton, N.J.: Princeton University Press, 1995.

Gutwirth, E. "Hispano-Jewish Attitudes to the Moors in the Fifteenth Century." *Sefarad* 49, 2 (1989): 237–62.

Habermann, Abraham Meir. "Haqdashot le-sefer *taḥkemoni* ve-reshimat tokhen maqamotav." *Maḥbarot le-sifrut* 5 (1953): 39–46.

——. *Sefer gezerot ashkenaz ve-ṣarfat.* Jerusalem: Ofir, 1971.

Haddawy, Husain, trans. *The Arabian Nights.* Based on the text of the fourteenth-century Syrian manuscript, ed. Muhsin Mahdi. New York: Everyman's Library, 1992.

——, trans. *The Arabian Nights II: Sindbad and Other Popular Stories.* New York: Everyman's Library, 1995.

Halevi, Judah. *Dīwān des Abū-l-Ḥasan Jehuda ha-Levi.* Ed. Ḥayyim Brody. 4 vols. Berlin: Schriften des Vereins Mekize Nirdamim, 1894–1930.

——. *Kitāb al-radd wa al-dalīl fī al-dīn al-dhalīl (al-kitāb al-khazarī).* Ed. David H. Baneth and Haggai Ben-Shammai. Jerusalem: Magnes, 1977.

——. *Shirei ha-qodesh le-rabi yehudah halevi.* Ed. Dov Jarden. Jerusalem, 1978–85.

Halkin, Abraham. "Le-toledot ha-shemad bi-yemei ha-almoḥadin." In *Joshua Starr Memorial Volume,* 101–10. New York: Conference on Jewish Relations, 1953.

Halkin, Abraham, and David Hartman, eds. *Epistles of Maimonides: Crisis and Leadership.* Philadelphia: Jewish Publication Society, 1985.

al-Hamadhānī, Badīᶜ al-Zamān. *Maqāmāt.* Ed. Muḥammad ᶜAbduh. Beirut: Al-maṭbaᶜah al-kathūlikiyah li-al-ābāᵓ al-yasūīyīn, 1889.

Hämeen-Anttila, Jaakko. *Maqama: A History of a Genre*. Wiesbaden: Harrassowitz, 2002.

Hamilton, Rita, and Janet Perry, trans. *El Poema de Mío Cid (The Poem of the Cid)*. London: Penguin, 1975.

Hamori, Andras. *On the Art of Medieval Arabic Literature*. Princeton, N.J.: Princeton University Press, 1974.

al-Ḥarīrī, Abū Muḥammad al-Qāsim Ibn ᶜAli. *The Assemblies of al-Ḥarīrī*. Ed. and trans. Thomas Chenery and F. Steingass. 2 vols. London: Williams and Norgate, 1867–98 (rpt. 1969).

——. *Maḥberot ittiᵓel*. Trans. Judah Ben Solomon al-Ḥarīzī, ed. Yiṣḥaq Pereṣ. Tel Aviv: Moledet, 1951.

——. *Sharḥ maqāmāt al-ḥarīrī al-baṣrī*, with commentary of Abū ᶜAbbās al-Sharīshī. 2 vols. Beirut: Al-maktabah al-thaqāfiyah, 1992.

al-Ḥarīzī, Judah. *The Book of Taḥkemoni: Jewish Tales from Medieval Spain*. Trans. David Simha Segal. London: Littman Library of Jewish Civilization, 2001.

——. *Taḥkemoni*. Ed. Y. Toporovsky. Tel Aviv: Mosad Harav Kook, 1952.

Harvey, L. P. "The Political, Social and Cultural History of the Moriscos." In *The Legacy of Muslim Spain*, ed. Salma Khadra Jayyusi, 201–34. Leiden: E. J. Brill, 1992.

Harvey, Steven. "Arabic into Hebrew: The Hebrew Translation Movement and the Influence of Averroes upon Medieval Jewish Thought." In *The Cambridge Companion to Medieval Jewish Philosophy*, ed. Daniel H. Frank and Oliver Leaman, 258–80. Cambridge: Cambridge University Press, 2003.

Heath, Peter. "Romance as Genre in *The Thousand and One Nights*." *Journal of Arabic Literature* 18 (1987): 1–21; 19 (1988): 3–26.

——. *The Thirsty Sword: Sīrat ᶜAntar and the Arabic Popular Epic*. Salt Lake City: University of Utah Press, 1996.

Heffernan, Carol F. *The Orient in Chaucer and Medieval Romance*. Woodbridge, England: Brewer, 2003.

Heijkoop, Henk, and Otto Zwartjes. *Muwaššaḥ, Zajal, Kharja: Bibliography of Strophic Poetry and Music from al-Andalus and Their Influence in East and West*. Leiden: E. J. Brill, 2004.

Heinrichs, Wolfhart. *The Hand of the Northwind: Opinions on Metaphors and the Early Meaning of Istiᶜāra in Arabic Poetics*. Wiesbaden: Steiner [in Komm], 1977.

——. "Literary Theory: The Problem of Its Efficiency." In *Arabic Poetry: Theory and Development*, ed. Gustave von Grunebaum, 19–69. Wiesbaden: Harrassowitz, 1973.

Hollier, Denis, et al. *A New History of French Literature*. Cambridge, Mass.: Harvard University Press, 1994.

Hooker, E. N. "Pope on Wit: The Essay on Criticism." In *The Seventeenth Century: Studies in the History of English Thought and Literature from Bacon to Pope*, ed. Richard Foster Jones et al., 225–46. Stanford, Calif.: Stanford University Press, 1951.

Horowitz, A. "ᶜAl mashmaᶜuyot ha-zaqan be-qehilot yisraᵓel be-mizraḥ u-be-eropa bi-yemei ha-beinayim u-ve-reshit ha-ᶜet ha-ḥadashah." *Peᶜamim* 59 (1994): 124–48.

Hubert, Merton Jerome, trans. *The Romance of Floire and Blanchefleur.* Chapel Hill: University of North Carolina Press, 1966.

Hughes, Aaron. *The Texture of the Divine: Imagination in Medieval Islamic and Jewish Thought.* Bloomington: Indiana University Press, 2004.

Hult, David F. "Jean de Meun's Continuation of *Le Roman de la Rose.*" In *A New History of French Literature,* ed. Denis Hollier et al., 97–102. Cambridge, Mass.: Harvard University Press, 1989.

Huss, Matti. "Alegoriyah u-bidayon: Sugiyot bi-qeviᶜat meᵓafyenav shel ha-modos ha-alegori be-sifrut ha-meḥorezet ha-ᶜivrit." In *Sefer yisraᵓel levin,* ed. Reuven Tsur and Tova Rosen, 1:95–126. Tel Aviv: Tel Aviv University, 1994.

——. "Ha-bidayon u-maᶜamado ba-maqāmah ha-ᶜivrit: Yehudah al-ḥarīzī ve-immanuᵓel ha-romi—hemshekh o temurah?" *Tarbiṣ* 67 (1998): 351–78.

——. "Loᵓ haya ve-loᵓ nivraᵓ: ᶜIyyun meshaveh me-maᶜamad ha-bidayon ba-maqāmah ha-ᶜivrit ve-ha-ᶜaravit." *Meḥqarei yerushalayim be-sifrut ᶜivrit* 18 (2001): 58–104.

——. "Minḥat yehudah, ᶜEzrat ha-nashim, ve-ᶜEin mishpaṭ—mahadurot madaᶜiyot bi-leviyat mavoᵓ, ḥilufei girsaᵓot, meqorot u-ferushim." Ph.D. diss., Hebrew University, 1991.

——, ed. *Meliṣat ᶜefer ve-dinah le-don vidal benveniste: Pirqei ᶜiyyun u-mahadurah biqortit.* Jerusalem: Magnes, 2003.

Ibn Ezra, Isaac Ben Abraham. *Yiṣḥaq ben avraham ibn ᶜezra: Shirim.* Ed. Menahem H. Schmelzer. New York: Jewish Theological Seminary, 1980.

Ibn Ezra, Moses. *Kitāb al-muḥāḍara wa al-mudhākara.* Ed. A. S. Halkin. Jerusalem: Mekize Nirdamim, 1975.

——. *Maqālat al-ḥadīqa fī maᶜnā al-majāz wa al-ḥaqīqa.* MS Oxford 1430.

——. *Shirei ha-ḥol.* Ed. Heinrich Brody. Vol. 1, Berlin: Schocken, 1935; vol. 2, Jerusalem: Schocken, 1941.

Ibn Gabirol, Solomon. *Shirei ha-ḥol le-rabi shelomo ibn gabirol.* Ed. Dov Jarden. Jerusalem: Hebrew Union College, 1975.

——. *Shirei ha-qodesh le-rabi shelomo ibn gabirol.* Ed. Dov Jarden. 2 vols. Jerusalem: Dov Jarden and the American Academy for Jewish Research, 1971–72.

Ibn Ḥazm, ᶜAlī Ibn Aḥmad. *The Ring of the Dove.* Trans. A. J. Arberry. London: Luzac Oriental, 1953.

Ibn Isḥaq, Ḥunayn. *Sefer musrei ha-filosofim* (Sinnsprüche der Philosophen). Trans. Judah al-Ḥarīzī, ed. A. Loewenthal. Frankfurt am Main: J. Kauffmann, 1896.

Ibn Jubayr, Abū al-Ḥusain Muḥammad. *Riḥlat Ibn Jubayr.* Ed. William Wright. 2nd ed., ed. M. J. De Goeje. Leiden: E. J. Brill, 1907.

Ibn Khalfūn, Isaac. *Shirei rav yiṣḥaq ibn khalfūn.* Ed. A. Mirsky. Jerusalem: Mosad Bialik, 1961.

Ibn al-Razzāz al-Jazarī. *The Book of Ingenious Mechanical Devices* (*Kitāb fī maᶜrifat al-ḥiyal al-handasiyya*). Trans. Donald R. Hill. Dordecht, Holland: D. Reidel, 1974.

Ibn Riḍwān, ᶜAli. *Iggeret ᶜali ha-ishmaᶜeli.* Trans. Judah al-Ḥarīzī, ed. M. Grossberg. London, 1900.

Ibn Ṣaddīq, Joseph. *Shirei yosef ibn saddīq*. Ed. Jonah David. New York: American Academy for Jewish Research, 1982.
Ibn Sahula, Isaac. *Meshal ha-qadmoni*. Ed. Yisrael Zamora. Tel Aviv: Mosad Bialik, 1952.
——. *Meshal ha-qadmoni: Fables from the Distant Past*. Ed. Raphael Loewe. 2 vols. Oxford: Littman Library of Jewish Civilization, 2004.
Ibn Saᶜīd, Abū al-Ḥasan ᶜAlī Ibn Mūsā. *Al-Mughrib fī ḥulā al-maghrib*. Ed. Shawqī Dayf. 2 vols. Cairo: Dār al-maᶜārif, 1955.
Ibn Ṣaqbel, Solomon. "Asher in the Harem." Trans. Raymond P. Scheindlin. In *Rabbinic Fantasies: Imaginative Narratives from Classical Hebrew Literature,* ed. David Stern and Mark J. Mirsky, 253–67. New Haven, Conn.: Yale University Press, 1990.
Ibn Zabarra, Joseph Ben Meʾir. *The Book of Delight by Joseph Ben Meir Ibn Zabara*. Trans. Moses Hadas. New York: Columbia University Press, 1932.
——. *Sefer shaᶜashuᶜim*. Ed. Israel Davidson. Berlin, 1925.
Idel, Moshe. "Zehuto shel metargem sefer ᶜarugat ha-bosem le-rav moshe ibn ᶜezra." *Kiryat sefer* 51 (1975–76): 484–87.
Irving, Washington. *The Alhambra*. London: Macmillan, 1931.
Irwin, Robert. "Andalusia of the Mind." *Times Literary Supplement,* August 13, 1993, 8.
——. *The Arabian Nights: A Companion*. London: Allen Lane, 1994.
Iser, Wolfgang. *The Act of Reading: A Theory of Aesthetic Response*. Baltimore: Johns Hopkins University Press, 1976.
al-Iṣfahānī, Abū al-Faraj. *Adab al-ghurabāʾ*. Ed. Ṣ. D. al-Munajjid. Beirut: Dār al-kitāb al-jadīd, 1972.
——. *Kitāb al-aghānī*. 24 vols. Cairo: Dār al-kutub, 1927.
Itzḥaki, Masha. *Elei ginat ᶜarugot: Shirat ha-gan ve-ha-peraḥim ha-ᶜivrit bi-sefarad*. Tel Aviv: Makhon Katz, 1988.
Ivry, Alfred. "Philosophical Translations from the Arabic in Hebrew During the Middle Ages." In *Recontres de cultures dans la philosophie médiévale,* ed. J. Hamesse and M. Fattori, 167–86. Louvain-la-Neuve, Belgium: Institut d'études médiévales de l'université catholique de Louvain, 1990.
Jacobi, Renate. "The Origins of the Qasida Form." In *Qasida Poetry in Islamic Asia and Africa,* ed. Stefan Sperl and Christopher Shackle, 21–34. Leiden: E. J. Brill, 1996.
——. "Qaṣīda." In *Encyclopedia of Arabic Literature,* ed. Julie Scott Meisami and Paul Starkey, 630–33. London and New York: Routledge, 1998.
——. *Studien zur Poetik der altarabischen Qaṣīde*. Wiesbaden: Steiner, 1971.
al-Jāḥiẓ, ᶜAmr Ibn Bakr. *Kitāb al-ḥayawān*. Ed. ᶜAbd al-Salām Muḥammad Hārūn. 8 vols. 2nd ed. Cairo: Maṭbaᶜat Muṣṭafā al-Bābī al-Ḥalabi wa-awlādihi, 1966–69.
——. *Rasāʾil al-Jāḥiẓ*. Ed. ᶜAbd al-Salām Muḥammad Hārūn. 4 vols. Cairo: Maktabat al-khānjī, 1964–79.
Jakobson, Roman, and Peter Colaclides. "Grammatical Imagery in Cavafy's Poem 'Remember Body.'" *Linguistics: An International Review* 20 (1966): 51–59.
Kee, Kenneth. "Two Chaucerian Gardens." *Mediaeval Studies* 23 (1961): 154–62.

Kelly, Douglas. *The Art of Medieval French Romance.* Madison: University of Wisconsin Press, 1992.

Kennedy, Philip. "Reason and Revelation or a Philosopher's Squib (The Sixth Maqāma of Ibn Nāqiyā)." *Journal of Arabic and Islamic Studies* 3 (2000): 84–113.

Khusraw, Nāṣir-i. *Safarnamah.* Trans. (into Arabic) Yāḥyā al-Khashshāb. Cairo: Maṭbaᶜat Lajnat al-Taʾlīf wa al-Tarjamah wa al-Nashr, 1945.

Kilito, Abdalfattah. "Le Genre séance: Une introduction." *Studia Islamica* 43 (1976): 25–51.

——. *Les Séances.* Paris: Sindbad, 1983.

Kilpatrick, Hilary. *Making the Great Book of Songs: Compilation and the Author's Craft in Abū al-Faraj al-Iṣbahānī's* Kitāb al-aghānī. London: Routledge Curzon, 2003.

Kobler, Franz. *A Treasury of Jewish Letters: Letters from the Famous and the Humble.* Philadelphia: Jewish Publication Society, 1952.

Kogman-Appel, Katrin. *Jewish Book Art Between Islam and Christianity: The Decoration of Hebrew Bibles in Medieval Spain.* Trans. Judith Davidson. Leiden: E. J. Brill, 2004.

Krueger, Roberta L. *Women Readers and the Ideology of Gender in Old French Verse Romance.* Cambridge: Cambridge University Press, 1993.

Kruk, Remke. "The *Arabian Nights* and the Popular Epics." In *The Arabian Nights Encyclopedia,* ed. Ulrich Marzolph and Richard van Leeuwen, 1:34–38. Santa Barbara, Calif.: ABC-CLIO, 2004.

——. "Warrior Women in Arabic Popular Romance." *Journal of Arabic Literature* 24 (1993): 213–40; 25 (1994): 16–33.

Lacy, Norris J. *The Craft of Chrétien de Troyes: An Essay on Narrative Art.* Leiden: E. J. Brill, 1980.

Lane, Edward William. *Arabic-English Lexicon.* 8 vols. London: Williams and Norgate, 1863–93.

Lassner, Jacob. *Demonizing the Queen of Sheba: Boundaries of Gender and Culture in Postbiblical Judaism and Medieval Islam.* Chicago: University of Chicago Press, 1993.

Lavi, Abraham. "A Comparative Study of al-Ḥarīrī's Maqamat and Their Hebrew Translation by al-Harīzī." Ph.D. diss., University of Michigan, 1979–81.

Leder, Stefan. "Conventions of Fictional Narration in Learned Literature." In *Story-telling in the Framework of Non-fictional Arabic Literature,* 34–60. Wiesbaden: Harrassowitz, 1998.

Leeuwen, Richard van. "Space as Metaphor in the *Alf laylah wa laylah:* The Archetypal City." In *Myths, Historical Archetypes and Symbolic Figures in Arabic Literature,* ed. Angelika Neuwirth et al., 493–505. Beirut: Deutsche morgenländische, 1999.

Lentricchia, Frank. "Representation." In *Critical Terms for Literary Study,* ed. Frank Lentricchia and Thomas McLaughlin, 14–15. 2nd ed. Chicago: University of Chicago Press, 1995.

Lentricchia, Frank, and Thomas McLaughlin, eds. *Critical Terms for Literary Study.* 2nd ed. Chicago: University of Chicago Press, 1995.

León Tello, Pilar. *Los Judíos de Toledo.* 2 vols. Madrid: Consejo Superior de Investigaciones Cientificas Instituto "B. Arias Montano," 1979.

Levin, Israel. *Avraham ibn ᶜezra: Ḥayyav ve-shirato.* Tel Aviv: Ha-Qibbuṣ ha-Meʾuḥad, 1966.

——. "Ha-bekhi ᶜal ḥorvot ha-meᶜonot ve-ha-demut ha-lailit ha-meshoṭeṭet." *Tarbiṣ* 36 (1966): 278–96.

——. *Ḥayy ben meqiṣ le-avraham ibn ᶜezra.* Tel Aviv: Makhon Katz, 1983.

——. *Meᶜil tashbeṣ.* 3 vols. Tel Aviv: Tel Aviv University Press, 1995.

——. "Ha-ᶜofer ve-ha-ṣipurim: ᶜAl megilat ha-ᶜofer le-rav eliyahu ha-kohen ve-iggeret ha-ṣipurim le-ibn sina." *Meḥqarei yerushalayim be-sifrut ᶜivrit* 10–11 (1987–88): 577–611.

——. "Ha-sevel be-mishbar ha-reqonqisṭa be-shirato shel yehudah halevi." *Oṣar yehudei sefarad* 7 (1964): 49–64.

——. *Yalquṭ avraham ibn ᶜezra.* New York: Keren Yisraʾel Maṣ, 1985.

——. "Zeman ve-tevel be-shirat ha-ḥol ha-ᶜivrit bi-sefarad bi-yemei ha-beinayim." *Oṣar yehudei sefarad* 5 (1962): 68–79.

Lewis, Bernard. "Raza y color en el Islam." *Al-Andalus* 33 (1968): 1–51.

Lewis, Clive S. *The Allegory of Love.* London: Oxford University Press, 1936.

López-Morillas, Consuelo. "Language." In *The Literature of al-Andalus,* ed. María Rosa Menocal, Raymond P. Scheindlin, and Michael Sells, 33–59. Cambridge: Cambridge University Press, 2000.

Lyons, M. C. *The Arabian Epic: Heroic and Oral Storytelling.* 3 vols. Cambridge: Cambridge University Press, 1995.

al-Maᶜarrī, Abū ᶜAlāʾ. *Risālat al-ghufrān.* Beirut: Dār al-ṣādir, 1964.

Mackay, Pierre. *Certificates of Transmission on a Manuscript of the Maqamas of Ḥarīrī. MS Cairo, Adab 105.* Philadelphia: American Philosophical Society, 1971.

Mahdi, Muhsin. *From History to Fiction: The Tale Told by the King's Steward in the Thousand and One Nights.* Cambridge: Cambridge University Press, 1997.

——. *The Thousand and One Nights (Alf Layla wa-Layla): From the Earliest Known Sources.* 3 vols. Leiden: Brill, 1994.

Makki, Mahmoud. "The Political History of al-Andalus (92/711–897/1492)." In *The Legacy of Muslim Spain,* ed. Salma Khadra Jayyusi, 1:3–87. Leiden: E. J. Brill, 1992.

Malakhi, Zvi. "Ha-maqāma ha-ᶜaravit ve-hashpaᶜatah ᶜal ha-alegoriya ha-ᶜivrit." *Maḥanayim* 1 (1992): 176–79.

——. "Megilat ha-ᶜofer le-rav elihu ha-kohen, maqāma alegorit mi-sefarad." In *Be-oreaḥ madᶜa, meḥqarim be-tarbut yisraʾel mugashim le-aharon mirski,* ed. Zvi Malakhi, 317–52. Lod: Makhon habermann le-meḥqarei sifrut, 1986.

——, trans. "Rabbi Elijah Ha-Kohen's Scroll of the Fawn: An Allegorical Maqama from Spain." In *Medieval and Modern Perspectives on Muslim-Jewish Relations,* ed. Ronald L. Nettler, 127–57. Chur, Switzerland: Harwood, 1993.

Mann, Jacob. *Jews in Egypt and Palestine Under the Fatimid Caliphs.* 2 vols. London: Oxford University Press, 1920–22.

al-Maqqarī al-Tilimsānī, Aḥmad Ibn Muḥammad. *Nafḥ al-ṭīb min ghuṣn al-andalus al-raṭīb.* Ed. Iḥsān ᶜAbbās. 8 vols. Beirut: Dār al-ṣadir, 1968.

al-Maqrīzī, Taqiyy al-Dīn Aḥmad Ibn ᶜAlī Ibn ᶜAbd al-Qādir. *Al-mawāᶜiẓ wa al-iᶜtibār fī dhikr al-khiṭaṭ wa al-athār.* Ed. Ayman Fuʾād Sayyid. 5 vols. London: Al-Furqān Islamic Heritage Foundation, 2002.

Marcus, Ivan G. "Beyond the Sephardic Mystique." *Orim: A Jewish Journal at Yale* 1, 1 (autumn 1985): 35–53.

——. "From Politics to Martyrdom: Shifting Paradigms in the Hebrew Narratives of the 1096 Crusade Riots." *Prooftexts* 2 (1982): 40–52.

——. "The Representation of Reality in the Narratives of 1096." *Jewish History* 13 (1999): 37–48.

——. *Rituals of Childhood: Jewish Acculturation in Medieval Europe.* New Haven, Conn.: Yale University Press, 1996.

Marʿī, ʿAbdal Raḥman. "Hashpaʿat maqamot al-ḥarīrī ʿal maḥbarot taḥkemoni." Ph.D. diss., Bar-Ilan University, 1995.

Martin, Wallace. *Recent Theories of Narrative.* Ithaca, N.Y.: Cornell University Press, 1986.

Marzolph, Ulrich, and Richard van Leeuwen, eds. *The Arabian Nights Encyclopedia.* 2 vols. Santa Barbara, Calif.: ABC-CLIO, 2004.

Mason, Eugene, trans. *Aucassin and Nicolette and Other Medieval Romances and Legends.* New York: E. P. Dutton, 1910.

McBride, M. F. *Folklore of Dryden's England: Gleanings from the Plays of Mac Flecknoe.* Washington, D.C.: University Press of America, 1982.

McGaha, Michael. *Coat of Many Cultures: The Story of Joseph in Spanish Literature 1200–1492.* Philadelphia: Jewish Publication Society, 1997.

Menéndez Pidal, Ramón, ed. *La leyenda de los Infantes de Lara.* Madrid: Impr. de Librería y Casa Editorial Hernando, 1934.

Menocal, María Rosa. *The Arabic Role in Medieval Literary History: A Forgotten Heritage.* Philadelphia: University of Pennsylvania Press, 1987.

——. *The Ornament of the World: How Muslims, Jews, and Christians Created a Culture of Tolerance in Medieval Spain.* Boston: Little Brown, 2002.

——. *Shards of Love: Exile and the Origins of the Lyric.* Durham, N.C.: Duke University Press, 1994.

Mintz, Alan. *Ḥurban: Responses to Catastrophe in Hebrew Literature.* New York: Columbia University Press, 1984.

Monroe, James T. *The Art of Badīʿ Az-Zamān al-Hamadhānī as Picaresque Narrative.* Beirut: American University of Beirut, 1983.

——. *Hispano-Arabic Poetry: A Student Primer.* Berkeley: University of California Press, 1974.

——. "Oral Composition in Pre-Islamic Poetry." *Journal of Arabic Literature* 3 (1972): 1–53.

——. "Al-Saraqusṭī Ibn al-Ashtarkūwī: Andalusī Lexicographer, Poet, and Author of *al-Maqāmāt al-Luzūmiyya.*" *Journal of Arabic Literature* 28, 1 (1997): 1–37.

——. "Al-Saraqusṭī Ibn al-Ashtarkūwī (Part II)." *Journal of Arabic Literature* 29 (1998): 31–58.

——. "*Zajal* and *Muwashshaḥa:* Hispano-Arabic Poetry and the Romance Tradition." In *The Legacy of Muslim Spain,* ed. Salma Khadra Jayyusi, 1:398–419. Leiden: E. J. Brill, 1992.

Montgomery, James E. "On the Unity and Disunity of the *Qaṣīdah.*" *Journal of Arabic Literature* 24 (1993): 271–77.

——. *The Vagaries of the Qaṣīdah: The Tradition and Practice of Early Arabic Poetry.* Cambridge: E. J. W. Gibb Memorial Trust, 1997.

Moore, Helen. "From the Greek." *Times Literary Supplement,* July 8, 2005, 5–6.

Mosher, Harold F. "A New Synthesis of Narratology." *Poetics Today* 1, 3 (1980): 171–86.

Nagid, Samuel the. *Dīwān (Ben Tehillim).* Ed. Dov Jarden. Jerusalem: Hebrew Union College, 1966.

Navarro Peiro, Ángeles. "Un cuento de Jacob ben Elazar de Toledo." *El Olivio* 15 (1982): 49–82.

——. "El 'mundus inversus' ('ʿolam hafuj') en el 'Séfer ha-meshalim' de Yaʿacob ben Elʿazar de Toledo." *Judaísmo hispano* 1 (2002): 209–15.

——. "La versión hebrea de *Calila y Dimna* de Yaʿaqob ben Elʿazar." In *Jewish Studies at the Turn of the Twentieth Century.* 2 vols. Ed. Judit Targarona Borrás and Angel Sáenz-Badillos, 1:468–75. Leiden: E. J. Brill, 1999.

Nemah, H. "Andalusian *Maqāmāt.*" *Journal of Arabic Literature* 5 (1974): 83–92.

Netanyahu, Benzion. *The Marranos of Spain: From the Late XIVth to the Early XVIth Century According to Contemporary Hebrew Sources.* 2nd ed. New York: American Academy for Jewish Research, 1973.

——. *The Origins of the Inquisition in Fifteenth Century Spain.* 2nd ed. New York: New York Review Books, 2001.

Neubauer, Adolf. *The Book of Hebrew Roots by Abū al-Walīd Marwān Ibn Janāḥ.* Oxford: Clarendon, 1875.

Neuwirth, Angelika, et al., eds. *Myths, Historical Archetypes and Symbolic Figures in Arabic Literature.* Stuttgart: Steiner [in Komm], 1999.

Nykl, Alois Richard. *Historia de los amores de Bayad y Riyad: Una chantefable oriental en estilo persa.* New York: Printed by order of the trustees, 1941.

Oettinger, Ayelet. "Criticism of the Social Classes in Yehudah al-Harīzī's 'Book of Tahkemoni' and in European Literature of the Thirteenth Century—Affinity and Distinction." Unpublished manuscript.

——. "Ziqato shel sefer taḥkemoni li-yehudah al-ḥarīzī, le-satirat ha-maʿamadot ha-noṣrit." Forthcoming in *Dapim le-sifrut.*

Orfali, Moisés. "Ecología y estrategias sociales en la jurisprudencia hispano-hebrea." In *Creencias y culturas: Cristianos, judíos y musulmanes en la España medieval,* ed. Carlos Carrete Parrondo and Alisa Meyuhas Gimio, 181–202. Salamanca: Universidad Pontificia de Salamanca, 1998.

Pagis, Dan. *Ḥidush u-masoret be-shirat ha-ḥol.* Jerusalem: Keter, 1976.

——. "Play and Substance: Aspects of Hebrew-Spanish Imagery." In *Hebrew Poetry of the Middle Ages and the Renaissance,* 25–43. Berkeley: University of California Press, 1991.

——. *Shirat ha-ḥol ve-torat ha-shir le-moshe ibn ʿezra u-venei doro.* Jerusalem: Mosad Bialik, 1970.

——. "Ṣiburei dimuyyim." In *Ha-shir davur ʿal ofnav,* 109–23. Jerusalem: Magnes, 1993 (originally printed in *Meḥqarei yerushalayim be-sifrut ʿivrit* 1 [1981]: 196–210).

——. "Trends in the Study of Medieval Hebrew Literature." *Association for Jewish Studies Review* 4 (1979): 125–41.

——. "Variety in Medieval Rhymed Narratives." *Scripta Hierosolymitana* 27 (1978): 79–98.

Paterson, Linda. "*Fin'amor* and the Development of the Courtly *Canso.*" In *The*

Troubadours: An Introduction, ed. Simon Gaunt and Sarah Kay, 28–46. Cambridge: Cambridge University Press, 1999.

Pinault, David. *Story-Telling Techniques in the Arabian Nights.* Leiden: E. J. Brill, 1992.

Prendergast, W. J. *The Maqāmāt of Badiᶜ al-Zamān al-Hamadhānī.* London: Curzon, 1915.

Propp, Vladimir. *Morphology of the Folktale.* Trans. Laurence Scott. Bloomington: Indiana University Center in Anthropology, Folklore, and Linguistics, 1958.

Qadi, Wadad. "Dislocation and Nostalgia: *Al-ḥanīn ilā l-awṭān,* Expressions of Alienation in Early Arabic Literature." In *Myths, Historical Archetypes and Symbolic Figures in Arabic Literature,* ed. Angelika Neuwirth et al., 3–31. Stuttgart: Steiner [in Komm], 1999.

Rabinovitz, M. D., ed. *Rabeinu moshe ben maimon: Haqdamot le-ferush ha-mishnah.* Jerusalem: Mosad Harav Kook, 1961.

Ramey, Lynne Tarte. *Christian, Saracen, and Genre in Medieval French Literature.* New York and London: Routledge, 2001.

Ratzaby, Yehudah. "Ḥolyo u-bediduto shel ibn gabirol le-or shirato." *Sinai* 84 (1979): 1–8.

——. "ᶜIyyunim be-darkhei shirateinu ha-sefardit." In *Baruch Kurzweil Memorial Volume,* ed. M. Z. Kaddari et al., 306–53. Tel Aviv: Schocken, 1975.

——. "Le-meqorotav shel taḥkemoni." *Tarbiṣ* 26 (1957): 424ff.

——. "Qinot ḥadashot le-rav yehudah halevi." *Sinai* 114 (1994): 1–23.

——. *Yalquṭ ha-maqāma ha-ᶜivrit.* Jerusalem: Mosad Bialik, 1974.

Ray, Jonathan. *The Sephardic Frontier: The Reconquista and the Jewish Community in Medieval Iberia.* Ithaca, N.Y.: Cornell University Press, 2006.

Ricoeur, Paul. *Time and Narrative.* Chicago: University of Chicago Press, 1984.

Robertson, Durant Waite, Jr. "The Doctrine of Charity in Medieval Literary Gardens: A Topical Approach Through Symbolism and Allegory." *Speculum* 26 (1951): 24–49.

Robinson, Cynthia. *In Praise of Song: The Making of Courtly Culture in al-Andalus and Provence, 1005–1134 A.D.* Leiden: E. J. Brill, 2002.

Rosen, Tova. *Unveiling Eve: Reading Gender in Medieval Hebrew Literature.* Philadelphia: University of Pennsylvania Press, 2003.

Rosen, Tova, and Eli Yassif. "The Study of Hebrew Literature in the Middle Ages: Major Trends and Goals." In *The Oxford Handbook of Jewish Studies,* ed. Martin Goodman et al., 241–94. Oxford: Oxford University Press, 2002.

Rosen-Moked, Tova (Tova Rosen). *Le-ᵓezor shir: ᶜAl shirat ha-ᵓezor ha-ᶜivrit bi-yemei ha-beinayim.* Haifa: Haifa University Press, 1985.

Rosen-Moked, Tova, and Eddy M. Zemaḥ. *Yeṣirah meḥukamah: ᶜIyyun be-shirei shmuel ha-nagid.* Jerusalem: Keter, 1983.

Rosenthal, Franz. "The Stranger in Medieval Islam." *Arabica* 44 (1997): 35–75.

Roth, Norman. "'Deal Gently with the Young Man': Love of Boys in Medieval Hebrew Poetry in Spain." *Speculum* 57 (1982): 20–51.

——. *Jews, Visigoths and Muslims in Medieval Spain: Cooperation and Conflict.* Leiden: E. J. Brill, 1994.

Ruggles, Fairchild. "The Gardens of the Alhambra and the Concept of the Garden in Islamic Spain." In *Al-Andalus: The Art of Islamic Spain,* ed. Jerrilynn D. Dodds, 163–71. New York: Metropolitan Museum of Art, 1992.

Sadan, Joseph. "Hārūn al-Rashīd and the Brewer: Preliminary Remarks on the *Adab* of the Elite versus *Ḥikāyāt.*" In *Studies in Canonical and Popular Arabic Literature,* ed. S. Ballas and R. Snir, 1–22. Toronto: York, 1998.

——. "Identity and Inimitability: Contexts of Inter-Religious Polemics and Solidarity in Medieval Spain, in the Light of Two Passages by Moshe Ibn ᶜEzra and Yaᶜaqov ben Elᶜazar." *Israel Oriental Studies* 14 (1994): 325–47.

——. "Maiden's Hair and Starry Skies: Imagery System and *Maᶜānī* Guides; the Practical Side of Arabic Poetics as Demonstrated in Two Manuscripts." *Israel Oriental Studies* 11 (1991): 57–88.

——. "Rabi yehudah al-ḥarīzī ke-ṣomet tarbuti: Biografiyah ᶜaravit shel yoṣer yehudi be-ᶜeinei mizraḥan." *Peᶜamim* 68 (1996): 18–67.

Sáenz-Badillos, Angel. "Hebrew Invective Poetry: The Debate between Todros Abulafia and Phinehas Halevi." *Prooftexts* 16 (1996): 49–73.

——. "Metrica romance y metrica hebrea." *Congreso Internacional "Encuentro de las Tres Culturas"* 3 (1988): 143–54.

Safran, Bezalel. "Bahya Ibn Paquda's Attitude Toward the Courtier Class." In *Studies in Medieval Jewish History and Literature,* ed. Isadore Twersky, 1:154–96. Cambridge, Mass.: Harvard University Press, 1979.

Safran, Janina M. "From Alien Terrain to the Abode of Islam: Landscapes in the Conquest of al-Andalus." In *Inventing Medieval Landscapes: Senses of Place in Western Europe,* ed. John Howe and Michael Wolfe, 136–49. Gainesville: University Press of Florida, 2002.

Sánchez, Elizabeth. "From World to Word: Realism and Reflexivity in Don Quijote and La Regenta." *Hispanic Review* 55, 1 (1987): 27–39.

al-Saraqusṭī, Abū al-Ṭāhir Muḥammad Ibn Yūsuf. *Al-maqāmāt al-luzūmiyya.* Ed. Aḥmad Badr Ḍayf. Alexandria, Egypt: Al-Hayᵓah al-Miṣrīyah al-ᶜĀmmah li-l-kitāb, 1982.

——. *Al-maqāmāt al-luzūmiyya.* Trans. James T. Monroe. Leiden: E. J. Brill, 2002.

Saunders, Corinne. *The Forest of Medieval Romance: Avernus, Broceliande, Arden.* Rochester, N.Y.: Brewer, 1993.

Schama, Simon. *Landscape and Memory.* New York: Knopf, 1995.

Scheindlin, Raymond P. "Fawns of the Palace and Fawns of the Field." *Prooftexts* 6 (1986): 189–203.

——. *Form and Structure in the Poetry of al-Muᶜatamid ibn ᶜAbbād.* Leiden: E. J. Brill, 1974.

——. *The Gazelle: Medieval Hebrew Poems on God, Israel, and the Soul.* Philadelphia: Jewish Publication Society, 1991.

——. "Al-Ḥarīzī's Astrologer: A Document of Jewish-Islamic Relations." *Studies in Muslim-Jewish Relations* 1 (1993): 165–75.

——. "The Hebrew Qasida in Spain." In *Qasida Poetry in Islamic Asia and Africa,* ed. Stefan Sperl and Christopher Shackle, 125–26. Leiden: E. J. Brill, 1996.

——. "Mid-Life Repentance in a Poem by Judah Halevi." *Maghreb Review* 29 (2004): 40–52.

——. "Moses Ibn Ezra." In *The Literature of al-Andalus,* ed. María Rosa Menocal, Raymond P. Scheindlin, and Michael Sells, 252–64. Cambridge: Cambridge University Press, 2000.

——. "Sipurei ha-ahavah shel ya^caqov ben el^cazar: Bein sifrut ^caravit le-sifrut romans." *Divrei ha-kongres ha-^colami ha-eḥad-^casar le-mada^cei ha-yahadut* 3, 3 (1994): 16ff.

——. "*Tawakkul* in the Poetry of Judah Halevi." In *Sasson Somekh Festschrift.* Forthcoming.

——. *Wine, Women, and Death: Medieval Hebrew Poems on the Good Life.* Philadelphia: Jewish Publication Society, 1986.

Schimmel, Annemarie. *Mystical Dimensions of Islam.* Chapel Hill: University of North Carolina Press, 1975.

Schippers, Arie. "Ibn Zabāra's *Book of Delight* (Barcelona, 1170) and the Transmission of Wisdom from East to West." *Frankfurter Judaistische Beiträge* 26 (1999): 149–61.

——. *Spanish Hebrew Poetry and the Arabic Literary Tradition: Arabic Themes in Hebrew Andalusian Poetry.* Leiden: E. J. Brill, 1994.

Schirmann, Jefim. "L'Amour spirituel dans la poésie hébraïque du moyen âge." *Les Lettres Romanes* 15 (1961): 315–25.

——. "Les Contes rimés de Jacob ben Éléazar de Toledo." In *Études d'Orientalisme dédiées à la mémoire de Lévi-Provençal,* 1:285–97. Paris: G.-P. Maisonneuve et Larose, 1962.

——. "The Ephebe in Medieval Hebrew Poetry." *Sefarad* 15 (1955): 55–68.

——. "The Function of the Hebrew Poet in Medieval Spain." *Jewish Social Studies* 16 (1954): 235–52.

——. "The Harmful Food: A Curious Parallel Between Cervantes and Joseph Zabarra." In *Romanica et Occidentalia,* ed. Moshe Lazar, 140–42. Jerusalem: Magnes, 1963.

——. *Die hebräische Übersetzung der Maqamen des Hariri.* Frankfurt am Main, 1930.

——. "Le-ḥeqer meqorotav shel sefer taḥkemoni li-yehudah al-ḥarīzī." *Tarbiṣ* 23 (1952): 198ff.

——. "Ma^caseh be-zaqen ṣavu^ca." In *Le-toledot ha-shirah ve-ha-dramah ha-^civrit,* 375–88. Jerusalem: Mosad Bialik, 1979.

——. "Der Neger und die Negerin." *Monatschrift für Geschichte und Wissenschaft des Judentums* 83 (1939): 481–92.

——. "Qinot ^cal gezerot be-ereṣ yisra^ɔel, afriqa, sefarad, ashkenaz, ve-ṣarfat." *Koveṣ ^cal yad* 3, 13 (1939): 31–35.

——. "Ha-sha^car ha-shemini me-'sefer ha-meshalim' li-ya^caqov ben el^cazar." *Qoveṣ ^cal yad* 8 (1975): 259–81.

——. *Ha-shirah ha-^civrit bi-sefarad u-be-provans* [*HHSP*]. 2 vols. Tel Aviv: Dvir; Jerusalem: Mosad Bialik, 1954–60.

——. *Shirim ḥadashim min ha-genizah.* Jerusalem: Ha-akademiya ha-le^ɔumit ha-yisra^ɔelit le-mada^cim, 1965.

——. "Sipurei ha-ahavah shel ya^caqov ben el^cazar." *Yedi^cot ha-makhon le-ḥeqer ha-shirah ha-^civrit* 5 (1939): 209–66.

——. *Toledot ha-shirah ha-ʿivrit bi-sefarad ha-muslemit.* Ed. Ezra Fleischer. Jerusalem: Magnes, 1995.

——. *Toledot ha-shirah ha-ʿivrit bi-sefarad ha-noṣrit u-bedarom ṣarfat.* Ed. Ezra Fleischer. Jerusalem: Magnes, 1997.

Schorsch, Ismar. "The Myth of Sephardic Supremacy." *Leo Baeck Institute Year Book* 34 (1989): 47–66.

Schwartz, Seth. *Imperialism and Jewish Society: 200 B.C.E. to 640 C.E.* Princeton, N.J.: Princeton University Press, 2001.

Segal, David S. "Mishlei yaʿaqov ben elʿazar: Le-mahut ha-maḥberet ha-shivʿit." In *Be-oreaḥ madʿa,* ed. Zvi Malakhi, 353–63. Jerusalem: Makhon habermann le-meḥqarei sifrut, 1986.

——. "Ha-petiḥa, ha-siyyum ve-ha-sipur ha-ʿotef be-sefer 'taḥkemoni' li-yehudah al-ḥarīzī." In *Meḥqarim be-sifrut ʿam yisraʾel u-be-tarbut teiman: Sefer ha-yuval le-profesor ratzaby,* ed. Judith Dishon and Efrayim Hazan, 415–17. Tel Aviv: Bar-Ilan University, 1991.

Septimus, Bernard. *Hispano-Jewish Culture in Transition: The Career and Controversies of Ramah.* Cambridge, Mass.: Harvard University Press, 1982.

——. "Hispano-Jewish Views of Christendom and Islam." In *In Iberia and Beyond: Hispanic Jews Between Cultures, Proceedings of a Symposium to Mark the 500th Anniversary of the Expulsion of Spanish Jewry,* ed. Bernard Dov Cooperman, 43–65. Newark, Del., and London: University of Delaware Press and Associated University Presses, 1998.

——. "'Open Rebuke and Concealed Love': Naḥmanides and the Andalusian Tradition." In *Rabbi Moses Naḥmanides (Ramban): Explorations in His Religious and Literary Virtuosity,* ed. Isadore Twersky, 11–34. Cambridge, Mass.: Harvard University Press, 1983.

——. "Piety and Power in Thirteenth-Century Catalonia." In *Studies in Medieval Jewish History and Literature,* ed. Isadore Twersky, 197–230. Cambridge, Mass.: Harvard University Press, 1979.

——. "Ha-shilton ha-ṣiburi be-barṣalonah bi-tequfat ha-polmos ʿal sifrei ha-rambam." *Tarbiṣ* 42 (1973): 389–97.

Shklovsky, Viktor. *Theory of Prose.* Trans. Benjamin Sher. Elmwood Park, Ill.: Dalkey Archive Press, 1990.

al-Sinjilāwī, Ibrāhīm. "The Lament for Fallen Cities: A Study of the Development of the Elegiac Genre in Classical Arabic Poetry." Ph.D. diss., University of Chicago, 1983.

Smith, Nathaniel B. "In Search of the Ideal Landscape: From 'Locus Amoenus' to 'Parc du Champ Joli' in the *Roman de la Rose.*" *Viator* 11 (1980): 225–43.

Solterer, Helen. "Figures of Female Militancy in Medieval France." *Signs* 16, 3 (1991): 522–49.

Southern, Richard W. *The Making of the Middle Ages.* New Haven, Conn.: Yale University Press, 1966.

Sperl, Stefan. *Mannerism in Arabic Poetry.* Cambridge: Cambridge University Press, 1989.

Sperl, Stefan, and Christopher Shackle, eds. *Qasida Poetry in Islamic Asia and Africa.* Leiden: E. J. Brill, 1996.

Spiegel, Gabrielle M. *The Past as Text: The Theory and Practice of Medieval Historiography.* Baltimore: Johns Hopkins University Press, 1997.

Spurgeon, Caroline Frances Eleanor. *Shakespeare's Imagery and What It Tells Us.* Cambridge: Cambridge University Press, 1935.

Stern, S. M. "Meqorah ha-ᶜaravi shel 'maqāmat ha-ternegol' le-al-ḥarīzī." *Tarbiṣ* 17 (1946): 100–187.

——. "Les Vers finaux en espagnol dans les muwaššaḥs hispano-hebraïques: Une contribution à l'étude du vieux dialecte espagnol 'mozarabe.'" *Al-Andalus* 13 (1948): 299–346.

Stetkevych, Jaroslav. "The Hunt in the Arabic *Qaṣīdah:* The Antecedents of the *Ṭardiyyah.*" In *Tradition and Modernity in Arabic Language and Literature,* ed. J. R. Smart, 102–18. Richmond, England: Curzon, 1996.

——. *The Zephyrs of Najd: The Poetics of Nostalgia in the Classical Arabic Nasīb.* Chicago: University of Chicago Press, 1993.

Stetkevych, Suzanne Pinckney. *Abū Tammām and the Poetics of the ᶜAbbāsid Age.* Leiden: E. J. Brill, 1991.

——. "Intoxication and Immortality: Wine and Associated Imagery in al-Maᶜarrī's Garden." In *Homoeroticism in Classical Arabic Literature,* ed. J. W. Wright and Everett K. Rowson, 210–32. New York: Columbia University Press, 1997.

——. *The Mute Immortals Speak: Pre-Islamic Poetry and the Poetics of Ritual.* Ithaca, N.Y.: Cornell University Press, 1993.

——. *The Poetics of Islamic Legitimacy: Myth, Gender, and Ceremony in the Classical Arabic Ode.* Bloomington: Indiana University Press, 2002.

——. "Structuralist Interpretations of Pre-Islamic Poetry: Critique and New Directions." *Journal of Near Eastern Studies* 42, 2 (1983): 85–107.

——. "The Ṣuᶜlūk and His Poem: A Paradigm of Passage Manqué." *Journal of the American Oriental Society* 104, 4 (1984): 661–78.

Suleiman, Susan R., and Inge Crosman, eds. *The Reader in the Text: Essays on Audience and Interpretation.* Princeton, N.J.: Princeton University Press, 1980.

Ṭaḥṭaḥ, Fāṭima. *Al-ghurba wa al-ḥanīn fī al-shiᶜr al-andalusī.* Rabat, Morocco: Al-Mamlakah al-Maghribīyah, 1993.

Tanenbaum, Adena. *The Contemplative Soul: Hebrew Poetry and Philosophical Theory in Medieval Spain.* Leiden: E. J. Brill, 2002.

Todorov, Tzvetan. *Mikhail Bakhtin: The Dialogical Principle.* Trans. Wlad Godzich. Minneapolis: University of Minnesota Press, 1984.

——. *The Poetics of Prose.* Ithaca, N.Y.: Cornell University Press, 1968.

Treece, Henry. *Dylan Thomas, "Dog Among the Fairies."* London: L. Drummond, 1949.

Twersky, Isadore. *Introduction to the Code of Maimonides* (*Mishne Torah*). New Haven, Conn.: Yale University Press, 1980.

Valle Rodríguez, Carlos del. "Nova et vetera in grammaticae hebraicae historia: La obra gramatical de Jacob ben Elazar." *Helmantica* 49 (1998): 139–73.

Van Dyke, Carolynn. *The Fiction of Truth: Structures of Meaning in Narrative and Dramatic Allegory.* Ithaca, N.Y.: Cornell University Press, 1985.

Von Grunebaum, Gustave E. "The Arabic Contribution to Troubadour Poetry." *Bulletin of the Iranian Institute* 7 (1946): 138–51.

Walker, Keith, ed. *John Dryden.* Oxford: Oxford University Press, 1994.

Wasserstein, David J. "The Language Situation in al-Andalus." In *Studies on the Muwaššaḥ and the Kharja (Proceedings of the Exeter International Colloquium),* ed. Alan Jones and Richard Hitchcock, 1–15. Reading, England: Ithaca, 1991.

——. *The Rise and Fall of the Party-Kings.* Princeton, N.J.: Princeton University Press, 1985.

Wasserstrom, Steven M. *Between Muslim and Jew: The Problem of Symbiosis Under Early Islam.* Princeton, N.J.: Princeton University Press, 1995.

Weever, Jacqueline de. *Sheba's Daughters: Whitening and Demonizing the Saracen Woman in Medieval French Epic.* New York: Garland, 1998.

Weimann, Robert. *The Structure and Society of Literary History: Studies in the History and Theory of Historical Criticism.* Charlottesville: University Press of Virginia, 1976.

Weiss, Joseph. "Tarbut ḥaṣranit ve-shirah ḥaṣranit." *World Congress of Jewish Studies* 1 (1947): 8–9.

Wellek, René, and Austin Warren. *Theory of Literature.* New York: Harcourt, Brace, 1949.

White, Hayden. *Metahistory: The Historical Imagination in Nineteenth-Century Europe.* Baltimore: Johns Hopkins University Press, 1973.

Wild, Stefan. "Die zehnte Maqāma des Ibn Nāqiyā: Eine Burleske aus Baghdad." In *Festschrift Ewald Wagner zum 65. Geburtstag, Band 2: Studien zur arabischen Dichtung,* ed. W. Heinrichs and G. Schoeler, 427–38. Beirut: Steiner, Stuttgart [in Komm], 1994.

Wilhelm, James J. *The Cruelest Month: Spring, Nature, and Love in Classical and Medieval Lyrics.* New Haven, Conn.: Yale University Press, 1965.

William of Tyre. *A History of Deeds Done Beyond the Sea.* Trans. Emily Atwater Babcock and A. C. Krey. 2 vols. New York: Columbia University Press, 1943.

Woods, William. "The Plot Structure in Four Romances of Chréstien de Troyes." *Studies in Philology* 50, 1 (1953): 1–15.

Yahalom, Joseph. "Judah Halevi: Records of a Visitor from Spain." In *The Cambridge Genizah Collections: Their Contents and Significance,* ed. Stefan C. Reif, 123–35. Cambridge: Cambridge University Press, 2002.

——. "New Clues from an Encounter with Old Spanish." In *Jewish Studies at the Turn of the Twentieth Century,* ed. Judit Targarona Borrás and Angel Sáenz-Badillos, 1:561–67. Leiden: E. J. Brill, 1999.

——. "Tafqido shel sipur ha-misgeret be-ʿibudim ʿivriyim shel maqamot." In *Sefer yisraʾel levin,* ed. Reuven Tsur and Tova Rosen, 1:136–54. Tel Aviv: Tel Aviv University, 1994.

Yellin, David. *Torat ha-shirah ha-sefardit.* 3rd ed. Jerusalem: Magnes, 1978.

al-Zayyāt, ʿAbd Allah Muḥammad. *Rithāʾ al-mudun fī al-shiʿr al-ʿarabi.* Bengasi, Libya: Qāryūnis Jāmiʿat, 1990.

Zemaḥ, Eddy. *Ke-shoresh eṣ: Qeriah ḥadashah be-11 shirei ḥol shel shelomoh ben gevirol.* Jerusalem: Akhshav, 1962.

Zink, Michel. *Medieval French Literature: An Introduction.* Trans. Jeff Rider. Binghamton, N.Y.: Center for Medieval and Renaissance Texts and Studies, 1995.

Zwettler, Michael. *The Oral Tradition of Classical Arabic Poetry.* Columbus: Ohio University Press, 1978.

Index

Index

JONATHAN P. DECTER is Assistant Professor and the Edmond J. Safra Professor of Sephardic Studies in the Department of Near Eastern and Judaic Studies at Brandeis University.

www.ingramcontent.com/pod-product-compliance
Lightning Source LLC
Chambersburg PA
CBHW060820310726
48980CB00002B/354

* 9 7 8 0 2 5 3 3 4 9 1 3 2 *